D0841829

Tax This!

An Insider's Guide to Standing Up to the IRS

Scott M. Estill

Self-Counsel Press Inc.
(a subsidiary of)
International Self-Counsel Press Ltd.

Copyright © 1999, 2002, 2005 by Scott M. Estill.

All rights reserved.

*No part of this book may be reproduced or transmitted in any form by any means —
graphic, electronic, or mechanical — without permission in writing from the publisher,
except by a reviewer who may quote brief passages in a review.*

Printed in Canada.

First edition: 2000
Second edition: 2002
Third edition: 2005

Library and Archives Canada Cataloguing in Publication

Estill, Scott M., 1961-
Tax this!: an insider's guide to standing up to the IRS / Scott M. Estill. -- 3rd ed.

(Self-counsel legal series)

ISBN 1-55180-596-0

    1. Tax protests and appeals--United States--Popular works. 2. Tax
courts--United States--Popular works. 3. Tax auditing--United States--Popular
works. I. Title. II. Series.

KF6324.Z9E87 2004   343.7304'2   C2004-906175-5

Self-Counsel Press Inc.
(a subsidiary of)
International Self-Counsel Press Ltd.

1704 N. State Street	1481 Charlotte Road
Bellingham, WA 98225	North Vancouver, BC V7J 1H1
USA	Canada

To Pat, my mom, for everything.

To Becky, my wife, for the typing and putting up with everything else.

To Sara and Caitlin, my daughters, for not wanting to be tax attorneys when they grow up.

Special thanks to:

Jon and Lisa, my friends at District Counsel and Coach;

Roger and Richard at Self-Counsel Press;

Audrey McClellan, my editor;

and everyone else who helped make this a reality.

NOTICE TO READERS

Laws are constantly changing. Every effort is made to keep this publication as current as possible. However, the author, the publisher, and the vendor of this book make no representation or warranties regarding the outcome or the use to which the information in this book is put and are not assuming any liability for any claims, losses, or damages arising out of the use of this book. The reader should not rely on the author or the publisher of this book for any professional advice. Please be sure that you have the most recent edition.

CONTENTS

INTRODUCTION   1

1   MEET THE IRS   3

     1.   A Brief History of Income Tax   3

     2.   So What Is the IRS?   5

     3.   How to Play with the IRS   9

         3.1   The rules   10

         3.2   Your rights   11

         3.3   Some useful publications   12

2   THE IRS RECORD-KEEPING SYSTEM: WHAT DOES THE IRS KNOW?   16

     1.   Understand the IRS Record-Keeping System   17

         1.1   Let the IRS know where you are   17

         1.2   Keep the IRS correctly informed   19

     2.   Know What the IRS Knows about You   19

     3.   Don't be Afraid to Request Information   20

         3.1   Freedom of Information Act requests   21

         3.2   IRS transcript of account requests   26

3   THE FILING PROCESS: WHO, WHAT, WHERE, WHEN, AND WHY   31

     1.   Who Doesn't File a Tax Return?   32

         1.1   Previous negative encounters with the IRS   32

         1.2   No money to pay   32

         1.3   Lack of records to prepare a return   34

    1.4   Personal problems   34

    1.5   Tax protests   35

    1.6   Did not earn minimum gross income   35

2. Preparing the Return   35

    2.1   Tax refunds   37

    2.2   Deductions   37

    2.3   Married filers — joint or separate?   38

3. Timely Returns, Late Returns, and Amended Returns   39

    3.1   Reasons to file tax returns on time   39

    3.2   Extensions to file   40

    3.3   Late-filed returns   41

    3.4   Amended returns   44

    3.5   Before filing a return   44

4   BUSINESSES AND THE IRS   **47**

1. Different Business Structures   49

    1.1   Sole proprietorships   49

    1.2   C corporations   51

    1.3   S corporations   52

    1.4   Partnerships   55

    1.5   Limited liability companies   56

2. Employment Taxes   57

5   THE AUDIT PROCESS: WHAT ARE THE ODDS?   **61**

1. What are the Odds of an IRS Audit?   62

2. How Can You Reduce the Odds of an Audit?   64

3. How are Tax Returns Selected for Audit?   66

    3.1   Statistical analysis   67

    3.2   IRS matching programs   68

    3.3   IRS special projects   69

    3.4   Informant tips   70

    3.5   Evidence of criminal activity   70

    3.6   Random audits   70

    3.7   Prior IRS audits   71

6 GOING THROUGH AN AUDIT   73

1. Understand Your Rights   74

2. Understand What the IRS Can Do During an Audit   75

    2.1 The IRS can examine books and records   75

    2.2 The IRS has access to other documents and information   76

    2.3 What does the IRS know?   76

3. Types of Audits   77

    3.1 Correspondence audit   77

    3.2 Office audit   78

    3.3 Field audit   79

    3.4 Repetitive audit   79

    3.5 Taxpayer Compliance Measurement Program (TCMP)
         National Research Program audits   80

4. Prepare for an Audit   80

    4.1 Keep all your records   80

    4.2 Know why your return was selected   82

5. The Audit Process   84

    5.1 The audit appointment   84

    5.2 Common audit questions   85

    5.3 What happens after an audit?   88

    5.4 What if the IRS is wrong?   90

    5.5 What does an IRS audit cost?   93

7 GENERAL AUDIT RULES   97

1. General Rules of IRS Audits   98

    1.1 Use all the time the IRS gives you   98

    1.2 Capitalize on the IRS's inability to communicate effectively   99

    1.3 Use the complex tax laws to your advantage   99

    1.4 Don't fight the IRS alone   100

    1.5 Don't volunteer information to the IRS   101

    1.6 Ask questions   102

    1.7 Never trust the IRS or anything that an IRS employee tells you 102

    1.8 Remember that appearances are important   103

    1.9 Don't let the IRS into your home   104

1.10 Never alter documents or lie to the IRS 104

1.11 Don't bribe or threaten IRS agents 105

1.12 Don't file any tax returns while an audit is pending 105

1.13 Stay focused 106

1.14 Be patient 106

2. Some Common Issues 106

2.1 What if I forgot to claim some deductions on my return? 106

2.2 What if I don't have any records? 107

2.3 How much time does the IRS have to audit my return? 110

2.4 Can the IRS audit me if I don't file a return? 111

2.5 Can the revenue agent settle a case? 113

2.6 What if I failed to appeal and the auditor was wrong? 114

8 HOW TO DEFEND YOURSELF IN AN AUDIT AND WIN 116

1. Standard of Living 117

2. The Search for Unreported Income 118

2.1 Direct (specific item) method 118

2.2 Indirect methods 119

3. Exemptions and Deductions 123

3.1 Medical expenses 124

3.2 Casualty and theft losses 125

3.3 Rental income and expenses 126

3.4 Miscellaneous deductions 126

3.5 Safe deductions 126

3.6 Questionable deductions 128

4. Economic Reality Audits 130

5. Tax Shelters 133

6. Tax Protestors 134

9 TAX AUDITS OF BUSINESSES 137

1. Odds of an IRS Audit 137

1.1 How to reduce the odds of an IRS audit 139

1.2 How business tax returns are selected for audit 140

2. Specific Business Tax Audit Issues 143

    2.1 The hunt for unreported business receipts 143

    2.2 Questions concerning business expenses 144

    2.3 Independent contractor versus employee 149

    2.4 Schedule C businesses (sole proprietorships) 152

    2.5 Hobby-loss businesses 153

    2.6 Other audit issues for small businesses 154

3. What to Expect During a Business Tax Audit 155

    3.1 What if I'm missing some records? 155

    3.2 What does the IRS know about my business? 156

    3.3 Where will the audit take place? 157

    3.4 Common questions during business tax audits 157

10 IRS PENALTIES AND NOTICES: WHAT THEY REALLY MEAN 160

1. IRS Notices 161

    1.1 Reasons IRS notices are wrong 161

    1.2 Fighting an IRS notice 163

2. IRS Penalties 163

    2.1 Inaccurate tax returns 163

    2.2 Failure to file/Late filing 166

    2.3 Fraud 167

    2.4 Fraudulent failure to file tax returns 169

    2.5 Late payment of tax 170

    2.6 Estimated tax penalty 170

    2.7 Trust fund recovery penalty 171

3. Penalty Abatement 186

    3.1 Reasonable cause 188

    3.2 Challenge penalties 190

11 THE IRS COLLECTION PROCESS: KEEP YOUR MONEY AND ASSETS 192

1. Assessments 193

2. The IRS Collection Division 193

    2.1 The Automated Collection System 194

	2.2	The revenue officer	196
	2.3	Basic rules	197
3.	Options when Dealing with the Collection Division		199
	3.1	Payment in full	200
	3.2	Installment Agreements	200
	3.3	Payments to the IRS	204
4.	Collection Forms		205
	4.1	Forms 433-A and 433-B	206
	4.2	Form 870	222
	4.3	Form 900	223
	4.4	Form 2261	224
	4.5	Form 2751	227
5.	Collection Powers		229
	5.1	Summons	229
	5.2	IRS levy and seizure powers and authority	232
	5.3	The Federal Tax Lien	248
	5.4	IRS accounts as currently not collectible	257

12 HOW TO PAY PENNIES ON THE DOLLAR: THE OFFER IN COMPROMISE PROGRAM

12	HOW TO PAY PENNIES ON THE DOLLAR: THE OFFER IN COMPROMISE PROGRAM		259
1.	When Can You Make an Offer in Compromise?		261
	1.1	Doubt as to collectibility	262
	1.2	Doubt as to liability	263
	1.3	Effective Tax Administration	265
2.	How Do You Make an Offer in Compromise?		266
	2.1	How do you decide how much to offer?	266
	2.2	Documents you need to submit an Offer in Compromise	272
	2.3	Disadvantages of filing an Offer in Compromise	272
3.	The IRS Investigation Process		273
	3.1	What if the IRS accepts the offer?	275
	3.2	Collateral agreements	276
	3.3	What if the IRS rejects the offer?	277

13 BANKRUPTCY LAW AND TAXES: 279
    FORCE THE IRS TO SAY YES

    1. Types of Bankruptcy   280

        1.1 Chapter 7 bankruptcy   280

        1.2 Chapter 13 bankruptcy   281

    2. Discharge of Taxes in Bankruptcy   282

        2.1 Taxes not dischargeable in bankruptcy   283

        2.2 Effect of bankruptcy on a Federal Tax Lien   283

    3. Advantages of Bankruptcy   284

        3.1 Automatic stay   284

        3.2 Redetermination of taxes due   284

        3.3 Elimination of tax debts after discharge is received 285

        3.4 Forcing the IRS to accept a payment plan   285

    4. Disadvantages of Bankruptcy   285

        4.1 Incurs expense   285

        4.2 Results in a negative credit report   286

        4.3 Increases IRS collection time   286

        4.4 Incurs trustee fees   286

14 THE CRIMINAL INVESTIGATION DIVISION: 288
    BEWARE THE AGENTS WITH GUNS

    1. How Many IRS Criminal Investigations Occur Each Year?   289

    2. IRS Criminal Investigation Procedures   290

        2.1 The referral process   291

        2.2 Rules for criminal investigations   293

        2.3 Types of IRS criminal investigations   294

    3. Types of Criminal Tax Violations   294

        3.1 Criminal tax evasion   295

        3.2 Filing a false return   297

        3.3 Criminal failure to file a tax return   298

        3.4 Other tax-related crimes   300

    4. Statute of Limitations   302

    5. Taxpayer Rights During Criminal Investigations   302

15 FIGHT THE IRS IN COURT 305

1. The US Tax Court 305

    1.1 Burden of proof issues 310

    1.2 Advantages to filing a tax court petition 311

    1.3 Disadvantages of filing a tax court petition 312

    1.4 Representing yourself in tax court 313

2. Types of Tax Court Cases 314

    2.1 Regular cases 314

    2.2 "S" cases 319

    2.3 Legal costs 322

3. US District Court 322

    3.1 Suits for refund 322

    3.2 Suits for improper disclosure under IRC §6103 324

    3.3 Suits to stop seizure or sale of assets 327

    3.4 Suits to stop IRS collection activities 327

    3.5 Suit when IRS fails to release a Federal Tax Lien 328

    3.6 Suit for improper browsing 328

    3.7 Suit for improper collection actions 328

4. Waiver of Rights 329

5. Termination of Employment 330

16 THE TAXPAYER ADVOCATE: WHEN ALL ELSE FAILS 332

1. The Taxpayer Advocate Program 333

2. Taxpayer Bill of Rights 336

3. Taxpayer Assistance Order 338

4. Use Your Representative in Congress 341

17 CONCLUSION 343

APPENDIXES

1 IRS Distribution and Service Centers 348

2 IRS District Offices (Taxpayer Advocate) 350

CHECKLISTS

1   Checklist for filing a tax return   45

2   Are you an employee or an independent contractor?   151

FIGURES

1   Organizational structure of the IRS   7

2   Income tax audit procedures flowchart   94

SAMPLES

1   Form 8822 (Change of address)   18

2   Freedom of Information Act request letter   22

3   Freedom of Information Act appeal letter   24

4   Request for transcripts of account   27

5   Form 4506 (Request for copy or transcript of tax form)   29

6   Form 1127 (Application for extension of time for payment of tax)   33

7   Form 4700 (IRS examination workpapers)   87

8   Form 870 (Waiver of restrictions on assessment)   89

9   Affidavit regarding business expenses   109

10 How the bank deposits method works   120

11 Form 8275 (Disclosure statement)   129

12 Form 4822 (Statement of annual estimated personal and
    family expenses)   132

13 How the bank deposits method works for business audits   145

14 Letter responding to an IRS notice   164

15 Form 4180 (Report of interview with individual relative to
    trust fund recovery penalty)   172

16 Form 4181 (Questionnaire relating to federal trust fund
    tax matters of employer)   179

17 Trust fund recovery penalty appeal letter   181

18   Form 843 (Claim for refund and request for abatement)   187

19 Form 433-A (Collection information statement for wage earners
    and self-employed individuals)   207

20 Form 433-B (Collection information statement for businesses)   213

21 Form 2261 (Collateral agreement for future income — individual)   225

22 Form 2751 (Proposed assessment of trust fund recovery penalty) 228

23 Form 6639 (Financial records summons) 231

24 Form 2433 (Notice of seizure) 238

25 Form 12153 (Request for a collection due process hearing) 241

26 Form 9423 (Collection appeal request) 243

27 Letter requesting discharge of a Federal Tax Lien 251

28 Letter requesting subordination of a Federal Tax Lien 254

29 Form 656 (Offer in compromise) 267

30 Determining the amount of your OIC 271

31 Tax court petition 307

32 Designation of place of trial 309

33 Trial memorandum 316

34 Appeal of tax court decision 320

35 Form 2848 (Power of attorney) 325

36 Form 911 (Application for taxpayer assistance order) 339

TABLES

1 Where the IRS gets its money 9

2 Minimun gross income needed to file a tax return 36

3 Percentage of individual tax returns audited
(by income level) 63

4 Tax returns audited by city 64

5 Average itemized deductions — 1999 68

6 Percentage of businesses audited 138

7 Number of penalties abated in 1995 – 2001 188

8 Monthy expenses allowed by the IRS 220

9 IRS collection statistics 233

10 Number of offers in compromise 260

11 Present value factors 270

12 Number of IRS criminal investigations 289

13 Taxpayer assistance statistics 334

INTRODUCTION

IRS. CID. DIF. RO. BLS. OIC. IA. CNC. TCMP. IRP. FICA. RA. FOIA. IRC. IRM. SA. AGI. TCM. USTC. LLC. SFR. DLN. DD. BMF. IDRS. IMF. PRO. FUTA. TC. MSSP. TAO. PRP. EA. CPI. FTL. ACS. CTR. EIN. ES. FOIA. DLN. SSN. NRP. CDP. TDP. CAP. ETA.

Dealing with the Internal Revenue Service is similar to waking up in a foreign country without speaking the language. Sure, you can often get by, but when push comes to shove, you know that you're going to be taken advantage of.

Anyone who deals with tax issues on a day-to-day basis understands that the vast majority of tax laws are hopelessly complex. For instance, the Economic Growth and Tax Relief Reconciliation Act of 2001, which President Bush signed into law on June 7, 2001, contained 85 major changes (and 441 total changes) to the Internal Revenue Code (IRC), all of which will be phased in (and possibly out) until 2011. The new law itself was 291 pages long! In addition, many tax law changes were proposed after the September 11, 2001 attacks on New York and Washington DC, in part to help the victims and also to stimulate a sluggish economy. As you can imagine, keeping track of all these changes is a major challenge — especially to the IRS! The IRS is often criticized, but in all fairness, its job is next to impossible to perform much of the time.

When I first began my employment with the IRS district counsel (the in-house legal staff for the IRS and now called "Area Counsel"), I was overwhelmed every day by the alphabet soup of acronyms, the piles of tax forms (of which at last count there were more than 1,000, with the number seeming to increase daily), and the fruitless attempt to interpret the IRC. Things never really got any better, only more manageable or tolerable.

This is what it's like on the inside. To you, the average American taxpayer who is undoubtedly on the outside, the bureaucratic maze of the IRS is downright impossible to figure out. The IRS knows it has the advantage if *it* makes the rules and keeps the other players (i.e., you, the taxpayer) in the dark, forced to learn those rules as the game is in progress. Since I left the IRS in 1994, there have been several internal reorganizations, moving employees from one old division to one new division, all in an attempt to find something that works. Of course, this has resulted in a great deal of confusion and stress for current IRS employees.

Imagine if a baseball player found out during the course of a baseball game that he or she has only three strikes before being out, while the pitcher knew this all along. Without a doubt, the pitcher would have a huge advantage. In the tax game, the IRS is the pitcher: the player that understands the game. The taxpayers are the batters: unsure how to play the game and not aware that three strikes make an out.

The purpose of this book is to update the rules and highlight the vast changes made since the second edition was published in early 2002, and to put you on a level playing field with the IRS. Once everyone understands the rules of the game, it becomes much easier for the taxpayer to win. And winning is the name of the tax game when the opponent is the IRS.

After discussing the history and organization of the IRS in the first few chapters of this book, I will take you step-by-step through the filing process, the audit, appeals, and court proceedings, and help you keep your hard-earned money and assets. I also include chapters on IRS penalties, collection and bankruptcy issues, and criminal investigations. I use real-life examples to explain many of the tax concepts and to demonstrate how to use various defenses and other weapons against the IRS. At the end of each chapter is a section called Tax Points. These sections provide a summary of the main points of the chapter and are an easy way to review and remember the information presented.

Education (or a lot of money to hire the best tax professionals!) is the only real chance you have to win the IRS game. I have written this book to give you the education you need to eliminate the fear of the IRS such that you will be able to fight and beat the IRS at both the administrative level and in the court system. Good luck!

CHAPTER 1

MEET THE IRS

The Congress shall have the power to lay and collect taxes on income, from whatever source derived, without apportionment among the several States, and without regard to any census or enumeration.

16th amendment to the United States Constitution (1913)

The taxpayer — that's someone who works for the federal government but doesn't have to take a civil service examination.

Ronald Reagan, United States president (1980-1988)

1. A Brief History of Income Tax

There has not always been an income tax in the United States, and George Washington or Thomas Jefferson could never have imagined anything remotely resembling today's IRS. The first tax on income in this country was put in place in 1862, and was used to finance the civil war. Not surprisingly, this tax proved highly unpopular with Americans, especially after the war had ended. It was discontinued in 1872.

It was not until 1913 that the United States again instituted an income tax. Ever since then, Congress, the president, and US citizens/taxpayers have been fighting over how to efficiently and fairly tax the citizens to finance the operations of the national government. Tax reform and tax reduction have been campaign themes in nearly every presidential election since 1913 because most politicians realize that running a campaign on increasing taxes is a sure way to get defeated. Yet, while no one publicly admits to wanting to increase taxes, the reality of nearly all "tax reforms" is that taxes rise and the tax laws get more complex.

Tax Freedom Day through
the years:
1984   April 15
2000   May 1
2002   April 27
2004   April 11

If anyone needs proof that revisions in the tax laws inevitably increase the average American's tax burden, all one has to do is look at the ever-changing Tax Freedom Day. This is the date each year when the average American has earned enough money to pay all federal, state, and local taxes. According to the Tax Foundation (a nonpartisan, nonprofit group that provides tax education to tax practitioners and the general public), in 1944, the average American had to work the first 90 days of the year (from January 1 to March 30) to pay all taxes owed to the government. By 1964, the number of days increased to 104 (all the way to April 13). Tax Freedom Day in 1984 was April 15 (106 days), and by 2000 the day was pushed back to May 1 (121 days). This day retreated back into April during 2002, primarily as a result of the US recession and the 2001 tax cuts. The April 11, 2004, Tax Freedom Day was the earliest since 1967! However, it does make a big difference where you live, as state and local tax rates can greatly affect when your particular Tax Freedom Day occurs. For instance, Conneticut (April 28) and New York (April 27) are the worst offenders, while people who live in Alaska (March 26) and Alabama (April 1) get off relatively easy. So when you are working in January, February, March, April, and possibly May this year, remember that every minute spent at the office, on the road, in the factory, or wherever your job is located is going to feed the government and not you and your family. And this is a lot of money. Again, thanks to the Tax Foundation, Americans spend more time working for tax than they do for any other expense, as the following chart demonstrates:

Expense	Days worked in 2004 to cover expense
Federal/State/Local Taxes	101
Housing	66
Medical Care	51
Food	31
Transportation	31
Recreation	22
Clothing	14
Savings	5
All Other Expenses	44
TOTAL	365

Politicians today continue to spread an anti-tax, anti-IRS message, presumably because such rhetoric is popular with the voters. However, in any alternative plan these politicians offer, the average American will continue to pay taxes to the government, possibly even more than he or she is paying today. Unless we adopt the Libertarian Party's position on taxes (reduce or eliminate nearly all taxes and the big government that goes with the higher tax revenues), there is going to be some federal government tax in this country in the future, and it is going to be awfully similar to what we have today.

Many campaign promises made during recent congressional and presidential elections have hinted that the IRS would no longer be necessary if a flat tax or national sales tax were implemented in place of today's income tax:

★ A *flat tax* is a tax on income where the tax is a certain percentage of income (unlike today's multiple levels of taxation, which vary depending on how much income is made), with fewer deductions than today's taxation system or possibly no deductions at all. For example, everyone might pay 20% of their income in tax. Individuals in favor of the flat tax claim it would make the tax laws much simpler and fairer than they are at present.

★ A *national sales tax* would be just like today's state and local sales taxes, except that it would be set at a much higher rate (one proposal from Rep. John Linder (R-GA) is for a 30% sales tax), given that it was intended to replace the income tax.

Under either of these proposed tax systems, there would still need to be some federal agency (like the IRS) to enforce the tax laws, whether through an increased effort to audit small businesses and the self-employed (who may be more likely to fail to report income under a flat tax system) or retailers who fail to report sales (under a national sales tax). Either way, the IRS as we know it is not likely to disappear at any time in the near future.

2. So What Is the IRS?

While the IRS is not responsible for the recent tax increases or the complexity of the tax laws, it gets most of the blame and it is undoubtedly an easy target. The IRS is the largest agency in the United States Department of the Treasury. Its mission, at least according to the IRS, is to "provide America's taxpayers top-quality service by helping them understand and meet their tax responsibilities and by applying the tax law with integrity

The IRS's mission is to collect the proper amount of tax revenues due, at the least cost to the public, in both a fair and impartial manner.

and fairness to all." The IRS has the very difficult task of trying to uphold the federal tax laws by encouraging the highest degree of voluntary compliance with the tax laws and regulations.

Most Americans do not disagree with this mission and do not have a problem with the IRS attempting to collect the proper amount of tax revenues due, at the least cost to the public, in both a fair and impartial manner. However, too often it seems that the IRS doesn't consider fairness, impartiality, and whether it is collecting the proper amount of tax. Instead, many IRS employees seem to want to collect as much tax as possible, in any way possible, regardless of the personal financial consequences and fairness to the taxpayer. Though this attitude is certainly not shared by every IRS employee, it is common enough that it creates a need for taxpayers to understand the tax laws, along with how the IRS is organized and operates in its attempt to administer the tax laws, so that they can stand up for their rights.

It should come as no surprise that the IRS is a hopelessly complex organization. It seems that not a year goes by without some new layer of bureaucracy being added to the already nightmarish bureaucratic system. Figure 1 is a brief and simplified illustration of the structure of the IRS.

Most of the layers of the bureaucracy shown in Figure 1 have no meaningful contact with taxpayers. Instead, the commissioner, deputy commissioners, and the National Office staff are primarily concerned with tax policy and management.

The IRS service centers are the initial contact point for most taxpayers, as these are the places where all tax returns get filed. After you file your tax return, most dealings you might have with the IRS will be at the local level (see the list of district offices in Appendix 2). As a result of the IRS reorganization (begun in 2001 and still being implemented!), you will likely come into contact with one of the four main operating divisions:

★ *Wage and Investment*: This division will handle more than 100 million taxpayers, including those who are employees and/or have home investment income.

★ *Small Business and Self Employed*: This division will handle more than 45 million taxpayers who are self-employed or own small businesses (annual gross receipts less than $5 million per year).

★ *Large and Mid-Size Businesses*: This division will handle businesses that gross more than $5 million per year.

FIGURE 1
ORGANIZATIONAL STRUCTURE OF THE IRS

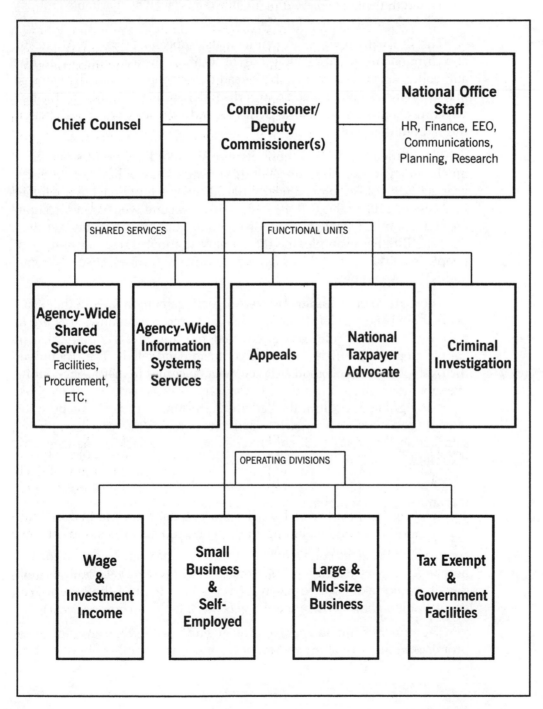

★ *Tax Exempt and Governmental Entities*: This division is responsible for handling employee benefit plans (such as 401(k) or other retirement plans), exempt organizations (such as charitable groups), and various governmental entities.

The IRS will continue to maintain its Appeals, Taxpayer Advocate, and Criminal Investigation Divisions. In addition, the examination (audits) and collection employees will be spread out among the four divisions so that they can develop specific expertise, depending on the type of taxpayer. Each of the various IRS divisions and functions will be discussed throughout this book.

It is difficult to believe how many offices and employees and how much money it takes to implement this country's tax policy. For the fiscal year 2004, the IRS employed nearly 100,000 people and had a total budget in excess of $10,185,000,000. By comparison, several well-known companies have a much smaller work force and annual operating budget than does the IRS. For example, the IRS employed about the same number of people in 2004 as did Dell Computers, Southwest Airlines, Cisco Systems, and NBC-TV combined.

There are so many different layers of management in the IRS that it appears there is no one left to do any work. As most companies that are in business to make a profit have discovered, multiple levels of management simply create an inefficient maze of confusion and chaos. The IRS proves the truth of this: it is as good as it gets when it comes to inefficiency. However, the IRS realizes it has these limitations, as in May of 2002 it received a passing grade of B- from the Federal Performance Project. Keeping the overall grade down were such negative factors as "decreased employee satisfaction, problems with computer systems, and lack of management flexibility."

Given the sheer size of the IRS, along with the size of its management, it is amazing that it manages to do a fairly decent job of collecting tax revenues. While there is no doubt that billions of dollars of income, from both legal and illegal sources, go untaxed and/or uncollected every year in this country, the IRS does collect over $2 trillion every year. To get an idea of how much money $2 trillion is, if you spent $1,000 every second of every day, it would take approximately 64 years before all of the money was spent. Table 1 shows where the IRS gets its $2 trillion from.

The numbers are staggering. And regardless of what any politician promises in the way of tax reform or tax relief, the numbers keep getting

The IRS collects over $1 trillion every year.

TABLE 1

WHERE THE IRS GETS ITS MONEY

Fiscal Year		How much the IRS collects from:			
	Individuals	Corporations	Employment	Other	Total
1993	586	132	412	47	1,177
1994	620	154	444	58	1,276
1995	675	174	465	62	1,376
1996	745	189	492	74	1,500
1997	825	204	529	79	1,637
1998	928	213	558	84	1,783
1999	1,002	216	599	101	1,918
2000	1,137	236	640	100	2,113
2001	1,178	187	682	98	2,145
2002	1,038	211	688	97	2034
2003	987	194	696	93	1,970

The amounts shown are in billions of dollars.

Employment tax numbers include Social Security, Medicare, Unemployment, and retirement-related taxes.

The "other" category includes excise, customs, estate, gift, and other miscellaneous taxes.

bigger. In general, as long as the numbers get bigger, so will the IRS. And as long as the IRS grows in size, US citizens will continue to have more tax problems. It is as simple as this.

3. How to Play with the IRS

Given the size of the IRS bureaucracy, you may feel intimidated or uncertain when dealing with its employees. But as a taxpayer, you should never feel this way. Despite the IRS's size and power, you have many opportunities to level the playing field and come out on top in the tax game.

3.1 The rules

There are four basic rules to keep in mind to help you avoid any misunderstandings or unnecessary problems when dealing with the IRS.

(a) *Strictly follow time deadlines to the day.* Many taxpayers get themselves in unnecessary trouble with the IRS because they don't do something when the IRS wants it done. While I'm not suggesting that you have no control over deadlines, missing an established deadline will certainly cause you more problems than it is worth.

(b) *Any time you communicate with the IRS, do it in writing.* Keep a copy of every communication for your records. If you must communicate orally, either in person or by telephone, follow up the conversation with a letter documenting what was said and agreed to. You will see how important this rule is when you realize that one division of the IRS often has no clue as to what another division of the IRS is doing. Furthermore, there are often massive communication failures within the same IRS division, perhaps even by employees in the same office. If there is conflict sometime down the road between what you and the IRS believed was orally communicated, the IRS will almost always believe its own personnel (to your disadvantage). If you have a written document to back up your position, you can make a stronger case.

(c) *Be specific.* When you must contact the IRS (whether in writing, in person, or by telephone), be specific about what you want to accomplish, what the facts are, and what the tax laws say regarding the issue. Many taxpayers create additional problems for themselves because they don't know what they want or what they are entitled to, or they are unclear on the facts or law. The IRS will use this uncertainty to your disadvantage.

As well, in many cases the biggest roadblock to finding a solution to the problem is finding the right person to deal with. The more specific you are, the more likely you are to find that person.

(d) *Get the IRS to agree.* Most IRS employees are trained to question and disagree. If you make statements rather than ask questions, you are more likely to get the IRS to agree with you. For example, a statement like "You would agree that an expense is deductible if it was incurred in the ordinary and necessary course of my business" will have much better results for you than a question like "Is this expense deductible?"

If you follow these rules, you should be in a much better position to fight the IRS and win. This being said, there is still one more rule that must never be broken:

> *Do not trust the IRS and its employees to do the right thing, and never rely on anything they say unless the statement is put in writing and signed.*

While many good people work for the IRS and try to live up to their word, many others do not. IRS employees often give incorrect tax advice or information, not because they are malicious, but because they do not fully understand the complex tax laws that they must interpret, administer, and enforce. When an IRS employee does provide incorrect information, that employee will often reverse himself or herself to cover up the error. If you have not got the statement or information in writing, it will be your word (that you were misinformed) against the IRS employee's word. It is not hard to figure out who will win the war of words when the IRS is the judge.

3.2   Your rights

It is also important for you to realize that you do have rights during every contact you have with the IRS. These rights are set out in IRS Publication 1 and include the following:

★ The IRS should explain to you what your rights are during any contact with the IRS. In reality, the IRS rarely does this, so it is up to you to know what your rights are during every phase of the tax game.

★ The IRS will always respect your right to privacy and the confidentiality of the information contained on any tax return. Given that there are severe penalties for violating the tax disclosure laws, the IRS is very good at observing your rights in this area.

★ You are always permitted to have professional representation (i.e., certified public accountant or CPA, tax attorney, or other tax professional) during any contact with the IRS. The IRS is typically very good at allowing taxpayers to exercise their right to professional representation. The basic difference between a tax attorney and a CPA is the formal education they undergo and the availability of confidentiality. The CPA is trained in accounting, which will include some tax training, while the tax attorney has a law degree and usually some formal training or experience with tax issues. An attorney can give you more confidentiality (called the attorney-client privilege) than can a CPA, which means he or she cannot be forced to reveal details of your case. The Tax Reform Act of 1998 recently added a limited practitioner privilege for discussions between a tax practitioner and a taxpayer concerning tax advice. The difference between the two privileges is that the new tax practitioner privilege does not extend to criminal matters. It is a step in the right direction but does not go nearly as far as does the attorney-client privilege.

★ You have the right to be treated courteously and professionally. Unfortunately, the IRS often completely fails when it comes to this basic taxpayer right. As a taxpayer, you do not have to tolerate rudeness or unprofessional treatment from any IRS employee. While you and the IRS may disagree about the facts and/or the law in your case, the IRS employee is aware that he or she must handle the disagreement in a professional and courteous manner. You have the right to demand (and receive) a new IRS employee should you ever be unhappy with your treatment.

★ You have the right to pay only the correct amount of tax due under the law. The IRS tries to observe this rule, although many audits are concluded with the taxpayer paying more in tax than the law actually requires.

★ You have the right to receive assistance from the Taxpayer Advocate Service when you reach a roadblock in normal IRS channels. This right is discussed in detail in chapter 16.

★ You have the right to ask for an appeals office review of your case whenever you disagree with the IRS relating to the amount of your tax liability or certain IRS collection actions. You should always take advantage of this opportunity, as most IRS Appeals Officers are highly trained employees with enough authority to correct any lower-level IRS mistakes. The IRS Appeals functions are discussed in detail throughout this book.

3.3 Some useful publications

Throughout this book I will refer to several publications and research materials concerning the IRS and the tax laws in general. The following is a list of frequently cited materials, with information on where they can be located:

(a) *Internal Revenue Code (IRC)*. This is the law under which the IRS and all taxpayers operate. It consists of Title 26 of the United States Code. The IRC can be found in many libraries and all law libraries. I will also refer to other sections of the United States Code throughout this book. For example, when I write about 5 USC §522, I am referring to Section 522 of Title 5 of the United States Code (USC). The USC, like the IRC, can be found in many general libraries and all law libraries.

(b) *Revenue Rulings (Rev. Rul.)*. This is the IRS interpretation of the IRC, which provides guidance to IRS employees and taxpayers about specific sections of the IRC. It can be found in most law libraries.

(c) *IRS Regulations (Regs)*. This is the official policy on how the IRS will administer specific tax laws. The Regs can also be found in most law libraries.

(d) *Internal Revenue Manual (IRM)*. This is the internal operating manual for the IRS. It does not have the full force of law and the IRS is not legally obligated to follow it. Not surprisingly, the IRS often chooses to ignore its own manual and rules, especially when doing so is to the taxpayers' disadvantage. You should not be discouraged by this and should always use the IRM if it is beneficial to do so. The IRM is available in most law libraries and can also be ordered directly from Tax Analysts, 6830 North Fairfax Drive, Arlington, VA 22213.

(e) *Court decisions*. Throughout the book I will make brief mention of various court decisions. These decisions can be found in any law library and some public libraries.

(f) *IRS publications*. The IRS publishes hundreds of different publications every year to assist you with questions you may have regarding all phases of the tax game. While many of these are highly specialized (covering such things as how to claim moving expenses and report gains from your mutual fund), many are general in nature and are quite valuable for nearly all taxpayers. Of the more general publications, I would recommend getting a copy of Publication 1 (*Your Rights as a Taxpayer*), Publication 17 (*Your Federal Income Tax for Individuals*), Publication 334 (*Tax Guide for*

Small Businesses), and Publication 910 (*Guide to Free Tax Services*). All IRS publications can be ordered directly from an IRS distribution center (see Appendix 1 for locations), and there is no cost for any of these.

I also refer to and explain three major tax reform bills that are now law: the Taxpayer Relief Act of 1997, the IRS Restructuring and Reform Act of 1998 (referred to throughout this book as the Tax Reform Act of 1998), and the Economic Growth and Tax Relief Reconciliation Act of 2001. Each of these new tax acts greatly strengthened the rights you have when dealing with the IRS. They should be used to your advantage whenever possible.

Tax Points

★ Understanding the massive IRS bureaucracy and complex tax laws permits you to even the playing field with the IRS.

★ Always follow all IRS deadlines to the day.

★ Keep accurate records of any communications with the IRS or any of its employees.

★ Make it easy for the IRS to agree, rather than disagree, with you.

★ Understand the facts and law before you contact the IRS.

★ Never trust the IRS or any of its employees to do the right thing.

★ You have many rights that the IRS must recognize. The most important of these rights is the right to privacy and confidentiality with respect to your return information.

★ You have the right to be treated professionally and courteously every time you have contact with any IRS employee.

CHAPTER 2

THE IRS RECORD-KEEPING SYSTEM: WHAT DOES THE IRS KNOW?

The purpose of the Internal Revenue Service is to collect the proper amount of tax revenue at the least cost to the public in a manner warranting the highest degree of public confidence in our integrity, efficiency, and fairness.

Margaret Richardson, former IRS Commissioner (1993-1997), as quoted on the IRS Internet site

It's hard to tinker with a monster.

Senator Sam Nunn (D-Georgia), discussing the United States Tax Code on October 5, 1993

Most Americans would challenge Ms. Richardson's statement; the taxpaying public has little or no confidence in the IRS's ability to treat taxpayers with integrity, efficiency, or fairness. With this in mind, it becomes important for all taxpayers involved with the IRS in any way (including the mere filing of tax returns) to understand all rules of the tax game before beginning to play the game at all.

One important way of leveling the IRS playing field is to know as much information about the IRS as possible before ever talking with an IRS employee. In particular, it is vital that you understand what the IRS knows about a taxpayer. In this chapter I discuss the IRS's system of maintaining information on taxpayers.

1. Understand the IRS Record-Keeping System

The IRS somehow manages to keep track of the financial information (income and expenses) for over 200 million taxpayers (including individuals and businesses). How it does this is anyone's guess because, generally, one division of the IRS is clueless about what any other IRS division is doing. According to the IRS's Office of Research for the 2000 tax year the IRS received approximately 226,564,000 tax returns, of which individual income tax returns accounted for approximately 127,657,000. Businesses filed approximately 36,378,000 returns, and the remaining returns represented a mixture of gift, estate, excise, amended, nonprofit, and requests for extensions to file tax returns. The IRS projects that the total number of tax returns to be filed will increase to almost 240 million by the year 2004. These numbers do not include the more than one billion Forms W-2 (Wage and Tax Statement) and 1099 (Miscellaneous Income) that employers and other businesses file with the IRS every year.

Given the amount of data and the number of forms that the IRS must keep track of on a yearly basis, it is remarkable that it does not make more mistakes than it actually does. What then can you do to reduce the odds of an IRS encounter as the result of an IRS mistake or miscommunication with the IRS?

1.1 Let the IRS know where you are

One of the more important things that you can do to prevent having to deal with the IRS is to keep the IRS informed of your current address. While this may go against your instinct (i.e., you may feel that if the IRS doesn't know where you live, it can't do anything bad to you), it is extremely important that the IRS has every taxpayer's correct address on record. This is because the IRS is permitted by law to use your last known address (according to IRS records) as the place to send you any important tax notices or information requests, many of which have severe time limitations with negative results if you don't respond. The IRS will also use your last known address for mailing tax refund checks, wh ich may not get properly forwarded. Of course, the IRS has a change-of-address form (Form 8822), shown in Sample 1.

You have nothing to gain by trying to hide from the IRS, and you have much to lose by doing so. It is almost always better to confront any problems as soon as possible rather than waiting for the IRS to catch up to you. And eventually, the IRS will catch up to you!

For the 2000 tax year, the IRS received approximately 226,564,000 tax returns:

Approximately 127,657,000 were individual income tax returns.

Approximately 36,378,000 were business returns.

The remaining returns represented a mixture of gift, estate, excise, amended, nonprofit, and requests for extensions to file tax returns.

The IRS projects that the total number of tax returns to be filed will increase to almost 240 million by the year 2004.

SAMPLE 1
FORM 8822 (CHANGE OF ADDRESS)

Form **8822** (Rev. December 2003) Department of the Treasury Internal Revenue Service	**Change of Address** ▶ Please type or print. ▶ See instructions on back. ▶ Do not attach this form to your return.	OMB No. 1545-1163

Part I   Complete This Part To Change Your Home Mailing Address

Check **all** boxes this change affects:

1   [X] Individual income tax returns (Forms 1040, 1040A, 1040EZ, TeleFile, 1040NR, etc.)
     ▶ If your last return was a joint return and you are now establishing a residence separate
     from the spouse with whom you filed that return, check here . . . . ▶ [ ]

2   [ ] Gift, estate, or generation-skipping transfer tax returns (Forms 706, 709, etc.)
     ▶ For Forms 706 and 706-NA, enter the decedent's name and social security number below.

     ▶ Decedent's name   ▶ Social security number

3 a Your name (first name, initial, and last name)	**3b Your social security number**
Sara Estill	123-45-6789
4 a Spouse's name (first name, initial, and last name)	**4b Spouse's social security number**

5   Prior name(s). See instructions.

6 a Old address (no., street, city or town, state, and ZIP code). If a P.O. box or foreign address, see instructions.	Apt. no.
321 Main Street, Denver, CO 80001	
6 b Spouse's old address, if different from line 6a (no., street, city or town, state, and ZIP code). If a P.O. box or foreign address.	Apt. no.
7 New address (no., street, city or town, state, and ZIP code). If a P.O. box or foreign address, see instructions. 123 Main Street Denver, CO 80001	Apt. no.

Part II   Complete This Part To Change Your Business Mailing Address or Business Location

Check **all** boxes this change affects:

8   [ ] Employment, excise, income, and other business returns (Forms 720, 940, 940-EZ, 941, 990, 1041, 1065, 1120, etc.)
9   [ ] Employee plan returns (Forms 5500, 5500-EZ, etc.).
10   [ ] Business location

11 a Business name	**11b Employer identification number**

12 Old mailing address (no., street, city or town, state, and ZIP code). If a P.O. box or foreign address, see instructions.	Room or suite no.
13 New mailing address (no., street, city or town, state, and ZIP code). If a P.O. box or foreign address, see instructions.	Room or suite no.
14 New business location (no., street, city or town, state, and ZIP code). If a foreign address, see instructions.	Room or suite no.

Part III   Signature

Daytime telephone number of person to contact (optional)   ▶ 303-555-1221

Sign Here	▶ _Sara Estill_ 1/2/05 Your signature Date	If Part II completed, signature of owner, officer, or representative Date
	▶ If joint return, spouse's signature Date	Title

For Privacy Act and Paperwork Reduction Act Notice, see back of form.   Form **8822** (Rev. 12-2003)
(HTA)

1.2 Keep the IRS correctly informed

Be sure to notify the IRS any time it receives incorrect information about you. This may be as simple as notifying the IRS when a Form W-2 or 1099 contains incorrect information (you should also notify the payor listed on the Form W-2 or 1099 so that he or she can prepare and file a corrected form). It may be as complex as filing an amended tax return. Many taxpayers suffer severe consequences based on information that, had it been correct, would have resulted in no problems at all. For instance, sometimes the IRS will "double count" income, disallow your children or spouse as dependents (perhaps as the result of an incorrect Social Security number or, as is often the case with recently married spouses, the failure to change a new last name with the Social Security Administration), or make a host of other improper changes to your tax return. The key is communication: keeping the IRS informed about its errors is the only way to ensure that the IRS keeps you informed.

2. Know What the IRS Knows about You

Many Americans have a misconception about the amount of information the IRS has about a taxpayer. While the IRS computer system has certainly improved over the last few years, thus providing today's IRS employee with a greater amount of instantaneous information than was available in the past, the IRS still has only a limited amount of information concerning you. It is reasonable to assume that an IRS employee has the following information available:

★ *Your tax return filing history.* The IRS computers maintain a database that permits the employee to see when and what type(s) of tax returns have been filed in the past, along with much information from the return itself (such as Adjusted Gross Income, Taxable Income, and the total tax due). This information is accessed based upon your Social Security or Employer Identification Number.

★ *Your source(s) of income.* The IRS computers keep track of how much income you received from wages, interest, and dividends and can access records about the payor of this income. The IRS will provide this information to you upon request. (This may be useful if you need to file some prior tax returns and are missing records to prepare accurate returns.) This request is known as an IRP (Information Return Program) request and is discussed in chapter 8.

★ *Personal taxpayer information.* This information includes your name, address, social security number, marital status, and number of children.

> Always inform the IRS of your current address. The IRS may legally use your last known address as the place to send important tax notices, information requests, or tax refund checks.

★ *The current balance you owe to the IRS.* The records reveal what, if anything, you owe the IRS for any prior tax years, including any penalties and interest that may have been added to the original debt. There is information on your payment history, including any amounts paid through an Installment Agreement (i.e., a payment plan) with the IRS. The IRS employee can also determine how much money it would take to pay off your entire IRS tax debt at any date in the future, including calculating interest.

★ *Notes from previous IRS contacts.* Given the sheer size of the IRS, it is likely that you will not speak with the same IRS employee twice concerning a particular tax matter (unless a specific employee has been assigned to your case). For example, when you contact the IRS by telephone, there may be hundreds of employees who potentially could handle the call. The IRS employee is trained to take accurate notes of the conversation so that the next IRS employee handling the case will be able to understand what was done in the past. These notes are usually entered into the IRS computer system, although they could be written down on work papers if there is an actual file on you. I have found that the accuracy of any IRS notes varies greatly depending upon the competency of the IRS employee. For this reason, it is important for you to keep accurate notes of any conversations you have with the IRS.

Most IRS paper files (as opposed to computer files) on taxpayers contain very standard information, such as copies of tax returns, Forms W-2 and 1099, documents provided by the taxpayer to the IRS, and miscellaneous notes and work papers.

Many taxpayers feel much more comfortable once they understand exactly what the IRS knows about them, because the information isn't as extensive or threatening as most people believe. Fortunately, the IRS does not generally know what our house looks like, what kind of car we drive, or who we had dinner with last Friday night.

3. Don't be Afraid to Request Information

Given that the IRS is supposed to be interested only in discovering the truth concerning the proper amount of taxes due, there is no reason why an IRS employee would refuse to disclose most, if not all, information in your file when you request it. (The only exception to this is when your file contains information the IRS employee is not permitted by law to disclose. This may include information gathered as part of a criminal investigation,

> The easiest and quickest way to obtain tax information is to request it directly from an IRS employee, either in writing or by visiting any IRS office.

from third parties who do not want their names disclosed, or information that would violate someone's right of privacy if it were disclosed.) Therefore, the easiest and quickest way for you to obtain any necessary tax information is to request it directly from an IRS employee, either in writing or by visiting any IRS office.

Should the IRS employee refuse to disclose any or all of your tax information, you should immediately find out why the employee is taking such an extreme position. If necessary, speak with the employee's manager about the refusal.

If you still can't get the information after a meeting with the manager, you should make sure that the IRS is not about to make a fraud referral, either criminal or civil. An IRS auditor is required to inform you if a fraud referral is about to be made. In such a case, the IRS usually will not turn over any tax information. If the IRS is about to make a fraud referral, the rules of the game change immediately (see the discussion of the fraud penalty in chapter 10).

If no fraud referral is being contemplated and the IRS still refuses to disclose any information, you still have a few other options. You can ask to speak to the manager's supervisor. Sometimes this is enough to get the information you desire. Many taxpayers overlook this step, believing that further management involvement will not result in any changes to the IRS position. However, remember that all IRS employees, including those in management, are employed to assist the taxpayers, who pay the employees' salaries through taxes.

If this still does not work and the IRS remains uncooperative, you should consider filing a request under the Freedom of Information Act (FOIA) to force the IRS to turn over the requested documents.

3.1 Freedom of Information Act requests

Under 5 USC §552, all Americans are entitled, with certain limited exceptions (i.e., those documents which relate to national security, are somehow confidential or privileged, or relate to ongoing law enforcement investigations), to find out what type of records the government is maintaining on them. The IRS is no exception to this rule.

When filing a Freedom of Information Act (FOIA) claim against the IRS, you must state specifically what documents are being requested and must agree to pay for any copy charges that the IRS may incur when providing the records to you. Sample 2 is the type of letter you should write to the IRS when making an FOIA request.

SAMPLE 2
FREEDOM OF INFORMATION ACT REQUEST LETTER

Internal Revenue Service
Attention: FOIA Officer
600 17th Street
Denver, CO 80202

December 27, 20—

Re: Freedom of Information Act Request

Dear IRS FOIA Officer:

Under the provisions of the Freedom of Information Act, 5 USC§552, I am requesting copies of:

- The revenue agent's report, including all notes and workpapers
- Any and all statements made by me or by any third party to the IRS relating to my audit
- [identify other records as clearly and as specifically as possible]

Before you fill the request, please inform me of any fees for searching for or copying the records I have requested, unless this amount is less than $50.

If all or any part of this request is denied, please cite the specific exemption that you think justifies the refusal to release the information and inform me of the appeal procedures available to me under the law.

I would appreciate your handling this request as quickly as possible, and I look forward to a response within 10 days, as stipulated in Section 552(6)(A)(I).

Sincerely,

Herman H. Munster
1313 Mockingbird Lane
Denver, CO 80222

After the IRS receives the FOIA request, it must decide the following within 10 days of receipt of the request:

★ What documents will and won't be released to the taxpayer

★ If any documents will not be released, the reason why the IRS will not release them

★ The amount of the fee, if any, to copy the documents requested

If you disagree with the IRS decision about which documents will not be released, you may appeal that decision. The IRS must explain your appeal rights in the letter denying you the documents. Sample 3 shows a model appeal letter to the IRS.

If you still are not satisfied after the initial appeal is filed, you may file a lawsuit in the district court within six years from the date when the IRS's 20-day response period expires. A lawsuit may be necessary because the IRS tends to err on the side of being too conservative with the release of documents.

To win in district court, you must be able to show that the IRS improperly withheld records that should have been given to you under the FOIA laws. If you win your lawsuit against the IRS, showing that the IRS did not have a reasonable basis for withholding the documents, the IRS must pay for your costs and attorney fees associated with the suit.

The taxpayer often requests the following documents in an FOIA request to the IRS:

★ A copy of the revenue agent's report. This report is created when an audit produces additional changes to the tax return(s) under examination.

★ Any statements, whether oral or written, made by the taxpayer to an IRS employee.

★ The transmittal letter that is used to send the file from the Examination Division to the Appeals Division. This letter may contain valuable information about the case from the IRS's perspective.

★ Any third-party records (such as bank statements, credit card invoices, business receipts) involved in the taxpayer's audit.

★ A special agent's report (if a criminal investigation took place and is over). If the criminal investigation is still ongoing, the IRS cannot be forced to turn over any records.

SAMPLE 3
FREEDOM OF INFORMATION ACT APPEAL LETTER

Internal Revenue Service
Attention: FOIA Officer
600 17th Street
Denver, CO 80202

January 5, 20—

Re: Freedom of Information Act Appeal

Dear IRS FOIA Officer:

   The purpose of this letter is to inform you that I wish to appeal the denial of my request for information pursuant to the Freedom of Information Act, 5 USC§552. On January 3, 20—, I received a letter from John Doe at the IRS denying my request for access to the following documents:

- Copy of the revenue agent's report, including all notes and workpapers
- Copies of any and all statments made by me or by any third party to the IRS relating to my audit

   I am enclosing a copy of this denial along with a copy of my request. Please review this matter and let me know when the information that I am seeking will be disclosed.

   As provided for in §552(6)(A)(ii), I will await a reply within 20 working days. Should this information not be disclosed to me, I will have no option but to file suit in the United States district court.

Sincerely,

Herman H. Munster
1313 Mockingbird Lane
Denver, CO 80222

★ Copies of the taxpayer's tax returns for any years involved in an audit or collection dispute. Copies of tax returns can also be requested from the IRS service center where the returns were filed by filling out and filing Form 4506 with the service center. This procedure is discussed in section **3.2** below.

★ The revenue agent's work papers, along with the index to the audit file (although the IRS may refuse to disclose these documents as being privileged).

★ The revenue agent's time log and daily activity record. These records will show what the IRS has done with respect to an audit and when it was done.

There are some documents that the IRS does not need to disclose to you in response to an FOIA request. Some of the more common exemptions include the following:

★ A computation of the DIF score in an audit (see chapter 5 for a discussion of the DIF scores)

★ Criminal investigation referral materials on specific taxpayers or taxpayers in general

★ Internal IRS documents relating to collection activities

★ Tax return information relating to other taxpayers, unless the information is in statistical form

★ Information received from confidential informants or persons other than the taxpayer who is seeking the material

★ Letters and other documents from the IRS attorneys (area counsel) to various divisions of the IRS (such as Collections or Examinations) (this information is protected under the attorney-client privilege)

★ Personnel files of IRS employees

If the IRS refuses to disclose any materials based on one of the available exemptions, it must first try to delete the confidential information from the document and give you a revised copy of the document. The IRS may, however, refuse to release the entire document if all, or a large portion, of the document is confidential or otherwise not permitted to be disclosed.

You have a legal right to most information in the government's possession, so there are really no disadvantages to you if you file an FOIA request, and there are advantages to filing the request. The most important

> You have a legal right to most information in the government's possession. By filing a Freedom of Information Act request you will know exactly what the IRS knows about you — and what the IRS does not know about you.

advantage is that you will know exactly what the IRS knows about you, including any facts or legal arguments that have not previously been shared with you. In addition, you will know what is *not* contained in the file, which can be important for preventing you from making any incorrect assumptions about what the IRS really knows.

3.2 IRS transcript of account requests

All taxpayers are permitted to obtain an IRS record of account (also called a transcript of account) from the IRS at no charge to the taxpayer. You can get a copy of this record by writing to your local IRS office or service center. (See Appendix 1 for a list of all IRS service centers, with addresses.) When requesting a transcript of account, you must provide your name, address, and social security number(s), and indicate the tax years requested. Sample 4 is an example of this type of request.

An IRS transcript of account will give you the following information:

★ The type of tax return filed (e.g., 1040, 1040X, 1040A) for each tax year

★ Your filing status (e.g., joint, single) for each tax year

★ The total amount of tax owed on the return, along with what has been paid to date

★ The Adjusted Gross Income and Taxable Income on the return

★ The self-employment tax on the return

★ The number of exemptions claimed on the return

★ A record of all payments made to the IRS for the tax year in question

★ The results of any audits (if any additional tax was due)

★ The amount of any penalties and interest assessed for the tax year on the total tax due (often as the result of an audit)

★ The current balance due, with interest calculated to the date when the transcripts were printed.

In addition, you may also get copies of any tax returns filed with the IRS in the past. Copies of tax returns are not free. You can request them by filling out and filing Form 4506 (see Sample 5), along with payment of the required fee (currently $39 for each tax return requested). You can also use Form 4506 to obtain copies of Form W-2 (wages) or verification that no return was filed. A safer route for confirming that no tax return was filed is to request a transcript of account from the IRS. This may be better than filing

SAMPLE 4
REQUEST FOR TRANSCRIPTS OF ACCOUNT

December 1, 20—

Internal Revenue Service
Attn: Mail Stop 6674DEN
600 17th Street
Denver, CO 80202

REQUEST FOR TRANSCRIPTS OF ACCOUNT

Re: Herman H. Munster; SSN: 123-45-6789

To the Commissioner:

Please provide me with a copy of my transcripts of account for the taxable years 1986 through 1995 (Form 1040 tax liability). Please send these to:

Herman H. Munster
1313 Mockingbird Lane
Denver, CO 80222

If you have any questions, please feel free to call me at (303) 555-1212. I thank you in advance for your consideration and assistance with this matter.

Sincerely,

Herman H. Munster

a Form 4506 because no one at the IRS will look to see whether a return was actually filed when only a computer transcript is requested. The IRS does not charge for either of these services.

Once you have used as many information sources as necessary in your case, you should have a firm understanding of what the IRS knows about you. This understanding allows you to level the playing field as much as is possible, and you will now be ready to begin to play the tax game with the IRS.

SAMPLE 5

FORM 4506 (REQUEST FOR COPY OR TRANSCRIPT OF TAX FORM)

Form **4506**

(Rev. January 2004)

Department of the Treasury
Internal Revenue Service

Request for Copy of Tax Return

▶ Do not sign this form unless all applicable parts have been completed.
Read the instructions on page 2.

▶ Request may be rejected if the form is incomplete, illegible, or any required
part was blank at the time of signature.

OMB No. 1545-0429

TIP: You may be able to get your tax return or return information from other sources. If you had your tax return completed by a paid preparer, they should be able to provide you a copy of the return. The IRS can provide a **Tax Return Transcript** for many returns free of charge. The transcript provides most of the line entries from the tax return and usually contains the information that a third party (such as a mortgage company) requires. See new **Form 4506-T**, Request for Transcript of Tax Return, to order a transcript or you can call 1-800-829-1040 to order a transcript.

1 a Name shown on tax return. If a joint return, enter the name shown first. Caitlin Estill	**1b** First social security number on tax return or employer identification number (see instructions) 123-45-6789
2 a If a joint return, enter spouse's name shown on tax return	**2b** Second social security number if joint tax return

3 Current name, address (including apt., room, or suite no.), city, state, and ZIP code
Caitlin Estill
123 Main Street, Apt. No. 101, Denver, CO 80001

4 Address, (including apt., room, or suite no.), city, state, and ZIP code shown on the last return filed if different from line 3

5 If the tax return is to be mailed to a third party (such as a mortgage company), enter the third party's name, address, and telephone number. The IRS has no control over what the third party does with the tax return.

CAUTION: *Lines 6 and 7 must be completed if the third party requires you to complete Form 4506.* **Do not** *sign Form 4506 if the third party requests that you sign Form 4506 and lines 6 and 7 are blank.*

6 **Tax return requested** (Form 1040, 1120, 941, etc.) and all attachments as originally submitted to the IRS, including Form(s) W-2, schedules, or amended returns. Copies of Forms 1040, 1040A, and 1040EZ are generally available for 7 years from filing before they are destroyed by law. Other returns may be available for a longer period of time. Enter only one return number. If you need more than one type of return, you must complete another Form 4506. ▶ 1040

Note: *If the copies must be certified for court or administrative proceedings, check here.* . . . . □

7 **Year or period requested.** Enter the ending date of the year or period, using the mm/dd/yyyy format. If you are requesting more than four years or periods, you must attach another Form 4506.

12/31/2002   12/31/2003   12/31/2004   _____

8 **Fee.** There is a $39 fee for each return requested. **Full payment must be included with your request or it will be rejected. Make your check or money order payable to "United States Treasury."** Enter your SSN or EIN and "Form 4506 request" on your check or money order.

a Cost for each return	$	39.00
b Number of returns requested on line 7		3
c Total cost. Multiply line 8a by line 8b	$	117.00

9 If we cannot find the tax return, we will refund the fee. If the refund should go to the third party listed on line 5, check here . . . . □

Signature of taxpayer(s). I declare that I am either the taxpayer whose name is shown on line 1a or 2a, or a person authorized to obtain the tax return requested. If the request applies to a joint return, **either** husband or wife must sign. If signed by a corporate officer, partner, guardian, tax matters partner, executor, receiver, administrator, trustee, or party other than the taxpayer, I certify that I have the authority to execute Form 4506 on behalf of the taxpayer.

		Telephone number of taxpayer on line 1a or 2a 303-555-1111
Sign Here	▶ *Caitlin Estill* Signature (see instructions)	5/5/05 Date
	▶ Title (if line 1a above is a corporation, partnership, estate, or trust)	
	▶ Spouse's signature	Date

For Privacy Act and Paperwork Reduction Act Notice, see page 2.   Form **4506** (Rev. 1-2004)

(HTA)

Tax Points

★ You have a right to know what the IRS knows about you.

★ Use the Freedom of Information Act to find out what information the IRS has on you.

★ Taxpayers who haven't filed tax returns should request an IRP printout from the IRS to make sure that all income is properly reported when the return is eventually prepared and filed (especially if the taxpayer is missing necessary records to prepare an accurate tax return).

★ Transcripts of account are free and can be ordered from the IRS to check the accuracy of tax information that the IRS computers have on a taxpayer, including any balances owed.

CHAPTER 3

THE FILING PROCESS: WHO, WHAT, WHERE, WHEN, AND WHY

The hardest thing in the world to understand is the income tax.
Attributed to Albert Einstein (1879-1955),
Nobel laureate in physics

As a citizen, you have an obligation to the country's tax system, but you also have an obligation to yourself to know your rights under the law and possible tax deductions. And to claim every one of them.
Donald Alexander, former IRS commissioner (1973-1977)

You know, it's against the law not to file tax returns. There is not an option. There is not a box that says "I would rather not."
Senator Don Nickles (R-Oklahoma) US Senator (1980-Present)

Most US taxpayers want to file an accurate and correct tax return — if only they could understand how to do so. IRS statistics for the 2002 tax year indicate that over 85,000,000 taxpayers telephoned the IRS (its toll-free telephone number is 1-800-829-FORM) with tax questions, and that the IRS home page on the Internet (www.irs.gov) received more than 2 billion hits (including nearly 78,000,000 hits on April 15, 2002 alone!). More than 9,000,000 taxpayers physically went to an IRS office to seek information. If we really didn't want to comply with the tax laws, why would so many of us attempt to contact the IRS for tax assistance?

You can call the IRS on its toll-free telephone number at 1-800-829-FORM, or visit its Web site at www.irs.gov.

1. Who Doesn't File a Tax Return?

The IRS has estimated that 6% of Americans, or approximately sixteen million people, do not file individual income tax returns, even though, according to the IRC, they are obligated to do so. The question the IRS has asked and never successfully answered is, Why? There are several reasons why average Americans fail to file returns.

1.1 Previous negative encounters with the IRS

At any given time, millions of Americans are fighting the IRS in several different arenas, whether in a current audit or a past collection dispute. When they are in the midst of such a battle, taxpayers' dislike of the IRS escalates and they stop wanting to cooperate with the IRS in other areas. Especially for those taxpayers who already owe the IRS a lot of money, the thought of filing another tax return and adding to the amount owed is not very attractive.

However, you must understand and accept that it is important to stay on top of all filing requirements and not compound the problem, no matter how unpleasant dealing with the IRS can be. Not filing a return will not make the problem any easier, no matter how much we may wish this to be the case.

1.2 No money to pay

Many taxpayers do not file tax returns after they have been prepared because there is a balance due on the return and the taxpayer cannot afford to pay the IRS. However, the filing and payment parts of the tax game are completely separate and should not be lumped together. You should always file timely tax returns, even if you cannot pay any or all of the taxes owed. By filing on time, you are avoiding a late filing penalty, discussed in detail in chapter 10.

The filing and payment parts of the tax game are completely separate. You should always file timely tax returns, even if you cannot pay any or all of the taxes owed.

Notwithstanding this advice, many taxpayers, and tax professionals for that matter, do not realize that it is possible to get an extension to pay any taxes owed. Simply file a completed Form 1127 (Application for Extension of Time for Payment of Tax) (see Sample 6). This extension is usually limited to six additional months, and it does not stop the interest from accruing on the unpaid tax deficiency.

To properly use this form, you must file it with the IRS before the tax return is due (usually before April 15). Furthermore, you must submit a statement with the form that explains how paying the tax will create an undue financial hardship for you.

SAMPLE 6

FORM 1127 (APPLICATION FOR EXTENSION OF TIME FOR PAYMENT OF TAX)

Form 1127
(Rev. 11-93)
Department of the Treasury
Internal Revenue Service

APPLICATION FOR EXTENSION OF TIME FOR PAYMENT OF TAX

(ATTN: This type of payment extension is rarely wanted because the legal requirements are so strict please read the conditions on the back carefully before continuing.)

Taxpayer's Name (include spouse if your extension request is for a joint return)
Mary Moneybags

Present Address
123 Main Street

City, Town or Post Office, State, and Zip Code
Denver, CO 80202

Social Security Number or Employer Identification Number
123-45-6789

Spouse's Social Security Number if this is for a joint return

District Director of Internal Revenue at   Denver, Colorado
(Enter City and State where IRS Office is located)

I request an extension from 4/15 , 19 99 , to November 1 , 19 99
(Enter Due Date of Return)

to pay tax of $ 7,500   for the year ended 12/31 , 19 98 .

This extension is necessary because *(If more space is needed, please attach a separate sheet):* I cannot pay my taxes due to a health emergency -- surgery -- which cannot be avoided or postponed. I can only pay for this necessary medical procedure or my taxes, not both.

I can't borrow to pay the tax because: My negative credit report, plus no equity in my real estate, wont permit me to borrow funds, and I have no friends / family to borrow from.

To show the need for the extension. I am attaching: (1) a statement of my assets and liabilities at the end of last month (showing book and market values of assets and whether securities are listed or unlisted); and (2) an itemized list of money I received and spent for 3 months before the date the tax is due.

I propose to secure this liability as follows:
My real estate located at 123 Main Street, Denver CO

Under penalties of perjury, I declare that I have examined this application, including any accompanying schedules and statements, and to the best of my knowledge and belief it is true, correct, and complete.

M. Moneybags   4/1/-
SIGNATURE (BOTH SIGNATURES IF YOUR EXTENSION REQUEST IS FOR A JOINT RETURN)   (DATE)

The District Director will let you know whether the extension is approved or denied and will tell you if you need some form of security. However, the Director can't consider an application if it is filed after the due date of the return. We will send you a list of approved surety companies if you ask for it.

(The following will be filled in by the IRS.)

This application is   ☐ approved   for the following reasons:
                      ☐ denied

Interest _____   Date of assessment _____   Identifying no. _____

Penalty _____   _____   _____
                               (SIGNATURE)   (DATE)

CAT. NO. 17238O   (over)   Form **1127** (Rev. 11-93)

The IRS does not automatically approve Form 1127 requests to extend the time to pay taxes. In fact, the IRS denies these requests far more often than it grants them. However, you should still try to obtain a payment extension. The IRS decision to grant the request generally depends on the severity of the financial hardship. For example, if you cannot sell any assets at fair market value to pay your tax bill, and if approving the extension to pay will permit you to sell property for market value and pay the IRS, the IRS is likely to approve your extension request. Like most IRS decisions, this one depends to a great extent on the reasonableness of the person reviewing the extension request.

You should use a Form 1127 request only when you are in dire financial straits and when there is a strong likelihood that the IRS will approve the request. This is because you must fill out a complete financial statement (Form 433, discussed in chapter 11) to accompany the Form 1127. By filing a financial statement, you are giving the IRS a lot of information that it would not otherwise have. Therefore, you should avoid using this form if it would be merely inconvenient or difficult to pay the taxes owed.

1.3 Lack of records to prepare a return

Many people do not file tax returns because they lack the records necessary to prepare an accurate tax return. However, you should treat the current lack of records as merely a delay to filing the return and not as an excuse not to file the return at all. If you cannot locate the records you need, you should first secure an extension of time to file the return. This process is discussed in section **3.** below.

If you are unable to gather the necessary records within the extension period, you should consider requesting information from the IRS to prepare the return. While this may sound strange, the IRS will provide this information at no charge to you, and it may contain enough detail to allow you to prepare the return. For instance, the IRS can provide information concerning many different sources of income that payers report (such as wages, nonemployee compensation, interest, dividends, etc.). At the very least, your tax return will contain all the information of which the IRS is aware.

1.4 Personal problems

Many taxpayers face difficult situations at home, such as divorce, a death or illness in the family, emotional stress, or some other situation that prevents them from filing a tax return on time. Unfortunately, many taxpayers fail to file the tax return after the personal problem(s) have been resolved, and they compound the problem by not filing future returns due to the fear factor that the IRS will get them for that one unfiled return.

The IRS will waive penalties for late filing when personal problems caused the failure to file on time. I discuss this in detail in chapter 10.

1.5　Tax protests

There is a growing movement in the United States today involving people whom the IRS and several courts have labeled as tax protestors. While I discuss many of the tax protestors' arguments in chapter 8, in general, tax protestors are people who believe that the tax laws are either unconstitutional or for some reason do not apply to them. Tax protestors do not usually file tax returns. When they do file returns, the returns do not contain information that would permit the IRS to accurately compute any taxes due.

Before you take such a position, I strongly advise you to consult with a competent tax professional. Taking a position of protest that is not founded in strong legal arguments is a good way to see the dark side of the IRS (i.e., potential criminal and civil fraud investigations).

1.6　Did not earn minimum gross income

Under the IRC, not every individual who earns income is obligated to file an income tax return. Table 2 shows the minimum gross income you needed to earn in a particular year before you were required to file an income tax return for that year. Gross income, for purposes of the filing requirements, means all income you received during the year that was not exempt from taxation. The most common types of income items include wages, bartering income, interest earned, dividends, bonuses, commissions, farm and rental receipts, capital gains, proceeds from illegal transactions, prizes, gambling winnings, royalties, alimony (or maintenance), and unemployment benefits.

> Under the IRC, not every individual who earns income is obligated to file an income tax return.

2.　Preparing the Return

For most Americans, preparing and filing a tax return is a relatively straightforward process (even taking into account the complex and often convoluted tax laws and forms). However, for millions of Americans, a trip to the dentist or funeral home is preferable to getting records together and preparing a tax return. There are several ways to make the tax return preparation process much easier come April 15:

★ If you have access to a computer, there are many software programs available that make filing an accurate return relatively easy.

TABLE 2
MINIMUM GROSS INCOME NEEDED TO FILE A TAX RETURN

Tax Year	Single	Married/Joint	Head of Household	Married/Separate
1993	6,050	10,900	7,800	2,350
1994	6,250	11,250	8,060	2,450
1995	6,400	11,550	8,250	2,500
1996	6,550	11,800	8,450	2,550
1997	6,800	12,200	8,700	2,650
1998	6,950	12,500	8,950	2,700
1999	7,050	12,700	9,100	2,750
2000	7,200	12,950	9,250	2,800
2001	7,450	13,400	9,550	2,900
2002	7,700	13,850	9,900	3,000
2003	7,800	15,600	10,050	3,050

This table is for taxpayers who are under age 65 and not dependents. Taxpayers over the age of 65 can often earn a slightly higher gross income before they trigger any tax return filing requirements.

★ Organize your tax records throughout the year rather than waiting until April and the pressure associated with last-minute preparation. There are many excellent software programs, such as Quicken, that can assist in this process.

★ Use a return preparer if the return is overly complicated. While this may be expensive, it may also be necessary to avoid future problems with the IRS. The professional fees can be money well spent if you avoid an audit or if you end up owing less tax. You can also claim the fees as an itemized deduction (along with safe-deposit box rental fees, investment expenses, and other miscellaneous expenses).

★ When selecting a return preparer (if one is necessary), be sure to seek referrals from friends, family members, or business associates. I would recommend that the return preparer be an accountant (preferably a CPA) or a tax attorney. If the individual has these credentials, he or she probably has at least a minimal amount of tax experience. I would strongly advise against using one of the tax preparation chains, as many of their preparers do not have enough training or experience to justify the cost. Of course, many employees at these and other national tax preparation firms are highly qualified; it's just that you cannot be sure who will actually prepare your return.

Once you have gathered all the information, you need to prepare the tax return itself. There are several issues that commonly arise at this time, among them tax refunds, deductions, and whether to file as a married or joint taxpayer.

2.1 Tax refunds

Many taxpayers find themselves receiving a large refund every tax year. This is generally a bad financial decision. It means you are, in effect, giving the US government an interest-free loan during the course of the year, a loan that is repaid, without interest, sometime around April 15 of the following year.

If you find yourself in this situation, the best course of action, assuming that you don't want to continue giving this interest-free loan to the government, is to adjust your federal withholdings (on Form W-4) to claim more exemptions (and thus have less taken out for federal taxes every payday). By having less money withheld, you will give yourself a raise with every paycheck, as well as eliminate the interest-free loan to the government.

2.2 Deductions

Perhaps the biggest problem that occurs during the return preparation period is trying to decide whether a particular expense is deductible or not. As I have previously stated, no one really understands the IRC. Thus, you are likely at some time to face a situation where you don't understand the tax law and do not know whether you are entitled to claim a certain deduction. If you claim it and are wrong (or at least if the IRS says you're wrong), you face paying additional amounts in tax, interest, and penalties. If you don't claim the deduction, you risk losing a deduction you may be entitled to and will pay more in tax for being too conservative.

What should you do in these circumstances? In general, I recommend claiming the unsure deduction for several reasons:

★ The chance of an IRS audit on a tax return is very small. (I discuss the odds of being audited in chapter 5.) If you are not audited, the deduction will not be noticed or questioned, and you will get away with claiming it.

★ The IRS usually won't penalize you for a good faith misinterpretation of the tax laws. Without the deterrence of being penalized, you have little downside risk (although the IRS will add interest to any amounts owed as the result of a disallowed deduction).

★ Perhaps most important, the deduction that you are now questioning may be perfectly legitimate and acceptable, even if the tax return is audited. Not claiming the deduction only benefits the IRS, and when only the IRS benefits, you have lost a part of the game.

Some tax practitioners recommend attaching an explanation to the return for any questionable deductions, reasoning that the IRS will not penalize you for claiming a questionable deduction when the IRS has been placed on notice concerning the deduction. While this advice is generally true, I do not recommend attaching any such explanations to the return because the simple act of attaching the explanation virtually guarantees that the return will be audited. As well, the IRS will reason that you must believe the deduction to be questionable or you would not have attached a statement. If the deduction is in fact questionable, the IRS will surely have a good basis to disallow it.

2.3 Married filers — joint or separate?

All married couples must decide whether it is better for them to file a joint return or to file separately. For most, the clear choice, based on the overall tax liabilities that they will owe, is to file a joint return. This is because the tax rates are generally lower for joint filers than they are for married people who file separately. However, as with everything else, there are exceptions to this general rule. Filing separately may be a better choice if:

(a) *One spouse has major medical bills and a relatively low income.* On a Schedule A, a taxpayer can deduct any medical expenses in excess of 7.5% of his or her Adjusted Gross Income (AGI). With a low income, it is much easier to meet the 7.5% expense threshold. The following example illustrates this:

Husband's AGI:	$25,000
Wife's AGI:	$25,000
Husband's medical expenses:	$3,000
Wife's medical expenses:	$0

If the couple files jointly, none of the medical expenses would be deductible ($50,000 combined AGI x 7.5% = $3,750), as the total medical expenses do not exceed $3,750. But if the couple files separate returns, the husband could deduct $1,125 ($25,000 AGI x 7.5% = $1,875; $3,000 of expenses minus $1,875 = $1,125).

(b) *One spouse has several miscellaneous deductions.* For similar reasons, if one spouse has more miscellaneous deductions subject to a 2% AGI limitation, it may be financially better for the couple to file separately. Miscellaneous deductions include investment expenses, tax advice and return preparation fees, employee business expenses, union dues, job-hunting expenses, and job-related education expenses.

(c) *One spouse owes the IRS a past-due tax liability and the married couple expects a refund this year.* For example, before the couple were married, the husband owed the IRS $5,000 that has not yet been paid. If the wife expects a $5,000 refund this year because too much money was withheld from her wages, the IRS will apply all of the refund to the husband's prior tax debt if they file jointly. By filing separately, the wife would get her entire refund and the husband would still owe the IRS. This may or may not be a good thing, but it is certainly something to understand and consider before filing any tax returns.

(d) *The married couple is having marital difficulties.* If divorce is a possibility, each spouse will not want to be responsible for the other spouse's tax liability. By filing separately, each spouse is responsible only for his or her tax liability.

There may be other situations where filing separately would be advantageous to a married couple. The only way to know for sure is to prepare the tax returns both ways and file the return (or returns) that, all things considered, produces the least amount of tax due.

3. Timely Returns, Late Returns, and Amended Returns

3.1 Reasons to file tax returns on time

There are numerous reasons why you should file all tax returns on time, and the tax laws certainly favor those taxpayers who do things when they're supposed to be done:

★ No criminal failure-to-file charges can be brought against you.

★ No late-filing penalties can be added onto any amounts owed.

★ The IRS audit period begins as soon as the return is filed (and will thus end sooner than if the return is late).

★ Most important, you don't have to think about filing taxes again for another year.

In addition, filing returns on time will increase the odds of you getting a refund if a refund is due. The reason for this is that under IRC §6511(a), a claim for refund must be made within three years from the date the return was filed or within two years from when the tax was paid, whichever is later. (The sections of the IRC dealing with refunds [IRC §6511 and §6513] are quite complicated, and you may need to get professional assistance to determine if you are legally entitled to a refund.)

A recent change in the tax laws provides a limited exception to this rule in cases where the taxpayer is physically or mentally impaired. In order to qualify under this exception (under IRC §6511(h)), the taxpayer must show that he or she could not manage his or her financial affairs due to a medical condition (either mental or physical) that is expected to result in death or at least one year of a disability. The IRS will require an affidavit from a physician or other qualified medical personnel to support this claim. In these instances, the three- or two-year rule will not apply (i.e., will be suspended) while the person suffers from the disability. It is important to understand, however, that this exception will *not* apply if the taxpayer's spouse, or another person acting under a Power of Attorney, is legally permitted to act on behalf of the taxpayer in financial matters.

If no return is ever filed, the two-year rule mentioned above applies. For example, if you had $1,000 withheld from your wages and owed $500 in tax, you would be due a refund of $500. If no return was filed, and assuming that you were not physically or mentally impaired, you would have two years from the payment date (generally considered to be April 15) to file a claim for refund.

Also, if you are due a refund, the refund will be sent to you shortly after the return is filed. Unless you owe the IRS money from prior tax years (in which case the IRS will apply the money to your debt rather than refunding it to you), there is no legitimate reason why a taxpayer who is owed a refund should be filing late (after any extensions have passed).

3.2 Extensions to file

If you cannot file your tax return by the due date (generally April 15), you are legally permitted to file a Form 4868 to obtain an automatic four-month extension of time in which to file. This extension does *not* extend the time to *pay* the tax. (This means that interest starts accruing on any tax you owe from April 15, even if you receive an extension and don't file your return until August 15.)

If, after receiving an additional four months, you still cannot file an accurate income tax return, you are permitted to file a Form 2688, which is

If you cannot file your tax return by the due date (generally April 15), you are legally permitted to file a Form 4868 to obtain an automatic four-month extension of time in which to file.

a request for up to two additional months to file the return. For a Form 2688, you must give a reason why you need the additional time, and the IRS does not automatically grant these requests for more time. However, I have never seen the IRS deny an additional extension request if the reason for it is the taxpayer's need to obtain necessary records in order to prepare and file an accurate tax return.

In addition, certain taxpayers who live in areas hit by a natural calamity (e.g., tornado, hurricane, fires, flooding), which the president has declared disaster areas, may qualify for additional time to file the return and pay any taxes due. The Tax Reform Act of 1998 also requires the IRS to abate (or eliminate) any interest that accrues during the disaster-mandated extension period.

3.3 Late-filed returns

You should make every attempt to file your tax returns on time, as a failure to do so could potentially result in both civil and criminal penalties.

It is a criminal offense not to file a tax return when a return is required to be filed. Under IRC §7203, the failure to file a return is considered to be a misdemeanor offense that could result in your spending up to one year in prison and/or paying a fine up to $25,000. If you are charged with violating this section, the government must prove, beyond a reasonable doubt, that you were required to file a tax return and failed to do so within the time allowed under the law, and that the failure to file the return was willful. There is a complete discussion of the potential criminal penalties in chapter 14.

Even though the chance of a criminal prosecution is remote, the civil penalties alone act as a significant incentive for taxpayers to file timely returns. For example, the IRS will nearly always assess the failure-to-file and/or failure-to-pay penalties when you fail to file a tax return on time. (These penalties are discussed in detail in chapter 10.) Even if you have no money to pay the tax owing, filing a return on time will eliminate the failure-to-file penalty and possible criminal prosecution.

3.3.a IRS procedures for locating nonfilers

The IRS has publicly stated that one of its main goals is to get nonfiling taxpayers back into the filing system and have them file returns on a timely basis in the future.

The primary way that the IRS locates nonfilers is through its computer matching program. Under this program, the IRS computer automatically

You should make every attempt to file your tax returns on time, as a failure to do so could potentially result in both civil and criminal penalties.

looks for taxpayers who earned income in a particular tax year but did not file a tax return. For example, if the IRS computer system does not find a tax return for someone who has received a Form 1099 or W-2, then this person is considered to be a nonfiler. If this person is you, the IRS will then send you as many as three notices requesting that you file a tax return or that you explain why you are not required to file a tax return. If you still do not file a return, you may receive several more letters from the IRS, spread out over a period of a few months, practically begging you to file the return. If the IRS does not receive a response, it will often prepare a return for you, using records and information that it has about you (generally from Forms W-2 and 1099).

These returns, called Substitute for Returns (SFR), are typically not favorable to you, because the IRS does not give you any of the tax breaks that you may be entitled to under the IRC. For example, the IRS may file a return for a married individual (who would be entitled to claim many deductions) as a return for a single person taking the standard deduction. (I cover SFRs in more detail in chapter 7.)

Instead of agreeing to the SFR, it would be best for you to review all records from the year in question and try to prepare your own tax return, taking advantage of every exemption, deduction, or other break the tax law permits in the process. The IRS must accept a filed return instead of the SFR, although like any other tax return, it is subject to audit.

If you determine that the SFR is a proper return, you can sign it, and the IRS will consider it your return. If you refuse to sign the return and also refuse to prepare another return, the IRS may sign the return for you. While this is a valid tax return for most purposes, the IRS cannot assess and try to collect any taxes due without first sending you a Notice of Deficiency. You can then petition the US tax court within 90 days to contest the matter (see chapter 15 for a complete discussion of the tax court procedures).

If the IRS cannot prepare an SFR (usually because it does not have sufficient financial information to do so), it can have a revenue agent or officer contact you or serve a summons on you to obtain information from which to prepare a return. You would be well advised never to let the situation deteriorate to this level; a fight over filing a tax return is not worth the pressures associated with a summons. If you have sufficient records to prepare a tax return, then you should prepare the return. If the records aren't available, you should try to collect them and prepare a return. It is rarely in your best interests to have the IRS prepare a return on your behalf.

3.3.b Filing late tax returns

Once you decide to file a late tax return, take care that you completely understand the process before actually filing the return. If you have a long history of nonfiling, I recommend that you look back a maximum of six years and file only those tax returns with the IRS. This is because the criminal statute of limitations for the failure to file tax returns is six years. Also, the IRS's general policy is not to seek enforcement of the filing rules beyond six years.

Of course, as with everything else, there are exceptions to this rule. Perhaps the most important exception is that the IRS will pursue returns over six years old when it suspects a taxpayer of committing some type of fraud. The IRS also looks at the reasons why a taxpayer failed to file for so many years (e.g., Was the taxpayer a tax protestor? What type of tax is involved? What is the taxpayer's occupation and education?) before deciding whether to pursue unfiled tax returns that were due more than six years ago.

When the IRS contacts a taxpayer concerning a failure to file past-due tax returns, the IRS (usually in the form of a revenue officer) will normally give that taxpayer a specific deadline by which to file the returns. This deadline is negotiable depending upon the unique facts of the case. While the IRS will not admit this, I have yet to see an IRS employee refuse to give as much time as is reasonably necessary to permit the taxpayer to gather the necessary records to prepare accurate and correct tax returns. However, once the deadline is set, the taxpayer should make sure that the returns are filed on or before the deadline date. If the taxpayer still misses the deadline, the revenue officer generally has the following choices available to him or her:

★ The revenue officer can refer the case to the Criminal Investigation Division for a criminal investigation.

★ The revenue officer can issue a summons to try again to get the returns filed.

★ The revenue officer can refer the case to the Examination Division for audit possibilities.

★ The revenue officer can try to prepare an SFR based upon the IRS records.

Each of these options is used frequently, with most revenue officers resorting to the summons procedure to "wake up" the taxpayer and get him or her to file the delinquent returns. None of the options are especially attractive to the taxpayer. Of course, the taxpayer should never let the situation get to the point where none of the options are attractive, as he or she cannot win at this point and can only hope to minimize the damage.

3.4 Amended returns

If you made an error on a tax return that has already been filed, usually by forgetting either to report some income or to claim a valid deduction, you are permitted (and may be required) to file an amended tax return (Form 1040X). You should file the amended return within three years from the due date of the original return or the actual filing date, whichever is later.

By filing an amended return, you are increasing the chance for an audit (although it is not a significantly higher audit risk). In many instances, you should include supporting documentation with the amended return, especially if the amendment will result in a refund. If you are concerned about the audit risk and are seeking a refund, one strategy to consider is to file the amended return just before the statute of limitations for the original return expires (three years after the original return was due or filed, whichever is later). By doing so, the IRS can only assess tax to the extent of the amended return and cannot assess any additional tax from the original return.

For example, the timing of amended returns for the taxable year 2004 is as follows:

Original tax return due:	April 15, 2005
Tax return filed:	April 15, 2005
Statute of limitations for audit changes:	April 15, 2008

If the taxpayer filed the amended tax return on April 10, 2008, it would be timely because it was filed within three years of the filing date of the original tax return. If the original return was not already being audited, it would be too late for the IRS to audit it after the amended return was filed. The only option for the IRS would be to deny any request for refund made on the amended return.

3.5 Before filing a return

Before filing any tax return, whether it is on time or late, original or amended, you should check the return to make sure it is as accurate as possible. Checklist 1 suggests a few areas to check before filing.

CHECKLIST 1
CHECKLIST FOR FILING A TAX RETURN

✓ Make sure that your filing status (married/single, etc.) is accurate and results in the least amount of tax due.

✓ Check all arithmetic, as mathematical errors give the IRS a reason to look at the return. The less the IRS looks at a tax return, the better for you.

✓ Make sure all income is reported. Verify all income against documents received from employers, banks, and mutual funds. In addition, it is important that all Forms W-2 and 1099 are accurate. If they are not, ask the preparer of the incorrect form to prepare a corrected form and file it with the IRS. The IRS is nearly certain to catch unreported income. This also gives the IRS a reason to look at the return, which again is never a good thing.

✓ Make sure that all Social Security numbers are correct, especially those for any children or other dependents listed on the return.

✓ Make sure that all payments made to the IRS are correct on the return. This is especially important for taxpayers who make estimated tax payments during the year.

✓ Make sure that all permissible deductions are claimed so that the tax liability is not overstated. Remember that you are not required to pay any more tax than the tax laws require.

✓ Make sure that the tax return is signed (by both spouses if it is a joint return).

✓ Make a copy of the final return and keep it for your records.

Tax Points

★ Only individuals who earn more than the minimum income in a particular year are required to file tax returns.

★ File all tax returns on time to avoid any additional penalties or being targeted for a criminal investigation.

★ The minimal chance of an audit should not deter you from filing a return and/or claiming all deductions permitted by law.

★ Don't let any previous IRS encounters influence your decision on whether or not to file any future tax returns.

★ Always file a tax return even if you owe money and cannot pay some or all of the balance due on the return.

★ Consider requesting an Extension to Pay (Form 1127) if you can demonstrate paying the tax due would cause you a severe financial hardship.

★ All married couples should prepare joint and separate returns, and compare the tax due on each, before filing any tax returns with the IRS.

★ It is better to file a return late than not file at all.

★ Carefully check all numbers on a tax return before signing it and filing it with the IRS.

★ Mistakes on tax returns can, and should, be corrected by filing an amended tax

CHAPTER 4

BUSINESSES AND THE IRS

If Patrick Henry thought that taxation without representation was bad, he should see how bad it is with representation.

The Old Farmer's Almanac (1881)

When there is an income tax, the just man will pay more and the unjust less on the same amount of income.

Plato (428 – 348? BC), the father of Greek philosophy, in *The Republic*

Owning a business is one of the best ways to remain in control of your finances, as you can set up transactions to minimize the inevitable tax hit. In this chapter I briefly discuss various types of business structures and the advantages and disadvantages of each structure from a tax perspective. In the chapters that follow, I address important business considerations with respect to audits and collections.

Since laws vary from state to state, tax implications are only one thing to consider when you are deciding how to set up a business. You should also think about what kind of liability protection you will need and what organizational structure will let you run the business properly. No matter how you set up your business, the following tax advantages apply to all businesses:

(a) *As a business owner, you can deduct all ordinary and necessary business expenses.* While the IRC does not specifically define what "ordinary and necessary" business expenses are, courts have determined that an expense meets this definition if the expense is common to the type of business and is appropriate or helpful to the development of the business.

If you were an employee of some other business, the law would allow you to deduct employee business expenses only if the expenses exceeded 2% of your Adjusted Gross Income (AGI). For example, if your AGI is $50,000 and you have business expenses of $1,200, you are allowed to deduct, on Schedule A, only $200 ($1,200 - [$50,000 x 2% = $1,000] = $200). If the same expenses are claimed by a business, the IRS permits a deduction of the full $1,200.

(b) *As a business owner, you can use tax-deferred retirement savings plans instead of simply having an Individual Retirement Account (IRA) available.* If you were an employee of some other business you could only have an IRA. Businesses are permitted to use a Simplified Employee Pension (SEP), Savings Incentive Match Plan for Employees (SIMPLE), or various other plans. You are also permitted to contribute much more to these plans each year than you can with a regular IRA. To make full use of these retirement plans, you should consult with a qualified financial planner.

(c) *You can make use of the home-office deduction.* This means you can also expense a portion of utilities and other expenses that would ordinarily not be deductible. However, there are limitations to this deduction, as I discuss in chapter 9.

(d) *You can hire your spouse and children to work for the business as long as the work is "real" and reasonable compensation is paid.*

(e) *You can deduct interest on loans, including credit cards, that are incurred for business expenses.* Individual taxpayers have not been able to deduct credit card interest — or any other interest that is not secured by real estate or used specifically for investments — for several years.

(f) *You can deduct some or all of the costs associated with insurance (including health insurance) and other employee benefits that would not have been deductible but for the business.*

As with any individual taxpayer, it is imperative to keep accurate records for the business. Businesses that end up reporting too much income nearly always do so because the business owner does not have complete records and so cannot accurately report all legitimate business expenses. It is important to have the following information or records for any business expense:

★ *Why* was the expense incurred?

★ *When* was the expense incurred?

★ *Where* was the expense incurred?

★ *Who* incurred the expense?

★ *How much* money was actually spent?

Generally, the IRS will accept a receipt, invoice, canceled check, credit card statement, or any other document that shows the date and amount of the expense, as long as the business reason is clear and can be demonstrated. It is helpful to maintain an accurate diary or other system to assist in proving the business purpose of the expense, as most audits occur a year or two after an expense was incurred, and relying on memory is an easy way to lose a legitimate deduction.

1. Different Business Structures

You can structure your business as a sole proprietorship, a C corporation, an S corporation, a partnership, or a limited liability company. Each structure has unique tax advantages and disadvantages.

1.1 Sole proprietorships

A sole proprietorship is a business that is owned by one person and is not considered to be a separate tax entity. The classic sole proprietorship is a person who wants to begin his or her own business with the least cost and paperwork. Many sole proprietorships begin as moonlighting businesses where the taxpayer starts the business while being employed by someone else. If the new business is successful, the employee usually will quit his or her job and concentrate on the new business full time.

For example, if a full-time computer programmer enjoys photography, the programmer can begin to operate a photography business while still employed as a computer programmer. If the photography business takes off and makes money, the programmer may decide to pursue the business full time, especially if he or she likes photography more than programming computers.

A sole proprietorship reports its receipts and expenses on a Schedule C (Profit or Loss From Business), which is attached to a taxpayer's Form 1040.

1.1.a Advantages of a sole proprietorship

A sole proprietorship has a number of advantages:

(a) This is the easiest type of business to form (although there may be a requirement to register with the state). There is no need to register the business with the IRS unless a tax identification number is required (i.e., if the business has employees, if it needs to register a retirement plan, or if there is some other reason for which the business needs its own identification number). If no tax identification number is required, the business simply uses the owner's social security number.

(b) There is little cost in establishing a sole proprietorship. You do not need to hire a lawyer or pay corporate filing fees.

(c) Losses can be used to offset other taxable income (e.g., wages, dividends, and interest). Note that you run the risk of an IRS audit if your business does not have an adequate and legitimate profit motive. For a discussion of these so-called "hobby loss" cases, see chapter 9.

1.1.b Disadvantages of a sole proprietorship

Disadvantages of sole proprietorships include the following:

(a) Unlimited personal liability. All your personal assets are at risk if the business is sued and loses in court. You can limit this disadvantage somewhat if you obtain appropriate business liability insurance.

(b) You are liable for self-employment tax — currently 15.3% of net profit.

(c) Only one owner (or husband and wife) is permitted.

(d) A loss may cause the IRS to disallow the loss as a hobby loss (see chapter 9).

(e) You must pay tax to the IRS on a quarterly basis if your business is earning a profit. Use Form 1040-ES, Estimated Tax Payments, for this.

(f) Sole proprietorships have a high audit rate with the IRS.

1.2 C corporations

A corporation is a separate business entity (sometimes called an artificial person) that is organized under the laws of a state and is completely distinct from its owners (called shareholders). All corporations are treated as separate entities for tax purposes and must file an income tax return (Form 1120) each year. The corporation is a very popular structure for conducting business: nearly six million corporations filed income tax returns with the IRS during 2003.

1.2.a Advantages of a C corporation

A C corporation has a number of advantages:

(a) A C corporation provides personal liability protection for its shareholders (owners).

(b) It's easy to sell or transfer shares of stock of a C corporation or to sell the entire company.

(c) The shareholders' only risk of loss is the amount they paid for the shares of stock. This is an extremely important advantage as a shareholder who invests $5,000 in a corporation knows that no matter how poorly the corporation does, the most money that can be lost is the original $5,000 investment. Had the taxpayer instead invested the $5,000 in a sole proprietorship, and the sole proprietorship ran up $50,000 in business debts, the taxpayer could be liable for the $50,000 in debt in addition to losing his or her original $5,000 investment in the business.

(d) A corporation may be able to borrow or raise money without any personal guarantee of the owner(s). This advantage is available only if the corporation has a financial history and is not a new company.

(e) A corporation will not be affected by the death, bankruptcy, or incompetency of a shareholder. In many other business structures, any one of these events could cause the business to end.

(f) A corporation is considered to be a separate legal entity under the law. This is important because it separates a taxpayer's business and personal affairs from each other.

(g) A C corporation has a low tax rate (15%) on the first $50,000 of net taxable income each year.

1.2.b Disadvantages of a C corporation

A C corporation has a number of disadvantages:

(a) A corporation can be expensive to set up. You may need to hire a lawyer to prepare the articles of incorporation, bylaws, and other necessary documents and pay filing fees to the state.

(b) A C corporation may be liable for double taxation. Double taxation occurs when any corporation declares a dividend. The corporation pays tax on its net profit without a deduction for the amount of the dividend, and then the shareholders pay taxes on the dividends received when they file their individual income tax returns. The IRS loves double taxation, which should be an immediate tip-off that it is probably *not* a good thing.

(c) Losses stay with a C corporation. Shareholders cannot personally deduct the losses for the business on their Forms 1040.

(d) A C corporation pays tax on its net profits as a separate taxable entity. For the taxable year 2003, the tax rates for corporations ranged from 15% to 39%, depending upon the corporation's taxable income.

(e) A C corporation may be subject to an accumulated earnings tax. An accumulated earnings tax occurs when the corporation keeps its profits within the corporation and allows them to "accumulate" rather than distributing the profits to its shareholders. (Distribution would result in double taxation, see above.) A corporation can avoid this additional tax if it can show that it was accumulating the money to meet the reasonable needs of the business. These "reasonable needs" of the business often involve money for future business expansion, to pay off debt, to buy other businesses, or to avoid having to borrow money from banks or other lenders in the near future.

(f) A corporation may have additional bookkeeping obligations and must obtain a tax identification number from the IRS. The tax identification number, also called an Employer Identification Number (EIN), is used by the corporation in much the same way that an individual uses a social security number.

1.3 S corporations

An S corporation is identical to a C corporation except that it elects to be treated as an S corporation by the IRS. You can elect to make your business an S corporation by filling out Form 2553. This must be done by the

15th day of the third month of a newly formed corporation's first year in order for the corporation to take advantage of the S election during its first year. If you do not meet this requirement, there is a one-year delay for the election to be valid (i.e., it will be valid for the second tax year but not the first tax year). Congress created S corporations as a way for small businesses to incorporate and get some tax advantages that C corporations do not have. All shareholders must agree to the S election before the election can be effective. Most corporations that meet the criteria for S corporation status usually benefit from making the S election.

1.3.a Advantages of an S corporation

An S corporation has a number of advantages:

(a) An S corporation provides personal liability protection for its shareholders.

(b) An S corporation avoids the double taxation problems of C corporations. The S corporation never needs to declare any dividends to its shareholders.

(c) There are no accumulated earnings tax issues.

(d) An S corporation avoids unreasonable compensation tax issues. Unreasonable compensation tax issues may apply to C corporations that pay their shareholders (who are also employees) salaries that may be too high. Under IRC §162, the business can deduct "a reasonable allowance for salaries or other compensation for personal services actually rendered." In an S corporation, all net income of the corporation passes directly to the individual shareholders and thus high (or low) salaries or other forms of compensation are not an issue. With a C corporation, the IRS can reclassify wages or other forms of compensation as dividends if it believes that the compensation is excessive. By doing so, the IRS can effectively trigger double taxation issues (the corporation is denied a salary expense and must pay additional tax, while the shareholders must also pay tax on the dividends that the IRS has now imposed).

(e) It is easy to transfer/sell ownership in a corporation or to sell the entire corporation.

(f) The corporation doesn't pay tax on profits. However, some states impose corporate income tax on S corporations. You should research any potential state tax issues before making the election as the laws vary greatly from state to state. With respect to federal taxes, any profits (or loses) that the S corporation may incur flow through to the shareholders' individual income tax returns, and the shareholders pay any tax owed or get the benefits of the loss that the corporation may have suffered. Each shareholder receives a Form K-1 from the corporation at the end of the corporation's tax year. This form tells the shareholder how much profit or loss he or she must report to the IRS.

1.3.b Disadvantages of an S corporation

An S corporation has a number of disadvantages:

(a) It can be expensive to set up. You may need to hire a lawyer to prepare the articles of incorporation, bylaws, and other necessary documents and pay state filing fees.

(b) There is a maximum of 75 shareholders. The maximum number of shareholders was recently raised from 35 to 75. A husband and wife are treated as one shareholder for purposes of this rule. Corporations with more than 75 shareholders must be C corporations for tax purposes.

(c) Only one class of stock is permitted. The S corporation cannot have common and preferred classes of stock.

(d) Shareholders are taxed on the income of the corporation, even if the shareholders do not actually receive the income. The reason for this is that most S corporations do not distribute the profits to the shareholders at the end of the year. Instead, they retain the earnings to provide for the financial needs of the business for the next year. Thus, if you are a 50% shareholder of an S corporation that has a net profit of $10,000, you will have to report $5,000 (50% of $10,000) on your personal tax return and pay income tax on this amount.

(e) There are some restrictions on who can be a shareholder. For example, most corporations, partnerships, limited liability companies, and any other entities that are not individuals cannot be shareholders of an S corporation.

(f) A corporation may have additional bookkeeping requirements and must obtain a tax identification number from the IRS (an EIN, just like a C corporation).

(g) Passive activity rules may apply. The passive activity rules limit a shareholder's loss when an S corporation has a loss, and not a profit, for a particular tax year. When a loss occurs, the loss can be used by the shareholders to reduce other taxable income, but only if the shareholders "materially participated" in the business. This area of the tax laws is hopelessly complex, but generally a person is considered to have "materially participated" in a business if he or she worked more than 500 hours for the business during the year of the loss, worked more than anyone else did for the business (but less than 500 hours), or worked at least 100 hours and at least as much as anyone else. I recommend that you contact a competent tax professional if the IRS is using the passive activity rules against you.

1.4   Partnerships

A partnership is a way for two or more persons to conduct business together for profit, without having to go through the process of incorporating the business. It is extremely easy to set up a partnership; nothing more is needed than an agreement between the partners (either in writing or verbal in most states). All partnerships must file tax returns (Form 1065) at the end of the year, and each partner receives a Form K-1 indicating how much income that partner must report on his or her personal tax return.

There are generally two different types of partnerships: general and limited. The basic difference is that certain partners in a limited partnership are able to limit their personal liability with respect to any partnership debts. Because the laws vary considerably from state to state, I would strongly recommend that you contact a lawyer before setting up a limited partnership.

This section discusses general partnerships.

1.4.a   Advantages of a general partnership

A general partnership has several advantages:

(a) A partnership is easy to form. Although it is not advisable, you can set up a partnership with no written agreement. This keeps set-up costs to a minimum because you do not incur additional attorney fees.

(b) There is no double taxation. The partnership itself does not pay any income tax. Instead, as in an S corporation, any profits or losses that a partnership incurs flow through to the individual partners' tax returns.

(c) There are no accumulated earnings tax problems.

(d) There are no unreasonable compensation tax issues.

1.4.b Disadvantages of a general partnership

There are several disadvantages to a general partnership:

(a) There is potential unlimited liability. This means, for example, that a judgment against a partnership can force a partner to use his or her personal assets to pay the partnership's debts.

(b) Partners are taxed on the profits of the partnership even if they don't actually receive their share of the profits. This disadvantage is exactly the same as one of the disadvantages of an S corporation.

(c) It can be very hard to sell or transfer a partner's interest in a partnership. This is because most people do not want to be partners with people that they do not know or trust. Also, many written partnership agreements contain provisions that prohibit the sale of one partner's interest in the partnership without the written consent of the other partner(s). These prohibitions on the transfer of an ownership interest are also often contained in a separate document called a buy-sell agreement. A buy-sell agreement is also common in corporations with a small number of shareholders.

(d) The actions of one partner can bind the other partners on partnership debts or transactions (even if the other partners weren't aware of the activity). For example, one partner can enter into a lease to rent an office, and the lease will be valid even if some or all of the other partners didn't want to lease the space.

(e) One partner can dissolve the partnership without the agreement of any of the other partners.

1.5 Limited liability companies

A limited liability company, or LLC, is a hybrid business entity with characteristics of both a corporation and a partnership. It is similar to a corporation because it limits the personal liability of its members, but it is taxed like a partnership. Given that this is a relatively new type of business entity, state laws vary considerably as to how LLCs will be treated as a separate business structure (and this should be researched thoroughly *before* setting up an LLC).

1.5.a Advantages of an LLC

A limited liability company has several advantages:

(a) No double taxation. Like a partnership or S corporation, any income that an LLC earns is taxed on the individual members' tax returns. The LLC does not need to declare dividends or generally pay any income tax.

(b) An LLC is taxed like a partnership if it has two or more members. This means losses are used to offset the taxpayer's other taxable income, such as wages, interest, and dividends. If an LLC has only one member (which most states permit), it may make an election with the IRS to be disregarded as a separate tax entity (by using Form 8832). If the LLC is disregarded for tax purposes, it reports its income and expenses on a Schedule C — just like a sole proprietorship. However, it still retains the limited liability protection afforded to an LLC.

(c) An LLC provides personal liability protection for its members.

(d) There are no accumulated earnings tax problems.

(e) There are no unreasonable compensation tax issues.

1.5.b Disadvantages of an LLC

There are a few disadvantages to an limited liability company:

(a) It can be expensive to set up. You may need to hire a lawyer to prepare the articles of organization, operating agreement, and any other necessary documents and pay any state filing fees.

(b) State laws vary considerably regarding LLCs. An LLC is a fairly new structure in which to conduct business. Because of this, there are not a lot of published court decisions to provide guidance on various legal and tax matters for LLCs. This is not a problem with corporations, which have been in existence since the creation of the United States.

(c) An LLC may cease to exist if a member files bankruptcy, dies, or becomes incapacitated.

2. Employment Taxes

All businesses that have employees must pay employment taxes. This is perhaps the area that causes businesses, no matter how they are organized, the greatest problem with the IRS. Employment taxes, basically taxes placed on an employee's wages, consist of the following:

(a) *Social security tax.* This tax is often referred to as the FICA tax (FICA stands for Federal Insurance Contributions Act). Both the employer and employee pay equal amounts of this tax; currently each pay 7.65% of the employee's gross income. The tax is broken down into two separate components: old-age, survivors, and disability insurance (6.2%) and the hospital insurance tax (1.45%). The hospital insurance tax applies to all wages, while the old-age portion of the tax is limited to a certain amount of wages an employee earns during a particular year. For example, in 2003, any wages earned up to $87,000 were subject to the 6.2% tax.

(b) *Federal unemployment tax.* This tax is often referred to as the FUTA tax (FUTA stands for Federal Unemployment Tax Act). Only the employer pays this tax, which currently is collected at the rate of 6.2% on the first $7,000 of wages every employee earns each year.

(c) *Income tax.* Employers are required by law to withhold income tax from an employee's wages at a rate based upon the employee's earnings and the number of exemptions claimed on his or her Form W-4.

An employer is required to withhold the money for each of these taxes from every paycheck, regardless of how often the employee is actually paid. The employer does not pay the withheld funds to the government immediately, but instead holds the funds in "trust" for the government. Most businesses are required to deposit the "trust funds" into a bank on a monthly basis (the deposit requirements are the same whether the business pays its employees on a weekly, monthly, or other basis). All employers must file a Form 941 tax return on a quarterly basis to account for all funds withheld from the wages during the quarter. Depending on the amount of the wages, most employers are required to make federal tax deposits on a monthly basis instead of waiting until the Form 941 is due to make a complete payment.

Many businesses that run into IRS trouble over employment taxes do so because the business fails to pay the IRS the money withheld from its employees' paychecks. Usually businesses get into this trouble because they use the withheld funds to pay creditors other than the IRS. For example, if a retail store owes its distributors money for last month's shipments, it knows it will not get any more products from the distributors until the old shipments are paid. The business takes the money which should go to the IRS and pays the distributor, hoping that sales will improve to cover the now-due tax bill. Often, unfortunately, the business doesn't get better and the IRS doesn't get paid. This is often the beginning of the end for the business.

Perhaps more than any other tax issue, the failure to pay the trust funds to the IRS on a timely basis upsets the IRS. There are several reasons for this, but the main one is that it appears as if the business is stealing from the IRS. The employee still gets to take a tax credit when he or she files the Form 1040 in April, but the IRS does not get the taxes which were withheld. In addition, the IRS never likes to be treated as the least important creditor, which is the message it believes the business is sending when it pays other creditors before the IRS.

The IRS has several weapons it can use when employment taxes are not paid. First, it can, and usually does, assess a trust fund recovery penalty against any of the business owners who were responsible for making the decision not to pay the IRS. This penalty, discussed in detail in chapter 10, is an extremely severe one. In addition, the IRS can make a demand for payment and can shut down the business if the payment is not made. While this is an extreme solution, the IRS will do this if it appears that the problem will occur again in the next quarter or in the near future. I will discuss the seizures of business assets (and businesses) in detail in chapter 11.

Businesses must make sure that all employment tax matters are handled correctly and in a timely manner. Without such compliance, the IRS can shut down the business and penalize those individuals who are responsible for the failure to pay the employment taxes. This is one area where IRS threats should always be taken seriously. It is also one of the two tax situations (the other is a criminal investigation) where professional tax assistance may be the only way to save the business and keep it operating.

Tax Points

★ Establishing a business is a good way to control the financial impact of taxes.

★ All businesses must maintain accurate records of all income and expenses.

★ All businesses are permitted to deduct all ordinary and necessary business expenses from the business' net income.

★ Different business structures result in different advantages and disadvantages, especially from a tax, administrative, and legal perspective.

★ Employment taxes must be paid to the IRS so the business can continue operating and to eliminate the owner's personal responsibility for the taxes.

CHAPTER 5

THE AUDIT PROCESS: WHAT ARE THE ODDS?

The avoidance of taxes is the only pursuit that still carries any reward.
> John Maynard Keyes (1883 – 1946), British economist

Read my lips — no new taxes.
> George Bush, at the Republican National Convention, August 18, 1988. He was subsequently elected president in November 1988 and forgot his now-famous quote. He did raise taxes.

An audit, as defined by *Webster's New Twentieth Century Dictionary*, is "an examination of an account or of accounts by proper officers or persons appointed for that purpose, who compare the charges with the vouchers, examine witnesses, and report the result." Under IRC §7602, the IRS may audit your books and records to make sure that you correctly reported your tax liability for the tax year in question.

The US tax system is based upon "voluntary" compliance. Unfortunately, this use of the word voluntary doesn't mean that you can choose whether or not you want to volunteer to pay taxes. Instead, it means that each US taxpayer must voluntarily (under the threat of criminal prosecution) tell the truth about his or her tax situation for a particular year. The voluntary nature of the US tax system means that each taxpayer makes a self-assessment of taxes owed when the return is prepared and filed.

The IRS believes that taxpayers are more likely to voluntarily comply with the tax laws and filing requirements if there is a threat of an audit in the back of their minds. The IRS Examination Division is responsible for conducting the often-dreaded tax audits of taxpayers. The division selects tax returns for examination and then conducts the actual examinations in the field or in IRS offices.*

1. What are the Odds of an IRS Audit?

The odds that the IRS will carry out an audit on a tax return are extremely small, primarily because the IRS does not have enough employees to audit a high percentage of yearly tax returns filed. For example, the IRS audited 1.38% of all returns filed during 1995 (a total of 2,136,819 audits out of 155,279,600 filed tax returns) and 1.36% of all returns filed in 1994 (a total of 2,100,144 audits out of 154,293,700 filed tax returns).

Recently, the numbers have dropped considerably, mainly due to reduced hiring and an IRS reorganization campaign that resulted in moving some tax auditors to different job duties. For instance, only 0.48% of all individual income tax returns were audited in 2002 (826,979 out of 171,140,558 tax returns). IRS Commissioner Mark Everson publicly stated that the IRS would audit many more tax returns from 2004 onward, and provided more money in the budget to hire new auditors. You would be wise to treat the Commissioner's statements very seriously on this point.

Also note that the percentages above are somewhat misleading because the total number of tax returns includes employment, gift, fiduciary (such as returns for estates and trusts), and partnership returns that the IRS rarely audits, the odds of an audit are still small. Table 3 shows the percentage of individual returns (i.e., Forms 1040, 1040A, and 1040EZ) audited from 1996 through 2002, broken down by income level.

The IRS claims that it audits a higher percentage of low-income taxpayers than middle-income taxpayers due to the recent IRS emphasis on individuals who do not file tax returns or who abuse the Earned Income Credit (a tax credit offered to low-income taxpayers only). However, low-income taxpayers are also easier audit targets because individuals who earn lower incomes are less likely to be able to afford legal or other professional assistance with the audit and are therefore less likely to be able to assert their rights during an audit.

> The odds that the IRS will carry out an audit on a tax return are extremely small, primarily because the IRS does not have enough employees to audit a high percentage of yearly tax returns filed.

---

* The terms "examination" and "audit" are used interchangeably in these chapters to indicate the inspection of books and records of a taxpayer.

TABLE 3

PERCENTAGE OF INDIVIDUAL TAX RETURNS AUDITED (BY INCOME LEVEL)

Taxable Income	Percentage Audited by Year						
	1996	1997	1998	1999	2000	2001	2002
$0 – $25,000	1.82	1.39	1.06	1.18	0.55	0.74	0.69
$25,000 – $50,000	0.95	0.70	0.58	0.36	0.21	0.22	0.23
$50,000 – $100,000	1.16	0.77	0.62	0.37	0.23	0.23	0.28
$100,000 and up	2.85	2.27	1.66	1.14	0.84	0.69	0.74

NOTE: These are individual tax returns only, not business returns.

In addition, contrary to what the IRS may claim, the odds of an audit vary depending on where the taxpayer lives. According to IRS statistics, the following cities have had the highest audit rates since 1988 (in this order): Anchorage, Las Vegas, Cheyenne, San Francisco, Laguna Niguel (near San Diego), Los Angeles, Boise, and Atlanta. The cities with the lowest audit rates were Albany, Milwaukee, Boston, Newark, Detroit, Philadelphia, Cincinnati, and Baltimore. A pattern clearly develops based upon this information: taxpayers who live in the western United States are much more likely to be exposed to an IRS audit than are those taxpayers who live in the eastern or Midwestern portions of the United States.

Table 4 shows the great variance between cities, though the percentages in the table are much lower than the actual audit figures for taxpayers in these selected cities because service center audits are not included in the city totals.

According to this chart, a taxpayer in Los Angeles is three times more likely to be audited than is a taxpayer in Philadelphia. Does this mean that there are more tax cheaters in Los Angeles than in Philadelphia? Or does it simply mean that the IRS is more aggressive and has more personnel in Los Angeles to perform the audits? The IRS does not provide the answer, and we can only speculate. Perhaps the IRS believes that taxpayers in the western regions are more likely to be anti-IRS than those in other parts of the United States. All things being equal, however, perhaps a move to Philadelphia, Boston, or another low-audit city is one way to decrease the risks of an IRS audit.

Cities with the highest audit rates since 1988:
Anchorage
Las Vegas
Cheyenne
San Francisco
Laguna Niguel
(near San Diego)
Los Angeles
Boise
Atlanta

Cities with the lowest audit rates since 1988:
Albany
Milwaukee
Boston
Newark
Detroit
Philadelphia
Cincinnati
Baltimore

TABLE 4

TAX RETURNS AUDITED BY CITY

City	Number of Returns	Number of Audits	Percentage
Boston	3,914,804	16,929	0.43
Chicago	5,553,787	27,770	0.50
Denver	2,503,387	14,965	0.60
Houston	2,669,810	17,512	0.66
Las Vegas	983,873	8,426	0.86
Los Angeles	4,313,553	56,244	1.30
New Orleans	2,321,562	20,666	0.89
Philadelphia	4,690,662	18,209	0.39
St. Louis	3,320,521	14,655	0.44
Seattle	3,396,024	19,355	0.57

NOTE: Statistics are from tax year 1996.

2. How Can You Reduce the Odds of an Audit?

The IRS will always try to perform as many audits each year as its resources allow, reasoning that the more audits it performs, the more tax dollars it will collect as a result of the audits and the easier it will be to increase next year's budget in Congress. With a bigger budget, the IRS can hire more auditors and collection agents, collect more money, increase its budget again, and so on. While nearly everyone fears the IRS, the IRS fears only Congress, because Congress has the power to appropriate funds and effectively determine how much power the IRS will have in any given year. Many members of Congress have recently considered reducing the IRS budget, which would reduce the IRS's size and overall power. This has, unfortunately, not yet happened. Until the IRS's budget, size, and power are reduced, you should expect an ever-larger and often out-of-control IRS, with the number of audits increasing every year.

In spite of this, there are ways to reduce the odds that you will be audited (although there is no way to eliminate the risk completely because some audits are truly random). The following are some tips for filing returns that are less likely to draw IRS attention:

(a) *Report all income that the IRS knows about or can find out about.* Using its computer system, the IRS has a tremendous ability to match income from sources it knows about (employers, banks, mutual funds, businesses, stock and real estate brokers, etc.) with the recipient, and it will nearly always catch you when you fail to report this income. Unreported income is the number one target in almost all audits and is the one area where taxpayers should be most cautious. In addition, beginning in 2003, the IRS computers will be able to match K-1 information (from certain corporations, LLCs, trusts, and partnerships) to your personal tax return information.

(b) *Do not use rounded numbers on the tax return.* The IRS is aware that a return that contains all rounded numbers (e.g., $2,000 for charitable contributions, $500 for office supplies) is likely to be an approximation that cannot be supported during an audit. The IRS audits these types of returns more frequently than other returns because the audits are almost certain to result in additional tax revenue for the government. Instead, use the actual amount paid or, if you must use approximate numbers (this is definitely not recommended), use figures such as $1,988 or $511 for the above examples.

(c) *Check carefully for math errors.* If the IRS computer catches a mathematical error on the return, the error will be corrected. However, this also gives the IRS a reason to look at the return in more detail. All taxpayers should try to limit the number of reasons the IRS has to look at a particular return.

(d) *File the tax return as close to April 15 as possible, or get an extension to file in August or October.* While the IRS denies that this will limit your audit chances, most practitioners disagree. (And when was the last time you believed what the IRS said anyway?) The reason many people believe that filing on or near April 15 will reduce the chance of an audit is that the tax return will be filed with a large number of other returns, and if the DIF score (discussed in section **3.1.** below) is higher than the national average, it may not stick out as much as it would if it was filed with few other returns on the same day. For example, if a return is filed on March 1, with a relatively small number of other returns, any deviation from what the IRS considers "normal" will increase the chance of the return being selected for audit.

Filing late (with an extension, of course) is believed to reduce audit chances because there is a limited number of returns the IRS can audit, and many of these will already have been selected before a late (after April 15) return is actually filed. If you do get an extension, remember that it only extends the time you have to file a tax return; it does not extend the time available to pay the tax you owe. You must pay at least 90% of the tax due by April 15 to avoid penalties for late payment of tax.

(e) *File a neat and organized tax return.* With all the inexpensive tax software out there today, there is no excuse for any taxpayer to file a return that the IRS has trouble reading or understanding. If the IRS is forced to examine a return more closely because it cannot read some of the information on the return, the odds of an audit increase tremendously. Why take this unnecessary risk?

(f) *Answer all questions on the tax return, even if a question does not apply to you.* Leaving a question blank invites the IRS to fill in an answer — an answer that you will often not like.

(g) *Attach explanations or documentation for unusual deductions on the return.* Though I wouldn't usually recommend attaching an explanation for any deduction that you yourself may question, you *should* attach an explanation to your return for an expense that you are sure you can deduct but that may be a bit unusual. For example, a casualty or theft loss should be supported with insurance and/or police claims or reports. This can lower the audit risk, because after the IRS computer flags any particular return as having a high audit potential, an IRS employee will review the return. If supporting documentation is attached to the return to explain the deduction, the audit risk is significantly lowered.

3. How are Tax Returns Selected for Audit?

There are several reasons why a tax return could be selected for audit. The following is a list of possibilities, with details to follow:

★ Statistical analysis (DIF)

★ IRS matching programs

★ IRS special projects on various occupations or professions

★ Informant tips

★ Evidence of criminal activity that produces probable unreported income (drugs, gambling, prostitution, etc.)

★ Random audits

★ Prior IRS audits with changes to return(s)

In recent years there were many rumors (some of them undoubtedly true) that the president of the United States, along with members of the executive branch of the US government (including the vice president and cabinet members) used IRS audits as a way to get even with their enemies (usually members of the opposite political party). In the Tax Reform Act of 1998, Congress enacted IRC §7217 and made it a crime for most executive branch members to interfere with an audit (whether the interference was forcing the IRS to begin an audit or to stop or alter an already pending audit). This law is at least a start to reassuring us that audits, or the threat of an audit, will not be done for any improper purpose.

3.1 Statistical analysis

The majority of audited income tax returns are selected by means of a computer-generated score, which the IRS calls the Discriminate Function System or DIF score. This score is a statistical profile that is computed by comparing the numbers (i.e., income, expenses, and deductions) on your income tax return with numbers generated using national statistics for taxpayers in a similar income tax bracket. If a number on your particular tax return is out of line, statistically speaking, from these national averages, the DIF score identifies the return as having audit potential. For example, if the national average for charitable contributions for a certain income group is $1,000 and your return contains $3,000 in charitable contributions, the computer will flag this entry for a potential audit.

Just because the IRS computer flags a particular entry on a return, it does not mean the entry is incorrect or that the return will actually be audited. Following the computer's audit flag, an IRS employee will manually review the return to determine if it has audit potential. Not every return that is statistically out of line with the national averages will be audited.

Table 5 contains some average itemized deductions figures the IRS has released for tax year 1999. The numbers are meant only to show IRS expectations based on statistical analysis. You should not use them as a substitute for actual amounts you spent on each of these expense items.

The IRS has never released the formula used for computing the DIF score, but certain items on a tax return are known to affect the score. For example, a loss on a sole proprietorship business (Schedule C) or expenses that are out of line with the numbers shown in Table 5 are known to increase the score and also the audit chances. Taxpayers should not worry about the actual numbers used for the DIF analysis, but they do need to be aware how the IRS uses the statistical information.

TABLE 5
AVERAGE ITEMIZED DEDUCTIONS — 2001

Adjusted Gross Income	Medical Expenses	Taxes	Interest	Contributions
$0 – $15,000	$7,281	$2,134	$6,884	$1,329
$15,000 – $30,000	5,616	2,311	6,406	1,875
$30,000 – $50,000	5,489	3,052	6,783	1,906
$50,000 – $100,000	5,532	5,108	8,330	2,429
$100,000 – $200,000	10,780	9,713	11,817	3,761
$200,000 or more	35,927	38,931	23,260	17,842

3.2 IRS matching programs

Many tax returns are selected for audit through a matching program that the IRS has developed using its computer system. The IRS reviews each information return it receives (i.e., from the millions of Forms W-2, 1099, and 1098 it receives) and compares the information on these returns to the return you have submitted, linking them via your social security number(s). The IRS receives tax information from the following common sources (although this is not a complete list):

★ Employers/wages (Form W-2)

★ Gambling/casinos (Form W-2 G)

★ Pensions/annuities (Form 1099-R)

★ Over $600 for services (Form 1099-MISC)

★ Banks/interest (Form 1099-INT)

★ Mutual funds/stockbrokers (Form 1099-DIV)

★ State unemployment (Form 1099-G)

★ State income tax refunds (Form 1099-G)

★ Real estate agents (Form 1099-S)

★ Corporations/dividends (Form 1099-DIV)

★ Mortgage interest (Form 1098)

★ Miscellaneous income (Form 1099-MISC)

★ Business (Schedule K-1)

For example, suppose that the IRS receives several Forms W-2 for your social security number, which add up to $30,000 in wages for the year. On your return you report $25,000 in wages. The IRS computer system will automatically adjust your income by $5,000 and send you a bill for the additional tax due on this alleged unreported income. While this may have been a mistake on your part, it is also possible that you reported the correct amount of wages and that one or more of the information returns the IRS received was incorrect (perhaps an employer listed the wrong social security number on one of the Forms W-2). For this reason alone, you should always check the accuracy of any IRS attempt to increase the amount of taxes due.

3.3 IRS special projects

The IRS routinely picks certain industries or professions (e.g., lawyers, nurses, ministers, construction workers, mechanics) and audits a large percentage of returns that fit its project criteria (either based on the profession listed on the signature line or the business code used on the Schedule C). The IRS calls this the Market Segment Specialization Program (MSSP). It has put together teams of agents to determine what type of audit issues exist for several different professions. It is amazing what they have come up with.

> You should always check the accuracy of any IRS attempt to increase the amount of taxes due.

For example, the IRS has developed audit strategies for targeting mobile food vendors, such as people who sell hot dogs on street corners in US cities. While the IRS believes that the food vendors are "generally unsophisticated and maintain poor records" (which makes them an easy target for the IRS because they probably cannot afford to hire legal representation and cannot support their tax returns with complete documentation), the MSSP guide goes on for several pages about how to attack the return and the taxpayer personally. Other recent IRS projects have included doctors and dentists (often for tax shelters and high expenses), salespersons (high expenses, especially travel and entertainment), airline pilots (tax shelters and commuting expenses), and ministers (mail-order ministry potential).

3.4 Informant tips

The IRS relies on information from informants to determine the audit potential of a tax return. Many informants provide the information to the IRS anonymously, although the informant must provide his or her identity to the IRS if he or she wants to collect any reward money for the information. Never discuss confidential tax information with anyone, including friends and family members. This is potentially inviting an IRS audit — one invitation that is better avoided.

3.5 Evidence of criminal activity

The IRS receives a great deal of information from a variety of sources concerning criminal activity and the likely unreported income associated with the criminal activity. While these sources include federal, state, and local law enforcement agencies, often the IRS will develop audit leads simply from reading the newspaper. For example, if a newspaper reports that "Lisa Smith, who resides at 112 Main Street, was caught late last night with two ounces of cocaine in her car," the IRS may well conclude that Ms. Smith was selling cocaine and probably not reporting the income on her tax return. While the IRS has no way of knowing whether this is indeed true, it will certainly want to investigate. Of course, the way the IRS investigates is via an audit.

3.6 Random audits

The IRS has always relied on the threat of conducting random audits to encourage "voluntary compliance" with the tax laws. The IRS reasons that if you believe that your tax return will be selected for audit solely on a random basis, you will be more likely to file correct returns, rather than risk being caught cheating on the return. This is one of the rare instances where the IRS is probably right. There is no way to avoid a random audit if a tax return is filed, although the odds that an audit will result from truly random selection are statistically very small.

The IRS has also announced its plans to begin conducting audits for its so-called "National Research Program" (NRP) tax compliance audits. These audits, which will number approximately 50,000 taxpayers, will be much more intrusive than a regular audit in that the IRS will be using the audits to gather statistical information to update its computer system for DIF-score purposes. It is unclear if this NPR audit program will become a regular, annual auditing strategy or used on a less frequent basis. Whatever the answer, it is not particularly good news for taxpayers.

3.7 Prior IRS audits

The IRS likes to pick on those taxpayers who have had the misfortune to be audited in the past and had to pay additional tax to the IRS. The IRS often performs follow-up audits on these taxpayers to make sure that the most recently filed returns do not contain the same mistakes found in the prior audit(s). Under any circumstances, taxpayers who have had a previous negative audit encounter with the IRS would be well advised to make sure that history does not repeat itself.

Tax Points

★ The IRS is allowed to audit your books and records to make sure that you correctly reported your tax liability for the tax year in question.

★ Each US taxpayer must voluntarily (under the threat of criminal prosecution) tell the truth about his or her tax situation in a particular year.

★ The odds that the IRS will carry out an audit on a tax return are extremely small but unfortunately are beginning to increase.

★ There are ways to reduce the odds that your tax return will be noticed by the IRS and chosen for an audit.

CHAPTER 6

GOING THROUGH AN AUDIT

I believe that the 16th Amendment has created a system that is economically destructive, impossibly complex, overly intrusive, unprincipled, dishonest, unfair, and inefficient.

Representative Sam Johnson (R-Texas), April 10, 1997

People who complain about taxes can be divided into two classes: men and women.

Anonymous

Indoors or out, no one relaxes in March, that month of wind and taxes. The wind will presently disappear, the taxes last us all the year.

(Ogden Nash (1902 – 1971), poet and humorist

During an audit, an IRS revenue agent, or a tax auditor on less complicated returns, will analyze both the income and deductions you have reported to make sure that your return is "substantially correct." The revenue agent does not have power to seize your assets, put a levy on your wages, make arrests, or do anything else that does not relate solely to determining the accuracy of a tax return. Because a tax auditor or revenue agent does not have any real power, there is nothing to fear from him or her (although a tax auditor can make your life miserable during the audit).

If you refuse to give in to the fear factor, you will be on a more level playing field with the IRS during the course of the tax audit. Always remember that even the IRS recognizes, in its Publication 1, that you are responsible only for paying "the correct amount of tax due under the law — no more, no less."

1. Understand Your Rights

It is important for you to understand that you, and not the IRS, have rights during an audit. While the IRS has the legal authority to do certain things, only you have legal rights. If you are, or may be, audited, you should obtain IRS Publication 556 (Examination of Returns, Appeal Rights, and Claims for Refund), which contains some valuable information concerning your rights during the audit process. The following is a list of the most important taxpayer rights during audits:

You, and not the IRS, have rights during an audit.

★ You are permitted to tape-record the audit interview so that no misunderstandings occur. You must give the IRS at least ten days' notification that you intend to record the interview, mainly so the IRS can also tape-record the appointment if it so desires. I would not recommend using this right at the initial appointment, as many IRS employees become uncomfortable when the meetings are tape recorded. Instead, I would recommend trying to establish an acceptable level of rapport with the employee and use your right to tape record any meetings only if you experience problems with communication.

★ You should insist that everything be put into writing, especially any requests for documentation.

★ You should ask questions (the IRS is not the only party in the audit game that is permitted to do this). If you do not understand something, you should always ask the examiner why he or she is requesting the information. If you don't agree with what is happening or where the audit is heading, you should tell the agent or ask why he or she is proposing to do something. The only sure way to protect all your rights is to be vocal at all stages of the audit.

★ All IRS employees are required to carry their identification badge with them during audits, and you have a right to ask to see the identification badge. By doing so, you can obtain information on how long the employee has worked for the IRS, which may be useful in determining the amount of experience he or she has. This will not tell you how much experience the person had before working for the IRS, but at least you will know the level of the employee's governmental experience.

★ You always have the right to be represented by counsel. If at any time during the examination you wish to seek professional counsel, the examiner must stop the examination and permit you to consult with a representative. A representative may be a lawyer, accountant, CPA, or enrolled agent. (Enrolled agents are people who have passed an examination on tax issues, law, and procedures, and are therefore allowed to represent taxpayers before the IRS. Unlike CPAs or attorneys, they do not necessarily have a professional degree.)

2. Understand What the IRS Can Do During an Audit

The IRS has several weapons available to it during the course of an audit; taxpayers should understand what these weapons are before they ever meet with an IRS employee.

2.1 The IRS can examine books and records

Under IRC §7602, the IRS has the authority to examine your books and records. The IRS may also get information from third parties (e.g., banks, brokerage houses, and business acquaintances) to assist in the audit.

If you refuse to allow the IRS to examine your books or records, the IRS may legally summon them. If you refuse to comply with the summons, the IRS can enforce the summons in the US district court. Before the IRS is permitted to do this, however, the examiner must inform you that this may happen and also must keep a list of any contacts made with third parties (whether made with a summons or without).

Forcing the IRS to use the summons procedures to get information is definitely *not* a good idea. An audit will rarely be resolved in your favor when you are unwilling to cooperate with the IRS. Most taxpayers benefit greatly by cooperating with the IRS during an audit, as long as the IRS is reasonable during the audit.

If you believe that you may have committed fraud (civil or criminal) or some other criminal violation, however, it may not be in your best interest to cooperate with the IRS. If you have committed fraud or a criminal violation, and the revenue agent doesn't know about it, providing records may be tantamount to giving the IRS the gun and ammunition to shoot you. Any cases in which fraud, whether criminal or civil, or any other criminal violation might be an issue should be handled by a tax professional, as the stakes are often too high for you to rely upon self-representation.

> You will benefit greatly by cooperating with the IRS during an audit, as long as the IRS is reasonable during the audit.

2.2 The IRS has access to other documents and information

The IRS has access to a wide variety of other documents and information during an audit. You should know exactly what types of information the IRS will rely on during an audit so that you can plan an effective audit strategy. The following are common types of information available to the revenue agent:

★ The original tax return(s) now under examination

★ Copies of your books and records for the years at issue

★ An interview with the taxpayer and the notes associated with the interview

★ Public records (e.g., recorded deeds and mortgage information, driver's license records, car registration forms, court documents)

★ IRS industry papers describing audit issues for hundreds of different types of businesses, professionals, and occupations

★ Newspaper articles

★ Information from informants (in a small number of cases)

★ Consultation with IRS attorneys (area counsel) and advice concerning the application of the tax laws to the issues in the audit

★ Information gathered by other revenue agents or IRS employees

★ Information gathered by special agents from the Criminal Investigation Division

★ The IRC, regulations, case law, and other tax research material that relates to the issues raised in the audit

Not all of this information applies in each audit, but the list suggests the scope of possible sources of information for the IRS auditor.

Information reported to the IRS by third parties (such as wage information, mortgage interest, bank interest earned, etc.)

2.3 What does the IRS know?

The IRS employee assigned to an audit generally knows very little about the taxpayer personally, unless an informant provided private information to get the audit started or the taxpayer is a public figure. The IRS employee, however, will never tell you just how little he or she knows about you. Instead, the examiner is trained to let you believe that the examiner

An IRS examiner knows only what information is provided on your tax return. However, IRS examiners are trained to let you believe that they know nearly everything about you.

knows nearly everything about you, mainly because most taxpayers believe this to be true.

In general, the examiner knows only what information is provided on your tax return. No more, no less. By examining the return, the examiner can determine the following:

(a) *Your occupation.* The examiner uses this information to make certain general assumptions, such as lifestyle expectations, types of common business expenses for the taxpayer's occupation, and stereotypes concerning the type of person engaged in the occupation. Contrary to popular belief, the revenue agents are human and have certain preconceived ideas about various occupations or professions (such as the idea that doctors are wealthy, professors are smart, and accountants are conservative).

(b) *Your income and expenses.* Using experience and extensive in-house training, many examiners have a pretty good idea as to what is reasonable, normal, or average, such as how much mortgage interest a family can typically afford if it earns $50,000 per year.

3. Types of Audits

3.1 Correspondence audit

The IRS conducts hundreds of thousands of tax audits by correspondence. The correspondence audit is the least threatening audit for you and the one in which you have the greatest chance of winning.

This audit process generally starts when you receive a notice from the IRS computer that your tax return has been changed, often as a result of the computer matching program. For example, if you report $50,000 in wages for the year, but the IRS receives Forms W-2 showing wages for you in the amount of $55,000, the IRS computer will catch the discrepancy, determine the correct amount of tax due on the additional $5,000 in wages, and send you a bill for the additional tax owing. Most correspondence audits are done by the service center where the return was filed. They often question only a small number of items on the return (generally one or two).

The main thing to remember if you find yourself the subject of a correspondence audit is this: do not automatically send the IRS a check for the amount that the notice says is owed. The IRS makes many mistakes in its correspondence audits, and there is no reason to believe that a bill increasing the taxes you owe is accurate. For example, there may be an incorrect social security number on the W-2 (Wages) or Form 1099 (such as Dividends from a Mutual Fund or Interest from Banks). If the number is off by only one digit, the IRS may believe that you received more taxable income than you actually did. Only after you have conducted a thorough review, comparing a copy of your tax return with the IRS notice, can you be certain that the IRS is either correct or incorrect.

Whether you agree or disagree with the contents of the notice, *do not ignore it.* Ignoring a notice will not make the problem go away. The IRS is like a disease that is curable if treated in time but fatal if left alone and ignored. If you do not respond to an IRS notice or letter, the IRS treats the lack of response as an agreement with its computations.

Should you agree with the IRS notice, you must sign and date the notice and pay the amount owed. If you are unable to pay, you can arrange an Installment Agreement (as described in chapter 11).

If you disagree with the IRS notice, there is a procedure in place to explain your disagreement. This procedure is explained in the notice you are sent from the IRS. Normally, your written explanation must be sent to the IRS within 30 days of the date of the IRS notice. The response should include copies of any documents that support your position as to the disagreement.

3.2   Office audit

An office audit is done in an IRS office and is usually carried out by less-experienced IRS employees, usually tax auditors. These audits are mostly concerned with simple tax matters (if there is such a thing) and are limited in scope to a few items on the return. Office audits are more complex than correspondence audits but are not complex enough to require a field audit. Most office audits concern common items found on tax returns, such as exemptions, travel and entertainment expenses, and casualty losses.

All office audits are scheduled during IRS business hours. If you are the subject of an office audit, you will receive a letter (often called an appointment letter) requesting you to bring in documentation supporting the items on the tax return(s) that are being questioned. If there are few documents needed, you can ask the IRS to handle the audit by mail. This effectively turns the office audit into a correspondence audit. If the IRS agrees, no actual meeting between you and the IRS official will take place. Generally, it is a benefit for you *not* to have a meeting with the IRS, and avoiding such a meeting should be your initial goal if you face an office audit.

Never ignore a notice or letter from the IRS. Lack of response indicates your agreement with the IRS's computations.

If you cannot escape a meeting during the office audit, your primary goal, other than paying no additional tax, is to complete the audit in one meeting with the IRS. This should be easy to accomplish, provided that you bring to the appointment all documents that the auditor requested. As in all other audits, you do not have to agree with the IRS findings and can exercise all appeal rights to challenge any proposed changes to your return.

3.3 Field audit

Field audits are usually the most complete IRS audits and are performed by a revenue agent. A revenue agent is usually experienced and is the IRS's best chance to assess additional tax revenues. If you are the subject of a field audit, I recommend you get professional assistance, as the issues can be complex and there is extensive interaction with the IRS.

The IRS usually conducts field audits when the issues require an on-site review of the taxpayer's books and records. You can request that the IRS change the audit site to an IRS office, which the IRS will often do if you can bring all books and records to an IRS office and can leave them there. The agent may still require an on-site visit during normal business hours if some audit issue requires an actual visit. You must make reasonable attempts to accommodate the revenue agent.

Like other types of audits, the IRS will present you with any proposed changes to the tax return at the end of the audit. You have all appeal rights available should you disagree with the proposed adjustments. These appeal rights are discussed in detail in section **5.4** below.

3.4 Repetitive audit

The IRS is known for auditing some of the same taxpayers over and over again. They can do this if each audit produces additional tax due. However, if you underwent a previous audit that produced little or no change to your return, and the IRS wants to audit you again (for the same reason or reasons), you can tell them that the proposed audit should be discontinued because it is a repetitive audit procedure. To support this request, you should send the auditor the following documentation:

(a) A copy of the last audit's appointment letter (or anything else that shows the issues involved)

(b) A copy of the no-change letter from the last audit

(c) A copy of the previous audit's tax return(s)

After the IRS receives this information, it will often agree that the situation represents a repetitive audit and will discontinue it promptly. Short of not being audited at all, this is the best of all possible worlds for the taxpayer.

3.5 Taxpayer Compliance Measurement Program (TCMP) National Research Program audits

In the past, the IRS has carried out Taxpayer Compliance Measurement Program (TCMP) audits. While it is not currently calling any "TCMP audits," it is conducting audits to collect statistical information. This is now called the National Research Program (NPR).

TCMP audits in the past were nothing more than a time-consuming, expensive, and intrusive way for the IRS to update its computer database at the taxpayers' financial and emotional expense. In a TCMP audit, the IRS asked you to verify every entry on the return. For example, it asked you to prove that you have a child, prove that you paid $5,000 in mortgage interest, or prove that you gave $200 to your church or synagogue. The IRS then used this information to update its computers for DIF score analysis purposes.

Although the IRS has promised that its NRP audits in 2002-03 (and possibly beyond) will be much less intrusive than were the TCMP audits, only time will tell. It seems likely, however, that the IRS will make these audits as intrusive as necessary to gather whatever information it seeks.

You cannot avoid a TCMP or NRP audit, even if the added burden of dealing with the audit, both in terms of time and money, is a hardship. Courts have determined that this is the price that we must pay as American citizens. Perhaps the courts would have a different view of the situation if all judges were the victims of these intrusive audits!

4. Prepare for an Audit

4.1 Keep all your records

As soon as you know you are going to be audited, you should begin to gather all records associated with the tax year(s) in question. When you are fighting an IRS audit, the most powerful weapons on your side, short of an incompetent auditor, are written records to support all entries on the return(s) in question.

Documentation to keep to prove tax deductions:

- Journals/ledgers
- Credit card bills
- Canceled checks
- Bank statements
- Brokerage account statements
- Invoices
- Receipts
- Mortgage statements
- Itemized accounts of your financial activity

The IRS wants to see some type of documentation to support anything in your favor. To prove a deduction, the IRS would like to see journals/ledgers, credit card bills, canceled checks, bank statements, brokerage account statements, invoices, receipts, mortgage statements, or any other itemized account of your financial activity for the year.

If for some reason you cannot locate any of these documents, you should immediately attempt to get the records from the third parties. Most banks will provide duplicate copies of bank statements to their customers for a nominal charge, and other institutions will do the same for many of the other types of documents mentioned above. Request duplicate copies as soon as possible, as delay is likely to make it more difficult to resolve the audit to your overall satisfaction. I discuss how a taxpayer should handle situations where there are a lack of records in chapter 7.

4.1.a How long should you keep tax records?

You should keep most tax records for at least three years and preferably for six years. The IRS has three years to audit most tax returns, and six years if it can demonstrate that you omitted at least 25% from your gross income as stated on the tax return. There is no limitations period if the IRS asserts, and can prove, fraud, or if you fail to file a tax return.

Some tax records should be kept forever. These records primarily relate to investments and are needed to compute how much the investment cost (known as the "basis") when the investment is sold. Examples of these records are stock, bond, mutual fund, and retirement account statements showing purchases, reinvested dividends, and/or interest and sale proceeds. Without these records, you inevitably pay more tax than is necessary. You can usually avoid this by keeping the necessary records.

For example, say that you purchased IBM stock at $1,000, reinvested $100 in dividends (basically taking the dividends in the form of more stock as opposed to cash) one year later, and then sold the stock for $1,050 another year later. Without any records to demonstrate that dividends were reinvested, you would be taxed on a capital gain of $50 ($1,050 sale price minus the $1,000 purchase price). If you had the records, you would not pay any tax on the transaction and would actually be able to deduct a loss of $50 on the sale ($1,100 purchase price including reinvested dividends minus the $1,050 sale price). The loss could then be used to reduce other taxable income such as wages or interest.

All records concerning real property, including purchase and sale information and all improvements, should be kept indefinitely. Again, this

Keep copies of your tax returns for at least six years, along with the proof of filing.

is so that you can properly account for all transactions and not pay any more tax than the IRS requires. This remains the case even after Congress raised the capital gain exclusions on the sale of personal residences in the Taxpayer Relief Act of 1997. While nearly every taxpayer will now be able to sell his or her home and not pay any capital gains tax (because single taxpayers can exclude up to $250,000 of gain, while married couples filing joint tax returns can exclude up to $500,000 of gain in most instances), you should not assume that Congress will not change this part of the tax code again in the future (and probably to your detriment).

Finally, keep copies of your tax returns for at least six years, along with the proof of filing (i.e., send all tax returns by certified mail, and request a return receipt).

4.1.b What do you do with the records you have?

Once you have located the records you need, organize them so that you can retrieve them quickly at any subsequent appointment with the IRS. Taxpayers who are organized and prepared during an audit will generally obtain more favorable audit results than will disorganized taxpayers.

In addition to securing and organizing records, you should locate and review copies of the tax return(s) in question, identifying any problem areas before your meeting with the auditor. The audit letter should set out the area(s) or issues on the tax return(s) that will be examined. If this was not done, you should ask the auditor for this information before your first meeting (see the next section).

Finally, if possible, research the appropriate areas of the tax law before your appointment with an auditor, or as soon after the appointment as possible. Chapter 1 outlines some useful publications for learning the tax law.

4.2   Know why your return was selected

All taxpayers have the right to know why their particular return was selected for audit. For some reason, many IRS revenue agents are secretive when it comes to answering this question. However, in its own Publication 1, the IRS states: "You have the right to know why we are asking for information, how we will use it, and what happens if you do not provide the requested information."

After asking the examiner why the return was selected, do not stop asking questions. You also have the right to know which part of the return is in question. The answer should not be "the entire return." Get a very

Ensure that the IRS uses an Information Document Request form to request specific documents from you. If you have the request in writing, there is less chance of problems arising due to miscommunication.

specific answer to this question, such as "the itemized deductions on Schedule A" or "the business expenses on Schedule C."

After finding out which part of the return is at issue, ask the examiner what documents he or she would like to see to verify the figures on the return. Asking this question gives you an advantage, because you only need to produce those documents that the IRS requests. It is generally not a good idea to volunteer any written documents or other information to the IRS if the information is not specifically requested. Information you volunteer may give the IRS a lead that the examiner would never have thought of had you not provided it.

The IRS should request specific documents from you in writing, using an Information Document Request (IDR). With an IDR, as opposed to an oral request, you are better able to limit the scope of the request and will generally be asked for fewer documents. In addition, a written request eliminates any problem due to miscommunication or misunderstanding of what was requested. Having a written IDR also means the IRS cannot accuse you of not cooperating with the audit, an assertion that the IRS will make if it does not get every document it later believes was necessary to accurately examine a particular return.

You should always make sure that the IRS is specific in its document requests, as doing so will keep the issues under examination as narrow as possible. It is critical to accomplish this early in the audit, as many revenue agents seem to turn routine audits into "lifestyle audits" (what used to be called "economic reality" audits, discussed in chapter 8).

Once the IRS gives you the IDR, you have the right to ask the revenue agent why the documents are being requested. While you could ask this about each document requested, I recommend limiting the "why" questions to those requests that don't seem to make any sense. If the revenue agent's answers don't satisfy you, your next step should be to find out what will happen if you do not produce the documents. You should be prepared for a negative answer, such as "I will disallow everything on the return and close my case unagreed." (If an audit is closed "unagreed," the IRS will send you a Notice of Deficiency, which states the amount of tax you owe and gives you 90 days to challenge the case in tax court or else pay the tax assessed.)

If you reach a roadblock with the revenue agent concerning the IDR, speak to the revenue agent's manager to clear up any misunderstanding or confusion. Make sure that the revenue agent understands that you are attempting to cooperate with the audit, even if this is not in fact the case.

If an audit is closed "unagreed," the IRS will send you a Notice of Deficiency, which states the amount of tax you owe and gives you 90 days to challenge the case in tax court or else pay the tax assessed.

Audits generally go from bad to worse when an examiner believes that the taxpayer is not cooperating during the course of the audit.

5. The Audit Process

Many taxpayers fear an IRS audit because they don't know the procedure the IRS follows and the appropriate response for the taxpayer to make. If you know what to expect during the audit process, you stand a better chance of winning the game.

5.1 The audit appointment

If you are involved in an IRS correspondence audit, you will not actually meet with an IRS employee. However, at some point during the course of nearly every field audit, and many office audits, the IRS auditor will want to interview you to obtain information concerning the tax year(s) at issue. You and the auditor must agree when and where the audit will occur. The choices for the time of the audit are limited to the business hours of the IRS. Most examiners will want to schedule the initial appointment for either 9:00 a.m. or 1:00 p.m. (i.e., first thing in the morning or after lunch). The *Internal Revenue Manual* states that the place should meet the "convenience" of the taxpayer.

Usually, you should ask to have the audit appointment at an IRS office, at the office of your tax representative (lawyer, accountant, etc.), or at any place other than your home or business. The IRS will generally agree to this as long as your books and records will be made available to the IRS wherever the audit is held.

While the IRS may prefer to have the audit at your home or business, you should resist this. The last thing most people want is to have the IRS sitting at their kitchen table or snooping around their business. Keep the following points in mind as you prepare for this appointment:

(a) *Reschedule the appointment if you need more time.* I have never been denied at least one postponement and sometimes have been granted several schedule changes. In some situations it is important to buy some additional time, especially if it is difficult to locate some of your tax records. The IRS will permit the rescheduling because it benefits by having a prepared and organized taxpayer; this way the audit usually goes much more smoothly and should take less overall time to complete. In order to have the greatest chance of getting the audit appointment postponed, you should give the auditor as much notice as is possible and should never cancel on the day of the appointment unless there is an emergency (illness, snowstorm, etc.).

(b) *Schedule the appointment for a Friday, or the day before a holiday weekend.* Scheduling an appointment at these times means you are meeting the auditor just before he or she gets some time off. This may put the auditor in a better mood, and he or she may be more willing to work with you to resolve questionable tax items.

(c) *Schedule the appointment for later in the morning (10:00 a.m. to 11:00 a.m.).* This may interfere with the auditor's lunch plans. Most government employees are regimented and programmed to eat lunch at a certain time and may cut the appointment short to be able to keep lunch plans. This is always worth a try, as a shorter appointment may work to your advantage if some questionable items are not discussed in much detail.

(d) *Always be on time or early for the appointment.* It is never a good idea to start the audit on a negative tone. The IRS expects you to be punctual, and you should be. Furthermore, if you are on time and the auditor is late, you start the audit off with a slight advantage. Any advantage, however slight it may be, should always be accepted with a smile.

5.2 Common audit questions

While each audit is unique due to the inherent differences between taxpayers, many audit interviews are remarkably similar. This may be partly due to the auditor's rigid application of what he or she learned during the in-house IRS training and also due to the presence of IRS Form 4700 (Examination Workpapers) (see Sample 7). Many, but not all, examiners use this form to make sure that they don't miss any potential audit issues. The agents are trained to check the following points:

★ Look for large, unusual or questionable items on the tax return.

★ Look for unreported income.

★ Make sure all tax returns currently due have been filed.

★ Decide if any penalties should be imposed.

★ Make sure any changes to the tax return are supported by the current law.

At the initial interview, the auditor is almost certain to ask you about the following information and types of income:

★ Personal information (i.e., name, address, city, marital status, children, occupation)

★ Prior IRS audit history, if any (if you have been audited in the past, the examiner will want to know the results of the audit)

★ Types of income received (i.e., wages, interest, tips, commissions, gambling, bonuses, alimony, rent, royalties, dividends, sale of assets)

★ Any bartering income — basically trading goods or services for other goods or services (the IRS asks about bartering because many people do not report these types of transactions as income and also because many tax protestors use bartering as a way to avoid a paper trail for their purchases and sales)

★ Any foreign bank accounts or foreign investments

★ Proof of expenses or deductions claimed on the tax return

After the auditor asks these questions, along with any other relevant questions, he or she will compare the answers with documents in your file and make audit recommendations concerning any proposed changes to the return. The auditor is trained to follow certain guidelines during audits to attempt to ensure uniformity. Many auditors use Form 4700 (Examination Workpapers) for this purpose (see Sample 7).

To reduce the chance of being caught off guard, you should anticipate the types of questions you will be asked. Taxpayers who are well prepared for the initial appointment generally obtain much better results than those who go into the appointment unprepared. Should the auditor ask any questions that you are not prepared to answer, it is perfectly acceptable to request some additional time to answer the question. Do not answer the question on the spot as you might say something that is not accurate. As well, you might give the auditor information you don't want the IRS to have.

View the initial appointment as a fishing expedition. The IRS auditor's goal is to catch as many fish (i.e., get as much additional tax revenue) as possible. The more the examiner learns about you, the more audit issues he or she will recognize, and the more potential revenue he or she will see. Don't make the examiner's job any easier unless you will directly benefit in some way.

Be prepared for your audit interview by anticipating the types of questions you will be asked. If the auditor asks a question that you do not know the answer to, request some additional time to answer the question. Do not answer the question on the spot as you might say something that is not accurate. Never volunteer information.

SAMPLE 7

FORM 4700 (IRS EXAMINATION WORKPAPERS)

Examination Workpapers

Taxpayer's name, address, SSN (*Use pre-addressed label or show changes for both spouses if a joint return audit*) Mary Moneybags 123 Main Street Denver CO 80202 SSN: 123-45-6789	Date 12/14/-99 — Year(s) 1997 Examiner Lou Snitch — Grade 11 Taxpayer(s) Home Phone (303) 555-1212 — Work Phone Reviewer Tina Tellall

Representative - Power of Attorney ☐ Yes ☒ No

Name

A

Initial Interview

1. Examination technique: ☐ Correspondence ☐ Undeliverable mail ☐ No show ☒ Interview with:
   Mary Moneybags
2. Receipt of Publication 1 ☒
3. Appeal rights and Privacy Act explained ☒
4. Innocent spouse (Pub. 971) ☐
5. Continue on Form 4700-A, B or C

B

Closed No Change

Issue: ☒ Letter 590 ☐ Letter 1156 ☐ Other

Examiner *Lou Snitch*

C

EQMS Auditing Standards (Rev. 5/95) — IRM Exhibit 4910-1

1. Consideration of Large, Unusual, or Questionable Items
2. Probes for Unreported Income
3. Required Filing Checks
4. Examination Depth and Records Examined
5. Continue on Form 4700-A, B or C

6. Penalties Properly Considered
7. Workpapers Support Conclusions
8. Report Writing Procedures Followed
9. Time Span/Time Charged

Was consideration given to all applicable auditing standards?

(YES)

If no, indicate the standard(s) not given consideration, and the reasons why consideration was not given: _____
_____
_____
_____

Service Center Tax Examiners—Refer to Center Examination Quality Measurement System (CEQMS) Auditing Standards in IRM Exhibit 4010-2

D

Examination Reminders

1. Proforma Worksheets utilized where applicable
2. Alternate minimum tax
3. Inspection of prior and subsequent year return, IRM 4215
4. Probe for unreported deductions and credits
5. Scope of Examination, IRM 4253.2
6. Automatic adjustments resulting from AGI change(s)
7. "Burned Out" Tax Shelters - IRM 4236(13)
8. Amounts claimed for See/Special Fuels - IRC 6426/6421
9. Health Care Continuation Coverage Under COBRA - IRC 49908

Case Processing Reminders

1. Claim Case - Forms 2297 and 3363
2. Information Reports (IRM 4219) - Form 5346
3. FICA, Self-Employment or Tip Income Adjustments . Forms 885-E, 885-F, and 885-T
4. Inequities, Abuses, Loopholes - Form 3558
5. Inadequate Records Notices (IRM 4271)
6. Special Handling Notice 3198

E

Required Filing Checks - IRM 4034

	CHECK COMPLETED			COMMENT IN:	
	YES	NO	N/A	F4700 SUPPLEMENT	F4700 BUSINESS SUPPLEMENT
1. All Required Returns (of THIS T/P)					
.. Prior	✔				
.. Subsequent	✔				
.. Compliance Items:					
Information Returns	✔				
Questionable W-4's	✔				
Forms 8300	✔				
Any Other Returns	✔				
2. All Related Returns (of ANOTHER T/P)			✗		

Form **4700** (Rev. 1-99) — Catalog Number 23315Y — Department of the Treasury—Internal Revenue Service

No matter what happens at the initial appointment, you should expect that the examiner will have unanswered questions or will need additional documentation. Most examiners will ask additional questions or request further information with an Information Document Request Form (IDR). You have plenty of time to comply with the IDR, and if your response is satisfactory to the auditor, this will be all the information that the IRS will receive to complete its audit of you and your tax return(s).

5.3   What happens after an audit?

At the end of an audit, you will be presented with a report that contains proposed changes to the tax return(s) under examination. If you agree with the report, you will usually be given a Form 870 (Waiver of Restrictions on Assessment and Collection of Deficiency in Tax and Acceptance of Overassessment) (see Sample 8). When you sign this form, the IRS is legally permitted to make an immediate assessment of the tax due and owing, without having to issue a Notice of Deficiency. Also, by signing you give up your right to challenge the tax adjustment in the US tax court.

Even though you have forfeited the right to go to tax court, you can still file a claim for refund with the IRS immediately after you pay the tax due. If this claim is denied, which it probably will be, you are legally permitted to file suit for refund in the US district or claims court. For a discussion of these options, see chapter 15. Of course, if the IRS is correct in asserting that additional tax is due, you would not have a legal basis for challenging the IRS in tax court and may be subject to a penalty (up to $25,000) for filing a frivolous tax court petition.

Remember that the IRS charges interest on overdue taxes. Interest is compounded daily from the date the return was due, not the date you agreed to pay the additional tax due.

When you agree that additional tax is due, you must realize that the IRS will compute interest on the tax owed at a rate defined in IRC §6621. This rate changes every six months and is computed by adding three percentage points to the Federal Reserve rate then in effect. While the rate is adjusted only every six months, the interest is compounded daily from the date the return was due, not the date that you agreed to pay the additional tax due. The compounded interest is what overwhelms many taxpayers.

For example, suppose that the audit has determined you owe an additional $5,000 in tax. While this amount may be difficult to pay, it becomes much more difficult, if not impossible, when the interest doubles the amount due (and the interest continues to accrue every day until the debt is paid in full). Because the interest is compounding, the taxpayer becomes responsible for the interest on the interest.

Unfortunately for the taxpayer, the examiner is not permitted to waive the interest unless the interest resulted from an unreasonable delay or

SAMPLE 8

FORM 870 (WAIVER OF RESTRICTIONS ON ASSESSMENT)

Form **870** (Rev. March 1992)	Department of the Treasury — Internal Revenue Service **Waiver of Restrictions on Assessment and Collection of Deficiency in Tax and Acceptance of Overassessment**	Date received by Internal Revenue Service

Names and address of taxpayers *(Number, street, city or town, State, ZIP code)* Mary Moneybags 123 Main Street Denver, CO 80202	Social security or employer identification number 123-45-6789

Increase (Decrease) in Tax and Penalties

Tax year ended	Tax	Penalties			
1997	$ 3,450.00	$ 480.00	$ 172.50	$	$
1998	$ 6,550.00	$ 1,310.00	$	$	$
	$	$	$	$	$
	$	$	$	$	$
	$	$	$	$	$
	$	$	$	$	$
	$	$	$	$	$

(For instructions, see back of form)

Consent to Assessment and Collection

I consent to the immediate assessment and collection of any deficiencies *(increase in tax and penalties)* and accept any overassessment *(decrease in tax and penalties)* shown above, plus any interest provided by law. I understand that by signing this waiver, I will not be able to contest these years in the United States Tax Court, unless additional deficiencies are determined for these years.

YOUR SIGNATURE HERE ➤	*Mary Moneybags*	Date 1/21/00
SPOUSE'S SIGNATURE ➤		Date
TAXPAYER'S REPRESENTATIVE HERE ➤		Date
CORPORATE NAME ➤		
CORPORATE OFFICER(S) SIGN HERE		Title	Date
		Title	Date

Catalog Number 16894U

Form **870** (Rev. 3-92)

error by an IRS employee (see IRS §6404(e)). Otherwise, interest on any tax debt is mandatory. The only way you can reduce the amount of interest owed is to reduce the amount of tax owed.

Before you agree to any additional tax, I recommend that you request an interest computation from the examiner. Once you have this information, you can make an informed decision about how much you will ultimately need to pay to clear up the overall balance due.

5.4   What if the IRS is wrong?

As difficult as it must be for the IRS to admit, it can be wrong. In fact, the IRS is wrong quite often. Considering that the IRS makes its living, so to speak, by accusing everyone but itself of being wrong, it is amazing to hear that the General Accounting Office (GAO), a congressional agency that oversees the financial activities of governmental agencies including the IRS, recently concluded that the IRS's own books and records were in such a hopeless mess that it could not perform an audit of the agency. On February 27, 2002, the GAO issued a statement that read as follows: "At present, IRS lacks timely, accurate, and useful financial information and sound controls from which to make fully informed decisions and ensure ongoing accountability."

While this information will not help a taxpayer in an audit (the IRS won't listen to any "My books are no worse than the IRS books" excuses and is likely to have a "Do as I say, not as I do" attitude), it is important to recognize that the IRS makes so many millions of mistakes or outright misapplications of the law that mistakes seem to be the rule rather than the exception. During audits, the examiner will often misconstrue the facts or the law in such a way that you would end up paying too much tax if you agreed with the examiner's proposed adjustments. This is why you should always be ready to question and argue with any IRS decision.

There are several different types of appeals available to the taxpayer who disagrees with a tax examiner's results.

5.4.a Talk to the supervisor

First, make an appointment to speak with the examiner's supervisor. Many times, this is all you will need to do, as the supervisor will see that any mistakes are corrected and any disagreements are resolved.

Should a meeting with the supervisor not result in a favorable outcome, you can move up the IRS management chain of command, first to the chief of the Examination Branch, then to the chief of the Examination Division.

The following rules apply whenever you want to go above the revenue agent for assistance with an audit:

★ Management will not provide you with any assistance if the dispute concerns an interpretation of the tax laws or facts of the case, unless the revenue agent's interpretation is unreasonable or clearly incorrect.

★ You should always inform the revenue agent of your intention to contact management and give the revenue agent an opportunity to correct the problem.

★ Involving management will often result in a solution to the problem, especially if the revenue agent is being unprofessional (i.e., rude and discourteous to you) or unreasonable in the management of the audit.

★ Management will make sure that the revenue agent follows the internal IRS rules and regulations for requesting documents and interviews.

★ You can always seek assistance from management when an audit is not proceeding to your satisfaction.

Simply contacting management, at whatever level, is no guarantee that an audit will end with you agreeing on all issues. Management personnel are still IRS employees and overwhelmingly tend to support other employees whenever a dispute does not reveal that the IRS is clearly wrong. You should not expect a manager to be any more competent or reasonable than the problem revenue agent, as the manager most likely was also a revenue agent once.

5.4.b The appeals officer

If you still do not agree with the IRS, the IRS will prepare and deliver what it calls a 30-day letter. The purpose of this letter is simple: to inform you of proposed changes to your tax return. You then have 30 days to file a written protest of these proposed changes.

There are many reasons why you may want to appeal the proposed changes. Perhaps the examiner didn't understand the facts or law. Or maybe the examiner chose to interpret facts or laws in a way that supported the IRS when there were at least two possible interpretations. Also,

Many taxpayers appeal because they believe the examiner was too stubborn, ignorant, or unintelligent, or simply would not listen to them and did not give them a fair examination.

many taxpayers appeal because they believe the examiner was too stubborn, ignorant, or unintelligent, or simply would not listen to them and did not give them a fair examination.

There are advantages to filing a protest. One is that you do not have to pay any portion of the disputed tax before filing the protest. However, the most important advantage is that the protest will be decided by an appeals officer at an informal hearing.

An appeals officer is an IRS employee who has the authority to settle cases for whatever he or she believes is a reasonable amount. The appeals officer has more discretion than revenue officers and their supervisors to resolve a case and will often exercise such discretion in the taxpayer's favor.

In determining what is reasonable, the appeals officer can consider the hazards of litigation (i.e., he or she weighs the probability that the IRS or the taxpayer will win if the case goes to trial in tax court). If the appeals officer believes that the IRS has only a 50% chance of winning in court, he or she will likely be willing to settle the case by conceding 50% of the additional tax that the examiner proposed. This means you would cut your tax bill in half simply by filing a protest letter.

The IRS discourages appeals because they eat up time and often result in the taxpayer paying less tax than was originally proposed. While the IRS would never publicly admit that it wants to make it difficult for taxpayers to exercise their appeal rights, there is one sure sign that this is the case: the IRS has no form for a taxpayer to file an appeal. The IRS has a form for nearly everything, so the lack of this form is its bureaucratic way of telling taxpayers not to file the appeals they have the legal right to make.

Keep the following rules in mind when meeting with an appeals officer:

★ Be prepared for the appointment. Perform all legal research on the tax laws and have a complete understanding of the facts *before* going to the appeals conference.

★ Know your ultimate settlement position *before* the appeals conference. You will not want to make a complex settlement decision in the pressure of the conference. For example, if the IRS believes that you owe $20,000 in additional tax, you should establish an amount (say $6,000) that you would be willing to settle for. If the settlement target is not met, you should refuse to settle and force the IRS to take the case to the next level if it wants to assess any additional tax. If the appeals officer agrees to an amount at or lower than

$6,000, you should agree and end the case. By deciding on a settlement amount before the meeting, you will not have to make a decision at the meeting and will be much less likely to second guess the decision in the future.

★ No case is a perfect case. Before you can emphasize the strong points and minimize the weak points of your case, you must objectively figure out which points are which. You can do this by evaluating your case from the IRS's perspective. Imagine that the roles are reversed and that you are the IRS employee.

5.4.c The Notice of Deficiency

If you still cannot agree with the IRS, the next step in the process is the issuance of a 90-day letter. This letter, also called a Notice of Deficiency, is your ticket to the US tax court. Many taxpayers get all the way to this point and then fail to file a petition with the tax court. This is nearly always a major mistake. If you do not file a petition within the 90-day period, the tax will be assessed against you and the IRS will start collection efforts.

By filing a petition, you get another chance to resolve the issues with the IRS, this time under the pressures of a trial date. Of course, there is also pressure on the taxpayer to settle, as the case will go to trial if no settlement is reached. A complete discussion of the tax court can be found in chapter 15.

Figure 2 shows the possible routes that an audit can follow.

5.5   What does an IRS audit cost?

It is generally quite expensive for a taxpayer to go through a full IRS audit. Before settling on your strategy, you should figure the overall cost of the audit into every decision. Unless there are potential criminal charges, you should think of an audit strictly in financial terms. When determining the cost of an audit, include the following considerations:

(a) Additional tax owed, plus

(b) Penalties and interest, plus

(c) Cost of representation (if any), plus

(d) Your time and effort

Remember to figure the overall cost of the audit into every decision you make. It may be more cost effective to settle an audit than to continue fighting.

FIGURE 2
INCOME TAX AUDIT PROCEDURES FLOWCHART

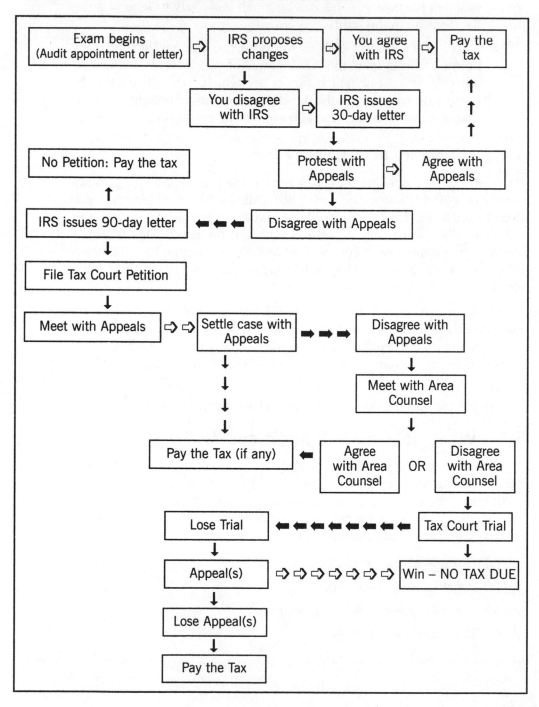

Only after you consider all four points can you calculate the real cost of an audit. For example, if an audit results in a $5,000 increase in tax (including interest and penalties) and it will cost you at least $5,000 in legal fees or lost wages, it is more cost effective to agree than to fight. While it can be difficult to remove the emotional aspects from the audit (i.e., many people want to fight the IRS on principle), you have to stick to the strict economic or financial view.

Most taxpayers eventually settle all audit issues with the IRS. The key is to settle the case as early as possible with the best possible results for you. You don't want to end up accepting the same settlement right before trial that was offered by the appeals officer after the 30-day letter protest was received.

Not considering settlement possibilities from the very beginning of the audit is perhaps the most common mistake that taxpayers make when they represent themselves during an audit. The goal for all taxpayers should be to emerge from the audit with the least possible financial damage. If this goal is accomplished, the taxpayer has won the audit game, even if additional tax, interest, and/or penalties must ultimately be paid.

Tax Points

★ You, and not the IRS, have rights during audits.

★ You must pay the correct amount of tax due and not a penny more.

★ Always report all income.

★ You have the right to know why your tax return was selected for audit and you should always be given an honest answer (the IRS should have nothing to hide).

★ Don't assume that the IRS knows anything about you except what was reported on your tax return.

★ Ask questions during an audit and be vocal about any disagreements.

★ You should not permit the IRS to conduct repetitive audits.

★ Be prepared for the initial audit appointment.

★ You always have the right to professional representation at any stage of the audit process.

★ Take advantage of any chances to settle the case with the IRS.

★ Use IRS management to resolve audit issues when the examiner is being unreasonable.

★ File a protest of any 30-day letter to have a chance to resolve the case with an appeals officer.

★ When all else fails, you should strongly consider filing a petition with the US tax court to get a final opportunity to clear up the tax controversy.

★ Stand up to the IRS during audits and don't be intimidated — the IRS can be beaten.

CHAPTER 7

GENERAL AUDIT RULES

The power to tax involves the power to destroy.
John Marshall, US Supreme Court Justice,
in *McCulloch v. Maryland* (1819)

For years, the IRS has run roughshod over the constitutional rights of our citizens.
Representative James A. Truficant Jr. (D-Ohio), introducing an
amendment in the United States House of Representatives on
February 8, 1995

An IRS audit is generally feared the same way death is, although it certainly doesn't need to be. Perhaps one reason why many taxpayers fear the IRS and its auditing powers so much is that the IRS takes the position during audits that the taxpayer is guilty and must prove his or her innocence. This is the case even though neither the IRS nor the taxpayer has any idea what the taxpayer is guilty of to begin with. Obviously, defending yourself when you don't know what you're defending yourself against is nearly impossible.

Luckily, an IRS audit usually follows a formal, standard procedure, whether the income on the return is $10,000 or $100,000. The IRS trains its agents to follow the procedure and to make sure that background information about the taxpayer is obtained, along with specific information concerning the return itself. Of course, the more complicated the return is, the greater detail the IRS agent will try to elicit from the taxpayer.

If you understand the rules and know what can and cannot happen during an audit, you will significantly level the playing field against the

IRS. This chapter covers the general rules that apply regardless of who the taxpayer is or how much he or she earns, and the most common audit issues that arise.

1. General Rules of IRS Audits

All taxpayers need to understand the significance of the sheer size of the IRS and its resulting inability to communicate effectively within its own bureaucracy. This affects everything from how well IRS employees understand tax laws to how quickly they can receive tax returns filed after the return they are auditing. The following rules suggest ways you can use this huge bureaucracy to your advantage.

1.1 Use all the time the IRS gives you

Many taxpayers take the position that the sooner the audit is over, the better for them, even if it ends up costing them more money. This strategy plays right into the hands of the IRS, as it means the IRS will be assessing a maximum amount of additional tax dollars within the shortest period of time, using a minimal number of employee hours.

The better way to play is: if the IRS gives you 30 days to comply with a document request, use the full 30 days (if not more time by requesting an extension). There is no reason why you should not eat up as much time on the audit as possible (although you should bear in mind that this will increase the interest due if you owe any additional tax after the audit concludes). The IRS works on the theory that the more audits it can perform, the more money it can collect and the better it looks to Congress come time for next year's budget. The IRS would certainly prefer a quick audit so that it can use the auditor or examiner assigned to your audit for auditing someone else.

Because there is pressure on each IRS employee to close as many cases as possible, it follows that any delay in the audit may eventually work in your favor. If a case is open for a long time, IRS managers are instructed to put pressure on their employees to get the case closed. If an auditor is under this type of pressure, he or she may be willing to make more concessions than usual to get your case closed.

While I am not suggesting that you use stalling tactics that might antagonize the auditor (which will force the auditor to close your case unagreed due to your lack of cooperation, something you certainly do not want to happen), I do believe that using the massive IRS bureaucracy against the IRS makes sense in most, if not all, audits. For example, if the

IRS sets an appointment date, you are permitted to postpone the date (to get records together, to develop strategy, to get a representative, etc.). If the IRS sets a deadline for you to get documents to the IRS, you can reschedule this date so as to get the necessary records.

Each extension is just that much more time your case is open and not agreed, adding to the auditor's already full inventory of cases. And remember, the auditor cannot add another case to his or her inventory of cases until your particular audit is closed. This may seem to be a small advantage, but you should use each advantage to level the playing field as much as possible.

1.2 Capitalize on the IRS's inability to communicate effectively

While the lack of communication can sometimes hurt you as a taxpayer and can be frustrating, there is no reason why you cannot turn this around to work to your advantage. Given that one IRS employee may not know what another employee is doing or has done, anything negative that has been threatened to date won't exist unless it was in writing or can be accessed on the computer. For example, if one employee does not know that you have been threatened with a tax lien, he or she may have to start the process over, which works in your favor.

By the same token, if you don't like the information or advice one IRS employee gives you over the telephone, hang up and try another employee. While this may be time consuming, the IRS computers do not update fast enough for the second employee to know what you discussed with the first one. Chances are you will get a better result the second time around, and any agreements can be binding on the IRS. And if the second employee doesn't offer any better solutions, you haven't lost anything but time by trying.

1.3 Use the complex tax laws to your advantage

Each year, *Money Magazine* does a survey of professional tax preparers in which each preparer receives the same set of facts about a hypothetical taxpayer and prepares a tax return based upon the information received. The resulting returns are then compared. The preparers rarely come up with the same amount of tax due.

In the March 1998 issue, for example, the preparers' total tax due for the hypothetical taxpayer ranged from $34,240 to $68,912. One taxpayer, 46 preparers, and 46 different results. None of the preparers hit the target

If you don't like the information or advice one IRS employee gives you over the telephone, hang up and try another employee.

tax due of $37,105. Thus, by using the preparer with the highest result, the taxpayer would have overpaid his or her tax by $31,807, while the lowest preparer would have set the taxpayer up for an audit by underpaying $2,865 in tax due. For these "professional" services, the hypothetical taxpayer would have paid anywhere from $300 to $4,950.

The moral of the story is that if these highly paid tax professionals do not understand the complex tax laws, it is safe to assume that no one else understands them either — including the IRS and its employees.

In the same issue of *Money Magazine*, Representative Bill Archer (R-Texas) stated that "mistakes are inevitable so long as we keep our ridiculously complex tax code."

If there is a gray area in the tax law concerning an issue on your return, do not allow the IRS to force an interpretation of the law that is beneficial to the IRS on you. Why should you give in to the IRS machine when no one really knows what the correct answer is? Instead, obtain time from the examiner to research the issue in order to present any legal citations (previous court cases, IRC, Regs., etc.) to the examiner (if any law in your favor indeed exists). Expect to get contrary legal citations thrown back (if there are any).

If the examiner does not want to resolve the impasse in your favor, you should let the examiner know that it looks like an appeals officer or tax court judge will have to decide the issue. By making this comment, you have indicated to the examiner that the case will not likely be closed agreed as it now stands, something the examiner does not want to hear. The examiner will then be forced to reconsider his or her position or will look to make other concessions to you with the hope of getting you to close the audit agreed. You should never give in to the IRS simply because the IRS will not give in to you.

1.4 Don't fight the IRS alone

All taxpayers should go into an IRS audit with as much understanding of the Internal Revenue Code as possible. Often, the best way to do this is to have a representative, either an attorney, CPA, or enrolled agent, who can accompany you throughout the course of the audit.

While this is certainly not required and often is not necessary, having an experienced representative is certainly the most common way of leveling the playing field with the IRS auditor assigned to your return. Presumably the tax professional will be familiar with the current tax laws and

IRS rules and procedures and will get you a better audit result. (Note that most attorneys and CPAs are *not* qualified to represent taxpayers in an IRS audit.)

It is your decision to hire or not hire a representative to handle the audit. Make that decision based on your confidence in your own ability to handle the audit, your fear of the IRS in general, and the complexity of your return and the corresponding audit issues. Many audits are relatively straightforward and can be handled by any taxpayer who has the determination and confidence to educate himself or herself prior to the initial audit appointment.

In order to use a tax professional, you must simply fill out a Power of Attorney (Form 2848) that gives the professional the authority and right to discuss your confidential tax information with the IRS (see Sample 35 in chapter 15). If you hire a representative, you are not required to attend any appointments with the IRS (unless there is a summons to appear).

1.5 Don't volunteer information to the IRS

You should never volunteer information to the IRS unless you are certain that the information can help, and not hurt, your position in the audit. I repeat this general rule several times in this book because it is extremely important. Always follow this rule.

When the examiner asks for information or documentation, give the examiner exactly what was requested — no more, no less. When the examiner asks a question, keep your answer to the point and as short as possible. IRS employees are trained to use silence as a tool and to let the taxpayer talk as much as possible, because the more a taxpayer says, the more information the IRS will have to work with. Continually remind yourself that silence should be welcomed and that all silent periods should be broken only by the auditor. While I'm not suggesting that you refuse to talk to the IRS, I am recommending that anything you say be a direct response to a question presented and that little or no information be volunteered to the IRS.

The same theory applies to document requests. A vague document request will often produce more documents for the IRS to look at than would a detailed request. For this reason, you should request that vague document requests be made more specific before you submit any documents.

Any additional information you give that was not specifically requested only gives the examiner more ammunition, something you don't want to give your enemy in times of battle.

> You should never volunteer information to the IRS unless you are certain that the information can help, and not hurt, your position in the audit.

1.6 Ask questions

The auditor is most comfortable when he or she is asking short questions and getting long answers. You should always try to reverse the role: give short answers and ask questions of the auditor.

For example, if the examiner asks you if you reported all income, you should respond, "I reported all the income I knew about. Do you have information that indicates that I didn't report all my income?" By responding in this manner you have not lied (assuming that you did in fact report all known income), you have not given the IRS much information, and you have put the auditor in the uncomfortable position of having to answer the question. If the auditor is not aware of any additional income, the income probe is closed and you can now discuss other issues.

This strategy works with nearly any type of question the auditor can ask you during an audit. However, you should be selective in answering questions with a question. The auditor may believe that you have something to hide or are not cooperating if you answer every question this way. For example, if you are being questioned about the expenses for a small business, you could respond as follows:

IRS auditor: "Why did you deduct $1,500 for advertising in 1997?"

Taxpayer: "Because it's an ordinary and necessary business expense. You would agree with that, wouldn't you?"

IRS auditor: "Perhaps. Do you have proof of the expense?"

Taxpayer: "Yes. Here are the receipts from the newspaper and Yellow Pages."

IRS auditor: "Fine. Thank you."

By handling the issue in this manner, the taxpayer was able to turn a question about whether an expense was deductible at all into proof that money was actually spent on advertising — a victory for the taxpayer.

1.7 Never trust the IRS or anything that an IRS employee tells you

The IRS works on a system of disinformation, meaning that it will usually tell you only what will benefit the IRS, nearly always at your financial expense. Contrary to what the IRS publicly claims ("provide America's taxpayers with quality service"), the IRS is not in the business of assisting taxpayers — its revenue (the amount it collects from taxes) would decrease if it informed taxpayers of all tax laws and rights in the taxpayers' favor.

In addition, there are some IRS employees who are either so incompetent or so malicious that they will tell taxpayers outright lies. I have seen IRS employees tell taxpayers that they could not deduct a loss on their business (not true), could not deduct expenses associated with rental property (not true), or that they were required to file an income tax return no matter what income they earned during the year (again, not true).

Thankfully, not all IRS employees treat taxpayers this way. There are many IRS employees who will give the taxpayer the benefit of most doubts, will inform taxpayers of their rights under the law, and will generally try to help confused taxpayers (which includes all of us at one time or another). The problem is that it is impossible to know before the audit begins whether the employee assigned to your case will be sympathetic or not. It is therefore best to err on the side of caution and not trust the IRS employee, as trusting an unfair employee can produce negative audit results.

Even if the IRS employee seems friendly, don't assume that you can win him or her over and develop a friendship. It won't work and will only leave you vulnerable to negative audit results. IRS auditors are not friends in a professional setting, even though the auditor certainly could be a nice person and a friend if he or she lived in your neighborhood. You should treat the auditor with professional respect; nothing more and nothing less.

1.8 Remember that appearances are important

The IRS has trained its employees to observe everything about you, including how you look and dress. For example, if you are claiming an income of $20,000 per year but are wearing a custom-made suit and a Rolex watch, the agent may suspect you are hiding income. While there may be perfectly legal reasons for declaring a small income but maintaining a wealthy lifestyle (you may have received gifts or an inheritance, for instance), there is certainly no reason to give the IRS any more reasons than it already has to look for unreported income or overstated deductions.

Always remember to meet IRS expectations during the audit, as the IRS may become suspicious if you deviate from its expectations. If you make $30,000 per year as an auto mechanic, the IRS does not expect you to be wearing a tailored suit to the audit appointment. Furthermore, if you are a banker earning $100,000 per year, the IRS does not expect you to show up wearing a mechanic's uniform.

No matter how much income you earn, dress conservatively. Flashy dressers attract attention, and attention is the last thing you want during

Even if the IRS employee seems friendly, don't assume that you can win him or her over and develop a friendship.

a tax audit. In addition, taxpayers who flash their wealth at an auditor may be in for a much longer audit than is necessary, as the examiner may try to find a way to take some of the wealth away from the taxpayer.

1.9   Don't let the IRS into your home

The last thing most people want is to have an IRS agent visiting their home or office. They fear that an agent will see something that may suggest they have a higher standard of living than what could reasonably be supported (in the IRS agent's opinion) on the amount of income reported on their return. In addition, all taxpayers have a right to privacy, and most of us would agree that having an IRS employee in our home is an invasion of privacy.

If you are faced with a field audit, you still can negotiate the location for the audit. Most tax auditors are completely reasonable if you ask to hold the examination at a place other than your home or office, as long as all records associated with the return will be at the place of the audit. The IRS itself states in its Publication 1 that you have the right to "ask that the examination take place at a reasonable time and place that is convenient for both you and the IRS." Unless your home is also your place of business (and you keep all business records there), there is generally no reason why the IRS ever needs to step into your home.

Remember, however, that the IRS is permitted to visit a business or residence, even if the audit is conducted somewhere else, if a visit is necessary for one or more issues in the audit. Thus, if an audit issue arises as to a business's inventory or an individual's assets, and the agent needs verification, the taxpayer must permit the agent to make an on-site inspection during normal workday hours. This visit is for a limited purpose and the visit should not deviate from this purpose (i.e., the agent should not be opening file drawers or interviewing employees).

1.10 Never alter documents or lie to the IRS

It is tempting to change a receipt or other document to match numbers on the tax return that you cannot precisely substantiate. Never give in to this temptation, as it can turn the audit into a criminal or civil fraud investigation.

The IRS usually is not concerned if receipts don't exactly match what was on the return, although large discrepancies will certainly result in an adjustment at the end of the audit. If a discrepancy is found, you should tell the auditor why the numbers don't match. A simple response that you did not obtain receipts for all business expenses may be enough for the auditor to move on to another issue. If the amount involved is small and you were able to substantiate your other expenses, the IRS auditor will usually give you the benefit of the doubt with respect to expenses that were not substantiated to the last cent.

Furthermore, you should never lie to the IRS, as lying is a sure way to experience the worst the IRS has to offer.

This can put you in some sticky situations. For example, if the IRS asks if you filed your 2001 tax return and you haven't yet filed the return, answering this question is a no-win proposition. If you say "Yes," you have lied and committed a criminal offense; if you say "No," you are opening yourself up to a prolonged audit investigation, which will not be closed until the unfiled return is filed. Instead of answering this question, you should tell the examiner, "I will get back to you on that after I've checked the status of this return with my attorney/accountant." By answering this way, you have not lied, and the examiner may never bring the issue back up. It is always better to answer a question by not answering the question than to answer with a lie in the hope of getting away with the lie.

1.11 Don't bribe or threaten IRS agents

For some reason, there are some taxpayers who want to resort to illegal means, including bribery, to close out an audit as early as possible. This temptation must be resisted, as very few auditors would ever consider a bribe as a means of supplementing their government salary. Offering a bribe is a sure way to turn a routine audit into a criminal investigation. Don't do it.

Threatening an auditor by saying you will do something violent if he or she does not close out the audit is also a terrible idea. Making a threat to an IRS employee is a federal criminal offense and will only make the matter much worse (no matter how bad it may already be).

1.12 Don't file any tax returns while an audit is pending

The examiner is trained to check for other tax years to determine whether returns have been filed and, if so, whether there is any audit potential on these other years. For example, if the IRS is auditing your 2001 tax return, the examiner may ask to see your 2002 tax return, as it is easy to audit other tax returns once the examiner is familiar with you. Again, this plays into the IRS mentality of seeking the easiest way to generate additional revenue for the government. If the 2002 return has not yet been filed, delay the filing until the audit has concluded (be aware that late filing penalties and interest may apply). It may be necessary to get extensions on a return in order to accomplish this strategy.

If you must file a return while an audit is pending, file it with the IRS Service Center and not with the auditor. It takes time for the auditor to get the return from the IRS Service Center (due to the bureaucracy), and often the auditor will forget about reviewing it in order to close the case. If the auditor continues to request the return and it is clear that the audit will not be closed without the return, it is then certainly in your best interests to provide the return to the examiner.

1.13 Stay focused

Look at all audits as a series of mini-audits, with each issue an audit within an audit. Rather than looking at the audit as one huge examination of an entire tax return, which may be overwhelming to you, it is much easier to look at each issue independently of the others. You also gain a psychological advantage by focusing on and winning several issues early in the audit. Many IRS auditors look closely at issues early in the audit, and if it appears that the taxpayer can support most of the issues, the examiner will be much less likely to examine issues later in the audit. Certainly, the less that an examiner looks at, the better for you and the greater chance that the end audit result will be in your favor.

1.14 Be patient

As I mentioned in rule 1, you should use all the time during the audit to your advantage. The IRS has trained its employees to be on the alert for impatient or nervous taxpayers. The theory is that impatient taxpayers may be pushing to get the audit over because they have something to hide. A taxpayer who is patient with the IRS as part of his or her overall audit strategy is much more likely to conclude the audit with a successful result than is the impatient taxpayer. This is another instance where appearances are important, as a calm taxpayer who doesn't push the examiner to conclude the audit conveys an appearance that everything is alright.

2. Some Common Issues

2.1 What if I forgot to claim some deductions on my return?

Remember that the purpose of an audit is to make sure that your tax return is substantially correct. Fortunately, this is a two-way street, as examiners are required to let you claim additional expenses or deductions that you are entitled to but failed to claim on the original return.

If you had not been audited, you would claim any forgotten deductions or other omissions by filing an amended tax return. (As I stated in chapter 3, a taxpayer has the right to file an amended tax return (Form 1040X) within a period of three years from the date the original return was due or filed, whichever is later. If you did not file a tax return, all claims for a refund must be made within two years from the date that the tax was paid.) However, most tax auditors do not want you to file amended tax returns during an audit, preferring instead to deal with any changes to the return(s) on the audit report. If the forgotten deductions become apparent during the audit, the IRS examiner must consider these additional deductions, even if a decrease in tax is the result.

While I have heard many reports of examiners telling taxpayers that the IRS is not permitted to consider additional deductions during the audit, examiners who say this are simply wrong. One thing you must always keep in mind is the overall purpose of the audit: to determine the correct amount of tax due and owing. If the IRS can disallow some deductions, it can certainly allow others, whether claimed on the original return or not. It works both ways.

2.2 What if I don't have any records?

Without records to support a particular deduction, many taxpayers believe that they cannot claim the deduction at all and will lose that particular audit issue. It doesn't help that many IRS employees also state that taxpayers are not entitled to deductions without the appropriate records.

However, the IRC is quite specific when it comes to what documentation is needed to support a deduction. For example, under IRC §274(d), you can establish the validity of a business expense deduction by using "adequate records" or other evidence to support your own statements concerning the deduction. For purposes of this section, "adequate records" are considered to be an account book, diary, journal, or similar document that answers the following questions:

★ What was the amount of the expense?

★ When and where was the money spent?

★ What was the business purpose of the expense?

★ If the expense was related to entertainment, what was the business relationship between the taxpayer and the person being entertained?

If for some reason you lack these "adequate records," you are still allowed a deduction if you can support your own statements with some type of evidence. For example, you can use an affidavit to support a properly deducted expense. An affidavit is a written statement made by a person under oath, affirming that certain facts are known to the person making the statement to be true.

Suppose at your audit you are required to support a deduction claimed for a business trip from New York to Boston. You cannot locate any receipts and have had only minimal success in getting records from other sources (i.e., securing a copy of a bill from the airline or hotel). Can you still deduct your meals, taxi rides, business entertainment expenses, or other ordinary and necessary expenses? The answer, regardless of what the IRS may claim, is yes. Sample 9 shows the type of affidavit that could be used in this instance.

This type of affidavit will help to prove the business purpose of your trip, along with the fact that certain expenses were incurred during the trip. Obtaining such an affidavit, in addition to providing an affidavit of your own and the copies of the hotel and airline bills, should be enough to support the deductions.

There are times, however, when no records are available and the best you can do is make reasonable estimates of the expenses incurred during the year(s) under audit. The tax court, along with the IRS, permits estimates under what is now known as the *Cohan* rule, although to use this rule the taxpayer must be able to prove that he or she is entitled to some deduction for the expense.

The following example illustrates how the *Cohan* rule works. Suppose that during an audit, you cannot locate any records to support a deduction for a computer purchased for your business. The computer store where you purchased the computer is no longer in business. Without any records, the IRS will try to disallow the entire expense. However, you know for certain that a computer was purchased. You can estimate the expense based upon the type of computer and work out some agreement with the auditor. While you may not get a complete deduction, at least you will be permitted some deduction. The amount of the deduction will often depend upon the knowledge and reasonableness of the examiner, along with the reasonableness of your estimate.

While the *Cohan* rule has saved many taxpayers during audits, the rule does not apply to travel, automobile, and entertainment expenses under IRC §274(d). Proper substantiation, using actual records and/or other evidence, is required under the current law.

> Even if you lack certain records, you are permitted to use estimates, reconstructions or affidavits to prove your entitlement to a specific deduction.

SAMPLE 9
AFFIDAVIT REGARDING BUSINESS EXPENSES

AFFIDAVIT

State of Colorado   )

)

County of Denver   )

I, C.W. Nagel, residing in Denver, Colorado, being first duly sworn on oath, depose and say that I personally know the taxpayer, Freddie Mack, of Denver, Colorado, and can affirmatively state that I was with Mr. Mack in Boston, Massachusetts, on May 1 and 2, 1996, for the purpose of securing business with Ben and Jerry's Ice Cream Company. Mr. Mack entertained myself and two Ben and Jerry's account executives on both days and we all came away from the meeting with additional business. I can personally remember going to the Boston Sea Party Restaurant on one evening and to a Boston Red Sox baseball game on the other evening.

C.W. Nagel
1111 16th Street
Denver, CO 80202

Before me, a notary public in and for the County of Denver, State of Colorado, personally appeared the above-named C.W. Nagel, who being duly sworn by me deposed and said that all the statements set forth above are true to the best of his own knowledge.

Witness my hand and seal on this _____ day of _____ 20_____.

_____, Notary Public

My Commission expires: _____

2.3　How much time does the IRS have to audit my return?

Under most circumstances, IRC §6501(a) gives the IRS three years from the due date of the tax return or from the actual filing date, whichever is later, to complete the audit and assess any additional tax due as a result of the audit. There are some exceptions to the three-year rule:

★ If the taxpayer commits fraud, and the IRS can prove the fraud, there is no time limitation on the IRS.

★ If the taxpayer omits more than 25% of his or her gross income, the three-year period is extended to six years pursuant to IRC §6501(e).

★ If the taxpayer fails to file a tax return, the limitations period doesn't begin and the IRS has no time limit to complete an audit (until a return is actually filed with the IRS).

★ If the taxpayer agrees to extend the statute of limitations, the period is extended to whatever date the IRS and the taxpayer agree to.

Even though the law provides for a three-year statute of limitations cycle with respect to returns and audits, the IRS does not work on a three-year cycle. Instead, understanding to some extent its own bureaucratic limitations, the IRS puts all taxpayers on a general 26-month schedule. The IRS does not want to be auditing a taxpayer when the three-year statute of limitations is due to expire, because it may not have enough time to complete the audit and will have wasted time and effort for nothing.

Even with these well-known time constraints, the IRS often does not have enough time to complete an audit and will ask a taxpayer to extend the statute of limitations under IRC §6501. You always have the right to refuse to extend the statute of limitations, and if you make this decision, the IRS is left with two choices:

(a) Do nothing and let the limitations period expire (not likely); or

(b) Issue a Notice of Deficiency based on the information currently known (very likely). At this point you have 90 days to file a petition with the tax court to challenge these changes. (Even if the IRS issues the Notice of Deficiency one day before the statute of limitations expires, you still have 90 days to file a challenge.)

In general, you should not extend the statute of limitations unless you believe that you will directly benefit by doing so. There are only two reasons why you should ever agree to extend the statute:

(a) You believe that extending the statute will result in less tax being due to the IRS. For example, if you know that you can produce documents to clear up the audit issues, then extending the statute certainly makes sense. Or if you and the examiner agree to close out some audit issues in exchange for your agreement to extend the statute, you have won a part of the audit and an extension would certainly make sense.

(b) You believe that additional time may allow you to resolve the case without having to file a petition with the tax court. This situation is likely if you have a good working relationship with the examiner. By extending the statute, the likelihood of a favorable resolution increases.

The bottom line, though, is still whether you will benefit from giving the IRS more time. In most cases I have found that you will not benefit. And if you will not benefit, there is no point in agreeing to any extension.

2.4　Can the IRS audit me if I don't file a return?

The IRS will often contact individuals it has identified as nonfilers in an effort to get them to file tax returns and get back into the tax system.

The IRS gets its nonfiler information from numerous sources, including its own matching program (for example, if the IRS receives a Form 1099 with your social security number on it, but you failed to file a tax return, the Form 1099 will flag your failure to file). In addition, various IRS employees, especially revenue officers handling tax collection cases, are trained to check for any unfiled returns. The IRS receives information from sources outside the IRS, including informers, concerning taxpayers who do not file tax returns.

Wherever the IRS gets the information from, the fact remains that it will pursue and audit taxpayers who do not file tax returns. In many instances, the taxpayer will continue to refuse to prepare a tax return despite several IRS notices and telephone calls. In these cases, the IRS may be forced to prepare a tax return (called a Substitute for Return, or SFR) for the nonfiler, often with negative results for the nonfiler.

The IRS uses several different sources of information to compute how much income the nonfiler earned during the year in question. First, it can use information submitted by employers and other business sources to determine income for any particular year. This is the most common method, and assuming that the IRS sources are accurate, is the least painful to the taxpayer, as he or she would have reported this income had a return been prepared and filed.

Wherever the IRS gets
the information from,
the fact remains that it will
pursue and audit taxpayers
who do not file tax returns.

The second method is not so kind to the taxpayer. The IRS has access to a wealth of statistics and will often use these statistics to approximate a person's income for any given year. The IRS will use a statistical method when it has no other evidence to indicate how much taxable income the nonfiling individual earned during the year in question. Two sources of statistics that the IRS commonly uses are the Consumer Price Index (CPI) and the Bureau of Labor Statistics (BLS).

The CPI is a monthly index the government publishes that attempts to determine the cost of common goods and services (e.g., food, clothing, gasoline) that an average consumer buys each month. It is often used to measure inflation as it relates to maintaining a household's standard of living. The IRS looks at the taxpayer's taxable income for the last year that a return was filed and then inflates the income by the percentage of growth in the CPI.

For example, suppose you reported a taxable income of $20,000 in 2000 and the CPI is 5% in 2001. The IRS will assert that your income in 2001 must have been at least $21,000 ($20,000 plus 5% of 20,000 ($1,000) equals $21,000). This is likely to be completely inaccurate, as you may not have made any money in 2001 and had to rely on support from family members to survive. However, without any information from you, the IRS will use whatever information it can, including the CPI, to compute your income.

If you have never filed tax returns or have not done so in any recent years, the IRS may use the BLS, rather than the CPI, to estimate your income in a tax year. The BLS takes into consideration average annual living expenses for food, clothing, taxes, housing, furnishings, transportation, medical care, social security, and personal care, based upon where an individual lives and how many people are in his or her family. Once the IRS determines how much it would cost to live in a certain city for a year, it will use this figure to estimate your minimum income for the year. For example, if it cost $20,000 for a family of three to live in Atlanta during a certain year, and if a taxpayer meeting this description fails to file a tax return or provide records of income for this year, the IRS can attribute income of $20,000 to the taxpayer and compute the tax on this amount. Courts have permitted the IRS to use the BLS method to determine an individual's taxable income in a year when the taxpayer fails to maintain accurate records of income, expenses, and deductions.

In spite of changes made in the Tax Reform Act of 1998, the IRS is still permitted to use statistical information. However, these recent changes place the burden of proof on the IRS when it uses statistical information based on unrelated taxpayers to claim any additional taxable income. I discuss burden of proof issues in chapter 15, but briefly what this means is that the IRS must prove that the income it is attributing to a taxpayer matches the taxpayer's lifestyle. Thus, under these circumstances, the IRS must now take a taxpayer's lifestyle or expenditures into account and show that they are consistent with the statistical information. While at first glance this would appear to favor the taxpayer, the reality is that an IRS employee may take it as an opportunity to examine the taxpayer's lifestyle more closely. This is not a particularly positive consequence of this change in the law.

In addition to estimating a taxpayer's income, the IRS will also compute the income tax due at the least favorable tax rate (either at the "Single" or "Married filing separately" rate) and will give the taxpayer only an exemption for himself or herself and the standard deduction (i.e., no itemized deductions). The IRS computations will result in the highest taxable income and tax due possible under the circumstances. Therefore, you should make sure that you, and not the IRS, control what information is used to prepare your tax return.

2.5   Can the revenue agent settle a case?

A revenue agent or tax examiner's job is to determine the correct amount of tax due based on the unique facts and law of each case. These IRS employees do not have the authority to "settle" cases for less than what they believe to be the correct amount of tax owed.

However, this does not mean there are no negotiations during the course of an audit. As I previously stated, many, if not most, areas of tax law are unclear and can be interpreted in two or more ways. Most revenue agents understand this and are willing to compromise some issues in exchange for your compromise on other issues.

In order to successfully negotiate with a revenue agent, you should be prepared to perform legal research on the issue(s) and/or come up with additional facts to support your position. Keep in mind that a revenue agent is required to use a "facts and law" approach. If the facts and law are clear (a rare case), the agent has little or no room to compromise. However, if either the facts or law, or both, are subject to more than one interpretation, the agent may be willing to accept your version if doing so means that the case can be closed as agreed. A revenue agent would much rather close a case agreed than have the case unagreed and go to appeals or tax court.

During any negotiation, you are really concerned only with the dollars of additional tax due, while the agent wants an acceptable agreement based on the law and facts. Only appeals officers and area counsel attorneys have actual settlement authority within the IRS.

2.6   What if I failed to appeal and the auditor was wrong?

The IRS may reopen any audit, even after the appeals period has expired, if the taxpayer makes a written request for it to do so. However, the IRS is not required to reopen an audit simply because a taxpayer wants the audit reopened. Instead, the IRS will reopen an audit if the taxpayer can demonstrate that the audit produced an inaccurate and unfair result through no fault of the taxpayer. The most common reason for an audit reopening is the discovery of additional records or documents that support the taxpayer's position (and that were not available to the taxpayer during the audit). A taxpayer should use the IRS's own mission statement (that a taxpayer is required to pay the correct amount of tax due — no more and no less) to obtain an audit reopening if the situation is appropriate.

The IRS, on the other hand, cannot generally reopen any audits without the taxpayer's consent. As with most issues surrounding the IRS, though, there are limited exceptions to this rule. The IRS may reopen an audit if it finds any of the following:

★ Evidence of fraud, concealment, or misrepresentation during the course of the original audit

★ Evidence that the original examiner made a substantial error based on an established IRS position in place at the time of the first audit

★ Other circumstances indicating the failure to reopen the case would be a serious administrative error

In reality, the IRS will typically reopen an audit to make an adjustment unfavorable to the taxpayer only if some evidence of fraud or the like comes to its attention. It is a relatively rare event for the IRS to reopen an audit on its own, as taxpayers would rebel if the IRS made a habit of putting them through multiple audits for the same tax year for no reason at all.

Tax Points

★ Use the IRS bureaucracy to your advantage.

★ Use all time allotted during the audit to your advantage, as a fast audit often favors the IRS.

★ Assume that the IRS does not understand the tax laws.

★ Do not volunteer information during an audit. Instead, cooperate completely with the auditor and provide only what was requested.

★ Ask many questions throughout the audit and make the auditor answer the questions.

★ Do not trust the IRS.

★ Dress conservatively and do not give the IRS any reason to assume that you have a higher standard of living than the income reported on the tax return.

★ Keep the IRS away from your home if at all possible.

★ Do not lie or do anything dishonest (such as falsifying documents) during the audit.

★ Do not extend the statute of limitations with respect to the time the IRS has to assess additional tax unless you will directly benefit.

★ Do not permit the IRS to prepare any Substitute for Returns if no tax returns were filed. Instead, get the necessary records together and prepare the returns for the IRS.

CHAPTER 8

HOW TO DEFEND YOURSELF IN AN AUDIT AND WIN

Logic and taxation are not always the best of friends.
Justice James C. McReynolds in the US Supreme Court
Concurring Opinion of Sonneborn Brothers v. Cureton,
262 US 506, 522 (1923)

If you get up early, work late, and pay your taxes, you will get ahead — if you strike oil.
J. Paul Getty (1892 – 1976), US billionaire

While not all audits are alike, many have the same or similar issues. In this chapter I discuss specific types of audit issues and, more important, how to defend yourself in an audit and come out on top of the IRS.

The IRS trains its employees to gather the following information during the initial phase of an audit:

★ Your standard of living

★ The potential that you may have unreported (usually cash) income

★ The correctness of the exemptions and dependents claimed on the tax return

★ Your employment history and education background

IRS employees will also be expected to verify the following:

★ All financial transactions reported on your return(s) or occurring during the tax year or years in question

★ Any nontaxable sources of income you received during the year(s) in question

If you are aware that your auditor is trying to gather this information, you can guard against giving him or her any details that might be used against you. This is the first line of defense in an audit.

Besides watching what you say or don't say, you should also be aware of how you appear to the auditor. Remember, the IRS is examining you in addition to the tax return. The IRS never informs you of this, always referring to the return itself. But while the auditor keeps one eye on the return, the other eye is trained directly on you. For example, the agent will look to see how you are dressed, how you respond to questions (do you make eye contact or look evasive when answering questions?), how nervous you appear (all taxpayers look nervous to some extent, but extreme nervousness may be a sign that the taxpayer has something to hide), and anything else you do that is different from the average person being audited. Much of the IRS employee's ability to evaluate any particular taxpayer will depend upon the employee's experience within the IRS — more experienced employees have seen a great deal more and have a better sense of when a taxpayer has something to hide than do less experienced employees.

1. Standard of Living

The IRS examiner will nearly always be concerned with how you lived during the year(s) in question. For example, the auditor will be suspicious if you claimed an income of $20,000 for the year, yet bought two new cars and a vacation home and traveled around the world. While there may be perfectly legitimate ways for this to happen (i.e., you might have received the cars as gifts, charged the vacation on credit cards, and bought the home with money accumulated during previous years), the fact that these big-ticket items were purchased in the same year will raise an audit red flag.

You are under the IRS microscope during all meetings with the IRS. As suggested in chapter 7, dress conservatively during any appointments with the IRS. This general rule bears repeating; don't show off expensive clothing and jewelry to the IRS unless you are a movie star, CEO of a large company, professional baseball player, or someone else who publicly leads a wealthy lifestyle.

As much as possible, your visible standard of living should match the numbers that appeared on the tax return. This way, you will meet the IRS employee's expectations, and he or she will move on to examine other issues. Most taxpayers are more comfortable when the audit moves away

Remember, the IRS is examining *you* in addition to the tax return.

from standard-of-living issues, as the audit tends to be less personal when typical tax-related issues are being reviewed.

2. The Search for Unreported Income

Perhaps the single greatest audit issue concerns your income, or more accurately, whether you correctly reported all income. Before jumping into this issue, you need to understand what constitutes income under the tax law. IRC §61 states that gross income is "income from whatever source derived" and commonly includes wages, commissions, some fringe benefits, business receipts, interest, dividends, rent, royalties, alimony, annuities, and dealings in property and pensions.

It is just as important to know what is not income. The IRS may not tax receipts of the following types of income because the IRC does not consider them to be "taxable" income:

★ Inheritances

★ Gifts

★ Proceeds from renting a vacation home (for 14 days or less per year)

★ Loans

★ Most damages for personal injury cases

★ Workers' compensation benefits

★ Federal income tax refunds

★ State income tax refunds (if the taxpayer didn't itemize deductions and list the state income tax paid as a Schedule A deduction)

★ Interest from municipal bonds

★ Life insurance proceeds

★ IRA or other retirement plan rollovers

★ Child support payments received

★ The sale of personal residences under most circumstances

The IRS uses a variety of investigative measures to determine whether you accurately reported all your income on the return under examination.

2.1 Direct (specific item) method

Perhaps the most common technique used by the IRS to determine whether you accurately reported your income is known as the specific item method. This is the simplest, most direct way for the IRS to challenge a taxpayer's income on a tax return. Under this method, the examiner has specific evidence, such as a Form W-2 or 1099, to demonstrate the existence of additional income. The IRS uses this method of proof whenever it has specific evidence of unreported or underreported income or when a case involves overstated deductions. This evidence is very difficult to dispute because the IRS will have evidence that directly conflicts with the tax return under audit. Unless the taxpayer didn't actually receive the income and can prove the Form W-2 is wrong, the taxpayer will have a very difficult time disputing the issue.

2.2 Indirect methods

Often, however, this direct, specific information is not available to the IRS. Instead, the IRS will be forced to use indirect methods to assert additional unreported income. Usually the IRS will resort to the indirect methods for taxpayers who are self-employed or who do not receive income from wages, bank interest, or other sources that are directly reported to the IRS and thus are easily traced. The indirect methods of checking the returns of self-employed taxpayers and businesses are discussed in detail in chapter 9.

2.2.a Bank deposits method

For individual taxpayers, the IRS often will review bank records to verify the accuracy of a tax return when adequate records are not otherwise available. Sample 10 shows how the bank deposits method works.

In this example, the IRS would subtract loans and/or gifts because they are not considered to be taxable income. Thus, you would have to be able to show that the $10,000 of proposed additional unreported income was in fact not taxable or else you would have to pay tax on it (along with penalties and interest). Before giving in and agreeing with the IRS, you should completely review all nontaxable sources of income to see if the alleged unreported income really is taxable.

In many instances you can successfully challenge the IRS when it uses the bank deposits method, especially if you are sure that all taxable income was reported properly. You will have to review each deposit made during the year and identify the source of the deposit. While the passage of time often makes this difficult to do, it is necessary to refute any IRS assertions of unreported income.

Be aware that the IRS often forgets to subtract transfers between accounts for taxpayers who have more than one bank account. For example,

SAMPLE 10

HOW THE BANK DEPOSITS METHOD WORKS

The IRS follows this formula to verify the accuracy of a tax return:

	Total deposits into all bank accounts
+	Cash spent during the year but not deposited into bank accounts
=	Total receipts
–	Nontaxable deposits (such as amounts received from gifts, loans, and inheritances)
=	Corrected gross income
–	Deductions and exemptions
=	Corrected taxable income
–	Taxable income per return
=	Understatement of taxable income

To show how the formula works, consider the following example:

$100,000	Total bank deposits for year
+ 10,000	Known cash spent during year but not deposited into bank account
$110,000	Total receipts
– 10,000	Loan from family (nontaxable deposit)
– 5,000	Gift from parents (nontaxable deposit)
$ 95,000	Corrected gross income
– 25,000	Deductions and exemptions
$ 70,000	Corrected taxable income
– 60,000	Taxable income on return filed
$ 10,000	Understatement of taxable income

if you receive a $5,000 paycheck and deposit all of it into your savings account, then two weeks later transfer $2,500 into your checking account to pay bills, the examiner may believe that this involves a total deposit of $7,500. However, the $2,500 transfer deposit should be subtracted from the total deposits because it has already been counted once.

The issues in a bank deposits case can get very complicated from a tax and accounting perspective. It is a good idea for you to get professional advice whenever you do not understand what the IRS is trying to do or if something doesn't seem quite right — for instance, if the IRS is alleging that you have $20,000 of unreported income and you know that all your income was reported on the return.

2.2.b Cash expenditures method

The IRS also likes to use the cash expenditures method to allege additional unreported income. This method, also referred to as the sources and applications of funds method, compares all known sources of income with all known expenditures made during a year. If the cash expenditures (purchases) for goods and services exceed your income, the difference, according to the IRS, represents unreported income. The burden then falls on the taxpayer to prove that the alleged unreported income was, in reality, from one or more of the nontaxable sources that were previously discussed.

The IRS uses this method if a taxpayer purchased assets and does not currently have records to support taxable income received during the year. The tax court has given its approval to the IRS's use of the cash expenditures method.

To defeat the IRS when it uses the cash expenditures method, you must be able to show that someone else made the expenditures and gave you the assets as a gift or loan or, if you made the expenditures, that you were using funds on hand from prior years (called a cash hoard defense) or were using nontaxable sources of income.

For example, if you spent $100,000 during 1999 and claimed $60,000 of income on your tax return, the IRS could claim that $40,000 of income was unreported during this year. If you can demonstrate that you received $10,000 from your father to buy a car, had $20,000 in savings at the beginning of the year, and received a $10,000 inheritance from your grandmother, you would be able to show that the alleged $40,000 in unreported income really wasn't taxable to you at all. In this instance, all income was reported correctly and what initially looked bad for the taxpayer was in reality no change from what was reported on the return.

2.2.c Net worth indirect method

Finally, the IRS also uses the net worth indirect method in an attempt to increase a taxpayer's taxable income. This method, which the tax court has approved many times, is based on the theory that any increases in a taxpayer's net worth (which is defined as total assets minus total liabilities) from one year to the next, after removing nontaxable items, have occurred as the result of the receipt of taxable income. The formula, while fairly complicated because all of the accounting additions and subtractions, can be understood in the following simplified example:

Net worth at beginning of year	$ 100,000
Net worth at end of year	150,000
Increase in net worth	$ 50,000
Minus deductions and exemptions	20,000
Corrected taxable income	$ 30,000
Minus taxable income on return	20,000
Additional unreported taxable income	$ 10,000

The net worth method is an approximation and can often be successfully challenged; not every increase in your overall net worth from one year to another is the result of taxable income. For example, if you own 100 shares of IBM stock worth $90 per share at the beginning of the year (or $9,000), and the stock rises to $110 per share at the end of the year (or $11,000), your net worth would increase by $2,000. However, the $2,000 would not represent an increase in taxable income unless you actually sold the stock during the year.

In all net worth cases, the IRS must establish an accurate opening net worth for the beginning of the first year in the audit. Courts require this because the opening net worth is the figure the IRS uses as a starting point to compute future increases in net worth. The opening net worth figure is the IRS's vulnerable point when it uses this method of proof. For example, using the previous example of an opening net worth of $100,000, if you could show that your net worth at the beginning of the year was at least $110,000, there would be no way for the IRS to claim any additional unreported income, because the alleged $10,000 in unreported income would be wiped out due to the miscalculation concerning the opening net worth.

You also can challenge the IRS if any increases in your net worth during the year in question came from nontaxable sources of income. As in the other indirect methods of proof, if you can demonstrate that the increase in your net worth was the result of a gift, loan, or other nontaxable source of income, the IRS will lose the unreported income issue.

2.2.d Guarding against IRS mistakes

While each of these indirect methods can be complex, remember that the IRS often makes mistakes, almost always at the taxpayer's expense, when using these methods. The most common error is the failure to account for all nontaxable sources of income (such as gifts and inheritances). Other common errors include the following:

★ The failure to accurately determine the amount of cash the taxpayer had in his or her possession

★ Simply failing to listen to the taxpayer's explanations or defenses concerning the alleged unreported income

A tax auditor might ask you how much cash you had on hand on a certain date. You should never answer this question immediately, but should instead provide the answer at a later date once you've had a chance to verify accurate amounts. Most taxpayers believe that admitting to the IRS that they had a lot of cash is the same as admitting that income was underreported. This is not true. If you had a great amount of cash available, this will likely destroy or weaken the government's case if the examiner is using an indirect method of proof. If you are going to use the cash hoard defense, you should be sure to think out answers carefully and analyze them before speaking to the IRS.

Whenever the IRS uses one of these indirect methods, you should be suspicious, as there is a great potential for errors. Under most circumstances you should dig in and fight rather than agreeing to what is likely a mistake. You certainly should not be afraid of the complexities of these methods, especially given that the IRS can often be defeated.

3. Exemptions and Deductions

After examining income issues, the IRS will turn to the exemptions and deductions claimed on the return to make sure they are all legitimate. For exemptions, the IRS will verify that you are entitled to claim an exemption for the person or persons you have claimed on the return. You are permitted an exemption for yourself and one for each dependent.

A dependent is a person for whom you pay more than half of all support and who is related to you in one of the following ways:

- ★ Son, daughter, grandchild, stepchild, or adopted child
- ★ Brother, sister, stepbrother, or stepsister
- ★ Mother, father, or ancestor of either
- ★ Stepfather or stepmother
- ★ Son or daughter of taxpayer's brother or sister
- ★ Brother or sister of taxpayer's father or mother
- ★ Any other person who lives in the taxpayer's home during the year and is a member of the taxpayer's household

The IRS may request proof that you supported the person claimed as a dependent, especially if the person is relatively far removed from your family (such as an uncle or nephew).

Once the IRS has verified the exemptions claimed, the examiner will turn to the deductions claimed on the return (or expenses if a Schedule C is used) to make sure that all are valid and proper. The IRS may examine any deduction claimed, although many, such as mortgage interest or property taxes, are easy to verify. Other deductions or expenses are often improperly claimed or inflated and receive a great deal of scrutiny during an audit. Included among these deductions are large medical expenses, casualty or theft losses, and rental income and expenses. In general, the IRS will challenge these deductions only if they appear to be out of line with your income (such as deducting $30,000 of medical bills when you made only $40,000 during the year) or to make sure that you can support the deduction with adequate documentation. The following are some of the more common deductions and what you can do to avoid another audit red flag.

3.1 Medical expenses

The IRS will permit a deduction for any medical expense that relates to the diagnosis, cure, prevention, mitigation, or treatment of any illness or disease affecting the human body. In addition, health insurance premiums and transportation expenses are covered as medical expenses.

However, it is difficult for most taxpayers to deduct medical expenses because the expenses must exceed 7.5% of a taxpayer's Adjusted Gross Income before they can be deducted at all. For instance, if your AGI is $20,000, you cannot deduct medical expenses until you have spent more than $1,500 ($20,000 x 7.5% = $1,500) on them.

When an IRS auditor looks at medical expenses, he or she is often checking to make sure that nondeductible expenses are not being improperly deducted. For example, some cosmetic surgery (that is undertaken without a valid medical reason), marriage counseling, weight reduction programs (without a prescription), and food for special diets are generally not deductible.

3.2 Casualty and theft losses

The IRS tends to audit casualty and theft losses, often because taxpayers lack the necessary records to support the deduction. A casualty or theft loss is basically any loss that occurs as the result of some unexpected or unplanned event, such as a fire, flood, hurricane, tornado, earthquake, theft, vandalism, or other sudden catastrophe.

According to IRC §165, you can deduct a loss in the year the loss is discovered (which may be different from the actual year of the loss in the case of a theft) and only when the loss exceeds 10% of your Adjusted Gross Income. You also have to reduce the amount of the loss by any amount you received from insurance companies to cover the loss.

You should use the following types of documentation to prove a casualty or theft loss:

(a) *Police reports*. For any vandalism, theft, or other loss caused by criminal activity, you should make a full report to the police. The failure to make a report can be used by the IRS as evidence that you really did not suffer any losses, because if you had suffered a loss, you would have filed a police report.

(b) *Insurance claims*. You should report all losses on property covered by insurance to the insurance company, as the IRS reasons that all insured individuals will do so if a serious or otherwise valid loss occurs.

(c) *Written witness statements*. Obtain written witness statements concerning the loss or damages at the time of the accident, theft, or other event. The IRS commonly accepts such statements, reasoning that witnesses unrelated to the taxpayer do not often have a reason to lie and that the statements are likely accurate because they were made when the event was fresh in the witness's mind.

(d) *Press coverage*. Keep newspaper or other press coverage of the casualty or theft. The IRS will accept this evidence as conclusive proof that the loss did indeed occur.

(e) *Photographs.* If possible, take photographs of the damage. A photograph is worth at least a thousand words with the IRS.

(f) *Appraisals.* Obtain qualified appraisals of the damages to any property. This is important to prove how much less the property was worth after the casualty occurred.

(g) *Receipts.* Keep receipts concerning repairs to the damaged property. The IRS permits taxpayers to deduct the costs associated with restoring the property to its condition before the loss occurred. Examples of the proof needed include canceled checks, receipts, invoices, estimates, and any other documents that show how much it cost to restore the property.

3.3   Rental income and expenses

Make sure you have adequate proof for all rental expenses and that you properly calculate depreciation.

The IRS will not often audit rental income and expenses reported on Schedule E unless the rental expenses greatly exceed rental income (for example, if income of $1,000 and expenses of $20,000 are reported, the IRS will want to make sure that all income is reported and that the expenses are not inflated). The IRS will make sure that you have adequate proof for all rental expenses and that you properly calculated depreciation. It will often look at how you treated improvements or repairs to the rental property: a repair cost (such as painting or normal maintenance) can be expensed, but an improvement (a new roof or furnace) must be depreciated. If you have a rental property, you should seek professional advice concerning deductible rental expenses, unless you are well-versed on the current tax law.

3.4   Miscellaneous deductions

The IRS will sometimes check to make sure that any miscellaneous amounts deducted on the Schedule A actually qualify for a deduction. The miscellaneous deductions include unreimbursed job-related expenses (e.g., training, clothing, union dues), tax preparation or legal fees, investment expenses, safety deposit box rentals, and professional dues. Under IRC §67, these expenses must exceed 2% of your AGI before they become deductible. The amounts are generally small and not often worth the examiner's time to review.

3.5   Safe deductions

The IRS's Information Return Program (IRP) gives it the ability to match information concerning income and deductions on your tax return with information received from other sources (e.g., banks, employers). Any deductions for which the IRS can use its IRP functions will rarely be challenged during an audit (unless there is a discrepancy). Thus, very rarely will the IRS audit a mortgage interest deduction or a deduction for real property taxes. Also, it is very unusual for the IRS to challenge dependent exemptions (i.e., for children) as, again, verification is relatively simple.

The IRS will not often challenge charitable contributions unless the deduction is well out of line with your income, mainly because any additional revenue that the IRS may receive as a result of disallowing the deduction would not make up for the amount of time needed to make the adjustment — in other words, it's not worth the time it takes to challenge the deduction.

However, in the event that the IRS does challenge a charitable contribution, you must be able to explain to the auditor how the amount of the contribution was computed (if the contribution was not made by cash, check, or credit card). In general, I have not seen the IRS argue with taxpayers who have assigned a fair market value of 25% of the original cost of the item (this is the garage-sale valuation approach for donated personal property). In addition, you should make sure that you receive a written receipt from the organization for any property donated.

> To determine the value of your charitable contributions, assign a market value of about 25% of the original cost of the item. Always make sure you receive a written receipt for any charitable donations you make.

There are two further requirements concerning charitable contributions that must be kept in mind. First, if you have made a contribution with a value greater than $500, you must file a Form 8283 with your return. Second, you must file an appraisal with your return for all donations worth more than $5,000. The IRS routinely questions charitable contributions in excess of $5,000 during audits, and such a contribution may be the reason the return was audited in the first place. It is therefore a good idea to have a qualified appraiser selected for the appraisal and to make sure that the appraisal filed with the tax return is accurate. This is because the IRS aggressively penalizes taxpayers who substantially misstate the value of their charitable contributions on a tax return (see IRC §6662(e)).

In order to claim a charitable contribution deduction, you should make sure that the charitable organization receiving the donation is a qualified organization. Nearly all nonprofit organizations, such as churches, synagogues, hospitals, research organizations, the Red Cross, cancer or other medical research societies, and Boy and Girl Scouts will qualify.

However, if you are in doubt, before you donate you can request a copy of the IRS letter approving the organization's ability to accept charitable contributions. Once you have determined that the organization is qualified, any donation that you are willing to make and the organization is willing to accept will qualify as a legitimate charitable contribution.

3.6 Questionable deductions

Many taxpayers wonder what to do with a deduction (or any other item on the tax return) when the tax law is unclear about whether the deduction is legitimate. You have two options when this happens:

(a) Claim the deduction and risk an audit and possible additional tax, penalties, and interest.

(b) Don't claim the deduction and pay more tax now, even though the deduction may have been valid.

You should make this decision on a case-by-case basis, depending on how conservative or aggressive your overall tax strategy is. I generally recommend you be as aggressive as possible when deciding whether or not to claim a questionable deduction. (This advice is based on the premise that the tax law is unclear about the legality of a deduction. You should never claim a deduction that is clearly not permitted under the law. For example, claiming a $3,000 donation to a church when the donation was actually $300 is not only improper, it is also fraudulent.)

The rationale for claiming a questionable deduction is simple: you have a small chance of being audited in any given year, and if you are audited, there is a reasonable probability that the IRS will permit the deduction. In my opinion, the downside of claiming a deduction that is later disallowed is far outweighed by the likelihood that the deduction will not be challenged.

Many tax professionals recommend that you file a Form 8275 (Disclosure Statement) when you take a position on a tax return that is marginal or that involves an area of tax law the IRS may disagree with (see Sample 11). These professionals reason that the IRS will not typically add a negligence (accuracy-related) penalty if a taxpayer makes this disclosure and is later wrong (at least wrong according to the IRS).

As I stated in chapter 3, I disagree with this advice. My view is that filing a Form 8275 with a tax return will greatly increase the audit risks and will likely result in an increase in taxable income and an increase in tax payable to the IRS. Why should you inform the IRS that you are taking a position that is questionable and with which the IRS may disagree? By putting the IRS on notice, it is reasonable to assume that they will disagree with your position. With the disagreement will come increased frustration, headaches, and expenses that may not have resulted if the Form 8275

SAMPLE 11

FORM 8275 (DISCLOSURE STATEMENT)

Form **8275** (Rev. May 2001) Department of the Treasury Internal Revenue Service	**Disclosure Statement** Do not use this form to disclose items or positions that are contrary to Treasury regulations. Instead, use Form 8275-R, Regulation Disclosure Statement. See separate instructions. ▶ Attach to your tax return.	OMB No. 1545-0889 Attachment Sequence No. **92**

Name(s) shown on return	Identifying number shown on return
Sara Estill	111-22-3333

Part I General Information (see instructions)

	(a) Rev. Rul., Rev. Proc., etc.	(b) Item or Group of Items	(c) Detailed Description of Items	(d) Form or Schedule	(e) Line No.	(f) Amount
1	N/A	Sch. C/ Travel + Entertainment	Entertainment Expenses	C	24	$8,221
2						
3						

Part II Detailed Explanation (see instructions)

1 These expenses relate to entertainment expenses incurred in Chicago, Las Vegas and Denver, along with travel expenses in Chicago and

(continued on back)

2

3

Part III Information About Pass-Through Entity. To be completed by partners, shareholders, beneficiaries, or residual interest holders.

Complete this part only if you are making adequate disclosure for a pass-through item.

Note: A pass-through entity is a partnership, S corporation, estate, trust, regulated investment company (RIC), real estate investment trust (REIT), or real estate mortgage investment conduit (REMIC).

1 Name, address, and ZIP code of pass-through entity	2 Identifying number of pass-through entity
	3 Tax year of pass-through entity / / to / /
	4 Internal Revenue Service Center where the pass-through entity filed its return

For Paperwork Reduction Act Notice, see separate instructions.   Cat. No. 61935M   Form **8275** (Rev. 5-2001)

Form 8275 (Rev. 5-2001)   Page **2**

Part IV   **Explanations** *(continued from Parts I and/or II)*

Las Vegas during the 2001 tax year. I have receipts and full documentation for all expenses, including airfare, hotel stays, meals and tickets to Chicago Bears football games and musical entertainment at Caesar's Palace. The amounts also include incidental expenses, including cab fares, tips, limousine rental and other client-related charges.

---

wasn't used in the first place. In my opinion (which is definitely not shared by all tax professionals), the risk of a negligence penalty is not a sufficient reason to file the Form 8275 with the return.

4. Economic Reality Audits

Economic reality, or lifestyle audits, are exactly what the names imply: the IRS wants to audit you and your lifestyle, not just the tax return. Normally these audits begin with the IRS asserting that the income reported on the return under audit was not enough to live on (or to use the IRS terminology, "the income was not sufficient to maintain your lifestyle") for any particular year.

Congress has only recently become involved in determining when the IRS can use these audits and has stated in IRC §7602(e) that the IRS is not permitted to use economic reality or lifestyle audits unless it has a reasonable indication that there is a likelihood of unreported income. Of course, Congress does not define what constitutes a reasonable indication of unreported income.

If, during the course of your audit, the examiner starts asking questions concerning your lifestyle, you should be suspicious and make the examiner explain why he or she is asking the questions (i.e., the examiner should tell you what reasonable indication there is that your lifestyle doesn't match your income reported on the tax return). In addition, many revenue agents and tax auditors will immediately request that you fill out Form 4822 (Statement of Annual Estimated Personal and Family Expenses) (see Sample 12). In fact, many examiners make filling out this form a routine part of their tax audits, even when it appears that the taxpayer reported a sufficient amount of income to maintain his or her standard of living. This form has spaces where taxpayers enter their estimated average monthly expenditures for various common expenses (e.g., housing, utilities, food, medical, transportation, entertainment, taxes).

You should never fill out this form during any audit. There are no exceptions to this rule. For instance, if your expense estimates are too low (in the examiner's opinion), the examiner will simply reject the estimation. If, however, you overestimate the expenses, you have potentially increased your taxable income, certainly to your financial disadvantage. You cannot win by completing this form, and when you cannot win, there's no point in playing the game.

Furthermore, the form requests estimates and is therefore not accurate. If the purpose of an audit is to determine the correct amount of tax due, and if the Form 4822 is not accurate, why should anyone (including the IRS) want to use it?

Finally, the IRS is often asking a taxpayer to fill out the form with estimates that are more than two years old. For example, most audits occurring during 2003 are for the 2000 and 2001 tax years. How many taxpayers can accurately remember what they spent on groceries, entertainment, or other expenses three years earlier?

You are under no legal obligation to fill out Form 4822, and the refusal to complete it cannot be used against you during the audit.

Some examiners, who realize that many taxpayers will not fill out this form, do not attempt to use it. This does not mean that the examiner is not interested in your lifestyle. Instead of using the form, many auditors will ask personal living expense questions during the audit. You should resist these questions as you do the Form 4822, unless there is some evidence that you failed to report taxable income on the return.

> There is never any reason why you should agree to complete a Form 4822 (Statement of Annual Estimated Personal and Family Expenses) during an audit.

SAMPLE 12

FORM 4822 (STATEMENT OF ANNUAL ESTIMATED PERSONAL AND FAMILY EXPENSES)

Form **4822** (Rev. 6-83)	Department of the Treasury - Internal Revenue Service **STATEMENT OF ANNUAL ESTIMATED PERSONAL AND FAMILY EXPENSES**			
TAXPAYER'S NAME AND ADDRESS Mary Moneybags 123 Main Street Denver CO 80202				**TAX YEAR ENDED** 1998

	ITEM	BY CASH	BY CHECK	TOTAL	REMARKS
1. PERSONAL EXPENSES	Groceries and outside meals	2,500		2,500	
	Clothing	750		750	
	Laundry and dry cleaning	250		250	
	Barber, beauty shop, and cosmetics	400		400	
	Education (tuition, room, board, books, etc.)				
	Recreation, entertainment, vacations	500		500	
	Dues (clubs, lodge, etc.)	50		50	
	Gifts and allowances	500		500	
	Life and accident insurance	350		350	
	Federal taxes (income, FICA, etc.)	4,000		4,000	
2. HOUSEHOLD EXPENSES	Rent				
	Mortgage payments (including interest)	12,000		12,000	
	Utilities (electricity, gas, telephone, water, etc.)	4,500		4,500	
	Domestic help				
	Home insurance	750		750	
	Repairs and improvements	2,500		2,500	
	Child care				
3. AUTO EXPENSES	Gasoline, oil, grease, wash	850		850	
	Tires, batteries, repairs, tags	1,000		1,000	
	Insurance	1,000		1,000	
	Auto payments (including interest)	3,800		3,800	
	Lease of auto				
4. DEDUCTIBLE ITEMS	Contributions				
	Medical Expenses — Insurance	1,400		1,400	
	Medical Expenses — Drugs	350		350	
	Medical Expenses — Doctors, hospitals, etc.	150		150	
	Taxes — Real estate (not included in 2. above)	1,750		1,750	
	Taxes — Personal property	100		100	
	Taxes — Income (State and local)	1,000		1,000	
	Interest (not included in 2. and 3. above)				
	Miscellaneous — Alimony				
	Miscellaneous — Union dues				
5. PERSONAL ASSETS, ETC.	Stocks and bonds				
	Furniture, appliances, jewelry				
	Loans to others				
	Boat				
	TOTALS ▶	40,450		40,450	

Cat. No. 23460C   *U.S. Government Printing Office: 1996 - 405-508/33726   Form 4822 (Rev. 6-83)

5. Tax Shelters

A tax shelter is an investment from which the taxpayer expects to acquire various expenses, depreciation allowances, and other deductions that the taxpayer hopes will reduce his or her tax due on a tax return. Tax shelters are often used by wealthy taxpayers for the tax benefits. They can involve investments in real estate, farming, natural resources (oil, gas, coal, gold, and other types of mining), and equipment leasing (such as computers).

The IRS requires that all tax shelters be registered with the IRS at all times. The IRS consistently audits tax shelters because the shelters, by definition, are set up to reduce tax liabilities. Anything that is used to reduce a taxpayer's taxable income and tax due is sure to be an IRS audit target.

There have been entire articles and books written on the subject of tax shelters, but briefly, a tax shelter will always involve at least one of the following:

(a) Tax deferral

(b) The use of borrowing or leverage to increase the amount of money at issue and the potential tax write-off

(c) The ability to convert ordinary income to capital gains for a lower tax rate

Most taxpayers will never invest or have anything to do with a tax shelter because of the amount of the investment required and the complexities of tax shelters in general. There is often a very fine line between a legitimate tax shelter and an abusive tax shelter. As one Federal Appeals Court has noted: "We recognize that in the bewildering world of tax shelter deductions, few experts, let alone lay persons, easily discern the difference between a fraudulent scheme and an exceptionally advantageous legal loophole in the tax code."

There are hundreds of cases in which the IRS has litigated tax shelter issues, with the IRS winning most of these cases. Given that the penalties for participating in abusive shelters can be severe, I recommend that any taxpayer thinking about making an investment in a tax shelter first consult with an experienced CPA or tax attorney and pay for a written opinion on the legality of the shelter. By doing so, you can be reasonably certain that the tax deductions associated with the investment are legitimate. In addition, the written opinion letter will serve as a legal basis for claiming the deduction should you be audited in the future. The letter won't necessarily mean that the deductions were legitimate, but it should serve to eliminate any penalties associated with the shelter should the IRS determine it to be abusive.

6. Tax Protestors

The IRS routinely targets individuals whom the IRS has labeled "tax protestors." While the Tax Reform Act of 1998 requires the IRS to stop labeling individuals as tax protestors in its master computer files, there is no reason to believe that this will have any impact on the IRS's attempt to track down individuals it believes are illegally avoiding tax reporting requirements.

Tax protestors (or whatever term the IRS will use now that this classification is prohibited) are individuals who do not believe that the US tax system, and/or the IRS in general, apply to them. The following are common reasons why protestors believe they are not required to pay income taxes (though the number of arguments is limited only by the imagination):

★ *Wages do not constitute taxable income.* Courts have routinely stated that wages are income and can therefore be taxed.

★ *Reporting and paying taxes is strictly voluntary* (and the protestor does not wish to volunteer, thank you).

★ *The Fifth Amendment to the US Constitution prevents the IRS from requiring a taxpayer to provide information and sign the return.* The Fifth Amendment provides that "no person shall be . . . compelled in any criminal case to be a witness against himself, nor be deprived of life, liberty, or property without due process of law." Courts have rejected this argument because filing a tax return is not a "criminal case" and does not violate any due process rights.

★ *The Sixteenth Amendment to the US Constitution was not properly ratified and therefore has no legal effect.* Courts have always found this argument to have no merit and it should never be raised in any dealings with the IRS.

★ *Wages do not represent a taxable gain because wages are equal to the fair market value of the labor and thus no gain is involved* (if the value of labor and the wages are equal). Courts have routinely rejected this argument.

★ *Only federal workers are employees subject to any tax on income under the tax laws.* Many protestors raise this argument based on IRC §3401(c), which states that "for purposes of this chapter, the term 'employee' includes an officer, employee, or elected official of the

United States, a State, or any political subdivision thereof." Courts have stated that this section does not exclude employees who do not work for the government.

★ *Residents of a state are not residents of the United States for income tax purposes and thus they do not have to pay federal income taxes.* The argument is based on the idea that if a taxpayer is a resident of a state and not the United States, the IRS will not have jurisdiction over the taxpayer and no tax will be owed to the IRS. While creative, no court has accepted this argument.

No court has found any of these arguments to have merit. If you are considering these, or similar arguments, I strongly recommend that you not advocate them, at least not publicly, when dealing with the IRS. If you are labeled a tax protestor (or whatever the new label is), you are sure to be subjected to repetitive audits and to have more court appearances than the average trial attorney. There are many legal ways to beat the IRS at the tax game. You should not resort to illegal methods to accomplish what often could be done legally.

> Courts routinely reject tax protestors' arguments. Don't resort to illegal methods to beat the IRS — there are many legal ways to win.

The IRS has been taking an aggressive position against tax protestors for several years now. In fact, it currently shows up on the IRS's "dirty dozen" tax scams and pobably will do so in the forseeable future (a list of these scams can be found at www.irs.gov). Unfortunately for tax protestors, so have the courts. Courts often state that tax protestors take up valuable court time that could go to those citizens who have valid lawsuits or complaints against the IRS. Whenever a court determines that a tax protestor is advancing a frivolous argument, the court will impose a sanction against the tax protestor. This sanction can involve a penalty up to $25,000 if the US tax court is involved. This is certainly an area where the tax protestor cannot win. And again, if there is no chance of winning, there isn't much point in playing the game.

Tax Points

★ The IRS audits the taxpayer in addition to the tax return at issue.

★ The IRS always checks for unreported income during a tax audit.

★ The IRS is permitted to use any reasonable method to reconstruct your income as long as it accurately reflects the income for a particular year.

★ When the IRS uses an indirect method of proving additional unreported income, you should always thoroughly review and challenge the results.

★ You should be immediately suspicious if the IRS tries to turn any audit into an economic reality or lifestyle audit.

★ Refuse to estimate personal living expenses during an audit, as you cannot benefit by doing so.

★ You must completely understand any tax shelter promotion before investing to gain any tax benefits.

★ Tax protestor arguments do not work and serve only to cause unneeded headaches and continual IRS problems.

CHAPTER 9

TAX AUDITS OF BUSINESSES

I prefer the IRS to be criticized as too tough.
> Senator Byron L. Dorgan (D-North Dakota), during a Senate
> Governmental Affairs Committee meeting, July 1994

From a tax point of view you're better off raising horses or cattle than children.
> Congresswomen Patricia Schroeder (D-Colorado)

All the Congress, all the accountants and tax lawyers, all the judges, and a convention of wizards all cannot tell for sure what the income tax law says.
> Walter B. Wriston, former chairman of Citicorp (1967 – 1984)

Like individual taxpayers, business entities, no matter how they are set up, all face the possibility that the IRS will examine their business tax returns in any given tax year. This chapter addresses issues that are common to business tax audits, including ways that the business can successfully prepare for and defend these often difficult audits.

1. Odds of an IRS Audit

The odds that the IRS will audit a business entity are small. Table 6 shows the odds based on the type of business structure and business assets or gross receipts. As you can see, the percentage of businesses that are audited increases greatly as the size of the business increases. This is somewhat misleading, as many of the largest corporations in the United States are part of the large case program or are involved in ongoing, multiple year audits.

TABLE 6

PERCENTAGE OF BUSINESSES AUDITED

Individuals with Schedule C (Sole Proprietorship Business)

Business Gross Receipts	Percent Audited by Year						
	1996	1997	1998	1999	2000	2001	2002
$0 – $25,000	4.21	3.19	2.37	2.69	2.43	2.72	2.67
$25,000 – $100,000	2.85	2.57	1.82	1.30	0.93	1.02	1.18
$100,000 and up	4.09	4.13	3.25	2.40	1.47	1.20	1.45

Corporations

Total Assets — Balance Sheet	Percent Audited by Year						
	1996	1997	1998	1999	2000	2001	2002
No balance sheet	1.13	1.17	0.96	0.67	0.62	0.66	0.93
$0 – $250,000	1.04	1.19	0.77	0.46	0.29	0.25	0.24
$250,000 – $1,000,000	2.76	3.52	2.52	1.68	1.10	0.78	0.76
$1 million – $5 million	6.64	7.78	6.40	4.93	2.96	2.04	2.08
$5 million – $10 million	14.08	16.02	13.52	10.30	6.99	5.33	4.63
$10 million – $50 million	19.88	20.10	18.02	14.90	11.67	9.66	7.80
$50 million – $100 million	21.29	19.59	18.19	16.49	14.68	12.32	10.74
$100 million – $250 million	27.57	22.88	19.61	18.83	17.42	17.55	15.98
$250 million and up	49.61	46.77	38.60	35.70	31.43	32.09	34.37

S-Corporations/Partnerships

Type of Business	Percent Audited by Year						
	1996	1997	1998	1999	2000	2001	2002
All S corporations	0.92	1.04	1.04	0.81	0.55	0.43	0.39
All partnerships	0.49	0.59	0.58	0.43	0.33	0.25	0.26

1.1 How to reduce the odds of an IRS audit

As I indicated in chapter 5, there is no way to completely eliminate the odds of a tax audit, as some audits are truly random. However, there are a few ways you can greatly reduce the odds of an audit on your business:

(a) *Always report all income that the IRS knows about or can find out about.* The IRS is constantly searching for unreported business income or receipts. For instance, it looks closely at the totals of Forms 1099 it receives. If your company does more than $600 worth of business with someone in a year, you will receive a Form 1099 from that company or individual. The party that pays the money files the Form 1099 with the IRS, but the recipient (you or your company) must report the income on the year's tax return. The gross income your business reports to the IRS must be at least as much as the total reported on all Forms 1099 for the year in question. There is no exception to this rule! In addition, business owners must carefully review all cash journals, ledgers, bank statements, and other documents listing business income to make sure that all income not recorded on Forms 1099 is also properly reported to the IRS.

(b) *Report actual business expenses and not "rounded" estimates.* Any business tax return that contains all nicely rounded numbers, such as $500 for advertising and $1,000 for insurance, is much more likely to be audited than a return that contains precise and accurate numbers. If the IRS believes that a business lacks the necessary records to prepare an accurate return (and thus had to use estimates), it will almost always audit the return.

(c) *Always double-check the return for mathematical errors.* Any return that contains mathematical mistakes is almost sure to be examined. Never be sloppy in this critical area.

(d) *Always answer all questions on the return, even if the question does not apply to your business.* It is always preferable to put "N/A" or "None" in the answer section than to have the IRS answer the question for you. If the IRS answers the question, you have lost control and you will probably not like the answer.

(e) *Structure the business so that you do not have to file a Schedule C.* Returns with a Schedule C have the highest audit rates, primarily because many taxpayers are tempted to deduct personal expenses as business expenses or do not have adequate records to support what should be the legitimate business expenses. For alternatives to the Schedule C, see the discussion under sole proprietorships and other businesses entities in chapter 4.

If a past audit
has uncovered additional
income or unsubstantiated
expenses, it is extremely
likely that the IRS will
revisit the same business
in the near future to make
sure that history does not
repeat itself.

1.2 How business tax returns are selected for audit

Many of the same audit selection techniques discussed in chapter 5 also apply to business tax returns. With specific respect to businesses, a few of the most common reasons returns are chosen for audit are the following:

★ Random audits

★ Prior IRS audits

★ Cash businesses

★ IRS matching programs

★ Special projects

★ Informant tips or information

1.2.a Random audits

Like individual taxpayers, a business cannot avoid the chance of a random audit whenever it files an income tax return. However, the number of truly random tax audits is statistically quite small, and they are used simply as a deterrent to reduce the number of businesses that are tempted to cheat. Of course, if you file as accurate a return as possible, you have nothing to fear from a random audit.

1.2.b Prior IRS audits with changes

If a past audit has uncovered additional income or unsubstantiated expenses, it is extremely likely that the IRS will revisit the same business in the near future to make sure that history does not repeat itself. For this reason, any time an audit of your business produces additional tax due, you should take great care to prepare highly accurate and conservative tax returns in the future.

1.2.c Cash businesses

All businesses that deal with a lot of cash — including bars, restaurants, vending machine operators, and laundromats — are more likely to be audited because there is a great temptation to keep the cash from ever seeing its way to the business records or bank account. During an audit of these types of businesses, the IRS will make sure that all cash income is accurately reported. For example, the IRS will closely examine the inventory of a bar or restaurant to get an idea of how many drinks or meals the business has served. Once this information is known, along with the retail price for the drinks or meals, it is relatively easy to detect skimming.

If this strategy is used for the audit of a tavern, for example, the examiner would determine how many beers the tavern purchased for sale to its customers during the period under review. Most bars will accurately report this information because the purchases are deductible when computing the tavern's cost of goods sold. If the audit determines that 1,000 cans or bottles of beer were purchased for resale at a cost to the bar's customers of $2.50 each, the IRS agent would expect to see $2,500 in receipts for the beer. If the tavern reports less than $2,500 and does not have a valid explanation for the difference (such as free drinks or spillage), the IRS will assume that the difference is the result of skimming and thus represents unreported income. Cash businesses need to be aware of the IRS audit techniques to avoid this potentially devastating audit issue of unreported income (along with a potential fraud referral).

> Businesses that deal with a lot of cash are more likely to be audited, as the IRS wants to make sure that all cash income is accurately reported.

1.2.d IRS matching programs

As I previously mentioned, the IRS computer system has a great ability to match income based upon information returns (usually Forms 1099) filed with the IRS. At a minimum, all businesses must make sure that any income reported to the IRS is also reported on the business tax return. If the business ever reports less than this amount, an audit is almost certain to occur, and the audit may include many other issues in addition to the unreported income analysis.

1.2.e IRS special projects

Many businesses are audited simply because of the type of business they are. For whatever reason, the IRS believes that many businesses in particular industries do not file accurate tax returns. As a result, the IRS has established a series of very detailed guidebooks that tell its agents and other employees in the Market Segment Specialization Program (MSSP) what to watch for when auditing returns from various industries. At the time of writing, the IRS has established MSSP guidelines on the following industries or professions (and is adding to this list every year):

★ Airplane charters

★ Architects

★ Artists and art galleries

- ★ Attorneys
- ★ Auto body and repair shops
- ★ Bail bondsmen
- ★ Bars and restaurants
- ★ Beauty and barber shops
- ★ Bed and breakfasts
- ★ Business consultants
- ★ Car Washes
- ★ Carpentry/Framing
- ★ Child-care providers
- ★ Commercial banking
- ★ Commercial fishing
- ★ Computers and electronics retailers and manufacturers
- ★ Drywallers
- ★ Farming
- ★ Furniture manufacturers
- ★ Garden centers/nurseries
- ★ Garment contractors and manufacturers
- ★ Gas retailers
- ★ Gift Shops
- ★ Hardwood timber industry
- ★ Laundromats
- ★ Masonry and concrete
- ★ Ministers
- ★ Mobile food vendors
- ★ Mortuaries
- ★ Music and entertainment
- ★ Oil and gas industry
- ★ Pizza restaurants
- ★ Printing
- ★ Reforestation industry

- ★ Retail liquor industry
- ★ Taxicabs
- ★ Tobacco industry
- ★ Tour bus industry
- ★ Trucking
- ★ Used car dealers
- ★ Veterinary medicine

The IRS does not audit all businesses in the categories listed, or even a majority of these businesses. But if your business should fall into one of these categories, be warned that it may come under a very different scrutiny than other businesses should an audit occur.

1.2.f Informant tips

While the IRS welcomes and relies upon tips from individuals and other businesses, this is the least likely way that your business tax return will be selected for an examination. About the only way to control this potential audit source is to remember never to discuss your business tax issues or obligations with anyone, including friends or family members.

2. Specific Business Tax Audit Issues

Although businesses have many of the same rights and responsibilities as individuals, discussed in chapters 6, 7, and 8, many business tax audits involve completely different issues.

2.1 The hunt for unreported business receipts

The IRS makes locating unreported gross receipts its number one priority in any business tax audit. Usually the IRS will not have specific evidence to dispute the gross receipts listed on the tax return in question, as nearly every business reports gross receipts that are at least equal to the total amount of income reported to the IRS on Forms 1099. Instead, the IRS will often need to resort to an indirect method of proving additional business gross receipts.

For example, in an audit of a mom-and-pop bakery, the examiner will focus a great deal of time on the small business enterprise if the common Schedule C is used. The first thing the agent will want to see is the business books and records. Most of the time, the books and records will substantially match what was reported on the return and the examiner's job will be relatively easy. However, what will the examiner do if the books and records do not match the return at all or if there are no books and records? The records may have been lost, destroyed in a flood or fire, or are somehow incomplete.

When the agent cannot audit the books, the IRS must resort to an indirect method of proving additional unreported income. IRC §446(b) gives the IRS the authority to use any method that will, in its opinion, accurately reflect the business's income for the year(s) in question.

One of these methods is known as the bank deposits analysis. The bank deposits method basically compares the total amount of bank deposits in any given year with the amount of income reported on the tax return. If the numbers don't match up after some accounting corrections, the difference is assumed to be unreported income. Sample 13 shows how this method works.

Should the IRS resort to using this type of analysis, it is vital that you make sure all calculations are accurate and that there aren't any nontaxable sources of income the auditor is attempting to tax. This often requires that you carefully review all deposits made during the year in question to insure that there weren't any additional loans, transfers or other nontaxable sources of bank deposits that could explain the difference between the alleged understatement and the amount of income reported on the tax return.

2.2   Questions concerning business expenses

The IRS will permit business expenses that are "ordinary and necessary," but often audits travel and entertainment, home-office, and automobile expenses.

After checking for unreported income, the IRS will next turn to the legitimacy of the expenses claimed on the business tax return. In general, the IRS will permit all business expenses that are considered to be "ordinary and necessary" to the business operations. Courts have determined that an expense is "ordinary" if it is "common and accepted in your field of business," while an expense is "necessary" if it is "helpful and appropriate for your business." The following types of business expense deductions frequently come under scrutiny during a business tax audit.

2.2.a Travel and entertainment

The IRS often audits businesses that claim travel and entertainment (T & E) expenses. The reason for this is that many business taxpayers (especially sole proprietorships) claim personal T & E expenses as business expenses in order to claim a tax deduction. To claim travel expenses as a business expense, you must be able to show that your business required

SAMPLE 13
HOW THE BANK DEPOSITS METHOD WORKS FOR BUSINESS AUDITS

The IRS uses this formula to determine income:

Total deposits into all bank accounts

\+   Cash spent during the year but not deposited into bank accounts

=   Total receipts

−   Nontaxable deposits (such as amounts received from gifts, loans and inheritances)

=   Corrected gross income

−   Deductions and exemptions

=   Corrected taxable income

−   Taxable income per return

=   Understatement of taxable income

To understand how the IRS uses the formula to compute additional taxable income, consider the following example:

$300,000	Total business bank deposits during 2003
+ 25,000	Known amount of cash spent during 2003 but not deposited into business bank account
$325,000	Actual business receipts in 2003
− 100,000	Loan from business shareholder/owner
$225,000	Corrected gross income for business in 2003
− 125,000	Business expenses claimed on 2003 tax return
$100,000	Corrected taxable income for business
− 70,000	Taxable income claimed on 2003 tax return
$30,000	Understatement of taxable income on 2003 tax return

you to be away from home for a period of time longer than an ordinary workday and that it was reasonable for you to sleep or rest before returning home. Your "home" is considered to be your regular place of business or, if you have no regular place of business, the place where you regularly live. If your "home" does not meet either of these rules — i.e., if you live wherever you happen to be working — you are not permitted a travel deduction because you would never be away from home.

The most common situation concerning T & E expenses involves overnight business trips. If you can show that the trip was necessary from a business standpoint, all ordinary expenses are deductible. These expenses include lodging, travel (car, plane, etc.), and meals, along with any miscellaneous expenses (such as telephone calls, cab rides, tolls, etc.).

Many taxpayers run into trouble with the IRS on T & E expenses because they fail to document the business purpose of the trip, fail to keep receipts, or try to deduct travel expenses for someone such as a spouse who is not traveling for the business. To avoid these problems with T & E expenses, I recommend the following:

Always document your business trips and keep all receipts. Remember to record:

Who

What

Where

Why

When

(a) *Document all business trips.* Use a journal or log that covers the five Ws: Who, What, Where, Why, and When. Many taxpayers, especially those who travel a great deal for business, forget the specifics of each trip, especially if two or three years have elapsed since the trip. A simple journal that states: "10/14/02 – 10/18/02. Travel to Denver/Brown Palace/meet with QWest and Denver Post concerning telephone and advertising accounts" will probably be sufficient to demonstrate the business purpose of the trip.

(b) *Keep all receipts.* The IRS requires receipts or other documentation for all travel expenses that are more than $75. In addition, it always requires receipts for you hotel/lodging expenses, even if this amount is under $75. I recommend keeping all receipts, no matter the amount, to support the deduction.

(c) *Do not claim T & E expenses for a spouse or travel companion who is not traveling for a valid business purpose.* This does not mean that a spouse cannot travel with the business taxpayer; it simply means that the spouse's expenses are not deductible.

With respect to meal and entertainment expenses, you must show that the expenses were ordinary and necessary to the business activity and that they were directly related to conducting the business. However, only half of any meal or entertainment expenses are deductible (under IRC §274(n)). For example, a taxpayer who takes a client to dinner and a professional baseball game may deduct only 50% of the cost of the meals and tickets, as long as some bona fide discussion of business was done at one or both events. Usually the business discussion must take place on the same day as the dining or entertainment activities, although there are numerous exceptions to this rule, such as when a taxpayer dines with a client on Monday night and discusses business the following morning. Meal and entertainment expenses can be claimed even if you are not traveling away from home.

The IRS likes to audit these expenses because taxpayers often include personal entertainment expenses as business expenses. For example, if a salesperson in Chicago takes her husband, brother, and his wife to a Chicago Bulls basketball game and deducts the cost of the tickets as a business expense, the IRS will disallow the deduction unless there is a valid business purpose for the basketball game entertaining.

Taxpayers claiming these types of entertainment expenses must keep accurate and detailed records concerning the purpose of the entertainment and the amount of money spent entertaining. By keeping records that state the names of persons entertained, the business purpose and relationship, the place of entertaining, and the amount spent, you will be able to defeat the IRS in this commonly audited area.

2.2.b Office in home

In the past, the IRS regularly audited taxpayers who claimed the home-office deduction. The IRS believed that many taxpayers were improperly deducting personal expenses (such as utilities and home repairs/maintenance) that they otherwise could not deduct, or that they were simply not permitted to claim the deduction at all under the current law. Thankfully, the IRS is not currently auditing taxpayers who claim a home-office deduction solely because of this deduction, although the tax auditor will almost certainly review this deduction if the return is selected for an audit for some other reason.

> You can deduct the cost of a home office if you regularly and exclusively use your home office for a trade or business purpose.

IRC §280A(c) allows a taxpayer to deduct the cost of a home office only if there is regular and exclusive use of the home office for a trade or business purpose. The US Supreme Court further restricted the use of this deduction when it ruled that Dr. Soliman, an anesthesiologist, could not claim a home-office deduction — even though he had no office outside his home — because a hospital, and not the home office, was his principal place of business. The court reached this decision even though the IRS did not dispute that Dr. Soliman used his home office exclusively and regularly for business. This was a strange result because it was also not disputed that Dr. Soliman would be permitted to deduct the costs associated with an office *outside* his home, even if he used the office solely for paper-work and never saw a patient there.

In the past, the IRS has looked at the relevance of the time spent in the home office, as opposed to the actual amount of time (i.e., it did not look at how many hours were actually spent in the office, but rather how important those hours were to the business). For example, using the rule in the *Soliman* case, if a plumber or electrician had a home office that was exclusively and regularly used for billing, returning customer telephone calls, keeping records, etc., the plumber or electrician would not be allowed to claim this deduction because the plumber's or electrician's main work (the work that actually generated the revenue) occurred outside of the home.

The Taxpayer Relief Act of 1997 changed this rule to permit a taxpayer who regularly and exclusively conducted management or administrative activities in a home office to deduct the home-office expenses if there was no other place to conduct such activities. Thus, for the previous example concerning the plumber or electrician, he or she would now be allowed to deduct home-office expenses as long as the plumber or electrician did not have any other office where he or she could manage his or her businesses.

Under any circumstances, the office will qualify for a deduction only if no personal use of the office occurs. For example, if you let your children use the office to watch television or do homework, you will defeat the business-only use requirement and will not be able to deduct the home office.

Given that the law concerning home-office deductions has been changing over time, if you face this audit issue, you would be well advised to research the current law before proceeding with the audit.

All taxpayers who claim a home-office deduction must file a Form 8829 (Expenses for Business Use of Your Home) with the Schedule C. The Form 8829 includes all deductible home-office expenses, including rent or mortgage interest, insurance, utilities, repairs, maintenance, and real estate taxes. The form also computes the percentage of business use of the home. For example, if a 2,000-square-foot home has a 500-square-foot office, only 25% (500/2000) of the home expenses can be deducted as home-office expenses.

The IRS can initiate a computer search that will pull out any tax returns that contain a Form 8829. Thus, in the future, the IRS may again decide to audit tax returns that claim home-office deductions. If you are going to use this form, be certain that you qualify for the deduction and that you can support all amounts deducted.

If you are going to claim the home-office deduction, consider incorporating your business. By doing this, you won't have to file a Form 8829 and thus lower the risk of being audited.

One way for small businesses to claim the same or a similar deduction without filing a Form 8829 is to incorporate the business. By incorporating, the corporation can take the same deduction without using the Form 8829. The taxpayer gets the same tax benefits without the audit trigger, and the IRS is frustrated in this area.

2.2.c Automobile expenses

Many taxpayers get into trouble with the IRS when they try to deduct miles spent commuting from home to work, reasoning that these miles are deductible because no money could be earned if the trips did not take place. Unfortunately, this is *not* a correct interpretation of the tax law. All commuting expenses, including mileage and tolls, are considered to be personal expenses and are not deductible anywhere on the tax return. However, miles spent commuting between two places of business are deductible as a valid business expense. In addition, self-employed taxpayers are not permitted to deduct mileage expenses associated with traveling from the home office to the taxpayer's principal office. However, if your primary office is the home office, all business trips from the home office would be deductible.

2.3   Independent contractor versus employee

The IRS routinely attempts to change a worker's status from "independent contractor" to "employee" during the course of an audit on a business taxpayer — either during an audit of the business paying the worker or of the worker claiming the income and expenses on a Schedule C.

An employee is basically any worker who receives wages or a salary from an employer who has the right to control what the employee does during the workday and when the employee performs the work. An independent contractor, on the other hand, generally receives a payment for a specific job and remains free of the control of the business that contracts for the worker's services. The key to determining the worker's status as an employee or independent contractor usually involves the amount of control that the business exercises over the worker. The more control the business has, the more likely the worker will be considered an employee for tax purposes.

The IRS is interested in reclassifying independent contractors as employees because of the potential increase in employment taxes that it could collect from the business employing the worker. If a worker is an independent contractor, the business hiring the contractor pays no taxes on the worker. However, if the worker is reclassified as an employee, the

The IRS will often try to reclassify an independent contractor as an employee, as the IRS can deduct more tax from an employee than it can from an independent contractor.

business now becomes responsible for social security (FICA), unemployment (FUTA), and hospital insurance taxes, along with potential federal income tax withholding.

In addition, many workers would rather be classified as independent contractors because of the potential tax savings to them. For example, an independent contractor is considered to be operating his or her own business and can therefore deduct all ordinary and necessary business expenses, can contribute to a tax-qualified retirement plan, can claim a home-office deduction, and can claim any other deduction that a business is permitted. The negative side for the independent contractor is that he or she will be responsible for self-employment tax, which would not be the case if the contractor was an employee. The self-employment tax is computed on the net income (gross income minus business expenses) of the business and consists of the FICA and hospital insurance taxes, which currently total 15.3%. An independent contractor is entitled to deduct half of the self-employment tax on his or her Form 1040 tax return.

Given that both the worker and the business hiring the worker usually prefer the worker to be considered an independent contractor, there is a possibility that workers who may really be employees are being labeled independent contractors to gain the tax advantages. The IRS, unfortunately, is very aware of this potential for abuse.

If the IRS is attempting to change your status from independent contractor to employee, you should use the IRS list of 20 factors to support the position you have taken. These 20 factors are listed in Checklist 2. Note that not all of these 20 factors are applicable in every case.

If, after reviewing this list, you determine that you qualify as an independent contractor, you should make sure of the following:

★ Always use a written contract that specifies you are an independent contractor.

★ You must be permitted to work for other companies and you should actually do so.

★ You should not receive any of the benefits that an employee would receive (such as vacation or sick days).

★ The contract should specify a total amount that you will be paid as opposed to an hourly rate (for example, $1,000 to paint the offices rather than $10 per hour).

CHECKLIST 2
ARE YOU AN EMPLOYEE OR AN INDEPENDENT CONTRACTOR?

1. *Instructions.* The more instructions you receive concerning when, where, and how you are to work, the more likely you are an employee.

2. *Training.* If you receive training, you are more likely to be an employee.

3. *Success of business.* If the success of the business depends greatly on you, you are probably an employee.

4. *Personal services.* If the business is interested in a specific worker, as opposed to any worker with similar skills, the worker is probably an employee.

5. *Hiring, supervising, and paying assistants.* If you need to hire additional workers to perform a job, you are probably an independent contractor.

6. *Continuing relationship.* The more often you work for the business, the more likely you are an employee.

7. *Set hours.* If you are required to work certain specified hours, you are probably an employee.

8. *Full-time work.* If you work full time for the business, you are probably an employee.

9. *Work done at employer's place of business.* If you must work at the employer's place of business, you are probably an employee, unless the work has to be done there (for example, building a house or painting an office).

10. *Order of work.* If you are told in what order the work must be done, you are probably an employee.

11. *Reports.* If you are required to provide written or oral reports, you are probably an employee.

12. *Payment by time.* If you are paid by the hour or week, instead of by the job or on a commission basis, you are probably an employee.

13. *Payment of expenses.* If you are reimbursed for any business expenses, you are probably an employee.

14. *Providing tools.* If you must provide your own tools or work materials, you are probably an independent contractor.

15. *Investment.* If you invest in a business facility to perform the services, you are probably an independent contractor.

16. *Profit or loss.* If you can lose money on a particular job, you are probably an independent contractor.

17. *More than one employer.* If you are working for more than one business at a time, you are probably an independent contractor.

18. *Services to the public.* If you make your services available to the public, you are more likely to be an independent contractor.

19. *Right to fire.* If you can be fired, you are probably an employee, as an independent contractor could sue the business for a breach of contract for terminating the business relationship.

20. *Right to quit.* If you can quit without being sued for a breach of contract, you are probably an employee.

★ The business should not tell you how or when to do the job, but should only provide you with instructions on what needs to be done and a deadline for completing the job (i.e., it is okay if the business tells you that the work must be done before February 15, but it must not tell you to begin work at 8:30 a.m. on February 1 and to leave at 5:00 p.m. every day).

★ You should already be trained to do the job.

The IRS has a special form (Form SS-8) that business owners can fill out in situations where a person's work status is questionable. I recommend *not* using this form. By using it, you are telling the IRS that you are unsure whether you are an independent contractor or an employee. By putting the IRS on notice, the IRS is almost certainly going to determine that you are an employee. Do not give the IRS an opportunity to make an advance ruling against you, as it has the ability to make enough rulings against you on its own.

2.4 Schedule C businesses (sole proprietorships)

The Schedule C tax form is used by individuals who are in business for themselves and have not incorporated or formed some other type of business organization (such as a partnership or limited liability company). These businesses are commonly referred to as sole proprietorships.

Without a doubt, the IRS loves to audit sole proprietorship businesses. The reasons are relatively simple: many taxpayers use this schedule to deduct personal expenses that would otherwise not be deductible, or to deduct costs associated with their hobbies, even though they may not have a legitimate profit motive for the hobby (see section **2.5** below).

For these reasons, along with other liability and legal reasons, I recommend that all Schedule C filers incorporate their businesses, usually as an S Corporation, or form a limited liability company (LLC). Once a business is incorporated, there is no need to ever file a Schedule C again for that business (it is treated as a separate taxpayer on Form 1120 or 1120S). The same is true for an LLC, which files a Form 1065 if it has two or more members (a Schedule C if only one member) and is also treated as a separate tax entity. Once it is a corporation, the business's audit risk decreases significantly (the same as if the business was formed as a partnership or LLC). These business entities are discussed in detail in chapter 4.

2.5 Hobby-loss businesses

The IRS is always on the lookout for individuals who consider their hobbies as a business for tax purposes only. In these hobby-loss cases, the IRS disallows any losses associated with the business because, in its opinion, the business was not operated with a profit motive.

For example, suppose your hobby is photography. If you claim that photography is now a business activity and file a Schedule C, you would be entitled to deduct the cost of the camera, film, developing, travel, and anything else associated with photography. Of course, if you sell few or no photographs, your income will be limited and the expenses will be great, thus producing a tax loss that you can use to reduce other taxable income (such as wages from your regular job).

The IRS is very well aware of this potential tax savings situation and audits a very high percentage of Schedules C that display losses. To avoid this hobby-loss designation, I recommend the following:

(a) *Incorporate.* This will mean there is less of a chance of an audit, even though the IRS could make the same hobby-loss determination under IRC §183.

(b) *Operate the business in a "businesslike" manner.* This is probably the best way to avoid an audit or to successfully fight the IRS during an audit on this issue. What this means is that you should get advice before beginning the business and should keep accurate books and records with proof of expenses. In addition, you should be prepared to spend a significant amount of time on the business and try to make a profit by advertising, marketing, and doing anything else that a successful business would do. You should have business cards printed, set up a business telephone line with an advertisement in the yellow pages, and register your company as a business with the state. Also, if the business has lost money in the past, it is important that you are able to show you are taking steps to correct any problems, with the goal of generating a profit in the near future.

(c) *Keep the business separate from any personal activities.* This means that the business should have its own bank account(s), insurance policies, identification number (from the IRS on Form SS-4), and anything else necessary to show it is a real business. Also, by keeping the business separate and apart from your personal financial activities, you are demonstrating a proper business purpose, as most taxpayers treat a hobby as a personal financial matter and not as a real business activity.

(d) *Be able to show a profit motive.* If the IRS ever questions your profit motive, you should be able to argue that even with the tax deductions, you would have been much better off had you never started the business to begin with. In addition, the IRS presumes that an activity is not a hobby and has a profit motive if it produced a profit in any three of the five years immediately before the year being audited, unless the IRS can prove otherwise. For horse breeding, showing, training, or racing, the profit requirement is two out of seven years.

2.6　Other audit issues for small businesses

If you are running a small business, you should be aware that the IRS is on alert for the following issues:

(a) *The IRS looks for expenses out-of-line with industry standards.* For example, if a small restaurant is claiming that 50% of its revenues went for advertising expenses, and the average in the restaurant business is 5%, the IRS is likely to question this expense (along with all others on the return).

(b) The IRS looks at transactions between a corporation and its shareholders or executives to make sure that corporate insiders are not abusing the tax laws and regulations. Any transactions like these must be extremely well documented (especially loans and other transactions involving money going between the corporation and its shareholders that are not easily understood from a review of the return).

3. What to Expect During a Business Tax Audit

It is reasonable to expect that the IRS will want to examine all books and records when it undertakes a business tax audit. The IRS has the authority under IRC §7602 to do this and nearly always exercises its authority. While the term "books and records" is somewhat vague, most examiners will request the following information:

★ Copies of various tax returns (including sales, use, employment, income, and excise returns)

★ Cash receipts ledger

★ Accounts receivable and payable ledgers

★ Balance sheets

★ Profit-and-loss statements

★ Shareholder or other owner records

★ Copies of contracts

★ Bank statements and canceled checks

★ Current asset schedule for business

★ Depreciation and amortization computation records and work papers

★ Promissory notes, lending agreements, and any other evidence relating to loans

★ Any other documents that support or otherwise verify tax return entries relating to business income or expenses

Given the large number of records that can potentially be required and examined, I strongly advise you to organize all business records when you are preparing a tax return and store them with a copy of the return after you file the return with the IRS. Keep these records at least six years, or longer if storage space is not a concern.

3.1 What if I'm missing some records?

During the course of an audit, many businesses realize that they cannot substantiate all expenses claimed on the tax return. In addition to using the estimates and affidavit procedures discussed in chapter 7, many businesses find it valuable to use reconstructions.

In general, reconstructions are permitted whenever a taxpayer's records have been lost or destroyed through no fault of the taxpayer, or when the expenses were obviously incurred but proper records were not maintained. It is very easy, for example, for a salesperson to forget to log automobile miles or business meals, even though the mileage or meals certainly qualified as legitimate business expenses. However, even if you don't have the proper records, you can reconstruct your activities and expenses from details in your appointment calendar or diary. While this is not an ideal method because it is very easy to overlook or underestimate the actual expenses, it is certainly preferable to not claiming the deduction at all (or not being able to support the deduction at an audit).

You should expect to meet IRS resistance when you use this or any method other than actual receipts to support a deduction claimed on a tax return. You should also realize that the IRS's own regulations do not require any documents to support business expenses in amounts less than $75 (for expenses incurred after October 1, 1995) unless the expenses related to travel. While I certainly recommend keeping all receipts that relate to a tax return, if you cannot locate a receipt or other documentation, you certainly can and should rely upon the less-than-$75 rule to support the deduction(s).

3.2   What does the IRS know about my business?

Contrary to popular belief, an IRS examiner generally knows very little about your business before beginning the audit. Most tax examiners have very limited experience when it comes down to specific audit issues for a particular business. For example, an examiner certainly understands what a plumber does for a living, but probably has no idea about the common business practices of a plumber (unless the examiner has audited other plumbers in the past). Given the large number of different types of businesses that exist, it would be unreasonable to expect the examiner to know whether a typical plumber spends 1% or 10% of his or her gross receipts on advertising or any other business expense. The same can be said about any other business or profession, and it is often up to the taxpayer to educate the examiner about any particular type of business.

Whenever you are given the opportunity to educate the examiner, you should always take advantage of the situation, as a chance to educate is a chance to limit the total number of audit issues and produce a favorable audit result.

3.3　Where will the audit take place?

As a business taxpayer, you can expect the audit to occur at the location where your books and records are located or at a location to where you can bring the books and records. While most individual taxpayers can request the audit be held at an IRS office because of the limited number of records involved, the rules change somewhat when a business taxpayer is being audited. Under IRC §7606, the IRS auditor is permitted to audit business taxpayers at the place of business. If this is not acceptable to you, you should ask for a different location and agree to the following:

★ That all books and records will be made available to the IRS at the place of the audit

★ That the IRS examiner will be permitted to tour the business at an agreed time in the future

★ That the business owner(s) will be available for an interview with the examiner

If you want the audit moved from your business location, you should tell the examiner that you want the audit away from your business so as to avoid any disruption or interference with the business, which is usually the case with a small business audit.

If the examiner does decide to visit your business, it is imperative that you make sure the examiner understands the visit is for a limited purpose and there must be no deviation from the actual purpose. For instance, it is reasonable for the auditor to want to see the business location, especially if the business is in your home and you are claiming a home-office deduction. However, this does not give the auditor the right to interrupt your business, interview your employees, or observe anything that is not in plain sight, without your express permission.

3.4　Common questions during business tax audits

No matter how your business is organized or structured, the IRS has specific questions for business taxpayers during an audit. These can be found in IRS Form 4700 (Business Supplement). The examiner will ask you for the following information:

★ A description of the business activity

★ The number of years in business

★ The number of paid employees

★ The name of the bookkeeper

★ The amount of cash on hand at the beginning and end of the year (You should answer this question carefully. The natural tendency is for taxpayers to err on the side of being too low, as it does not seem to be a good idea to tell the IRS how much money you have. However, the IRS may later use this too-low amount against you if an indirect method of proof of income is used — see section **2.1**).

★ The name of your bank or financial institution

★ Proof of filing of all tax returns currently due (including income, employment, and other returns and forms, including Forms W-2 and 1099)

★ The method of accounting for all income and expenses

★ Loans to and from business owners

★ Inventory issues, including valuation and accounting methods

★ Verification of business expenses

The IRS will use this information to make sure that you are correctly reporting all business income and expenses on the business tax return.

Tax Points

★ Always report all income that the IRS knows about or can find out about.

★ Do not use rounded numbers on the return. Instead, use the actual expenses incurred.

★ Always double-check the accuracy of the tax return before filing it, including any mathematical calculations.

★ If your business is in one of the industries listed in the IRS MSSP guidelines, be especially careful. You may find it beneficial to get a copy of the guidelines from the IRS.

★ Do not discuss your business or personal tax situation with anyone, including friends, family members, and business associates.

★ Report only those business expenses that are both ordinary and necessary to the operation of your business.

★ Document all expenses with the following information: who, what, when, where, and why.

★ Keep all receipts and other business records at least six years.

★ Use the IRS 20-factor test to determine whether you, or any individual, are an employee or independent contractor of your business.

★ Sole proprietors should consider incorporating their business to reduce the audit risk.

★ The IRS probably knows very little about your particular business prior to initiating the audit.

★ The IRS is permitted to examine all your business books and records during the audit.

★ The IRS is permitted to view your business location at some point during the audit, even if the audit is not being conducted at your business location.

★ A business must be able to show a profit motive before it is allowed to deduct any business losses (otherwise it runs the risk of a hobby-loss audit from the IRS).

CHAPTER 10

IRS PENALTIES AND NOTICES: WHAT THEY REALLY MEAN

The current tax code is a daily mugging.
President Ronald Reagan, speech in Independence, Missouri, on
September 2, 1985

IRS agents strike fear into the hearts of the little people of America.
Senator David H. Pryor (D-Arkansas),
quoted in the *Washington Post*, May 4, 1987

*Wherever a discretionary power is lodged in any set of men over
the property of their neighbors, they will abuse it.*
Alexander Hamilton (1755 – 1804), first Secretary of the US
Treasury under President George Washington

The IRS loves to assert penalties, or what it calls "additions to tax," against taxpayers, and with over 150 penalties to choose from (at last count), the IRS can penalize you for almost any reason imaginable. Once you know what penalty the IRS is attempting to assert and why, you can develop a strategy or defense based on whether the penalty is legitimate and must be paid, or if it can be abated (eliminated) because it should not have been imposed in the first place. If a penalty is abated, the interest associated with the penalty is also abated. In this chapter I discuss IRS penalties and strategies for defeating the IRS when it tries to assert any penalties against you.

1. IRS Notices

Before discussing the various common penalties that the IRS can assert, you need to first understand the IRS notice system. A notice is simply the IRS's way of informing you that there has been some change to your account for a specific tax year. Usually, but not always, this means the amount of money that you owe the IRS has increased.

The number of penalty notices the IRS sends to taxpayers every year is, without a doubt, excessive. For example, in 2003 the agency sent out 28,767,480 notices to taxpayers, with additional amounts due ranging from a few pennies to hundreds of thousands of dollars.

The first thing to bear in mind is that an IRS notice is not always correct. The IRS itself admits that many of these notices are incorrect in some manner. Unfortunately for taxpayers, the IRS is doing little if anything to correct the vast problems. It has little incentive to fix the system, because taxpayers often respond to the notices by paying the incorrect penalty. This means the IRS collects more revenue and looks better when it asks Congress for increased operating funds during the next year's budget discussions.

> The IRS sends out over 33 million penalty notices a year — many of them incorrect. Many taxpayers simply pay the incorrect penalty, and the IRS wins.

The IRS makes millions of mistakes every year. An IRS notice does not necessarily mean that more tax will be due, and IRS notices informing you of additional tax, penalties, and/or interest due can be successfully fought. One thing you must remember, however, is that *an IRS notice cannot be ignored.*

All IRS notices contain the following information:

★ Your name, address, and identification number (usually your social security number)

★ The date of the notice

★ The tax form and year (for example, Form 1040, 2001) in question

★ The document locator number (DLN), which the IRS uses to track every tax transaction with which it is involved

★ The amount of any tax, penalties, and interest owed (according to IRS records)

1.1 Reasons IRS notices are wrong

There are many reasons why IRS notices might be wrong, including the following possibilities:

(a) *You did not receive proper credit for all tax payments made.* This is often the case with estimated tax payments. The IRS is also known to post tax payments to the wrong year, which would result in a refund for one year and an amount due for another. It is usually relatively easy to fix this problem. If you receive a notice and suspect this is the situation, you should call the IRS and request a copy of your transcript of account. The transcript will show if payments were applied to the wrong tax years. You always have the right to receive this information and the IRS does not charge you for it.

Whenever the IRS sends a notice, you should first determine if the notice is accurate.

(b) *The IRS has information concerning income reported to the taxpayer, but you are not the right taxpayer.* For example, if an employer incorrectly prepares a Form W-2 by using the wrong social security number for an employee, the person who has the social security number used on the incorrect W-2 will receive a notice from the IRS concerning unreported income. The notice will demand payment concerning the additional tax due as a result of the "unreported income." This also is usually easy to correct, as long as you do not ignore the notice.

(c) *The income the IRS claims was not reported is not taxable.* The income could be a gift, a loan, or an inheritance. In any event, you should always make sure the income is in fact taxable before you agree to pay any additional amounts.

(d) *The income the IRS says was not reported was actually reported on the return, but in the wrong place.* For example, you might have listed business income, which should go on Schedule C, as "other income," or dividends might have been incorrectly listed as interest. If you do not challenge this kind of notice, the IRS will succeed in double counting income (it's bad enough to pay tax on the income once).

(e) *The IRS has no record of receiving the tax return.* This is one reason, among many, that you should always send tax returns to the IRS by certified mail, return receipt requested, as it is up to you to prove that a return was actually filed.

Whenever the IRS sends a notice, you should first determine if the notice is accurate. If it is accurate, the amount should be paid in full or a payment plan worked out with the IRS (see chapter 11 for a discussion of ways to resolve tax bills with the IRS). If the notice is not accurate, it is up to you to fight back, as ignoring the problem will not correct the problem.

1.2 Fighting an IRS notice

To fight an IRS notice, you should first respond to the notice in writing. Your letter to the IRS should be short, simple, and to the point, and should include the following information:

★ Your name, address, and social security number

★ The tax form and year being challenged

★ A copy of the notice that the IRS sent to you

★ A brief paragraph explaining why the IRS is wrong, with copies of any documents that support your position — for example, copies of canceled checks, Forms W-2 or 1099, or contracts

★ A brief paragraph telling the IRS what you want it to do to fix the problem (you should always request that the IRS remove all interest and penalties associated with the incorrect notice)

★ A telephone number where the IRS can reach you for further information

The tone of the letter should be polite but firm. Remember that the IRS employee reading the letter will not have any knowledge of the notice or your tax situation in general. You should make it easy for the employee to correct the problem. If it is not clear what is wrong with the notice or what you want the IRS to do, the employee is less likely to be able to fix the problem. Sample 14 is an example of a letter responding to an IRS notice.

2. IRS Penalties

Many notices that the IRS sends to taxpayers include IRS additions to tax, or what are commonly known as penalties. The IRS imposes penalties to encourage compliance with the tax laws and to ensure consistency and fairness in the application of the tax laws.

2.1 Inaccurate tax returns

Under IRC §6662, the IRS can apply a penalty when it believes that a taxpayer failed to file an accurate tax return. The penalty under this section is 20% of any additional tax due after the audit has concluded. While there are five different penalties in this section, the two most common are negligence and substantially understating the income tax due.

> The IRS imposes penalties to encourage compliance with the tax laws and to ensure consistency and fairness in the application of the tax laws.

SAMPLE 14
LETTER RESPONDING TO AN IRS NOTICE

Internal Revenue Service
Attention: Mail Stop 5000DEN
600 – 17th Street
Denver, CO 80202

January 15, 20—

Dear IRS:

Re: Penalty Notice for Herman H. Munster, SSN: 123-45-6789

On January 10, 20—, I received a copy of Notice Number ___ (copy enclosed), which indicates that according to the IRS records I owe an additional $1,400 for filing my 1998 tax return late. Please be advised that this notice is not correct, as my return was mailed to the IRS on April 12, 1999. In support of my position, I submit the following:

(a) Taxpayer information: Herman H. Munster, 1313 Mockingbird Lane, Denver, CO 80222. My SSN is 123-45-6789

(b) Tax year: 1998 Form 1040

(c) A copy of the IRS notice is enclosed

(d) Telephone number during the day: (303) 555-1212

(e) A copy of my return receipt from the US Postal Service concerning the 1998 tax return is enclosed. This copy clearly shows that I mailed my tax return on April 12, 1999, and that the IRS service center in Ogden, Utah, received the return on April 16, 1999.

Inasmuch as my return was mailed on time, I am not subject to any penalty for late filing. Therefore, please abate this penalty, along with all interest associated with this penalty. If you need any further information, please contact me at the address or telephone numbers listed above. I thank you in advance for your assistance in getting this matter resolved.

Sincerely,

_____

Herman H. Munster
1313 Mockingbird Lane
Denver, CO 80222

Enclosures: As stated

2.1.a Negligence

Negligence simply means that a taxpayer failed to do what a reasonable and ordinary taxpayer would do under the same or similar circumstances. It uses a "reasonable person" standard and penalizes those taxpayers who are not "reasonable." The IRS usually asserts this penalty when it believes that a particular taxpayer is taking an unreasonable position on a tax return — such as deducting his or her hobby expenses as business expenses — or does not have any records to support the tax return during an audit.

The taxpayer's conduct does not have to be intentional (if the IRS believed that the taxpayer intentionally omitted income or claimed an invalid deduction, the IRS would likely assert that the taxpayer committed fraud); a simple error or mistake is enough to warrant the imposition of the negligence penalty.

In general, all defenses to a negligence penalty are based on the taxpayer's attempt to comply with the tax laws. You can successfully fight a negligence penalty if you can show that you contacted a tax professional and followed the professional's advice. A simple claim that you read the IRC and attempted to follow it is often enough to abate the penalty, as the IRS is aware that the tax laws are very difficult to understand.

The IRS asserts this penalty quite often, because it believes that many taxpayers are negligent when it comes to preparing and filing tax returns. The IRS often loses this penalty when a case goes to tax court, as the tax court judge often finds that the mistake on the taxpayer's return did not result from the taxpayer's negligence. In addition, the IRS itself will often concede this penalty during the appeals process, either through the appeals officer or the area counsel attorney.

> You can successfully fight a negligence penalty if you can show that you followed professional advice or attempted to read and follow the Internal Revenue Code.

2.1.b Substantial understatement

The IRS uses the substantial understatement penalty when it believes that a taxpayer failed to report the correct amount of tax by a substantial amount. For purposes of this penalty, "substantial" means a difference of at least 10% between what was reported and what should have been reported, or $5,000 — whichever is more.

For example, if the IRS determines that your correct tax due for 1998 was $60,000, and you show less than $54,000 on the return, you may be charged with a substantial understatement penalty (10% of $60,000 is $6,000). Likewise, if the correct tax is $100,000 and you report tax of $92,000, the IRS will most likely assert a penalty because more than $5,000 of tax due was not reported.

Because this penalty is primarily a mathematical calculation, it is difficult to successfully fight. You can still argue "reasonable cause" (see section **3.**), although the chances of success are slim. Other possible defenses include the argument that you acted in good faith and there was reasonable cause for the understatement; that the understatement was based upon substantial authority (such as the IRC, IRS Regulations, Rulings or Procedures, Court cases, Congressional intent or other tax law sources); or that you made an adequate disclosure on form 8275 that was filed with your tax return indicating the questionable nature of the position you took with respect to the issue on the return.

2.1.c Frivolous Tax Returns

As if all the other penalties are not sufficient, the IRS also has the authority to fine taxpayers an additional $500 for filing a frivolous tax return. This penalty is in addition to any other penalties the IRS may choose to assert.

For the purposes of this penalty (IRC §6702), "frivolous" means any tax return that omits the information necessary to determine an accurate tax liability, or shows a tax amount that is —

★ substantially incorrect,

★ based upon a legal position that has no legal authority (such as the 16th Amendment was not properly ratified or that wages do not constitute taxable income), or

★ based upon the taxpayer's desire to delay or otherwise impede the IRS from collecting the tax or performing its duties.

In addition, the IRS will assert this penalty if you cross out or alter the "penalties of perjury" language that appears on Form 1040 directly above the signature lines. This penalty is just one more reason why you definitely do not want to raise or assert tax protestor types of arguments with the IRS. Not only will you lose, you will also be $500 poorer for your efforts.

2.2 Failure to file/Late filing

Under IRC §6651, the IRS can penalize taxpayers 5% per month, up to a maximum of 25%, for failing to file a tax return when it is due (taking into account any extensions that were given). If you can convince the IRS that the failure to file the return was due to "reasonable cause" and not to "willful neglect," you may be able to get this penalty removed. Courts have determined that "reasonable cause" means the taxpayer was unable to file timely returns despite using ordinary business care, while "willful neglect" is a conscious, intentional failure or reckless indifference. Reasonable cause could be the case if you were relying upon your return preparer's professional advice that no return was required (because there was no taxable income), or if a personal tragedy prevented you from filing on time (death, serious illness, divorce, flood, fire, etc.).

Be on the lookout for IRS mistakes with this penalty, because the IRS sometimes misplaces tax returns and then tries to place the blame on the taxpayer. The IRS will remove this penalty if you can prove that the return was filed on time and that it was the IRS's fault that the return was not correctly processed.

2.3 Fraud

Fraud is an intentional act committed by the taxpayer in hopes of improperly lowering his or her tax bill. Under IRC §6663, the IRS can assert a penalty for fraud that will add 75% to any amounts owed to the IRS as a result of a tax deficiency.

The IRS asserts the fraud penalty when it believes that the taxpayer has intended to evade taxes that he or she knows are due and owing. To impose a fraud penalty on a taxpayer, the IRS must prove he or she intended to conceal, mislead, or otherwise do something to avoid paying taxes that were owing, or that the taxpayer had knowledge of what was being improperly claimed on the tax return.

Because fraud is a serious assertion, the IRS has the burden of proving, by clear and convincing evidence, that the failure to pay the taxes owing was not simply an honest mistake or ignorance. The clear and convincing standard of proof is less than the criminal case standard of "beyond a reasonable doubt" but is greater than the normal civil case standard of "preponderance of the evidence." It is a difficult burden for the IRS to prove, but certainly not impossible.

If you are involved in an IRS fraud investigation you should contact an attorney for advice if you do not feel absolutely confident about handling the investigation by yourself. There is a very real possibility that a fraud investigation will lead to a criminal investigation, which is one of the few areas of dealing with the IRS in which you should never rely upon self-representation.

The IRS will look for the following types of conduct when it tries to prove fraud:

(a) *A pattern of understating income (usually for three or more years).*

(b) *Keeping two or more sets of books.* One set of books will accurately reflect the business operations and the other set will be for the IRS.

Always send your tax return by registered mail, receipt requested. This will provide you with proof of prompt filing.

(c) *Concealing assets or sources of income.*

(d) *Engaging in illegal activities (and not reporting the income).* The IRS often uses this type of conduct as proof of fraud because many people assume that a taxpayer who would engage in illegal activities would also try to commit tax fraud by not reporting the income associated with the illegal activities.

(e) *Extensive use of cash to avoid a traceable paper trail.* This assumes there is no proper business reason that would justify using cash.

(f) *Altering or creating false documents.*

(g) *Lying to the IRS.* It is difficult for the IRS to successfully use lying as proof in a court case involving tax fraud because the IRS must prove that the taxpayer's fraudulent conduct occurred at or near the time that the return was prepared and filed and not at some point after the return was filed. On its own, this type of conduct will rarely support IRS fraud allegations. However, when there is proof of other fraudulent conduct as well as lying, the taxpayer will have a difficult time overcoming the combination. And even if the IRS cannot successfully use the taxpayer's lies to prove a fraud case, the IRS still can use the lies to support a variety of possible criminal charges. It does not pay to lie to the IRS under any circumstances.

(h) *Failing to cooperate with the IRS.* It is also difficult for the IRS to use failure to cooperate on its own to prove fraud. For one thing, no one really knows what "failure to cooperate" really means. The taxpayer may be trying to cooperate even when the auditor thinks he or she is not cooperating. Also, the conduct (lack of cooperation) is not occurring at or near the time that the tax return was prepared and filed. For these reasons, the IRS will usually use this allegation of fraud when other indications, such as keeping two sets of books, are present.

(i) *Filing false Forms W-4 (for tax withholding on wages).* According to the IRS, the only reason that a taxpayer would file a false Form W-4 is to lower or eliminate any taxes being withheld from the taxpayer's wages and therefore deprive the IRS of tax revenues. Unless the taxpayer can come up with another reason for the false Form W-4, the IRS is probably accurate more often than not on this assumption.

To defend yourself against a fraud charge you must demonstrate that you did not intend to evade taxes. The following are some of the defenses you can use:

(a) *Cash hoard.* Use this defense when the IRS is trying to assert that all purchases or expenditures made with cash during a year must have come from unreported taxable income. The defense works if you can show that you had a large amount of money (i.e., the cash hoard) accumulated in the years prior to actually spending the cash.

(b) *Nontaxable sources of income.* If you had gifts, loans, or other non-taxable sources of income that the IRS did not properly consider, you can often dodge a fraud assertion.

(c) *Honest or no mistake.* Remember, without intent to improperly reduce the taxes due, there cannot be any fraud, even if you failed to report income or claimed an improper deduction. A mistake or error is negligence at the most and can never be fraud.

(d) *No intent to evade taxes due and owing.* With tax fraud, the IRS must show that the fraudulent conduct related to taxes. If the taxpayer can demonstrate another reason for the fraud, there may not be any tax fraud. For example, if the taxpayer submitted a false tax return to a mortgage company to get a loan, the taxpayer may have committed bank fraud but not tax fraud. Likewise, if a taxpayer hid assets so that his ex-wife could not get them, the taxpayer may have violated one of his state's divorce laws but not the federal tax laws.

2.4 Fraudulent failure to file tax returns

The IRS has recently added a new penalty (under IRC §6651(f)) to its arsenal for those taxpayers whom it believes fraudulently failed to file tax returns. While the IRS must prove the fraud allegations, it penalizes taxpayers 15% per month, up to a maximum of 75%, if it can show that the taxpayer's reason for not filing the tax returns was fraudulent. The same type of evidence discussed in the fraud section above applies to the fraudulent failure to file tax returns. The IRS usually uses this version of the fraud penalty against tax protestors, high-income or well-known taxpayers, and also those taxpayers who fail to file tax returns for two or more consecutive years.

If the IRS alleges a fraudulent failure to file, you should immediately stop talking to the IRS and seek competent tax counsel (as you should do with any fraud allegations). The IRS can use anything that you say against you in court, but it does not need to warn you of this fact or tell you that you don't have to talk to the IRS. Also, there is a very real possibility that the case could be referred to the Criminal Investigation Division for a complete criminal investigation. A fraud case is no place for a taxpayer to make a mistake, because a taxpayer's potential freedom at the most and very large dollar amounts at the least are involved.

2.5   Late payment of tax

Under IRC §6651, the IRS can penalize taxpayers for failing to pay a tax when the tax is due. This penalty adds 0.5% for each month that the tax is not paid, up to a maximum penalty of 25%. Again, you should use the "reasonable cause" rule (see section **3.**) as a defense whenever the facts allow its use.

2.6   Estimated tax penalty

Under IRC §6654, the IRS can penalize taxpayers when they are required to make estimated tax payments to the IRS but do not do so. This penalty usually applies to self-employed taxpayers, but it can also apply to employees if the employer does not withhold enough from their wages. There are several defenses available to fight this. There is no penalty in the following circumstances:

★ If the total tax due is less than $500

★ If you did not have any tax liability in the previous tax year

★ If the full amount of the tax due is paid by January 31 of the year in which the return is being filed

★ If you retired or became disabled in the year that the estimated tax payments became due

★ If it would be "against equity and good conscience" (i.e., unfair) to hold you liable for the penalty

★ If the underpayment of taxes was due to a casualty, disaster, or another unusual circumstance (such as a fire; the September 11, 2001 terrorist attacks; an extreme illness; etc.)

From the taxpayer's perspective, it is worthwhile to fight this penalty because a fight can often be won. You should review the list of potential defenses carefully and challenge the penalty if any of the defenses remotely apply.

2.7 Trust fund recovery penalty

The trust fund recovery penalty is one of the most severe and dangerous penalties that the IRS can assert against a taxpayer. Such a penalty is usually applied when an employer who withholds taxes from employees fails to pay those withheld taxes to the government. While these taxes may be withheld on a weekly basis (or any other period depending on how often the employees are paid), the employer usually pays these funds to the government on a monthly or quarterly basis and holds the funds "in trust" until they are paid. Hence the name of the penalty.

After the net wages are paid to an employee, the government credits that employee with the tax payments, even if the employer fails to pay the taxes. Often the employer fails to pay the taxes due to major financial problems with the business. Regardless of the reason, the IRS will try to collect the money that should have been paid to the government from the responsible persons with the employer (assuming that the employer cannot pay the taxes). The penalty can be assessed against more than one person or entity, and the IRS will often assert the penalty against several individuals in the hopes of getting payment from at least one of them.

> For a person to be liable for a trust fund recovery penalty, he or she must be both responsible and willful in the failure to pay the taxes to the IRS.

Under IRC §6672(a), a person is liable for the penalty if he or she is both responsible and willful in the failure to pay the taxes to the IRS. The two relevant terms under the statute and the court cases interpreting this statute are "responsible" and "willful." A responsible person is often the person who has the authority to control how money is paid, and to whom, in a business. Included in this responsibility is the control to pay (or not pay) the IRS. Usually this involves high-ranking corporate officers or actual owners of the business. However, it can also involve persons not employed by the business (for example, outside accountants or payroll departments). For the person to be willful, all that must be shown is that the person knew about the tax liabilities and knowingly and intentionally used available funds to pay operating expenses or other debts of the business. If the taxpayer is not both responsible and willful, there can be no trust fund recovery penalty against that taxpayer.

Before assessing the penalty, a revenue officer will request an interview with the potentially responsible person and will complete a Form 4180 (Report of Interview with Individual Relative to Trust Fund Recovery Penalty) (see Sample 15). You may also have to fill out a Form 4181 (Questionnaire Relating to Federal Trust Fund Tax Matters of Employer) (see Sample 16). The interview can be lengthy and will include the following types of questions:

SAMPLE 15

FORM 4180 (REPORT OF INTERVIEW WITH INDIVIDUAL RELATIVE TO TRUST FUND RECOVERY PENALTY)

Report of Interview with Individual Relative to **Trust Fund Recovery Penalty or Personal Liability for Excise Tax** Notice 609 was furnished during the interview. (Check here) ☒ (See instructions below.)	Date of Interview March 3, 1999 Name of Interviewer Albert Snitch

INSTRUCTIONS TO INTERVIEWER: The questions which follow are to be used as a guide as you conduct the interview. Other questions may be asked. You must prepare this form personally, recording the interviewee's answers. Where a question is not applicable, write "N/A." Do not leave any blocks or lines blank. Attach additional sheets if necessary.

Notice 609, Privacy Act and Paperwork Reduction Act Notice, must be given to persons who haven't received notice of their right to privacy. If furnished during the interview, check the box above. If not, explain in the case history.

IRC 6672, failure to collect and pay tax from *(date)* __4/1/98__ to *(date)* __12/31/98__

IRC 4103, failure to pay tax from *(date)* _____ to *(date)* _____

Section I—Background Information

1.	a.	Person interviewed *(name)*	Mary Moneybags
	b.	*(address)*	123 Main Street, Denver CO 80202
	c.	Telephone number *(home)* (303) 555-1212	d. Telephone number *(work)*
	e.	Social Security number	123-45-6789
2.	a.	Taxpayer (Corporation) *(name)*	MM Restaurant Supply, Inc.
	b.	*(address)*	123 Main Street, Denver CO 80202
	c.	Incorporation *(date)* 4/1/98	d. State where incorporated Colorado
	e.	Has the state revoked the corporation franchise?	☐ yes ☒ no f. If so, when?
	g.	Has the corporation ever filed bankruptcy?	☐ yes ☒ no h. If so, when?
3.		Was any of the property of the corporation sold, transferred, quitclaimed, donated or otherwise disposed of, for less than fair market value, since the accrual of the tax liability? ☐ yes ☒ no What happened to the corporate assets?	
4.	a.	How were you associated with this corporation?	President and CEO
	b.	Describe your duties/responsibilities. Ran company on a day-to-day basis.	
	c.	By whom were you hired? Self	
	d.	What were the dates of your employment with the corporation? 4/1/98 to present	

Form **4180** (Rev. 2-93) Cat. No. 22710P   Department of the Treasury — Internal Revenue Service

Page 1

SAMPLE 15 — CONTINUED

e.	Did you resign from the corporation? ☐ yes ☒ no		f. In writing?		☐ yes ☐ no
g.	When? 　　N/A		h. Is a copy of your resignation available? ☐ yes ☐ no		
i.	To whom was your resignation submitted?				
j.	Did you have your name removed from the bank signature cards? ☐ yes ☒ no			k.	When?
h.	Do you have any money invested in the corporation? ☒ yes ☐ no			m.	Amount $50,000

5.

a.	Have you ever been involved with another company which had tax problems? ☐ yes ☒ no	
b.	If so, explain. *(Corporate name, EIN, etc.)* 　　N/A	

6. With what banks or financial institutions did the corporation have transactions such as checking and other accounts, loans, financing agreements, etc.? *(attach additional sheet, if necessary)*

Financial Institution	Transaction(s)	Address	Date(s)
Denver Bank	Checking account	100 First Avenue	4/1/98 to present

7. Where are the financial records located?　123 Main Street, Denver CO 80202

8. Please indicate the names, dates of service and percentage of ownership for the positions indicated below.

Position	Name	Dates of Service	% Ownership
Chairman of the board	Mary Moneybags	4/98 to present	25
Other Directors *(list)*	Michael Night	4/98 to 10/98	25
	Jake Bates	4/98 to present	25
	Matt Lamm	4/98 to present	25
President	Mary Moneybags	4/98 to present	25
Vice President	Matt Lamm	4/98 to present	25
Secretary	Jake Bates	4/98 to present	25
Treasurer	Michael Night	4/98 to 10/98	25
Others *(shareholders, owners)*			

Page 2

SAMPLE 15 — CONTINUED

Section II—Ability to Direct	Interviewee

Please indicate whether you performed any of the duties/functions indicated below for the corporation and the time periods during which you performed them. If another person performed these duties, please list names and time periods.

Did you...	Yes	No	Dates from	Dates to	Did anyone else? (name)	Dates from	Dates to
1. Hire/fire employees	X		4/98	present	Michael Night	4/98	10/98
2. Manage employees	X		4/98	present	Michael Night	4/98	10/98
					Jake Bates	4/98	present
3. Direct (authorize) payment of bills	X		4/98	present	Michael Night	4/98	10/98
4. Deal with major suppliers and customers	X		4/98	present	Matt Lamm	4/98	present
5. Negotiate large corporate purchases, contracts, loans	X		4/98	present	Matt Lamm	4/98	present
6. Open/close corporate bank accounts		X			Michael Night	4/98	10/98
7. Sign/countersign corporate checks	X		4/98	present	Michael Night	4/98	10/98
					Matt Lamm	4/98	present
8. Guarantee/co-sign corporate bank loans		X			Michael Night	4/98	10/98
9. Make/authorize bank deposits		X			Michael Night	4/98	10/98
10. Authorize payroll checks		X			Michael Night	4/98	10/98
11. Prepare federal payroll tax returns							

Page 3

SAMPLE 15 — CONTINUED

Did you...	Yes	No	Dates from	to	Did anyone else? (name)	Dates from	to
12. Prepare federal excise tax returns		X					
13. Sign federal excise tax returns		X					
14. Authorize payment of federal tax deposits		X			Michael Night	4/98	10/98
15. Review federal income tax returns		X			Michael Night	4/98	10/98
16. Determine Company financial policy	X				Michael Night	4/98	10/98
					Jake Bates	4/98	present
					Matt Lamm	4/98	present

17. Please provide the information requested below for each person, other than yourself, listed for the above questions. Also, please provide any additional information indicating their knowledge and/or control over the corporation's financial affairs. *(Attach additional sheets if necessary.)*

Name	Address
Michael Night	100 North Fish Street
Phone Number (303) 666-1200	**Social Security number** 321-54-9876
Additional information	

Name	Address
Jake Bates	250 South Fish Street
Phone Number (303) 331-1000	**Social Security number** 231-54-7698
Additional information	

Name	Address
Matt Lamm	100 North Broadway
Phone Number (303) 455-2500	**Social Security number** 213-45-6897
Additional information	

Name	Address
Phone Number	**Social Security number**
Additional information	

Page 4

Section III—Knowledge	Interviewee
	Mary Moneybags

1. When and how did you first become aware of the delinquent taxes?

In October 1998, when we caught Michael Night embezzling funds from the company.

2. What action did you take to see that the tax liabilities were paid?

We tried to see if we had sufficient funds, but the embezzlement caused us to nearly file for bankruptcy.

3. Were discussions or meetings ever held by stockholders, officers or other interested parties regarding the non-payment of the taxes? ☒ yes ☐ no
Identify who attended, the dates of the meetings, and any decisions reached.
(Attach additional sheets, if necessary.)

In October, November, and December.
All other shareholders attended.
Michael Night was arrested and not present.

4. Are minutes available from any meetings described in question 3 above? ☒ yes ☐ no

5. Who maintained or has access to the books and records of the corporation? When?
(Please provide name, address and phone number, if possible)

All four shareholders.

6. Were financial statements ever prepared for the corporation? ☒ yes ☐ no
If so, by whom? Who reviewed them and to whom were they submitted?
(Please provide time periods.)

Michael Night prepared them.

7. Did the corporation employ an outside accountant? ☐ yes ☒ no
If so, please provide the name, address and phone number of the person or firm.

Page 5

SAMPLE 15 — CONTINUED

8. Who in the corporation had the responsibility of dealing with the outside accountant?

  N/A

9. Did you personally have discussions with the accountant or bookkeeper of the corporation regarding the tax liability?

  ☒ yes ☐ no

  If so, when?
  What was discussed?

  After the embezzlement was uncovered, Mr. Night confessed.

10. Who reviewed the payroll tax returns or tax payments?

  No-one other than Mr. Night.

11. Who reviewed the excise tax returns or tax payments?

  N/A

12. Who handled IRS contacts, such as IRS correspondence, phone calls from IRS, or visits by IRS personnel?

  Mary Moneybags

  When?
  What were the results of these contacts?

  Unknown

13. During the time the delinquent taxes were increasing, or at any time thereafter, were any financial obligation of the corporation paid?

  ☐ yes ☐ no

  If so, which ones?

  To supplies and current employees

14. Which individual or individuals authorized or allowed any of these obligations to be paid?

  Michael Night, myself, Matt Lamm

15. During the time that the delinquent taxes were increasing, or at any time thereafter, were all or a portion of the payrolls met?

  ☒ yes ☐ no

16. When there was not enough money to pay all the bills, what decisions were made and what actions were taken to deal with the situation? Who made the decisions?

  All the board members made the decisions.

17. Did any person or organization provide funds to pay net corporate payrolls? ☐ yes ☒ no
  If so, explain in detail.

Page 6

Section IV—Special Circumstances

1. Is the corporation required to file federal excise tax returns? ☐ yes ☒ no
   If so, are you aware of any required excise tax returns which have not been filed? ☐ yes ☒ no
   (If either response is negative, do not complete remaining questions in Section IV.)

2. With respect to excise taxes, were the patrons or customers informed that the tax was included in the sales price? ☐ yes ☒ no

3. If the tax liability is one of the so-called "collected" taxes—transportation of persons or property and communications:

   a. Was the tax collected?   N/A   ☐ yes ☐ no

   b. Were you aware, during the period tax accrued, that the law required collection of the tax? ☐ yes ☐ no

Continue answers from Sections I through III below. Identify by section and item number.

Section V—Additional Comments

Is there anyone else who may have been involved or who could provide additional information regarding this matter? ☒ yes ☐ no

Mrs. Night

Please add any comments you may wish to make regarding this matter.

I declare that I have examined the information given in this statement and, to the best of my knowledge and belief, it is true, correct and complete.

Person interviewed *(signature)*	Date
M. Moneybags	3/4/99

Interviewer *(signature)*	Date
A. Snitch	3/4/99

Date copy given to person interviewed
3/4/99

Form **4180** (Rev. 2-93)   Page 8   *U.S. Government Printing Office: 1997 - 417-702/74814

SAMPLE 16
FORM 4181 (QUESTIONNAIRE RELATING TO FEDERAL TRUST FUND TAX MATTERS OF EMPLOYER)

Form **4181** (November 1989)	Department of the Treasury - Internal Revenue Service
	Questionnaire Relating To Federal Trust Fund Tax Matters Of Employer

Note: If you do not know the answer to a question, please write "unknown." Continue answers on the back of this form, if necessary, and number them to correspond to the question being answered.

1. Name and address of corporation	2. Your name, address, and social security number
ABC, Inc. 10 South Federal # A-100 Denver, CO 80011	Caitlin Estill 123 Main Street Denver, CO 80111

3. Date of employment by corporation named *(Give beginning and ending dates, using month, day, and year)*	4. My job title or position
June 1, 2001	Administrative Assistant

5. The business was operated by the following individuals *(Give full name and job title, if known)*

a. Jake Bates, President

b. Nick Bates, Secretary/Treasurer

c.

d.

6. The payroll records were maintained by the following person(s)	7. I was paid by *(circle answer)*
Nick Bates	(check) cash other *(specify)* _____

8. The person(s) who directed me in my duties was	9. I received my pay from *(name)*
Nick Bates	Nick Bates

10. When a problem arose regarding payments of bills or debts of the business, I referred the matter to or contacted *(name)*	11. Payment of the obligations of the business was authorized by *(name)*
Nick Bates	Nick Bates

I have read the foregoing questions and answers. I fully understand this questionnaire, and it is true, accurate, and complete to the best of my knowledge and belief. I made the corrections shown and placed my initials opposite each. I made this statement freely and voluntarily, without any threats or promise of reward.

Signature Caitlin Estill   Date 11-11-02

Continue answers in this space. Number answers to correspond to question being answered.

U.S. Government Printing Office: 1990-717-016/03605

(a) What are your duties and responsibilities with the company that now owes past-due employment taxes?

(b) What is your job title and responsibilities?

(c) What are the names of the officers, directors, and/or managers of the company?

(d) Who are the persons responsible for making financial decisions for the company, including who was paid and when?

(e) What types of meetings does the company hold relating to financial matters, including taxes?

(f) Who is the person responsible for preparing and filing income and employment tax returns, along with preparing the accounting books and records?

(g) Who is or are the person or persons responsible for hiring and firing employees, along with seeing that all employees were paid?

(h) Who had access to the company's checking and other financial accounts?

The person being interviewed may also attach a statement to the interview form explaining anything that he or she believes to be important.

Rather than agreeing to a formal interview, I recommend that you offer to fill out the Form 4180 and submit it to the revenue officer at a later date. By handling the interview this way, you can complete the form in familiar surroundings (such as your office or home) and can consult with a tax professional, if necessary, before submitting the document to the IRS. You will also have time to locate records to support your position concerning willfulness or responsibility. However, many revenue officers will not agree to this procedure but will insist on a live interview. Whatever the circumstances, be sure to thoroughly review the Form 4180 before signing it. If there are errors on the form, you should refuse to sign it until the errors are corrected. After this form is submitted and reviewed, the revenue officer will make a determination as to whether or not the penalty will be asserted.

If the revenue officer decides to assert the penalty, IRC §6672(b) requires that the IRS give you at least 60 days' written notice before the penalty can be assessed and any collection efforts initiated. The notice can either be personally delivered or sent to your last known address. If you disagree with the notice, you can appeal the trust fund recovery penalty to the appeals office. Sample 17 is an example of a trust fund recovery penalty appeal letter.

TRUST FUND RECOVERY PENALTY APPEAL LETTER

June 16, 20—

Internal Revenue Service
ATTN: Alan Capone, Revenue Officer
1075 South Yukon Street
Lakewood, CO 80226

Dear Mr. Capone:

Re: XYZ Corporation Inc., EIN: 11-1112223

Herman H. Munster, SSN: 123-45-6789

This is formal notification to you that the above-referenced taxpayer hereby appeals the proposed assessment of a trust fund recovery penalty for the tax periods 9609, 9612, 9703, 9706, and 9709. The letter proposing the assessment of this penalty was dated May 10, 20—, and the 60-day appeal period expires on July 10, 20—. In support of this appeal I submit the following:

Taxpayer information:

XYZ Corporation Inc.
11 North 43 Street
Denver, CO 80203
EIN: 11-1112223

Person alleged to be responsible:

Herman H. Munster
1313 Mockingbird Lane
Denver, CO 80222
SSN: 123-45-6789

The taxpayer hereby formally requests an appellate conference in reference to this protest.

Date and number of the letter:

May 10, 20—
Letter 1153 (DO)

SAMPLE 17 — CONTINUED

Tax periods involved:

9609, 9612, 9703, 9706, and 9709

Issues the taxpayer disagrees with:

The taxpayer respectfully disagrees with the assertion that he was in any way responsible or willful in the nonpayment of trust fund taxes with respect to XYZ Corporation, Inc., and the tax periods stated above.

Legal arguments relied upon:

Internal Revenue Code (IRC) Section 6672 requires that the taxpayer be both a responsible party and willful in the nonpayment of trust fund taxes before the penalty will apply. As one court has stated, "the key to liability under Section 6672 is control of finances within the employer corporation: the power to control the decision-making process by which the employer corporation allocates funds to other creditors in preference to its withholding tax obligations." (*Haffa v. United States*, 516 F.2d 931, 936 7th Cir. 1974)

I. Responsibility

A "responsible" person is one who is required to collect, truthfully account for, or pay over any employment tax due to the Internal Revenue Service. *United States v. Carrigan*, 31 F.3d 130, 133 (3d Cir. 1994). A "responsible" individual is one who also has significant decision-making authority over a corporation's tax or other financial matters. *Barton v. United States*, 988 F.2d 58, 59 (8th Cir. 1993); *United States v. Vespe*, 868 F.2d 1328, 1332 (3d Cir. 1989). As *Barton* indicated, simply having the authority to sign checks and/or prepare tax returns is not enough. *Barton*, 988 F.2d at 59; see also *Matter of Elms*, 156 B.R. 519 (E.D. La. 1993) (the "mechanical duties" of compiling wage information, generating reports, and cutting paychecks are not enough to determine responsibility under IRC §6672; *Fiaturuolo v. United States*, 8 F.3d 930 (2d Cir. 1993) (co-signing checks is not significant control over corporate finances). In addition, simply inquiring into an individual's title or corporate status does not demonstrate responsibility if that individual lacked taxpaying authority. *Barton*, 988 F.2d at 60; *Godfrey v. United States*, 748 F.2d 1568, 1575 (Fed. Cir. 1984).

To determine responsibility, courts have typically looked at several different factors, including the following:

   (a) Is the individual an officer or director of the corporation?

   (b) Does the individual own a substantial amount of stock in the corporation?

   (c) Does the individual manage the day-to-day operations of the business?

   (d) Does the individual have the authority to hire and/or fire employees?

SAMPLE 17 — CONTINUED

(e) Does the individual have the authority to sign company checks?

(f) Who in the corporation makes decisions with respect to the disbursements of funds and payments to creditors?

See *Barnett v. Internal Revenue Service*, 988 F.2d 1449, 1455 (5th Cir. 1993); *George v. United States*, 819 F.2d 1008, 1011 (11th Cir. 1987).

As was stated in *Barnett*, no single factor is determinative; instead, all factors must be looked at as a whole in making this determination. *Barnett*, 988 F.2d at 1455; see also *Hochstein v. United States*, 900 F.2d 543 (2d Cir. 1990), *cert. denied*, 112 S.Ct. 2967 (1991). Using these guidelines, courts have determined that several high-ranking executives of various corporations or businesses were not responsible parties under IRC §6672 for purposes of the trust fund recovery penalty. For example, a president of a corporation (*Alesheskie v. United States*, 31 F.3d 837 (9th Cir. 1994)), vice president and director (*In re Taylor*, 140 B.R. 294 (N.D. Ok. 1992)), treasurer/controller (*Heimark v. United States*, 18 Cl. Ct. 15 (1989)), and controller (*Graunke v. United States*, 711 F.Supp. 388, (N.D. Il. 1989)) were all deemed not responsible notwithstanding their corporate titles.

II. Willfulness

"Willfulness" in the failure to pay the employment trust fund taxes requires the taxpayer's failure to be "voluntary, conscious and intentional." *Domanus v. United States*, 961 F.2d 1323 (7th Cir. 1992); *Barnett v. United States*, 594 F.2d 219 (9th Cir. 1979). Often, it is a conscientious and intentional decision to prefer other creditors over the Government (Internal Revenue Service). See *Quattrone Accountants, Inc. v. Internal Revenue Service*, 895 F.2d 921, 928 (3d Cir. 1990). In general, a willful failure to pay the trust fund taxes usually results when a responsible person has knowledge of the unpaid taxes but chooses to pay the withheld amounts to some entity or person other than the Internal Revenue Service. See *Newsome v. United States*, 431 F.2d 742 (5th Cir. 1970). Simply because an individual is a "responsible" person and a stockholder or owner of a business does not equate to a finding that the failure to pay the trust fund taxes was willful. *Vespe v. United States*, 868 F.2d 1328 (3d Cir. 1989). Furthermore, mere negligence is not enough to satisfy the willfulness requirement. *Alten v. Ellin and Tucker Chartered*, 854 F. Supp. 283 (D. Del. 1994); *Cooke v. United States*, 796 F. Supp. 1298 (N.D. Cal. 1992).

Application of law to facts:

I. Responsibility

Specifically, it is the taxpayer's position that the Internal Revenue Service is improperly attempting to asses a trust fund recovery penalty against an individual who was in no way responsible for the collection, accounting for, and/or the payment of the employment taxes. Analyzing the factors set forth in *Barnett* and several other cases mentioned above reveals the following:

(a) Mr. Munster was the payroll supervisor of XYZ Corporation and made sure that all employees were paid their correct wages. In addition, Mr. Munster made sure that each employee was paid on the appropriate payday. However, he was in no way responsible for any financial matters of the corporation (this responsibility falls on the treasurer and chief financial officer, neither of whom were Mr. Munster).

(b) Mr. Munster owned no stock in the company and does not own any stock at this time.

(c) Mr. Munster did not manage the day-to-day business operations and did not supervise any employees of the corporation. Instead, Mr. Munster was an employee of the corporation himself and received compensation in the form of wages from the corporation. As such, Mr. Munster did not have the responsibility to manage the business on a day-to-day basis and was unaware of the financial conditions of the corporation.

(d) Mr. Munster had no authority to hire and/or fire employees and did not make any general or specific business decisions. As such, Mr. Munster never had any involvement with the corporation's employees other than to do his job with respect to processing the payroll.

(e) Mr. Munster did not have the authorization to sign any company checks, but instead prepared the checks for the signature of Mr. Kincaid, the corporate treasurer.

(f) Mr. Munster did not make any decisions with respect to the disbursements of funds to creditors or employees and did not negotiate any business contracts or otherwise deal with suppliers.

(g) Perhaps most importantly, Mr. Munster did not become aware that there was an employment tax problem with the corporation until he received notification from the IRS this past May.

Under these circumstances, it is difficult to understand why Mr. Munster is being treated as a responsible party with respect to the trust fund taxes at issue in this appeal. Certainly, he had no knowledge of the problem until very recently. As such, the attempt to assess a trust fund recovery penalty against Mr. Munster does not appear to be at all warranted and is inconsistent with the Internal Revenue Service's mission to collect taxes and/or penalties due and owing from "responsible" individuals. Mr. Munster was not a "responsible" individual for any of the quarters at issue in this proposed assessment.

II. Willfulness

Furthermore, Mr. Munster was not "willful" in the failure to pay the trust fund taxes. This is not a situation where Mr. Munster directed the business to pay other creditors instead of the Internal Revenue Service (he did not direct the business to pay any creditors as he did not have this authority or responsibility in his extremely limited involvement with the business's decisions). Simply put, Mr. Munster did not even know about the tax problem until well after it was too late to do anything about it. Thus, he was neither willful nor negligent regarding the trust fund taxes at issue in this case.

Conclusion:

Herman H. Munster was neither a responsible party nor willful in the nonpayment of trust fund taxes due for the periods at issue in this appeal. It is the taxpayer's position that the proposed assessment is erroneous and improper for the reasons stated above. For these reasons, it is respectfully requested that the Internal Revenue Service withdraw this proposed assessment against Herman H. Munster.

Under the penalties of perjury, I declare that I have examined the facts presented in this statement and any accompanying information, and, to the best of my knowledge and belief, they are true, correct, and complete.

Respectfully submitted,

_____

Herman H. Munster
1313 Mockingbird Lane
Denver, CO 80222

It is usually a good idea to file an appeal and assert that the revenue officer was wrong (as long as it would not be considered "frivolous" to file an appeal). Even if the appeals officer sides with the revenue officer, the appeal will buy time and delay any potential collection activity. During this period it is possible that the business or another responsible party will pay the trust fund taxes, thus eliminating the need for the IRS to collect the penalty from anyone else. Also, if the appeal is unsuccessful, you are allowed to pay the tax for one employee for one quarter (which could be a very small amount) and file suit in district court.

3. Penalty Abatement

The IRS often imposes penalties improperly, usually because the IRS employee does not understand the facts of the case, the law, or both. When this happens, it is imperative that you do not meekly accept the penalty as correct but that you fight the issue. There are three common ways to fight the IRS on the imposition of penalties:

(a) *Review the penalty prior to the penalty being assessed.* You would usually do this review with the IRS employee proposing the penalty (often a revenue agent), through the IRS Appeals Division. For a discussion of the appeals procedure, see chapter 6.

(b) *Request a penalty abatement after the penalty is assessed.* You do not have to pay the penalty to do this.

(c) *Pay the penalty and request an abatement by filing a claim for refund.*

Assuming that the IRS does not agree to the first option and remove the penalty before it is ever really asserted, you are left with the abatement process to get the penalty removed.

The abatement process is the most common way to challenge IRS penalties. Abatement requests are made after the IRS sends a notice to the taxpayer informing him or her of the penalty. Remember that some abatement requests have a strict 60-day limitation (especially if there is a Notice of Deficiency involved — discussed in chapter 15), so you should always file an abatement request as soon as you discover the existence of an inappropriate penalty. Delay may only result in more problems for you in the future.

You begin the process by submitting a Claim for Refund and Request for Abatement (using Form 843 — see Sample 18). Under IRC § §6213(b) and 6404, the IRS is permitted to abate penalties for errors that the IRS makes with respect to any tax return. On the abatement request form, you

SAMPLE 18

FORM 843 (CLAIM FOR REFUND AND REQUEST FOR ABATEMENT)

Form **843** (Rev. November 2002) Department of the Treasury Internal Revenue Service	**Claim for Refund and Request for Abatement** ► **See separate instructions.**	OMB No. 1545-0024

Use Form 843 only if your claim involves **(a)** one of the taxes shown on line 3a or **(b)** a refund or abatement of interest, penalties, or additions to tax on line 4a.

Do not use Form 843 if your claim is for –
- An overpayment of income taxes;
- A refund for nontaxable use (or sales) of fuel; or
- An overpayment of excise taxes reported on Form(s) 11-C, 720, 730, or 2290.

Type or print

Name of claimant Sara Estill	Your SSN or ITIN 123-45-6789
Address (number, street, and room or suite no.) 123 Main Street	Spouse's SSN or ITIN
City or town, state, and ZIP code Denver, CO 80001	Employer identification number (EIN) 84-1234567
Name and address shown on return if different from above	Daytime telephone number 303-555-1111

1 Period. Prepare a separate Form 843 for each tax period
From 10/1/2003 to 12/31/2003

2 Amount to be refunded or abated
$ 2,455.00

3a Type of tax, penalty, or addition to tax:
[X] Employment   [ ] Estate   [ ] Gift   [ ] Excise (see instructions)
[ ] Penalty-IRC section ►

b Type of return filed (see instructions):
[ ] 706   [ ] 709   [ ] 940   [X] 941   [ ] 943   [ ] 945   [ ] 990-PF   [ ] 4720   [ ] Other (specify)

4a Request for abatement or refund of:
[ ] Interest as a result of IRS errors or delays.
[X] A penalty or addition to tax as a result of erroneous advice from the IRS.

b Dates of payment ► 1/15/04

5 Explanation and additional claims. Explain why you believe this claim should be allowed, and show computation of tax refund or abatement of interest, penalty, or addition to tax. If you need more space, attach additional sheets.

The IRS informed me that employment tax payments were not due until 2004 when in reality they were due during the Fourth Quarter of 2003. I operate a new business and relied upon this erroneous advice. Please abate the late payment penalty and interest, along with any other penalties associated with this erroneous advice.

Signature. If you are filing Form 843 to request a refund or abatement relating to a joint return, both you and your spouse must sign the claim. Claims filed by corporations must be signed by a corporate officer authorized to sign, and the signature must be accompanied by the officer's title.

Under penalties of perjury, I declare that I have examined this claim, including accompanying schedules and statements, and, to the best of my knowledge and belief, it is true, correct, and complete.

Signature (Title, if applicable. Claims by corporations must be signed by an officer.)	Date 10/15/2004
Signature	Date

For Privacy Act and Paperwork Reduction Act Notice, see separate instructions.   (HTA)   Form **843** (Rev. 11-2002) should indicate the reasons why the penalty should be abated and attach a copy of the penalty notice along with copies of documentation to support the abatement request, if any such documents exist.

If this abatement request is denied, the IRS will send you a letter stating that you have the right to appeal the denial of the request for abatement to the appeals office. If the appeals officer also denies the penalty abatement request, your only remaining choice is to pay the penalty and underlying tax deficiency and file a claim for refund.

In all instances you should exercise your right to appeal the IRS's refusal to abate the penalties, as you really have nothing to lose by doing so. The IRS, contrary to what it may inform the public, does abate a large number of penalties every year, as Table 7 demonstrates.

In Table 7, had taxpayers not filed abatement requests in the years since 1995, the IRS would have collected more than $64 billion to which it was not entitled under the law. Penalty abatement requests do work and should be used whenever the facts permit.

TABLE 7
NUMBER OF PENALTIES ABATED IN 1995 – 2001

Year	Number of Penalties	Number Abated	Percentage Abated	Dollar Value of Abatements
1995	34,013,588	4,201,294	12.35	$5,548,044,000
1996	33,984,689	4,214,033	12.39	$5,728,833,000
1997	33,486,314	4,107,084	12.26	$5,086,070,000
1998	34,157,063	4,441,165	13.00	$4,625,910,000
1999	32,316,758	4,390,443	13.59	$9,436,765,000
2000	30,861,612	4,166,386	13.50	$10,547,834,000
2001	32,494,027	4,360,983	13.42	$6,904,276,000
2002	28,299.002	4,109,815	14.52	$9,155,868,000
2003	28,767,480	5,082,371	17,67	$8,454,335,000

3.1   Reasonable cause

The IRC lists numerous situations in which penalties may not be imposed, all of them centering on reasonable cause. Although the IRC does not define "reasonable cause," the IRS regulations indicate that reasonable cause exists if you exercised ordinary business care and prudence and were nevertheless unable to file the return or pay the tax within the prescribed time.

The IRS has accepted the following as evidence of reasonable cause:

(a) Death or serious injury/trauma in family

(b) Divorce

(c) Destruction of records (i.e., a flood, fire, or other casualty destroyed the tax records)

(d) The tax return was filed in the wrong IRS district (for a late filing penalty)

(e) The tax return was mailed on time but received late (you will need proof of the postmark to prove the date of mailing)

(f) You were away from home due to an emergency (personal, military, or business)

(g) The tax records were stolen

(h) You relied on erroneous advice from the IRS (In the instructions for the 1996 Form 1040, the IRS indicates that it will cancel any penalties it asserted if the taxpayer can demonstrate that he or she received inaccurate tax information from an IRS "tax assister." Of course, nowhere in the instructions are you told that the IRS can, and does, cancel penalties for other reasons. Interestingly, there is no mention of this "inaccurate information" penalty cancellation in the 2001 Form 1040 instructions.)

(i) You cannot get access to necessary tax records, through no fault of your own

(j) You relied on a tax professional who provided improper advice (Reliance on a tax advisor to prepare a tax return is not reasonable cause for the failure to file the return, as the duty to file a return rests solely on the taxpayer.)

(k) The tax return was mailed but never received (with proof of mailing)

> You have nothing to lose by requesting an abatement. The possible reasons for abatement are limited only by your creativity — as long as the reasons are truthful.

These reasons are not the exclusive list of "reasonable cause" excuses. That list is only limited by the creativity and imagination of the person requesting the penalty abatement. You have nothing to lose by requesting the abatement, as long as the reasons you present are truthful. (Do not lie to the IRS when making an abatement request or in any other correspondence with the IRS.) The IRS will review any requests based upon reasonable cause with the following questions in mind:

(a) Do the taxpayer's reasons explain why the penalty should not be assessed? If not, the abatement request may not be legitimate.

(b) Does the length of time between the event cited as a reason and the filing or payment date negate the event's effect? For example, if illness is the excuse used and it's been two years since the taxpayer recovered from the illness, the IRS will want to know why the illness should still be used as reasonable cause. In general, a taxpayer must file his or her tax returns as soon as the problem is resolved, whether the problem was divorce, illness, destruction of records, or anything else.

(c) Should the taxpayer have anticipated the event that caused the problem? If so, the penalty may not be abated.

(d) Was the taxpayer careless or negligent, or did the taxpayer make an honest mistake?

(e) What proof does the taxpayer have of the reasonable cause? For example, the IRS will want to see hospital bills, death certificates, police reports, insurance claims, written advice from the IRS, or a statement from a CPA before allowing the penalty abatement.

(f) Is there a prior history of problems with this taxpayer? If yes, then this penalty may not be the result of reasonable cause but instead may be due to a dislike of the IRS and its practices.

3.2 Challenge penalties

The penalties discussed in this chapter are the most common penalties in the IRS bag of weapons. Most taxpayers do not challenge penalties, often because they don't understand why the penalty was applied in the first place or how to fight it (either within or outside the IRS). In my experience, penalty issues give you one of the best chances to beat the IRS. Do not roll over and pay whenever the IRS wants to penalize you. Instead, stand up and fight back. Challenging a penalty is the only way to get it removed, as the IRS is not likely to remove a penalty on its own.

Tax Points

★ IRS penalty notices are often wrong and should be challenged whenever possible.

★ Closely examine any penalty notices you receive before you make any payments to the IRS.

★ Respond to IRS penalty notices in writing and offer the IRS an easy solution to correct the problem.

★ If the IRS accuses you of fraud, you should immediately stop talking to the IRS and seek professional assistance and advice.

★ All penalties that cannot be resolved with the IRS employee handling the penalty should be appealed to the IRS Appeals Division.

★ The IRS can and does abate (eliminate) millions of penalties every year, saving taxpayers billions of dollars in overcharged penalties and interest.

★ The IRS will not impose a penalty on you if you can demonstrate that there was reasonable cause for your conduct.

CHAPTER 11

THE IRS COLLECTION PROCESS: KEEP YOUR MONEY AND ASSETS

The art of taxation consists in so plucking the goose to obtain the largest amount of feathers with the least amount of hissing.
Jean Baptiste Colbert (1619 – 1683), French statesman

There is one difference between a tax collector and a taxidermist — the taxidermist leaves the hide.
Attributed to Mark Twain (1835 – 1910), writer and humorist

I don't suppose we will ever get to the point where people are pleased to pay taxes, but we owe it to them to see that the collection is done as efficiently as possible, as courteously as possible, and always honestly.
Lyndon Johnson, US president (1963 – 1968)

When we think of the IRS's power to collect money, we are often seized by feelings of fear and utter hopelessness. We have probably all seen the newspaper headlines: IRS SEIZES LOCAL RESIDENT'S HOME or IRS PUTS ABC COMPANY OUT OF BUSINESS. The IRS Collection Division is the dream of every private collection agency in the United States, as it has access to a great deal of private, confidential financial information and has the ability to seize assets, sometimes without first getting permission from a court.

However, while it is certainly true that IRS collection personnel, called revenue officers, have a great deal of power (they can seize assets, garnish wages and bank accounts, and generally make your life miserable), a revenue officer's power is not absolute and you do have rights. The problem with revenue officers, and with the IRS collection system in general, is that the IRS will not tell taxpayers what rights they do have and how to use these rights. Once you know what these rights are, your playing field with the revenue officer will be almost level (although the rules are always stacked against the taxpayer in the area of collections). In this chapter I discuss IRS collection procedures and, more important, what your rights are and what you can do to protect your assets from the IRS.

1. Assessments

Before the IRS may legally collect any taxes alleged to be due and owing, it must first make an assessment. A tax assessment simply means that the IRS has determined, and recorded, that you owe the IRS money for taxes now currently due.

The most common way that the IRS assesses taxes is when you file a tax return showing that taxes are owed. For example, if you file a return showing $10,000 in taxes owed and $5,000 in taxes paid for any particular year, the IRS will make an assessment of $5,000 against you.

The other common assessment technique is when the IRS determines that you owe additional taxes for a particular year, usually the result of an examination of a tax return (audit).

You may challenge any assessment made by the IRS except when the IRS simply corrects a mathematical error. (You cannot challenge assessments you made yourself when you filed a return showing a tax due, but you can amend your return by filing a form 1040X.) The methods of challenging assessments, or proposed assessments, are discussed in the Audit and Court chapters (chapters 6 and 15 respectively).

2. The IRS Collection Division

The IRS Collection Division is primarily responsible for collecting overdue taxes and getting taxpayers to file tax returns that are now past-due. The Collection Division does not conduct audits or criminal investigations. You are most likely to talk to someone in the Automated Collection System (ACS) — generally by telephone after you have received a threatening, computer-generated notice demanding payment in full — or to a revenue officer, who will take over cases that cannot be handled by the ACS and are sent to the field for investigation.

No matter what part of the Collection Division is handling a case, the goal for the IRS always remains the same: collect as much money as possible with the least amount of effort. The taxpayer's goal is exactly the opposite: make the Collection Division collect as little money as possible with the maximum amount of effort. As is usually the case when two opponents have opposing goals, there is a great deal of conflict between taxpayers and the IRS when it comes to collection issues.

2.1   The Automated Collection System

The Automated Collection System is the computer collection arm of the IRS, responsible for handling the overwhelming majority of collection cases. The ACS is set up to handle all initial telephone contacts with taxpayers and to work out arrangements to get the most amount of money into the US Treasury in the shortest amount of time possible. The ACS deals with accounts that have a relatively small balance (it won't handle an account where a taxpayer owes the IRS more than $75,000, for instance), and it attempts to resolve cases without the involvement of a revenue officer.

Avoiding revenue officer involvement should also be the goal of most taxpayers, as it is usually better for you if the case stays with the ACS. While all IRS collection efforts require you to complete a financial disclosure form (usually 433-A or 433-B), the ACS uses an abbreviated version of the Form 433-A for financial information (cleverly called a Form 433-F). A complete Form 433-A, however, will provide all information necessary for you to discuss a possible Installment Agreement or other solution with the ACS employee. (These forms and the Installment Agreement are discussed later in this chapter.)

When dealing with the ACS, it is imperative that you keep accurate written notes of each telephone call, especially remembering to get the name and employee number of the IRS employee you talk to. This information is important because it is unlikely that you will ever talk to the same person twice. Without these notes, you are at the mercy of the IRS and its notoriously inaccurate record-keeping systems.

2.1.a Notice of nonpayment of taxes due

The ACS is the part of the IRS that will send you a series of threatening notices, usually one right after the other, concerning your nonpayment of taxes due. The IRS computers have been programmed to send a series of four different notices to a taxpayer who currently owes money to the IRS.

These notices, usually sent approximately one month apart, are the series of Form 500 notices, beginning with a Reminder (Form 501), followed by an Urgent notice (Form 503) and a Final Notice (Form 504), ending with the Notice of Intent to Levy (Form 523), which is sent by certified mail. As the titles indicate, these notices get progressively more threatening.

You should take the Form 523 very seriously, as once this form has been sent, the IRS can seize your assets. While you shouldn't ignore any of these notices, you must *never* ignore the Form 523 notice.

2.1.b What can the ACS do?

The ACS can file a Federal Tax Lien, seize assets, garnish wages, and set up an Installment Agreement (these tools will be described later in the chapter). ACS employees have access to the IRS computer system, which contains information on a number of sources of assets that can be seized.

ACS employees most commonly seize bank account funds, mainly because these seizures can be done through the mail and are relatively simple from the IRS's perspective. The IRS has access to information returns (sent in by financial institutions to report interest earned) and also to bank account information from checks sent in by the taxpayer to pay the taxes due. (It is a good idea to pay the IRS with funds from one bank account only, so that it does not have information about your other accounts. You may want to close the account you use to pay your taxes if you run into collection problems with the IRS).

For the same reason, the ACS also likes to attack a taxpayer's wages, because wages are relatively easy for it to locate and garnish.

ACS employees follow the IRS procedures and file a Federal Tax Lien when the taxpayer's balance with the IRS is greater than $25,000. If you find yourself in this situation, you should try to bring the balance under $25,000 to avoid the lien.

2.1.c When should you ask for a revenue officer?

While most taxpayers will have more success dealing with the ACS than with a revenue officer, there are some situations where it is better to request that the ACS transfer the case to a revenue officer in the field. You may be getting nowhere dealing with a different person at the ACS for each telephone call, you may have special circumstance requiring discretion that is better exercised in the field, or you may simply need to slow down the

> The IRS commonly seizes bank account funds. It is a good idea to pay the IRS with funds from one bank account only, so that it does not have information about your other accounts.

collection process by using the delay associated with a transfer from the ACS to a revenue officer to buy some time to resolve the tax liability.

2.2 The revenue officer

When the public hears about the vast abuses of power within the IRS, most of the time the IRS employee responsible for the abuses is the revenue officer. The revenue officer is the IRS employee who is primarily responsible for collecting taxes and getting taxpayers to file late tax returns (to get "back in the system" as the IRS likes to put it).

No matter what the IRS claims in public relations statements or press releases, the revenue officer is taught to use whatever means are necessary to collect taxes. In most instances, this means trying to figure out what assets and sources of income the taxpayer has and how the IRS can get its hands on these potential sources of revenue. Once these two pieces of information are known, the revenue officer can begin seizing assets, garnisheeing paychecks, or using any other means to squeeze money out of the taxpayer. In short, the revenue officer is the strong arm of the IRS, and his or her power must be respected.

Congress recognized the IRS's vast powers and large-scale abuses of power when it enacted the Tax Reform Act of 1998. One of the changes that attempted to reduce the large number of abuses was the addition of IRC §6304 and of some provisions in the Fair Debt Collection Practices Act (FDCPA) being made applicable to the IRS. Before this change, the FDCPA applied only to private collection agencies. Now the following provisions apply to the IRS collection practices:

★ The IRS is not permitted to contact you at any time other than between 8:00 a.m. and 9:00 p.m.

★ The IRS cannot contact you at any place that is known or should be known to be inconvenient or unusual, except with your consent or a court order. This could include your business/work location (inconvenient), a public location (inconvenient), a church/synagogue/mosque (unusual), or any other place that meets this definition.

★ The IRS cannot contact you at your place of employment if your employer prohibits the contact.

★ The IRS cannot contact you directly if you have a representative (unless the representative consents).

★ The IRS is not permitted to harass, oppress, or abuse you in connection with any collection activities.

> In an attempt to limit the power of the IRS, Congress has made the IRS Collection Division abide by the same rules as private collection agencies.

The IRS will claim that these provisions were already in place, but the reality is that these changes should slow down or eliminate the widespread abuses that have occurred in the past.

You have other options available in the IRS collection arena, and while the revenue officer is powerful, you must always remember that you do have rights during the collection game.

First, as with any other dealings with the IRS, it is imperative that you deal honestly with the revenue officer from the very beginning. If the revenue officer ever suspects that you are trying to deceive him or her, the communications and negotiations will be over and you will be hit with every weapon available to the revenue officer. By staying in close contact with the revenue officer and being honest at all times, you have a chance to level the playing field and come out with a deal fair to both the IRS and you. You must realize that getting to the "win-win outcome" in any negotiations with a revenue officer is the name of the collection game.

When dealing with revenue officers, it is important to understand what they want and what they can do if they don't get what they want. Once you have this information, you must be willing to do whatever is necessary to satisfy the revenue officer and stay in control of the situation. Nearly every revenue officer is concurrently working on a large number of cases, but a revenue officer will not actively work any case in which the taxpayer is attempting to cooperate. The bulk of a revenue officer's time is spent on cases in which the taxpayer will not cooperate with the revenue officer.

> Try to obtain a win-win outcome in any negotiations with a revenue officer.

2.3 Basic rules

The following basic rules apply when dealing with the IRS Collection Division (I refer to revenue officers in this section, but the guidelines refer to your dealings with ACS personnel as well):

(a) *Be current with all tax return filings.* It is always better for you to be able to tell the ACS or revenue officer that all tax returns have been filed, as this eliminates the need for them to set deadlines for you to file the returns and then monitor the situation to make sure that you comply with the deadline.

(b) *Make all agreed-to payments (under an Installment Agreement) on time.* The revenue officer is trained to begin enforced collection procedures (i.e., seizure of assets) whenever the taxpayer defaults on an Installment Agreement. You never benefit when the IRS uses enforced collection measures, as you immediately lose control of the situation and will have to work extremely hard to get back the control from the revenue officer. Should you ever realize that you will not be able to make a payment on time, contact the revenue officer *before* the payment is due to warn him or her of the missed payment and work out a new payment agreement. There is no way that you can miss a payment without a revenue officer finding out about it.

(c) *Do not miss any deadlines that the IRS imposes.* While this includes making all agreed-to payments on time, it also includes providing financial information (Forms 433-A and/or B); proof of income, expenses, or assets (e.g., copies of deeds, bank statements, utility bills, mortgage statements); or any other information that the revenue officer requests on a timely basis.

(d) *Always be prepared to explain why you owe the taxes now due and why it won't happen again in the future (i.e., why the problem was a one-time problem).* I have seen many instances where taxpayers have one bad year — perhaps they go through a divorce, a death, or serious illness in the family, or some other event that can cause great financial stress — and end up owing tax as a result of this problem. This then causes them to get behind the next year as they attempt to pay off the earlier year. One year of owing taxes can lead to two years, and the snowball effect starts. Once the snowball effect comes into play, it becomes impossible for taxpayers to pay for the multiple years of tax liabilities. The revenue officer needs to understand the situation, even if he or she shows little sympathy or concern. Regardless of the appearance many revenue officers convey to the public, they are still human and will respond to the cause of the tax problems.

(e) *You should be the first to offer the IRS solutions to your tax problems.* Don't wait for the revenue officer to offer a solution. Undoubtedly, your solution will be better than the revenue officer's solution from your perspective. It may even be acceptable to the IRS without any counter offer from the IRS. You remain in control by making the first offer, and this usually makes the revenue officer's job easier (a good thing for you). All revenue officers like to hear solutions to the problem because it shows that you are serious about resolving the problems. If you are serious, the revenue officer will be serious and will usually treat you with a great deal more respect than if you had not shown any interest in resolving the problem. Most important, the revenue officer will try to work with you, and not against you, if you show a serious desire to get the tax problem straightened out.

(f) *Prepare any documents, including financial statements (Forms 433-A and/or B), at home and not in the IRS office during an interview with the revenue officer.* Most taxpayers are nervous during the interview and may tend to inflate their income and forget some of their legitimate expenses, obviously to their financial detriment. The stress imposed on you in the often-hostile environment of an IRS office means this is no place for you to make any decisions that could have long-term financial implications for you.

You will regain a great deal of control over your tax liability situation if you follow the above six rules, and this will give you the greatest likelihood of success. A taxpayer succeeds in the collection game if he or she keeps all or most of his or her assets and pays the tax liabilities on his or her own terms. Above all else, revenue officers like to see the taxpayer attempting to cooperate with them and trying to get the problems cleared up in as short a time as possible. The sooner you resolve the situation, the sooner the revenue officer can close your case (which both you and the revenue officer should want to see happen).

3. Options when Dealing with the Collection Division

There are three cardinal rules for dealing with the IRS Collection Division:

(a) *Delay collection activities for as long as possible.* By doing so, you will have as much time as possible to get the tax debt paid or to develop another strategy for keeping the IRS at bay.

(b) *Never ignore IRS collection notices.* The IRS Collection Division will not go away, and ignoring notices is a sure way to meet with IRS resistance in the future. In addition, if you ignore these notices, you face the very real possibility of being hit with enforced collection activities (such as seizures or garnishments).

(c) *Always respond in writing.* This way you can document your case for any potential future problems.

When you face a battle with the IRS Collection Division, I encourage you to first obtain IRS Publications 594 (Understanding the Collection Process) and 1660 (Collection Appeal Rights), as the price is right (both publications are free) and they both contain valuable information.

In general, you have five choices when the Collection Division handles a case:

(a) Pay the taxes owed in full immediately to get the IRS out of your life.

(b) Pay the taxes owed in full over time using an Installment Agreement.

(c) Pay a reduced amount of the total taxes owed through an Offer in Compromise with the IRS (see chapter 12).

(d) Pay nothing now and hope for the best in the future by having the account put on hold as currently not collectible (see section **5.4** below).

(e) File bankruptcy and force the IRS to discharge the tax debts or accept a payment plan through the bankruptcy court (see chapter 13).

3.1 Payment in full

Owing the IRS is worse than owing any other creditor, with the possible exception of a loan shark.

Any time you owe the IRS money, you should make every attempt to get the bill paid in full as soon as possible (assuming that you agree with the amount of the bill). Owing the IRS is worse than owing any other creditor, with the possible exception of a loan shark, as the IRS has more weapons available to it than any other creditor or private collection agency currently has: the interest rates are high, the debt is difficult to eliminate in bankruptcy, the agency can seize assets without first going to court, the collection costs are not considered (i.e., the IRS doesn't care if it costs it $5 to collect $1 of additional tax), and there is a huge in-house legal staff available to fight any battles with you that may arise.

Unfortunately for most taxpayers, payment in full, especially after the interest and penalties are added to the tax liability, is simply not an option. Most taxpayers do not have the funds available, either through savings, gifts, or borrowing, to pay for an unexpectedly large tax bill. Thus, one of the other four previously mentioned options becomes the only real choice for taxpayers in most instances.

3.2 Installment Agreements

Under the IRC §6159, the IRS can let you to pay your tax debt over a period of time if this allows the IRS to collect the greatest possible amount of tax. Therefore, the IRS usually agrees to an Installment Agreement, as long as the Installment Agreement is set up so you will pay the tax due in the shortest amount of time possible and so the monthly payment is realistic based on your overall financial situation.

In fact, the most recent Taxpayer Bill of Rights actually requires the IRS to explore the possibility of entering into an Installment Agreement any time the taxpayer is unable to immediately pay the full amount of taxes owed, especially if the total amount that you owe the IRS is not more than $10,000 (not including penalties or interest). The Tax Reform Act of 1998 now specifically requires the IRS to set up a payment plan if the following conditions are met:

★ All tax returns currently due have been filed.

★ You haven't entered into any other Installment Agreements with the IRS in the previous five taxable years.

★ You haven't failed to pay any taxes owed on previous returns.

★ You cannot pay this tax bill in full now that it's due.

★ You will be able to pay the entire balance now due within three years of making the monthly payments.

You may not be able to get an Installment Agreement set up in the following circumstances:

(a) If you owe more than $10,000

(b) If it will take more than three years to pay the tax bill in full

(c) If the IRS believes that you can immediately pay the taxes due in full

The IRS has also established a streamlined Installment Agreement program which, although at the discretion of the IRS, is nearly always approved. In order to qualify, the following must be present:

(a) The assessed tax liability is under $25,000.

(b) Full payment will be made within five years.

(c) The taxpayer pays a $43 Installment Agreement fee.

(d) The taxpayer is currently in compliance (i.e., all tax returns have been filed).

(e) The taxpayer can pay at least $25 per month to the IRS.

The reality is that most taxpayers do not want to owe the IRS (a fate nearly as bad, or possibly worse, than owing the Mafia) and would pay the IRS in full if they could.

In determining how much you should pay each month, the IRS will usually require you to pay the difference between your monthly income and expenses. To compute these amounts, you will be asked to make a complete disclosure of your financial picture to the IRS. This is done on Forms 433-A (individuals) and 433-B (businesses). These forms are discussed in detail later in this chapter.

You can certainly negotiate the amount of this monthly payment, as there are often disagreements over the amount of expenses that are allowable. For example, some revenue officers will allow you more expenses than will others. It is up to you to convince the revenue officer that the expense is both legitimate and necessary before it is allowed. It is very important to negotiate expense amounts as high as possible; you will want to be sure that enough money is available to pay for necessary expenses (food, shelter, clothing, transportation, medical bills, etc.).

It is also important that you realize most Installment Agreements are short-term solutions to what is often a long-term problem. This is generally the case unless you can afford large enough payments to eliminate the tax liabilities in one year or less. If it appears that it will take more than one year to pay off the IRS, you should use the Installment Agreement to buy time before a solution to the problem, such as an Offer in Compromise, full payment, or bankruptcy, can be realized.

In addition, simply applying for an Installment Agreement brings you several benefits, as the IRS is not legally permitted to seize your assets while they are considering your Installment Agreement request, while the payment plan is in effect, for 30 days after your payment request is denied, or for any period during which you are appealing the rejection of your payment-plan proposal.

3.2.a Requirements to get an Installment Agreement

In order for you to get an Installment Agreement, you must demonstrate that you cannot immediately pay the full amount of taxes owed, that all tax returns have been filed (to use the IRS terminology, that you are "current" on your filing requirements), and that you will file all future tax returns on time and pay them in full when filed.

The IRS may also require that you sell assets to raise money to pay part of the tax bill. For example, if you own a $15,000 automobile, you may have to sell the vehicle and buy a cheaper one, with the difference in price between the two vehicles going to the IRS to satisfy a portion of the taxes owed.

In addition, you will have to make a complete financial disclosure to the IRS, which you will have to update every 12 months or so to show any changes in your financial situation, either positive or negative, that occurred in the previous year. Once all these conditions have been met, you

> If you cannot make a payment on your Installment Agreement, always contact the IRS *before* the payment due date.

most likely will be placed on an Installment Agreement and must make sure that all monthly payments are made on time.

3.2.b Modifying an existing Installment Agreement

In many instances, after you agree to pay the IRS a certain amount per month, you discover at some point in the future that you cannot continue to pay this amount. This is often the result of a change in circumstances, such as the loss of income or an increase in some expense (such as unexpected medical bills).

When this occurs, make sure you contact the IRS *before* you miss a payment due date. If you default on the agreement, it is often difficult (and sometimes impossible) to obtain a new Installment Agreement. As long as you are honest with the IRS and explain in detail the reasons why the payment plan needs to be changed, the IRS will usually agree to the change.

If you do in fact miss a payment, the IRS will consider the Installment Agreement to be in default and will usually send you a notice indicating that a default has occurred. The IRS may also try to seize one or more of your assets or garnishee wages or bank accounts as a result of the default. Always respond immediately to any default notices and suggest to the IRS how the default can be cured. You should always ask the IRS to reinstate the Installment Agreement, which the IRS will often do at least once.

The IRS can also modify, or even cancel, an Installment Agreement on its own. It is permitted to do either of these for any of the following reasons:

★ If the IRS determines that you can pay more due to a change in your financial picture

★ If the IRS finds out that you lied or provided inaccurate information on the collection forms dealing with financial information (Forms 433-A or 433-B)

★ If the IRS believes that you are about to do something that will jeopardize the collection of the tax (e.g., selling or transferring all your assets, quitting your job, and leaving the country)

3.2.c Advantages of an Installment Agreement

IRS Installment Agreements are very valuable from the taxpayer's perspective, but you must understand the pros and cons of such agreements.

These are some of the advantages:

★ An Installment Agreement provides you with a fixed monthly payment to the IRS.

★ An Installment Agreement prevents the IRS from using any enforced collection to collect the tax debt, such as seizures and garnishments, as long as you continue to make all your payments on time. This is perhaps the most important benefit to you and the reason why many taxpayers agree to make a monthly payment to the IRS.

3.2.d Disadvantages of an Installment Agreement

Some disadvantages of an Installment Agreement include the following:

★ Interest will accrue on the tax debt even though you are making monthly payments.

★ If the payments are not high enough, you may owe the IRS more money than you owed when the Installment Agreement began. This can happen if the interest accruing on the debt is more than the monthly payments. For example, if you owe the IRS $20,000 and the interest on the tax debt is $150 per month, any payments of less than $150 per month will actually result in you owing the IRS more than $20,000 at the end of the first year of making payments (even if all payments were made on time during the year). This is sometimes referred to as negative amortization and is very common with IRS payment plans. This obviously is not a good long-term solution to the problem, as the tax debt is increasing and not decreasing over time.

★ The IRS will likely file a Federal Tax Lien against you. A Federal Tax Lien has extremely negative implications for your credit rating and may in fact make it impossible for you to borrow any funds to pay the IRS.

3.3   Payments to the IRS

Any time you make a payment to the IRS, you have the right to tell the IRS what the payment is for and where it should be applied. If you fail to do this, the IRS will apply the payment any way it wants, which under nearly all circumstances means it will be applied to the benefit of the IRS, even if it is harmful to you.

By law, the IRS applies payments in the following order:

(a) To tax, penalty, and interest, in this order, for the earliest tax period.

(b) To tax, penalty, and interest, again in this order, for each subsequent year, until the entire amount of the payment is used up.

For example, if you make a payment to the IRS in the amount of $1,000 and fail to tell the IRS how to apply the payment, the IRS will apply it first to any tax, penalty, and interest for 1998 before applying any of the $1,000 to amounts owed for 1999 or later years.

To avoid having the IRS decide where the payment should be applied, you have the legal right to designate what year and type of tax the payment should be applied to. In order to designate a payment to the IRS, I recommend sending a cover letter with the payment, stating exactly how the payment is to be applied (such as "payment for 1998 Form 1040 liability"). In addition, you must, on the memo line of the check, write in the specific designation (such as "1998 Form 1040, SSN:111-11-1111"). This way, should the IRS fail to honor your wishes, you will have a record of the designation via the canceled check and a copy of the cover letter.

It is important for you to designate most tax payments to the IRS. For strategy reasons, you are better off telling the IRS that the payments should be applied to the most recent tax year, especially if you are considering bankruptcy in the near future (where the most recent three years would not be dischargeable anyway) or if the ten-year collection statute has almost expired (the most recent year would be the last to expire).

Furthermore, you should make any payments to the IRS with a money order or check from an account that the IRS already knows about. Paying with a check from an account the IRS doesn't know you have will simply provide the IRS with another future source to levy (or seize).

> You have the legal right to designate what year and type of tax your tax payment should be applied to. Always send a cover letter with the payment, stating exactly how the payment is to be applied.

4. Collection Forms

One of the main problems average taxpayers have when dealing with the IRS Collection Division is trying to understand the forms that they are asked to sign (and trying to figure out what will happen to them after they do sign the forms). Revenue officers understand this and will often try to use these forms to their advantage (i.e., intimidating you with threats like "If you don't sign this form, I will seize your car or bank account").

In the following sections I describe some of the more common IRS forms, along with the pros and cons (from the taxpayer's perspective) of signing, or refusing to sign, each of them.

4.1 Forms 433-A and 433-B

Forms 433-A and 433-B are the IRS's most important collection of forms and are used to determine a taxpayer's complete current financial picture, whether the taxpayer is an individual (Form 433-A) or a business (Form 433-B). See Samples 19 and 20.

From your perspective, the main purpose of the financial forms is to demonstrate to the IRS that you cannot pay the full amount of tax due and that an Installment Agreement is appropriate.

When filling out either of these forms, take your time and be accurate and honest (the forms are signed under the penalties of perjury, which means that if there is any intentional omission of information or any false information, you, as the signor of the form, can be subject to a criminal investigation).

Forms 433-A and 433-B are divided into two sections. The first section concerns your assets and liabilities, while the second section deals with your monthly income and expenses. For any assets that you list on the form, you should compute the value as if the asset was to be sold at a garage sale (sometimes called the "quick sale value") or auction (sometimes called the "forced sale value"). Do not list the market value. If you or the IRS had to sell the asset quickly, the asset would not generally command fair market value (which is often defined as the amount of money that a willing seller would take from a willing buyer for some property such as a house or car, with neither the buyer nor the seller forced to engage in the sale transaction). In fact, the instructions for Form 433-A state that you should use "the amount you could sell the asset for today" as its value.

As you might expect, the value that you place on any particular asset is subject to interpretation and negotiation. The IRS has often been known to disagree with the value that a taxpayer claims an asset is worth. If the disagreement is substantial and the value of the asset is great (as with real property such as a house, condominium, or rental property, or a collectors item such as a car, coin collection, or piece of artwork), it may be necessary to get an appraisal of the property from a qualified appraiser to resolve the disagreement.

The liability portion of this section gives you an opportunity to explain what liabilities you owe to creditors other than the IRS. These liabilities often include credit card debt, student loans and other loans, judgments, and state tax liabilities. Be sure to get the current amount owed on each liability, along with the actual monthly payment you are making on each debt. The IRS will usually ask you for proof that you are really making the payment(s) on a monthly basis.

FORM 433-A (COLLECTION INFORMATION STATEMENT FOR WAGE EARNERS AND SELF-EMPLOYED INDIVIDUALS)

☆ U.S. GOVERNMENT PRINTING OFFICE 2002-717-763

IRS

Department of the Treasury
Internal Revenue Service

www.irs.gov

Form 433-A (Rev. 5-2001)
Catalog Number 20312N

Collection Information Statement for Wage Earners and Self-Employed Individuals

Complete all entry spaces with the most current data available.
Important! Write "N/A" (not applicable) in spaces that do not apply. We may require additional information to support "N/A" entries.
Failure to complete all entry spaces may result in rejection or significant delay in the resolution of your account.

Section 1
Personal Information

☒ Check this box when all spaces in Sect. 1 are filled in.

1. Full Name(s) **Sara Estill**

Street Address **111 North Third Street**
City **Denver** State **CO** Zip **80123**
County of Residence **Denver**
How long at this address? **2 years**

1a. Home Telephone (**303**) **555 1111**
Best Time To Call: **10** am **2** pm (Enter Hour)

2. Marital Status:
☐ Married   ☐ Separated
☒ Unmarried (single, divorced, widowed)

3. Your Social Security No.(SSN) **111 22 3333**   3a. Your Date of Birth (mm/dd/yyyy) **01/02/66**
4. Spouse's Social Security No. **N/A**   4a. Spouse's Date of Birth (mm/dd/yyyy) **N/A**

5. ☒ Own Home   ☐ Rent   ☐ Other (specify, i.e. share rent, live with relative) _____

6. List the dependents you can claim on your tax return: (Attach sheet if more space is needed.)

First Name	Relationship	Age	Does this person live with you?	First Name	Relationship	Age	Does this person live with you?
N/A			☐ No ☐ Yes / ☐ No ☐ Yes	**N/A**			☐ No ☐ Yes / ☐ No ☐ Yes

---

Section 2
Your Business Information

☒ Check this box when all spaces in Sect. 2 are filled in and attachments provided.

7. Are you or your spouse self-employed or operate a business? (Check "Yes" if either applies)

☐ No ☒ Yes If yes, provide the following information:
7a. Name of Business **Sara's Marketing**
7b. Street Address **111 N. Third Street**
City **Denver** State **CO** Zip **80123**

7c. Employer Identification No., if available : **N/A**
7d. Do you have employees? ☒ No ☐ Yes
7e. Do you have accounts/notes receivable? ☒ No ☐ Yes
If yes, please complete Section 8 on page 5.

ATTACHMENTS REQUIRED: Please include proof of self-employment income for the **prior 3 months** (e.g., invoices, commissions, sales records, income statement).

Section 3
Employment Information

☒ Check this box when all spaces in Sect. 3 are filled in and attachments provided.

8. Your Employer **CD Spectrum**
Street Address **PD Box 215**
City **Conifer** State **CO** Zip **80433**
Work telephone no. (**303**) **555-1212**
May we contact you at work? ☒ No ☐ Yes
8a. How long with this employer? **2 years**
8b. Occupation **Sales Associate**

9. Spouse's Employer **N/A**
Street Address _____
City _____ State _____ Zip _____
Work telephone no. (_____)
May we contact you at work? ☐ No ☐ Yes
9a. How long with this employer? _____
9b. Occupation _____

ATTACHMENTS REQUIRED: Please provide proof of gross earnings and deductions for the past 3 months from each employer (e.g., pay stubs, earnings statements). If year-to-date information is available, send only 1 such statement as long as a **minimum of 3 months** is represented.

Section 4
Other Income

☒ Check this box when all spaces in Sect. 4 are filled in and attachments provided.

10. Do you receive income from sources other than your own business or your employer? (Check all that apply.)

☐ Pension   ☐ Social Security   ☐ Other (specify, i.e. child support, alimony, rental) _____

ATTACHMENTS REQUIRED: Please provide proof of pension/social security/other income for the past 3 months from each payor, including any statements showing deductions. If year-to-date information is available, send only 1 such statement as long as a **minimum of 3 months** is represented.

Section 5 begins on page 2 → (Rev. 5-2001)

Collection Information Statement for Wage Earners and Self-Employed Individuals					Form 433-A

Name __Sara Estill__   SSN __111-22-3333__

Section 5

Banking, Investment, Cash, Credit, and Life Insurance Information

Complete all entry spaces with the most current data available.

11. CHECKING ACCOUNTS. List all checking accounts. (If you need additional space, attach a separate sheet.)

	Type of Account	Full Name of Bank, Savings & Loan, Credit Union or Financial Institution	Bank Routing No.	Bank Account No.	Current Account Balance
11a.	Checking	Name __First Bank__	80020601	3332221	$ 100 —
		Street Address __123 Main Street__			
		City/State/Zip __Denver, CO 80111__			
11b.	Checking	Name			$
		Street Address			
		City/State/Zip	11c. Total Checking Account Balances		$ 100 —

12. OTHER ACCOUNTS. List all acounts, including brokerage, savings, and money market, not listed on line 11.

	Type of Account	Full Name of Bank, Savings & Loan, Credit Union or Financial Institution	Bank Routing No.	Bank Account No.	Current Account Balance
12a.		Name			$
		Street Address			
		City/State/Zip			
12b.		Name			$
		Street Address			
		City/State/Zip	12c. Total Other Account Balances		$

ATTACHMENTS REQUIRED: Please include your current bank statements (checking, savings, money market, and brokerage accounts) for the past three months for all accounts.

13. INVESTMENTS. List all investment assets below. Include stocks, bonds, mutual funds, stock options, certificates of deposits, and retirement assets such as IRAs, Keogh, and 401(k) plans. (If you need additional space, attach a separate sheet.)

¤ Cur ent Value: Indicate the amount you could sell the asset for today.

	Name of Company	Number of Shares / Units	¤ Current Value	Loan Amount	Used as collateral on loan?	
13a.	VANGUALD	100	$ 1,000 —	$ 0	☒ No	☐ Yes
13b.					☐ No	☐ Yes
13c.					☐ No	☐ Yes
		13d. Total Investments	$ 1,000 —			

14. CASH ON HAND. Include any money that you have that is not in the bank.

14a. Total Cash on Hand $ 25 —

15. AVAILABLE CREDIT. List all lines of credit, including credit cards.

	Full Name of Credit Institution	Credit Limit	Amount Owed	Available Credit
15a.	Name __Discover Card__	1,000 —	1,000	$ 0
	Street Address __111 Main Street__			
	City/State/Zip __Denver, CO 80111__			
15b.	Name			$
	Street Address			
	City/State/Zip	15c. Total Credit Available		$ 0

Section 5 continued on page 3 →
(Rev. 5-2001)

SAMPLE 19 — CONTINUED

Collection Information Statement for Wage Earners and Self-Employed Individuals   **Form 433-A**

Name _Sara Estill_   SSN _111-22-3333_

Section 5
continued

16. LIFE INSURANCE. Do you have life insurance with a cash value?   ☒ No ☐ Yes
(Term Life insurance does not have a cash value.)
If yes:
16a. Name of Insurance Company _N/A_
16b. Policy Number(s) ....
16c. Owner of Policy ....
16d. Current Cash Value $ ....   16e. Outstanding Loan Balance $...............

Subtract "Outstanding Loan Balance" line 16e from "Current Cash Value" line 16d = 16f $ _-0-_

☒ Check this box when all spaces in Sect. 5 are filled in and attachments provided.

ATTACHMENTS REQUIRED: Please include a statement from the life insurance companies that includes type and cash/loan value amounts. If currently borrowed against, include loan amount and date of loan.

Section 6
Other Information

17. OTHER INFORMATION. Respond to the following questions related to your financial condition: (Attach sheet if you need more space.)

17a. Are there any garnishments against your wages?   ☒ No ☐ Yes
If yes, who is the creditor?...............   Date creditor obtained judgement ....   Amount of debt $...............

17b. Are there any judgments against you?   ☒ No ☐ Yes
If yes, who is the creditor?...............   Date creditor obtained judgement ....   Amount of debt $...............

17c. Are you a party in a lawsuit?   ☒ No ☐ Yes
If yes, amount of suit $...............   Possible completion date ....   Subject matter of suit ....

17d. Did you ever file bankruptcy?   ☐ No ☒ Yes
If yes, date filed _1/8/88_   Date discharged _5-1-88_

17e. In the past 10 years did you transfer any assets out of your name for less than their actual value?   ☒ No ☐ Yes
If yes, what asset? ....   Value of asset at time of transfer $...............
When was it transferred?...............   To whom was it transferred? ....

17f. Do you anticipate any increase in household income in the next two years?   ☒ No ☐ Yes
If yes, why will the income increase? ....   (Attach sheet if you need more space.)
How much will it increase? $...............

17g. Are you a beneficiary of a trust or an estate?   ☒ No ☐ Yes
If yes, name of the trust or estate...............   Anticipated amount to be received $...............
When will the amount be received? ....

☒ Check this box when all spaces in Sect. 6 are filled in.

17h. Are you a participant in a profit sharing plan?   ☒ No ☐ Yes
If yes, name of plan ....   Value in plan $...............

Section 7
Assets and Liabilities

⊐ Current Value: Indicate the amount you could sell the asset for today.

18. PURCHASED AUTOMOBILES, TRUCKS AND OTHER LICENSED ASSETS. Include boats, RV's, motorcycles, trailers, etc.
(If you need additional space, attach a separate sheet.)

Description (Year, Make, Model, Mileage)	⊐ Current Value	Current Loan Balance	Name of Lender	Purchase Date	Amount of Monthly Payment
18a. Year _1999_ Make/Model _Subaru_ Mileage _61,000_	$ _10,000_	$ _11,000_	_First Bank_	_2/1/02_	$ _302-_
18b. Year _____ Make/Model _____ Mileage _____	$	$			$
18c. Year _____ Make/Model _____ Mileage _____	$	$			$

Page 3 of 6

Section 7 continued on page 4 →
(Rev. 5-2001)

Collection Information Statement for Wage Earners and Self-Employed Individuals   **Form 433-A**

Name _Sara Eskll_   SSN _111-22-3333_

Section 7 continued

19. LEASED AUTOMOBILES, TRUCKS AND OTHER LICENSED ASSETS. Include boats, RV's, motorcycles, trailers, etc. (If you need additional space, attach a separate sheet.)

Description (Year, Make, Model)	Lease Balance	Name and Address of Lessor	Lease Date	Amount of Monthly Payment
NONE				
19a. Year				
Make/Model	$			$
19b. Year				
Make/Model	$			$

ATTACHMENTS REQUIRED: Please include your current statement from lender with monthly car payment amount and current balance of the loan for each vehicle purchased or leased.

20. REAL ESTATE. List all real estate you own. (If you need additional space, attach a separate sheet.)

◻ Current Value: Indicate the amount you could sell the asset for today.

✱ Date of Final Payment: Enter the date the loan or lease will be fully paid.

Street Address, City, State, Zip, and County	Date Purchased	Purchase Price	◻ Current Value	Loan Balance	Name of Lender or Lien Holder	Amount of Monthly Payment	✱ Date of Final Payment
20a. 111 N. Third Street Denver, CO 40123 Denver County	2/1/02	$150,000	$150,000	$140,000	First Bank	$1,025-	2/1/32
20b.		$	$	$		$	

ATTACHMENTS REQUIRED: Please include your current statement from lender with monthly payment amount and current balance for each piece of real estate owned.

21. PERSONAL ASSETS. List all Personal assets below. (If you need additional space, attach separate sheet.) *Furniture/Personal Effects* includes the total current market value of your household such as furniture and appliances. *Other Personal Assets* includes all artwork, jewelry, collections (coin/gun, etc.), antiques or other assets.

Description	◻ Current Value	Loan Balance	Name of Lender	Amount of Monthly Payment	✱ Date of Final Payment
21a. Furniture/Personal Effects	$500	$ 0		$	
Other: (List below)					
21b. Artwork	$ 0	$ 0		$	
21c. Jewelry	100	100			
21d.					
21e.					

22. BUSINESS ASSETS. List all business assets and encumbrances below, include Uniform Commercial Code (UCC) filings. (If you need additional space, attach a separate sheet.) *Tools used in Trade or Business* includes the basic tools or books used to conduct your business, excluding automobiles. *Other Business Assets* includes any other machinery, equipment, inventory or other assets.

Description	◻ Current Value	Loan Balance	Name of Lender	Amount of Monthly Payment	✱ Date of Final Payment
22a. Tools used in Trade/Business	0	0		$	
Other: (List below)					
22b. Machinery	$	$		$	
22c. Equipment – Computer	$ 5	$ 0			
22d.					
22e.					

☒ Check this box when all spaces in Sect. 7 are filled in and attachments provided.

Page 4 of 6

Section 8 begins on page 5 →
(Rev 5-2001)

Collection Information Statement for Wage Earners and Self-Employed Individuals   Form 433-A

Name _Sara Eskill_   SSN _111-22-3333_

Section 8 Accounts/ Notes Receivable	**23. ACCOUNTS/NOTES RECEIVABLE**. List all accounts separately, including contracts awarded, but not started. (If you need additional space, attach a separate sheet.)

	Description NONE	Amount Due	Date Due	Age of Account

Use only if needed.

☑ *Check this box if Section 8 not needed.*

23a. Name _____ $ _____ _____ ☐ 0 - 30 days
Street Address _____ ☐ 30 - 60 days
City/State/Zip _____ ☐ 60 - 90 days
☐ 90+ days

23b. Name _____ $ _____ _____ ☐ 0 - 30 days
Street Address _____ ☐ 30 - 60 days
City/State/Zip _____ ☐ 60 - 90 days
☐ 90+ days

23c. Name _____ $ _____ _____ ☐ 0 - 30 days
Street Address _____ ☐ 30 - 60 days
City/State/Zip _____ ☐ 60 - 90 days
☐ 90+ days

23d. Name _____ $ _____ _____ ☐ 0 - 30 days
Street Address _____ ☐ 30 - 60 days
City/State/Zip _____ ☐ 60 - 90 days
☐ 90+ days

23e. Name _____ $ _____ _____ ☐ 0 - 30 days
Street Address _____ ☐ 30 - 60 days
City/State/Zip _____ ☐ 60 - 90 days
☐ 90+ days

23f. Name _____ $ _____ _____ ☐ 0 - 30 days
Street Address _____ ☐ 30 - 60 days
City/State/Zip _____ ☐ 60 - 90 days
☐ 90+ days

23g. Name _____ $ _____ _____ ☐ 0 - 30 days
Street Address _____ ☐ 30 - 60 days
City/State/Zip _____ ☐ 60 - 90 days
☐ 90+ days

23h. Name _____ $ _____ _____ ☐ 0 - 30 days
Street Address _____ ☐ 30 - 60 days
City/State/Zip _____ ☐ 60 - 90 days
☐ 90+ days

23i. Name _____ $ _____ _____ ☐ 0 - 30 days
Street Address _____ ☐ 30 - 60 days
City/State/Zip _____ ☐ 60 - 90 days
☐ 90+ days

23j. Name _____ $ _____ _____ ☐ 0 - 30 days
Street Address _____ ☐ 30 - 60 days
City/State/Zip _____ ☐ 60 - 90 days
☐ 90+ days

23k. Name _____ $ _____ _____ ☐ 0 - 30 days
Street Address _____ ☐ 30 - 60 days
City/State/Zip _____ ☐ 60 - 90 days
☐ 90+ days

23l. Name _____ $ _____ _____ ☐ 0 - 30 days
Street Address _____ ☐ 30 - 60 days
City/State/Zip _____ ☐ 60 - 90 days
☐ 90+ days

☐ Check this box when all spaces in Sect. 8 are filled in.

Add "Amount Due" from lines 23a through 23l = 23m $ ▒▒▒▒▒

Page 5 of 6

Section 9 begins on page 6 →
(Rev. 5-2001)

Collection Information Statement for Wage Earners and Self-Employed Individuals   **Form 433-A**

Name _Sara Estil_   SSN _111-22-3333_

Section 9

Monthly Income and Expense Analysis

If only one spouse has a tax liability, but both have income, list the total household income and expenses.

Total Income

Source	Gross Monthly
24. Wages (Yourself)[1]	$ 3,200
25. Wages (Spouse)[1]	0
26. Interest - Dividends	0
27. Net Income from Business[2]	0
28. Net Rental Income[3]	0
29. Pension/Social Security (Yourself)	0
30. Pension/Social Security (Spouse)	0
31. Child Support	0
32. Alimony	0
33. Other	0
34. Total Income	$ 3,200

Total Living Expenses

Expense Items [4]	Actual Monthly
35. Food, Clothing and Misc.[5]	$ 554
36. Housing and Utilities[6]	1,250
37. Transportation[7]	450
38. Health Care	125
39. Taxes (Income and FICA)	750
40. Court ordered payments	0
41. Child/dependent care	0
42. Life insurance	0
43. Other secured debt	0
44. Other expenses	0
45. Total Living Expenses	$ 3,129

[1] **Wages, salaries, pensions, and social security:** Enter your gross monthly wages and/or salaries. Do not deduct withholding or allotments you elect to take out of your pay, such as insurance payments, credit union deductions, car payments etc.
To calculate your gross monthly wages and/or salaries:
    If paid weekly - multiply weekly gross wages by 4.3. Example: $425.89 x 4.3 = $1,831.33
    If paid bi-weekly (every 2 weeks) - multiply bi-weekly gross wages by 2.17. Example: $972.45 x 2.17 = $2,110.22
    If paid semi-monthly (twice each month) - multiply semi-monthly gross wages by 2. Example: $856.23 x 2 = $1,712.46

[2] **Net Income from Business:** Enter your monthly net business income. This is the amount you earn after you pay ordinary and necessary monthly business expenses. This figure should relate to the yearly net profit from your Form 1040 Schedule C. If it is more or less than the previous year, you should attach an explanation. If your net business income is a loss, enter "0". Do not enter a negative number.

[3] **Net Rental Income:** Enter your monthly net rental income. This is the amount you earn after you pay ordinary and necessary monthly rental expenses. If your net rental income is a loss, enter "0". Do not enter a negative number.

[4] **Expenses not generally allowed:** We generally do not allow you to claim tuition for private schools, public or private college expenses, charitable contributions, voluntary retirement contributions, payments on unsecured debts such as credit card bills, cable television and other similar expenses. However, we may allow these expenses, if you can prove that they are necessary for the health and welfare of you or your family or for the production of income.

[5] **Food, Clothing and Misc.:** Total of clothing, food, housekeeping supplies and personal care products for one month.

[6] **Housing and Utilities:** For your principal residence: Total of rent or mortgage payment. Add the average monthly expenses for the following: property taxes, home owner's or renter's insurance, maintenance, dues, fees, and utilities. Utilities include gas, electricity, water, fuel, oil, other fuels, trash collection and telephone.

[7] **Transportation:** Total of lease or purchase payments, vehicle insurance, registration fees, normal maintenance, fuel, public transportation, parking and tolls for one month.

ATTACHMENTS REQUIRED: Please include:

≠ A copy of your last Form 1040 with all Schedules.

≠ Proof of all current expenses that you paid for the past 3 months, including utilities, rent, insurance, property taxes, etc.

≠ Proof of all non-business transportation expenses (e.g., car payments, lease payments, fuel, oil, insurance, parking, registration).

≠ Proof of payments for health care, including health insurance premiums, co-payments, and other out-of-pocket expenses, for the past 3 months.

≠ Copies of any court order requiring payment and proof of such payments (e.g., cancelled checks, money orders, earning statements showing such deductions) for the past 3 months.

☐ Check this box when all spaces in Sect. 9 are filled in and attachments provided.

☐ Check if is box when all spaces in all sections are filled in and all attachments provided.

⚠ **CAUTION**

Failure to complete all entry spaces may result in rejection or significant delay in the resolution of your account.

Certification: *Under penalties of perjury, I declare that to the best of my knowledge and belief this statement of assets, liabilities, and other information is true, correct and complete.*

✎ _Sara Estil_   _____   _12/5/02_
Your Signature   Spouse's Signature   Date

Page 6 of 6

(Rev. 5-2001)

FORM 433-B (COLLECTION INFORMATION STATEMENT FOR BUSINESSES)

☆ U.S. GOVERNMENT PRINTING OFFICE: 2002-716-887

IRS Collection Information Statement for Businesses

**Department of the Treasury
Internal Revenue Service**

www.irs.gov

Form 433-B (Rev. 5-2001)
Catalog Number 16649P

Complete all entry spaces with the most current data available.
Important! Write "N/A" (not applicable) in spaces that do not apply. We may require additional information to support "N/A" entries.
Failure to complete all entry spaces may result in rejection or significant delay in the resolution of your account.

Section 1
Business Information

☑ Check this box when all spaces in Sect. 1 are filled in.

1a. Business Name _Caitlin's Consulting_
Business Street Address _111 North Main Street_
City _Denver_ State _CO_ Zip _80111_
County _Denver_
1b. Business Telephone (303) 555-1212
2a. Employer Identification No. (EIN) _84-1111111_
2b. Type of Entity (Check appropriate box below)
☐ Partnership ☐ Corporation ☑ Other _LLC_
2c. Type of Business _Sales + Consulting_

3a. Contact Name _Caitlin Estill_
3b. Contact's Business Telephone (303) 555-1212
Extension _123_
Best Time To Call _8_ am _5_ pm (Enter Hour)
3c. Contact's Home Telephone (303) 555-2121
Best Time To Call _____ am _____ pm (Enter Hour)
3d. Contact's Other Telephone (____)
Telephone Type (i.e. fax, cellular, pager)
3e. Contact's E-mail Address _caitlin@_

Section 2
Business Personnel and Contacts

☑ Check this box when all spaces in Sect. 2 are filled in.

4. PERSON RESPONSIBLE FOR DEPOSITING PAYROLL TAXES
4a. Full Name _Caitlin Estill_ Title _Manager_ Social Security Number _111 22 3333_
Home Street Address _123 First Street_ Home Telephone (303) 555-1111
City _Denver_ State _CO_ Zip _80111_ Ownership Percentage & Shares or Interest _50%_

5. PARTNERS, OFFICERS, MAJOR SHAREHOLDERS, ETC.
5a. Full Name _Caitlin Estill_ Title _Manager_ Social Security Number _111 22 3333_
Home Street Address _123 First Street_ Home Telephone (303) 555-1111
City _Denver_ State _CO_ Zip _80111_ Ownership Percentage & Shares or Interest _50%_

5b. Full Name _Sara Estill_ Title _Owner_ Social Security Number _123 45 6789_
Home Street Address _125 First Street_ Home Telephone (303) 555-2222
City _Denver_ State _CO_ Zip _80111_ Ownership Percentage & Shares or Interest _25%_

5c. Full Name _Griffin Estill_ Title _Owner_ Social Security Number _111 11 2222_
Home Street Address _127 First Street_ Home Telephone (303) 555-3333
City _Denver_ State _CO_ Zip _80111_ Ownership Percentage & Shares or Interest _25%_

5d. Full Name _____ Title _____ Social Security Number _____
Home Street Address _____ Home Telephone (____)
City _____ State _____ Zip _____ Ownership Percentage & Shares or Interest _____

Section 3
Accounts/ Notes Receivable

See page 6 for additional space, if needed.

☑ Check this box when all spaces in Sect. 3 are filled in.

6. ACCOUNTS/NOTES RECEIVABLE. List all contracts separately, including contracts awarded, but not started.

Description	Amount Due	Date Due	Age of Account
6a. Name _NONE_	$	_____	☐ 0 - 30 days ☐ 30 - 60 days ☐ 60 - 90 days ☐ 90+ days
Street Address _____			
City/State/Zip _____			
6b. Name _____	$		☐ 0 - 30 days ☐ 30 - 60 days ☐ 60 - 90 days ☐ 90+ days
Street Address _____			
City/State/Zip _____			

6a + 6b = 6c **6c** $
Amount from Page 6 + **6p**
6q. Total Accounts/ Notes Receivable = **6c + 6p = 6q** $ -0-

Page 1 of 6

Section 4 begins on page 2 →
(Rev. 5-2001)

Collection Information Statement for Businesses

Form 433-B

Business Name   Caitlin's Consulting   EIN   84-111111

Section 4	7.	OTHER FINANCIAL INFORMATION. Respond to the following business financial questions.

Other Financial Information

7a. Does this business have other business relationships (e.g. subsidiary or parent, corporation, partnership, etc.)? .... ☒ No ☐ Yes
If yes, list related EIN _____   Additional EIN _____

7b. Does anyone (e.g. officer, stockholder, partner or employees) have an outstanding loan borrowed from the business? .... ☒ No ☐ Yes
If yes, amount of loan $ _____   Date of loan _____   Current balance $_____

7c. Are there any judgments or liens against your business? .... ☒ No ☐ Yes
If yes, who is the creditor?_____   Date creditor obtained judgment/lien _____   Amount of debt $ _____

7d. Is your business a party in a lawsuit? .... ☒ No ☐ Yes
If yes, amount of suit $ _____   Possible completion date _____   Subject matter of suit_____

7e. Has your business ever filed bankruptcy? .... ☒ No ☐ Yes
If yes, date filed _____   Date discharged _____   Petition No._____

7f. In the past 10 years have you transferred any assets from your business name for less than their actual value? .... ☒ No ☐ Yes
If yes, what asset? _____   Value of asset at time of transfer $_____
When was it transferred? _____   To whom or where was it transferred?_____

7g. Do you anticipate any increase in business income (e.g. contracts bid but not yet awarded)? .... ☒ No ☐ Yes
If yes, why will the income increase? _____ .... (Attach sheet if you need additional space.)
How much will it increase? _____   When will the business income increase?_____

7h. Is your business a beneficiary of a trust, an estate or a life insurance policy? .... ☒ No ☐ Yes
If yes, name of the trust, estate or policy? _____   Anticipated amount to be received?_____
When will the amount be received? _____

☒ Check this box when all spaces in Sect. 4 are filled in.

Section 5	8.	PURCHASED AUTOMOBILES, TRUCKS AND OTHER LICENSED ASSETS. Include boats, RV's, motorcycles, trailers, etc. (If you need additional space, attach a separate sheet.)

Business Assets

☒ Current Value: Indicate the amount you could sell the asset for today.

	Description (Year, Make, Model, Mileage)	☒ Current Value	Loan Balance	Name of Lender	Purchase Date	Amount of Monthly Payment
8a.	Year NONE Make/Model Mileage	$	$			$
8b.	Year Make/Model Mileage	$	$			$
8c.	Year Make/Model Mileage	$	$			$

9. LEASED AUTOMOBILES, TRUCKS AND OTHER LICENSED ASSETS. Include boats, RV's, motorcycles, trailers, etc.
(If you need additional space, attach a separate sheet.)

	Description (Year, Make, Model)	Lease Balance	Name of Lessor	Lease Date	Amount of Monthly Payment
9a.	Year 2001 Ford Make/Model Mustang	$15,000	Ford Motor Co	2/1/01	$318-
9b.	Year Make/Model	$			$

ATTACHMENTS REQUIRED: Please include your current statement from lender with monthly car payment amount and current balance of the loan for each vehicle purchased or leased.

Page 2 of 6

Section 5 continued on page 3 →

(Rev 5-2001)

Collection Information Statement for Businesses

Form 433-B

Business Name Caitlin's Consulting   EIN 84-1111111

Section 5
continued

10. REAL ESTATE. List all real estate owned by the business. (If you need additional space, attach a separate sheet.)

¤ **Current Value:** Indicate the amount you could sell the asset for today.

✱ **Date of Final Payment:** Enter the date the loan or lease will be fully paid.

	Street Address, City, State, Zip, and County	Date Purchased	Purchase Price	¤ Current Value	Loan Balance	Name of Lender or Lien Holder	Amount of Monthly Payment	✱ Date of Final Payment
10a.	NONE							
			$	$	$		$	
10b.								
			$	$	$		$	

📎 **ATTACHMENTS REQUIRED:** Please include your current statement from lender with monthly payment amount and current balance for each piece of real estate owned.

☑ Check this box if you are attaching a depreciation schedule for machinery/ equipment in lieu of completing line 11.

11. BUSINESS ASSETS. List all business assets and encumbrances below, include Uniform Commercial Code (UCC) filings. (If you need additional space, attach a separate sheet.)   Note: If attaching a depreciation schedule, the attachment must include all of the information requested below.

	Description	¤ Current Value	Loan Balance	Name of Lender	Amount of Monthly Payment	✱ Date of Final Payment
11a.	Machinery	$	$		$	
	Equipment					
	3 Computers	$1,500	-0-			
	Printers/Fax	$1,000	-0-			
	Merchandise					
	Other Assets: (List below)					
11b.		$	$		$	
11c.						

☑ Check this box when all spaces in Sect. 5 are filled in and attachments provided.

📎 **ATTACHMENTS REQUIRED:** Please include your current statement from lender with monthly payment amount and current loan balance for assets listed which have an encumbrance.

Section 6

Investment, Banking and Cash Information

12. INVESTMENTS. List all investment assets below. Include stocks, bonds, mutual funds, stock options and certificates of deposits.

	Name of Company	Number of Shares / Units	¤ Current Value	Loan Amount	Used as collateral on loan?	
12a.	NONE		$	$	☐ No	☐ Yes
12b.					☐ No	☐ Yes
	12c. Total Investments		$ -0-			

Page 3 of 6

Section 6 continued on page 4 →
(Rev. 5-2001)

Collection Information Statement for Businesses

Form 433-B

Business Name **Caitlin's Consulting**   EIN **84-1111111**

Section 6 continued	**13. BANK ACCOUNTS.** List all checking and savings accounts. (If you need additional space, attach a separate sheet.)			

Complete all entry spaces with the most current data available.

	Type of Account	Full Name of Bank, Savings & Loan, Credit Union or Financial Institution	Bank Routing No.	Bank Account No.	Current Account Balance
13a. Checking		Name **First Bank** Street Address **112 Main Street** City/State/Zip **Denver, CO 80123**	**6662233**	**114488**	$ **350 —**
13b. Checking		Name _____ Street Address _____ City/State/Zip _____			$
13c. Savings		Name _____ Street Address _____ City/State/Zip _____	**13d. Total Bank Account Balances**		$ **350 —**

ATTACHMENTS REQUIRED: Please include your current bank statements (checking and savings) for the past three months for all accounts.

14. OTHER ACCOUNTS. List all accounts including brokerage accounts, money market, additional checking and savings accounts not listed on line #13 and any other accounts not listed in this section.

	Type of Account	Full Name of Bank, Savings & Loan, Credit Union or Financial Institution **N/A**	Bank Routing No.	Bank Account No.	Current Account Balance
14a.		Name _____ Street Address _____ City/State/Zip _____			$
14b.		Name _____ Street Address _____ City/State/Zip _____	**14c. Total Other Account Balances**		$

ATTACHMENTS REQUIRED: Please include your current bank statements (checking, savings, money market, and brokerage accounts) for the past three months for all accounts.

15. CASH ON HAND. Include any money that you have that is not in the bank.

15a. Total Cash on Hand $ **100 —**

16. AVAILABLE CREDIT. List all lines of credit, including credit cards.

Full Name of Credit Institution	Credit Limit	Amount Owed	Available Credit
16a. Name **First Bank** Street Address **112 Main Street** City/State/Zip **Denver, CO 80123**	**$5,000**	**$1,000**	$ **4,000**
16b. Name _____ Street Address _____ City/State/Zip _____		**16c. Total Credit Available**	$ **4,000 —** $

☑ Check this box when all spaces in Sect. 6 are filled in and attachments provided.

Page 4 of 6

Section 7 begins on page 5 →
(Rev. 5-2001)

SAMPLE 20 — CONTINUED

Collection Information Statement for Businesses

Form 433-B

Business Name _Caitlin's Consulting_   EIN _84-1111111_

Section 7

Monthly Income and Expenses

Complete all entry spaces with the most current data available.

17. The following information applies to income and expenses from your most recently filed Form 1120 or Form 1065.
Fiscal Year Period _1/1/02_ to _11/30/02_

18. Accounting Method Used: ☒ Cash   ☐ Accrual

The information included on lines 19 through 39 should reconcile to your business federal tax return.

Total Income		Total Expenses	
Source	Gross Monthly	Expense Items	Actual Monthly
19. Gross Receipts	$ 21,000	27. Materials Purchased [1]	$ 1,000
20. Gross Rental Income		28. Inventory Purchased [2]	0
21. Interest	0	29. Gross Wages & Salaries	$ 15,000
22. Dividends	0	30. Rent	$ 2,000
Other Income (specify in lines 23-25)		31. Supplies [3]	$ 500
23.	0	32. Utilities / Telephone [4]	$ 500
24.		33. Vehicle Gasoline / Oil	$ 1,000
25.		34. Repairs & Maintenance	$ 250
(Add lines 19 through 25)		35. Insurance	$ 250
26. TOTAL INCOME	$ 21,000 —	36. Current Taxes [5]	$ 100
		Other Expenses (include installment payments, specify in lines 37-38)	
		37.	
		38.	
		(Add lines 27 through 38)	
		39. TOTAL EXPENSES	$ 20,600

[1] **Materials Purchased:** Materials are items directly related to the production of a product or service.

[2] **Inventory Purchased:** Goods bought for resale.

[3] **Supplies:** Supplies are items used in your business that are consumed or used up within one year, this could be the cost of books, office supplies, professional instruments, etc.

[4] **Utilities:** Utilities include gas, electricity, water, fuel, oil, other fuels, trash collection and telephone.

[5] **Current Taxes:** Real estate, state and local income tax, excise, franchise, occupational, personal property, sales and the employer's portion of employment taxes.

☒ Check this box when all spaces in Sect. 7 are filled in.

☒ Check this box when all spaces in all sections are filled in and all attachments provided.

⚠ **CAUTION** *Failure to complete all entry spaces may result in rejection or significant delay in the resolution of your account.*

Certification: Under penalties of perjury, I declare that to the best of my knowledge and belief this statement of assets, liabilities, and other information is true, correct and complete.

Caitlin Estill   _Manager_
Print Name   Title

🖎 _Caitlin Estill_   _12/11/02_
Your Signature   Date

Accounts/Notes Receivable Continuation on page 6 →
(Rev. 5-2001)

Collection Information Statement for Businesses

Form 433-B

Business Name ___Caitlin's Consulting___ EIN ___84- 111111___

Section 3	ACCOUNTS/NOTES RECEIVABLE CONTINUATION PAGE. List all contracts separately, including contracts awarded, but not started. (If you need additional space, copy this page and attach to the 433-B package.)

Accounts/ Notes Receivable continued

Use only if needed.

☑ *Check this box if this page is not needed.*

	Description	Amount Due	Date Due	Age of Account
6d.	Name _____ Street Address _____ City/State/Zip _____	$		☐ 0 - 30 days ☐ 30 - 60 days ☐ 60 - 90 days ☐ 90+ days
6e.	Name _____ Street Address _____ City/State/Zip _____	$		☐ 0 - 30 days ☐ 30 - 60 days ☐ 60 - 90 days ☐ 90+ days
6f.	Name _____ Street Address _____ City/State/Zip _____	$		☐ 0 - 30 days ☐ 30 - 60 days ☐ 60 - 90 days ☐ 90+ days
6g.	Name _____ Street Address _____ City/State/Zip _____	$		☐ 0 - 30 days ☐ 30 - 60 days ☐ 60 - 90 days ☐ 90+ days
6h.	Name _____ Street Address _____ City/State/Zip _____	$		☐ 0 - 30 days ☐ 30 - 60 days ☐ 60 - 90 days ☐ 90+ days
6i.	Name _____ Street Address _____ City/State/Zip _____	$		☐ 0 - 30 days ☐ 30 - 60 days ☐ 60 - 90 days ☐ 90+ days
6j.	Name _____ Street Address _____ City/State/Zip _____	$		☐ 0 - 30 days ☐ 30 - 60 days ☐ 60 - 90 days ☐ 90+ days
6k.	Name _____ Street Address _____ City/State/Zip _____	$		☐ 0 - 30 days ☐ 30 - 60 days ☐ 60 - 90 days ☐ 90+ days
6l.	Name _____ Street Address _____ City/State/Zip _____	$		☐ 0 - 30 days ☐ 30 - 60 days ☐ 60 - 90 days ☐ 90+ days
6m.	Name _____ Street Address _____ City/State/Zip _____	$		☐ 0 - 30 days ☐ 30 - 60 days ☐ 60 - 90 days ☐ 90+ days
6n.	Name _____ Street Address _____ City/State/Zip _____	$		☐ 0 - 30 days ☐ 30 - 60 days ☐ 60 - 90 days ☐ 90+ days
6o.	Name _____ Street Address _____ City/State/Zip _____	$		☐ 0 - 30 days ☐ 30 - 60 days ☐ 60 - 90 days ☐ 90+ days

☐ Check this box when all spaces in Sect. 3 are filled in

Add lines 6d through 6o = 6p $ -0-   *(Add this amount to amount on line 6c, Section 3, page 1)*

Page 6 of 6

(Rev. 5-2001)

This section is very important because it often has a direct impact on how much money will be available every month to pay the IRS. While the IRS will allow most payments to creditors, it does not permit taxpayers to pay more than the minimum monthly payment to any unsecured creditors (such as credit cards).

While most parts of Form 433-A or B are self-explanatory, be extremely careful when filling out the monthly income and expense sections. Many taxpayers seem to take an optimistic view of their income (and thus overstate it), while at the same time forgetting some monthly expenses (and thus understating the expense section). In these instances, the taxpayer will be left with an Installment Agreement that is not realistic, leading to an eventual default and many more problems with the IRS. It is much more beneficial for you to accurately state all income and expenses to come up with a realistic amount to be paid to the IRS on a monthly basis. It is always better to agree to pay the smallest amount possible so you won't default the agreement, as you can always pay an additional amount each month you are financially able to do so (the IRS will gladly take more money from you but will not be happy with less money than you agreed to pay). It is important to remember that the interest continues to accrue so there is most definitely an incentive to pay off the IRS in the shortest amount of time possible without having to default on your payment plan.

In most instances, the IRS will allow all expenses that are both reasonable and necessary. However, it will not permit you to claim $500 per month in entertainment expenses (even if this amount is truthful), as these expenses are not necessary. Instead, the IRS will demand that you forego an afternoon at a football game or a night at the opera so that you can pay more money to the IRS to be applied to the tax debt.

Often the IRS and the taxpayer will argue about what is a "necessary" expense. The Internal Revenue Manual provides guidance on what is an allowable expense. In general, these expenses include the following:

(a) Expenses that permit you to continue working or running a business

(b) Basic necessities, such as food, clothing, and the like, to be computed based upon current national standards (averages) for these expenses (As of this writing, the IRS bases the amounts allowed for food, clothing, personal care products, housekeeping supplies, and miscellaneous expenses on the size of the taxpayer's family and the current monthly income, as shown in Table 8. You should obtain a copy of the current monthly standards from the IRS before submitting any financial statements to the IRS.)

> When listing your assets on an IRS form, compute the value as if the asset was to be sold at a garage sale (the "quick sale value") or auction (the "forced sale value"). Do not list the market value.

(c) Transportation expenses (within limits, as the IRS will not permit you to own a Rolls Royce if you cannot pay the taxes you owe)

(d) Current tax payments (including state tax payments)

(e) Secured expenses (usually loans, secured credit cards, or judgments)

(f) Insurance

(g) Alimony, child support, or other court-ordered payments (if you can prove that the payments are really being made)

(h) Minimum payments on unsecured debts (usually credit cards)

TABLE 8
MONTHLY EXPENSES ALLOWED BY THE IRS

Monthly Income	Number of Persons in Household				
	1	2	3	4	Over 4
Less than $833	$367	$599	$732	$859	+$132
$833 – $1,249	420	606	774	934	+143
$1,250 – $1,666	456	651	801	942	+153
$1,667 – $2,499	513	727	838	947	+164
$2,500 – $3,333	619	801	905	985	+174
$3,334 – $4,166	689	904	1030	1,202	+185
$4,167 – $5,834	722	1005	1,085	1,257	+196
Over $5,834	976	1,271	1,407	1,561	+206

The "Over 4" column applies to families comprising more than four individuals. The amounts listed in this column are added for each individual over four in the family. For example, if a household has an income of $2,000 per month and there are six people in the household, the National Standards expenses would be $1,279 ($830+$166+$166).

If you decide to provide the financial information (often the only way to get an Installment Agreement and avoid enforced collection), it is important that you make a complete financial disclosure. If the IRS determines that assets or sources of income were omitted, whether intentionally or otherwise, the revenue officer typically has four options:

(a) The revenue officer can immediately seize your assets or wages.

(b) He or she can summons you to appear before the IRS to provide the correct information.

(c) He or she can make a criminal referral to the IRS Criminal Investigation Division for lying to the IRS.

(d) The revenue officer can do nothing.

Unless the revenue officer is inexperienced, overwhelmed with a large caseload, or simply not doing his or her job, the last option will not be used. And from your perspective, none of the first three options are very attractive. The moral is: if you are going to submit financial information to the IRS, make sure that it is accurate to the very best of your ability.

In order to have the best chance at complete accuracy, *do not*, under any circumstances, fill out financial forms at an IRS office (even if an revenue officer wants the forms to be filled in there). As mentioned earlier, taxpayers consistently omit important information concerning assets, liabilities, income, and expenses due to the pressure and stress associated with being at an uncomfortable IRS office. Instead, fill out all forms at home or wherever your financial records are located, as the surroundings will be more comfortable and you will be much less likely to make any major mistakes.

After the IRS receives the financial information and completes its investigation, it will generally do one of the following:

(a) Require full payment (if there are enough assets or you possess the ability to borrow funds to cover the tax liability)

(b) Consider the account currently not collectible (if you have no available funds to pay the IRS)

(c) Set up an Installment Agreement at a monthly payment amount agreeable to both you and the IRS

(d) File a Notice of Federal Tax Lien

(e) Suggest that you consider filing an Offer in Compromise with the IRS (discussed in detail in the next chapter)

(f) Begin enforced collection — seizures or garnishment (the revenue officer will use this option only if he or she believes you were not truthful in filling out the financial forms)

4.1.a Advantages of using Forms 433-A and B

Forms 433-A and B are necessary if you wish to have the revenue officer work with you to resolve the tax liability, either by having the account placed in an uncollectible status, to obtain an Installment Agreement, or to work an Offer in Compromise. It is reasonable to expect that the IRS must have an accurate picture of your overall financial status prior to figuring out a way to resolve the tax controversy. If you do not want to reach some type of an agreement with the IRS concerning your tax liability, you should never provide the IRS with either of these financial forms.

4.1.b Disadvantages of using Forms 433-A and B

The forms are an invasion of your privacy, as they disclose a great deal of financial information to the revenue officer and the IRS. Specifically, these forms give the IRS a complete listing of your assets, which it may use at a future date to seize the assets (should you stop cooperating with the IRS). As well, the IRS will know about all your sources of income, such as wages, interest, and dividends. It is generally not a good idea for the IRS to know how you are making money when you owe the IRS money.

4.2 Form 870

Form 870 (see Sample 8) is used to obtain a waiver of the restrictions on the assessment and collection of tax. Simply put, the IRS uses this form to assess an agreed tax liability against a taxpayer without having to issue a Notice of Deficiency (commonly called a 90-day letter). Although the form is usually completed and used by the Examination Division, I have included it in this chapter because it really relates to the collection of taxes and not to audits. When you sign this form, the IRS must bill (assess) the tax deficiency against you within 30 days from when you signed the form. No additional interest will accrue if you pay the full amount owed within 10 days of receiving the demand for payment.

For example, if you signed a Form 870 on January 2, 2002, additional interest would not accrue until after February 1, 2002 (30 days later). If the IRS demanded payment from you on March 1, 2002, you would have until March 11, 2002, to pay the full amount without any additional interest being due. If you don't pay the full amount of tax due, interest will begin to accrue as of March 1, 2002.

4.2.a Advantages of using a Form 870

Signing Form 870 stops the accrual of interest if the taxpayer can pay in full within ten days of the date of the IRS demand letter. Obviously you will benefit immensely because the interest due on the tax liability is kept as low as possible.

4.2.b Disadvantages of using a Form 870

You have no opportunity to challenge the IRS in tax court with a petition of the Notice of Deficiency. This is not a negative factor if you would not have challenged the IRS anyway (remember, the IRS is not always wrong!).

4.3   Form 900

By signing a Form 900 (Extension of Statute of Limitations), you agree to extend the statute of limitations to collect a tax that you owe. A statute of limitations is simply the period of time that the IRS has to do something before the law will not permit the IRS to do anything further. For collecting a tax obligation, IRC §6502 states that the IRS has ten years from the date that the tax is assessed to collect any taxes from the taxpayer. What Form 900 does is extend the statute of limitations beyond the ten years that the IRS has to legally collect the tax.

Be certain that you understand what this form actually does before you consider signing it, as it has some very serious ramifications. If you refuse to sign this form, the IRS may not be able to do anything to you in retaliation (i.e., the IRS cannot seize assets if you have no assets to seize and cannot garnishee any wages if you are not currently employed). In addition, the IRS cannot force you to sign the extension request to avoid any levies or property seizures. In most cases, extending the time for the IRS to collect an old tax debt serves no real purpose for you.

Congress made an important change to the ten-year collection statute in the Tax Reform Act of 1998. Specifically, it told the IRS that after December 31, 1999, it no longer has the authority to request an extension of the statute from taxpayers. Any extensions of the collection statute of limitations already in place on this date will automatically expire on December 31, 2002. Of course, there is one major exception to this change, and this involves Installment Agreements. Congress has given the IRS the authority to seek an extension from the taxpayer whenever there is a payment plan in place and for which the full tax liability will not be paid in full within the ten-year collection period. However, the IRS employee must inform taxpayers that they may refuse to sign this extension request.

4.3.a Advantages of using a Form 900

It is rarely beneficial for you to sign a Form 900 to extend the collection period. However, signing this form may prevent an immediate seizure of real or personal property that you own (the IRS is more likely to seize property as the ten-year statute of limitations draws near). If the IRS is ready to seize any property, you should try to work with the revenue officer to prevent the seizure without agreeing to extend the period of time to collect the taxes.

4.3.b Disadvantages of using a Form 900

Why would you want to give a creditor more time than the law permits to collect a debt? In general, there are few legitimate situations when you would benefit from signing this form. And if you will not benefit, you should not agree to the IRS's desires.

4.4 Form 2261

Form 2261 (Collateral Agreement for Future Income — Individual) (see Sample 21) gives the IRS the right to use a portion of your future income to satisfy a past-due tax obligation. The IRS will often use this form in an Offer in Compromise situation, or in any other situation in which the taxpayer owes the IRS money and has an income that varies greatly from year to year. Some common occupations that are typically subject to a Future Income Collateral Agreement include real estate or stock brokers, actors, salespersons, or auctioneers. The IRS and the taxpayer will agree to a sliding scale to deal with the possible increases in future income, such as the following:

★ The IRS will receive 0% of any income that you earn up to $25,000 per year.

★ The IRS will receive 10% of any income that you earn between $25,001 and $50,000 per year.

★ The IRS will receive 20% of any income that you earn above $50,001 per year.

Usually the IRS will request that the agreement run for a period of five years, although this is not always the case. You are never required to sign this form, although it may be necessary in order to get the IRS to agree to something that it also is not required to do.

SAMPLE 21

FORM 2261 (COLLATERAL AGREEMENT FOR FUTURE INCOME — INDIVIDUAL)

Form **2261** (Rev. 04-95)	DEPARTMENT OF THE TREASURY — INTERNAL REVENUE SERVICE **Collateral Agreement** Future Income — Individual
Names and Address of Taxpayers Mary Moneybags 123 Main Street, Denver CO 80209	**Social Security and Employer Identification Numbers** 123-45-6789

To: Commissioner of Internal Revenue

The taxpayers identified above have submitted an offer dated __6/10/99__ in the amount of $ __5,000__ to

compromise unpaid __Form 1040__ tax liability, plus statutory additions, for the taxable periods __1995 & 1996__

The purpose of this collateral agreement (hereinafter referred to as this agreement) is to provide additional consideration for acceptance of the offer in compromise described above. It is understood and agreed:

1. That in addition to the payment of the above amount of $ __5,000__, the taxpayers will pay out of annual income for the years __2000__ to __2001__, inclusive.

   (a) Nothing on the first $ __30,000__ of annual income.

   (b) __5__ percent of annual income more than $ __30,001__ and not more than $ __50,000__ .

   (c) __10__ percent of annual income more than $ __50,001__ and not more than $ __75,000__ .

   (d) __12.5__ percent of annual income more than $ __75,001__

2. That the term annual income, as used in this agreement, means adjusted gross income as defined in section 62 of the Internal Revenue Code (except losses from sales or exchanges of property shall not be allowed), plus all nontaxable income and profits or gains from any source whatsoever (including the fair market value of gifts, bequests, devises, and inheritances), minus (a) the federal income tax paid for the year for which annual income is being computed, and (b) any payment made under the terms of the offer in compromise (Form 656), as shown in item 5, for the year in which such payment is made. Annual income shall not be reduced by any overpayments waived in item 7g, Form 656. The annual income shall not be reduced by net operating losses incurred before or after the period covered by this agreement. However, a net operating loss for any year during such period may be deducted from annual income for the following year only. It is also agreed that annual income shall include all income and gains or profits of the taxpayers, regardless of whether these amounts are community income under state law.

3. That in the event close corporations are directly or indirectly controlled or owned by the taxpayers during the existence of this agreement, the computation of annual income shall include their proportionate share of the total corporate annual income in excess of $10,000. The term corporate annual income, as used in this agreement, means the taxable income of the corporation before net operating loss deduction and special deductions (except, in computing such income, the losses from sales or exchanges of property shall not be allowed), plus all nontaxable income, minus (a) dividends paid, and (b) the federal income tax paid for the year for which annual income is being computed. For this purpose, the corporate annual income shall not be reduced by any net operating loss incurred before or after the periods covered by this agreement, but a net operating loss for any year during such period may be deducted from the corporate annual income for the following year only.

4. That the annual payment provided for in this agreement (including interest at the rate established under section 6621 of the Internal Revenue Code (compounded under Code section 6622(a)) on delinquent payments computed from the due date of such payment) shall be paid to the Internal Revenue Service, without notice, on or before the 15th day of the 4th month following the close of the calendar or fiscal year, such payments to be accompanied by a sworn statement and a copy of the taxpayers' federal income tax return. The statement shall refer to this agreement and show the computation of annual income in accordance with items 1, 2, and 3 of this agreement. If the annual income for any year covered by this agreement is insufficient to require a payment under its terms, the taxpayers shall still furnish the Internal Revenue Service a sworn statement of such income and a copy of their federal income tax return. All blocks, records, and accounts shall be open at all reasonable times for inspection by the Internal Revenue Service to verify the annual income shown in the statement. Also, the taxpayers hereby expressly consent to the disclosure to each other of the amount of their respective annual income and of all books, records, and accounts necessary to the computation of their annual income for the purpose of administering this agreement. The payment (if any), the sworn statement, and a copy of the federal income tax return shall be transmitted to:
   Address:
         IRS, Service Center, Ogden, Utah 84201

Cat. No. 18243R	*(Over)*	Form **2261** (Rev. 04-95)

5. That the aggregate amount paid under the terms of the offer in compromise and the additional amounts paid under the terms of this agreement shall not exceed an amount equivalent to the liability covered by the offer plus statutory additions that would have become due in the absence of the compromise.

6. That payments made under the terms of this agreement shall be applied first to tax and penalty, in that order, due for the earliest taxable period, then to tax and penalty, in that order, for each succeeding taxable period with no amount to be allocated to interest until the liabilities for taxes and penalties for all taxable periods sought to be compromised have been satisfied.

7. That upon notice to the taxpayers of the acceptance of the offer in compromise of the liability identified in this agreement, the taxpayers shall have no right, in the event of default in payment of any installment of principal or interest due under the terms of the offer and this agreement or in the event any other provision of this agreement is not carried out in accordance with its terms, to contest in court or otherwise the amount of the liability sought to be compromised; and that in the event of such default or noncompliance or in the event the taxpayers become the subject of any proceeding (except a proceeding under the Bankruptcy Act) whereby their affairs are placed under the control and jurisdiction of a court or other party, the United States, at the option of the Commissioner of Internal Revenue or a delegated official, may (a) proceed immediately by suit to collect the entire unpaid balance of the offer and this agreement, or (b) proceed immediately by suit to collect as liquidated damages an amount equal to the tax liability sought to be compromised, minus any payments already received under the terms of the offer and this agreement, with interest at the rate established under section 6621 of the Internal Revenue Code (compounded under Code section 6622(a)) from the date of default, or (c) disregard the amount of such offer and this agreement, apply all amounts previously paid thereunder against the amount of the liability sought to be compromised and, without further notice of any kind, assess and collect by levy or suit (the restrictions against assessment and collection being waived) the balance of such liability. In the event the taxpayers become the subject of any proceeding under the Bankruptcy Act, the offer in compromise and this agreement may be terminated. Upon such termination, the tax liability sought to be compromised, minus any payments already received under the terms of the offer and this agreement, shall become legally enforceable.

8. That the taxpayers waive the benefit of any statute of limitations applicable to the assessment and collection of the liability sought to be compromised and agree to the suspension of the running of the statutory period of limitations on assessment and collection for the period during which the offer in compromise and this agreement are pending, or the period during which any installment under the offer and this agreement remains unpaid, or any provision of this agreement is not carried out in accordance with its terms, and for 1 year thereafter.

9. That when all sums, including interest, due under the terms of the offer in compromise and this agreement, except those sums which may become due and payable under the provisions of item 1 of this agreement, have been paid in full, then and in that event only, all federal tax liens at that time securing the tax liabilities which are the subject of the offer shall be immediately released. However, if, at the time consideration is being given to the release of the federal tax liens, there are any sums due and payable under the terms of item 1, they must also be paid before the release of such liens.

This agreement shall be of no force or effect unless the offer in compromise is accepted.

Taxpayer's Signature *M. Moneybags*	Date January 8, 2000
Taxpayer's Signature	Date

I accept the waiver of statutory period of limitations for the Internal Revenue Service.

Signature and Title	Date

Cat. No. 18243R

Form **2261** (Rev. 04-95)

4.4.a Advantages of using a Form 2261

Signing Form 2261 may be a relatively small price to pay to get an Offer in Compromise accepted, especially if your income fluctuates a great deal from year to year. The IRS is aware that many taxpayers file an Offer in Compromise when their income is at a low point and earn a considerably greater income after the Offer is accepted. This may be for psychological reasons, as taxpayers generally feel better when IRS problems are resolved and they can devote more attention to earning a living.

4.4.b Disadvantages of using a Form 2261

It is generally not a good idea to give the IRS a percentage of future income, especially when the amount of the future income is unknown. Many taxpayers find that agreeing to collateral agreements lowers their incentive to earn more money, knowing the IRS will get a percentage. Their reasoning is, Why should I, in effect, work for the IRS after a certain income level is attained? You should be certain that a collateral agreement is necessary before you sign this form.

4.5 Form 2751

Form 2751 (Proposed Assessment of Trust Fund Recovery Penalty) (see Sample 22) is an agreement by the taxpayer that he or she is liable for what is known as the 100% penalty (also called the Trust Fund Recovery Penalty). This penalty is applied to business owners or other responsible individuals for their failure to withhold and pay over to the IRS the employees' share of employment taxes (FICA, Medicare, etc.). These taxes are also known as "trust fund" taxes. A complete discussion of this penalty is found in chapter 10. There are few reasons why you should sign this form, as refusing to sign it usually provides you with more options.

4.5.a Advantages of using a Form 2751

Signing a Form 2751 may provide you with more options in negotiating a resolution of the tax problems with the revenue officer. For example, the revenue officer may work out a more favorable Installment Agreement or may recommend that the IRS accept a very marginal Offer in Compromise if you sign the Form 2751.

4.5.b Disadvantages of using a Form 2751

If you sign a Form 2751 you waive your privilege of filing a claim for a penalty abatement (elimination). This is because you have agreed to the

FORM 2751 (PROPOSED ASSESSMENT OF TRUST FUND RECOVERY PENALTY)

*U.S. GPO: 1998-438-020/80044

Form **2751** (Rev. January, 1998)	Department of the Treasury–Internal Revenue Service **Proposed Assessment of Trust Fund Recovery Penalty** (Sec. 6672, Internal Revenue Code, or corresponding provisions of prior internal revenue laws)

Report of Business's Unpaid Tax Liability

Name and address of business

Mary's Laundry and Drycleaning, 600 First Avenue S., Denver CO 80228

Tax Return Form No.	Tax Period Ended	Date Return Filed	Date Tax Assessed	Identifying Number	Amount Outstanding	Penalty
941	12/31/99	1/22/00	3/15/00	84–1234567	$ 3,022.15	$ 3,022.15
					Total Penalty	$ 3,022.15

Agreement to Assessment and Collection of Trust Fund Recover Penalty

Name, address, and social security number of person responsible

Mary Moneybags, 123 Main St., Denver CO 80202   SSN: 123-45-6789

I consent to the assessment and collection of the total penalty shown, which is equal either to the amount of Federal employment taxes withheld from employees' wages or to the amount of Federal excise taxes collected from patrons or members, and which was not paid over to the Government by the business named above. I waive the 60 day restriction on notice and demand set forth in Internal Revenue Code § 6672(b) and I waive the privilege of filing a claim for abatement after assessment.

Signature of person responsible

M. Moneybags

Date 5/22/00

Part 1—This copy to be signed and returned to Internal Revenue Service

Form **2751** (Rev. 1-98) Cat. No. 21955U

legitimacy of the penalty and cannot later change your mind. The signing of this form does not, however, waive a claim for abatement based upon payments made by other responsible parties or the business. For example, if you agree to a penalty in the amount of $15,000 and the business pays $10,000 of the employment taxes owed, you would now have your penalty reduced by the $10,000 payment.

Signing this form also means you cannot appeal the proposed penalty to the IRS Appeals Office. This is a major disadvantage, as many taxpayers benefit greatly by appealing their cases. While the success rate with Appeals in the Trust Fund Recovery Penalty area is less than with audits or other appeal issues, the fact remains that most appeals officers are much more reasonable than revenue officers.

Finally, interest starts accruing immediately after the assessment is made, which is very close in time to when you sign the Form 2751. If you refuse to sign the form, the interest does not begin to run until the actual assessment is made.

5. Collection Powers

Taxpayers frequently ask, "What can the IRS do if I can't pay the taxes and don't cooperate with the IRS in paying the taxes owed?" The answer is: The IRS can do a lot. In this section I discuss the enforcement measures the IRS has available in its arsenal to obtain complete taxpayer compliance with its demands.

5.1 Summons

A summons is a formal demand from the IRS that you appear in person, with or without documents, and testify or otherwise provide information relating to certain matters that the IRS is investigating. The IRS will only use a summons when it believes that you are refusing to cooperate with an investigation it is conducting. While many IRS divisions have the authority to use a summons, the Collection Division uses summons quite often, as many taxpayers seem to stop cooperating with the IRS as soon as the IRS Collection Division wants to get into their wallets.

The IRS can also issue a summons to third parties, such as banks or other financial institutions, during the collection process when the taxpayer will not provide the financial information requested. When the IRS issues a summons to any third party (i.e., any party that is not the taxpayer in question), the IRS must inform you and give you an opportunity to object or work out an agreeable solution to the problem. In addition, as required by the Tax Reform Act of 1998, the IRS must notify you at the beginning of the collection process (or the beginning of an audit) that it may contact third parties. The IRS must keep a list of any third-party contacts and provide this list to you on a periodic basis or if you request the information. You should take advantage of this provision and request the information from the IRS every two to three months to see exactly who the IRS is discussing your tax situation with.

The Collection Division has several summons tools available to it, including Form 6637 (Collection Information Statement), which is used to obtain financial information about you. This form is almost always used when a taxpayer will not submit financial statements voluntarily. In addition, a revenue officer will use Form 6638 (Collection Summons: Income Tax Return) to obtain information when you will not voluntarily prepare a tax return that is due but has not yet been filed. However, the IRS cannot use Form 6638, or any other IRS form for that matter, to force you to file a tax return. Finally, a revenue officer will use Form 6639 (Financial Records Summons) to get financial records concerning a taxpayer from banks or other financial institutions (see Sample 23).

Always do whatever is necessary to avoid becoming involved with any IRS summons, as a summons escalates the situation to one of confrontation and not cooperation. You rarely, if ever, benefit when your relationship with the IRS becomes confrontational.

Any summons must be hand delivered and given to you directly. In order for the notification to be effective, the IRS must do one of the following:

(a) Give the summons directly to you.

(b) Leave the summons at your residence. If the summons is left with someone other than you, the person who receives the summons must be over 16 years of age.

(c) Mail the summons by certified or registered mail to your last known address. The summons cannot be sent by regular mail, as the IRS needs proof that it was actually received.

After the summons has been served, you must appear at the time and place listed in the summons and comply with the summons. If you wish to challenge the summons, there are several defenses available. You can make one of the following arguments:

(a) *The documents requested are irrelevant.* For example, if the IRS is investigating the 2002 tax year, it would generally be irrelevant to know how much you earned from wages during 2000.

(b) *The information requested is protected by the attorney-client privilege (or any other legally recognized privilege).* You are never required to give the IRS privileged information, even if the information is sought in a summons.

(c) *The material is sought for an improper purpose.* While this may seem to be difficult to prove, the IRS must have a legally recognized reason before it can request any information from you.

(d) *The production of the requested documents would violate your Fifth Amendment right against self-incrimination.* This argument would apply if you could face a potential criminal conviction as a result of providing the information to the IRS. For example, if you listed $50,000 of income on a tax return but did not disclose the source

SAMPLE 23

FORM 6639 (FINANCIAL RECORDS SUMMONS)

Financial Records

Summons

In the matter of _Sara Estill_

Internal Revenue Service *(Identify Division)* _Denver, Colorado Collection Division_

(Identify industry or area by number or name) _____ ,

Periods _1999, 2000 and 2001_

The Commissioner of Internal Revenue

To: _Nick Bates_

At: _Bank of America_
111 North Main Street, Denver, CO 80111

You are hereby summoned and required to appear before _Sam Martens_ ,
an officer of the Internal Revenue Service, to give testimony and to bring with you and to produce for examination the
following books, records, papers, and other data relating to the tax liability or for the purpose of inquiring into any offense
connected with the administration or enforcement of the internal revenue laws concerning the taxpayer identified above
for the periods shown.

**Copies of documents and records that you possess or control that concern banking matters of the taxpayer
named above, as described in the subparagraphs checked below for the periods shown:**

☒ Bank signature cards in effect of *(Entity Name)* _Sara Estill_
from _1/1/98_ to _12/31/01_

☐ Corporate resolutions in effect of *(Entity Name)* _____
from _____ to _____

☒ Bank statements of *(Entity Name)* _Sara Estill_
from _1/1/98_ to _12/31/01_

☒ *(Number)* _____ Cancelled checks issued by taxpayer for *(Entity Name)* _Sara Estill_
during each month of the period from _1/1/98_ to _12/31/01_

☒ Loan applications, agreements, and related records *(including corporate financial statements)*
submitted by, entered into by, or in effect regarding *(Entity Name)* _Sara Estill_
from _1/1/98_ to _12/31/01_

Do not write in this space

Business address and telephone number of IRS officer before whom you are to appear:
600 17th Street, Denver, CO 80202 _(303) 446.1111_

Place and time for appearance at _600 17th Street, Denver, CO 80202_

IRS

Department of the Treasury
Internal Revenue Service
www.irs.ustreas.gov

Form 6639 (Rev. 7-2000)
Catalog Number 25004I

on the _15_ day of _March_ , _2003_ at _10_ o'clock _A_ m.

Issued under authority of the Internal Revenue Code this _20_ day of _January_ , _2003_ .
(year)   (year)

Sam Martens
Signature of issuing officer

Jeff
Signature of approving officer *(if applicable)*

Revenue Officer
Title

Manager
Title

Original — to be kept by IRS

of the income, you would not have to provide the source of the income to the IRS if it was from an illegal enterprise such as gambling or prostitution.

(e) *You cannot comply because you do not possess the requested documents.* Of course, you should make sure that this is absolutely true before using this defense.

(f) *You do not understand the request because it is vague or doesn't describe the documents in enough detail.* You are never required to guess at what the IRS wants. If you do not understand the summons, the IRS should be willing to clear up any misunderstandings by issuing a new summons.

(g) *The summons request is repetitive (i.e., the documents have already been given to the IRS).* The IRS is not permitted to use the summons process to harass you.

I strongly recommended that you be represented by an experienced tax attorney during any summons proceeding, because the IRS is clearly elevating the stakes in the game. Should you ever refuse to appear or comply with a summons, the IRS will attempt to enforce the summons in district court. If you do not have a valid defense, the IRS will likely win the enforcement proceedings. After the district court enforces the summons request, any future failure to comply with the summons will result in a contempt of court proceeding. You have no hope of winning should a contempt of court proceeding be initiated.

5.2 IRS levy and seizure powers and authority

Under IRC §6331, the IRS has the right to levy (seize) property that a taxpayer owns in order to satisfy a tax liability, either in full or in part. Most of the time the IRS uses its levy power when a taxpayer refuses to cooperate or does not respond to IRS attempts to contact him or her. Many revenue officers believe that the use of a levy will "wake up" the taxpayer and will ultimately force him or her to cooperate.

However, before the IRS is permitted to levy any assets, it must first provide you with notice of its intent to levy and give you an opportunity for a hearing. Under this new IRC §6330, you have 30 days to request this hearing. The hearing is held in the Appeals Division and permits you to raise the following issues:

★ Appropriate defenses, including innocent spouse

★ Appropriateness of the collection activity

In 2000, the IRS carried out 220,000 third-party levies and 174 property seizures. In 2001, the IRS carried out 447,000 third-party levies and 225 property seizures.

★ Solutions or alternatives to use of the levy to collect the tax due and owing

If you lose your hearing with Appeals, you are permitted to challenge the IRS levy decision in the tax court or district court.

Under all circumstances, when the IRS threatens a levy, you should definitely listen. In nearly all cases, you are better off to work with the revenue officer to avoid any levies, as you lose control of the situation the minute a levy is issued. Once you lose control, you will be forced to act defensively, which is a bad negotiating position to be in with the IRS.

The IRS makes frequent use of levies on taxpayers. Third-party levies involve any seizures of the taxpayer's money or property that are in the hands of a party other than the taxpayer. The two most common types of third-party levies are seizures of a taxpayer's wages and bank accounts.

In 2000, it carried out 220,000 third-party levies and 174 property seizures (these numbers are much lower than any year from 1990 to 1999), while in 2003, the numbers jumped to 1,680,844 third-party levies and 399 property seizures. Table 9 shows IRS Collection statistics from 1997 to 2003.

TABLE 9
IRS COLLECTION STATISTICS

Types of Action	1997	1998	1999	2000	2001	2002	2003
Number of Federal Tax Liens Filed	544,000	383,000	168,000	287,517	426,166	482,509	548,683
Number of Property Seizures	10,090	2,259	161	174	234	296	399
Number of Notices of Levy issued to Third Parties	3,659,000	2,503,000	504,000	219,778	674,080	1,283,742	1,680,844

Whenever the IRS serves a levy on a bank or other third party, you should immediately contact the third party and ask that it hold the property until you can negotiate with the IRS to obtain a release of the levy. Once the IRS has the property, it is very difficult, if not impossible, to get the property back. The IRS will usually only release a levy in situations where the levy will impose a severe financial hardship on you or when the release of the levy will make it easier for the IRS to collect more money from you in the future.

5.2.a Wage levies

It is usually easy for the IRS to determine where you work, as the IRS receives copies of Forms W-2 from employers on a yearly basis (in January). In addition, you must list your employer on a Form 433-A financial statement. Once your employer is known to the IRS, the IRS can serve a Form 668-W (Wage Levy) on him or her, and the employer must honor the levy until the IRS gives notification that the levy has been released. You are permitted to claim a small amount of your wages to cover necessary living expenses, but the amounts are minimal.

Under exempt IRS rules and regulations, you can claim the following amount of exempt wages: the sum of your standard deduction plus the amount of additional deductions for personal exemptions allowable. For example, in 2003, the standard deduction was $9,500 for those taxpayers who file as joint, with a personal exemption of $3,050 per person. For a family of four, the exempt wages would be $21,700 ($9,500 + 4 x $3,050) per year, or $417,31 per week. Any income over this amount would go to the IRS to satisfy the tax debt, regardless of the financial impact on the family.

If a wage levy is issued, you should immediately contact the IRS employee who issued the levy and attempt to get the levy released. It generally takes complete cooperation with the IRS to get the levy released, as the IRS does not have to release a levy until you provide a reason for it to do so.

5.2.b Bank account levies

The IRS can serve a Form 668-A on a bank or other financial institution to obtain all the funds in any account in the bank under your name. Once the IRS serves a levy on a bank, the bank cannot pay the funds in the account to the IRS until 21 business days have passed. The 21-day period gives you time to be informed of the pending bank levy and to try to get the IRS to release the levy (especially if the funds are in a checking account and there are outstanding checks that will not be paid if the levy goes through).

A bank account levy only affects funds in the account on the day when the levy is served on the bank. It does not apply to any deposits made after the levy was served. Unfortunately, there is nothing to prevent the IRS from serving multiple levies on the same bank in an attempt to get money from your account(s). Once the IRS issues one bank levy, you should expect future levies to occur at that bank and should proceed accordingly (i.e., don't use the account any longer and/or open a new account at a new bank).

5.2.c Is any property exempt from IRS levy?

Not all property that you own is fair game to an IRS levy. Under IRC §6334(a)(1), the following property is exempt from an IRS levy:

★ Clothing and school books

★ Fuel, furniture, and personal effects (not over $6,250 in value)

★ Books and tools used in a trade or business (not over $3,125 in value. This amount, like the $6,250 for fuel, above, will increase after 2003 in an amount to match the rate of inflation.)

★ Unemployment benefits

★ Undelivered mail (which may include checks or money orders)

★ Annuity and pension payments from railroad retirement, military, and other very limited sources (most pension and other retirement accounts are not exempt from an IRS levy proceeding)

★ Workers' compensation benefits

★ Judgments for child support

★ A minimum exemption from your wages, salary, and other income, plus an additional amount for each legal dependent (discussed above)

★ Certain service-connected disability and public assistance payments

★ Assistance under the Job Training Partnership Act

★ Your principle residence, without written approval of the district director (and a district court per the changes in the Tax Reform Act of 1998) or in jeopardy situations

With respect to your personal residence, the IRS will, in very limited circumstances, try to seize your home to satisfy an unpaid tax bill. Usually the IRS will use "jeopardy" as its reason for wanting to seize your personal residence. A jeopardy situation is one in which the IRS believes that you are doing something to avoid paying the IRS, such as hiding assets or converting assets to cash before you leave the country or otherwise become difficult to locate.

If the IRS believes that collection of the tax liabilities is in jeopardy, it will move quickly to collect the taxes owed. However, the revenue officer must first obtain the approval of area counsel (the IRS's in-house legal staff) before any jeopardy levies are made.

It is hard to imagine how a jeopardy situation could arise over a personal residence. First, the IRS could simply file a Notice of Federal Tax Lien on the property and be guaranteed to receive any proceeds from the future sale of the property. Second, it is difficult to sell a personal residence quickly and without the IRS noticing and still pass good title to the buyer. There are always a few weeks at a minimum between the contract date to purchase the property and the actual closing of the sale.

Finally, the district director must approve these seizures, and, under the Tax Reform Act of 1998, the seizure must also be approved by a district court. This is a major change in the law and is extremely beneficial to taxpayers because a district court judge is much more likely to rule in the taxpayer's favor than would a district director.

If the IRS is attempting to seize your personal residence, you should immediately seek competent tax counsel to help you resolve the situation, and you should also set up a meeting with the district director or the person who approved the seizure to discuss alternatives. It is always a good idea to try to get the IRS administration to decide not to go forward with the seizure rather than relying upon the district court to deny the IRS's request to seize. The seizure of a personal residence is, of course, very serious and should be treated this way.

5.2.d How does the IRS seize property?

The US Constitution, specifically the Fourth Amendment prohibition on unreasonable searches and seizures, does not apply to IRS levies. While most law enforcement agencies need to obtain a search warrant before seizing any property, the IRS is not required to go to court before issuing a levy and seizing property. The IRS must fulfill the following requirements before it can seize property:

(a) There must have been an assessment of the tax due.

(b) It must have sent a notice of the assessment to the taxpayer.

(c) It must have demanded payment of the taxes owed.

(d) The taxpayer must have neglected or refused to pay the assessed tax within 30 days after the notice and demand were sent.

The IRS can levy property you own, whether it is in your actual possession (e.g., a car, house, boat) or in the possession of a third party (e.g., a bank account, accounts receivable, wages).

Once the IRS decides to seize property, its employees have the authority to enter your public or private premises (if the private premises are open to the public) to enforce the tax laws. However, if the IRS wants to seize your private residence, it can enter only after obtaining your permission to do so. If you request the IRS employee (usually a revenue officer) to leave, the employee must leave.

Unless you want the IRS to seize your property (or don't mind if it happens), there is generally no reason why you would permit the IRS to enter your private property. This is another instance where you should "just say no" to the IRS. If you refuse the IRS permission to enter, the IRS employee must obtain a search warrant before entering your private property.

Before using the levy process, the IRS must inform you that a levy is about to occur and must provide you with the section of the IRC that permits it to levy. The IRS must also explain the appeal rights available to you and let you know if there are any other options that would prevent the levy.

The IRS must also provide you with a Notice of Seizure (Form 2433), which describes in detail the property that is about to be seized (see Sample 24). On this form, the IRS will notify you of the property's value (based upon a "forced sale value," which is usually 10% to 25% less than its fair market value). In addition, the IRS must establish a minimum bid price for the asset to be sold at an auction sale and must provide this information to you. You should review the calculations used to determine the minimum bid price very carefully. You have a strong incentive to make sure that this number is as high as possible. If you are going to lose the asset, you might as well get the most for it, and any proceeds will be credited to your account balance with the IRS.

5.2.e What happens to seized property?

Whenever the IRS seizes any property other than cash or negotiable instruments, it is ultimately sold at a public auction sale. The taxpayer is credited with the amount of the sale proceeds, less the expenses associated with the sale. For example, if the asset brings in $10,000 at an auction and the expenses of the sale were $1,000, the taxpayer's tax liability will be reduced by $9,000 ($10,000 − $1,000).

Recent tax law changes require the IRS to release the property to you if no one at the sale (including the IRS) bids the minimum amount. If the

The IRS can only enter your private residence if you give the revenue officer permission to enter. If you say no, the revenue officer must get a search warrant before entering your private property.

FORM 2433 (NOTICE OF SEIZURE)

Department of the Treasury
Internal Revenue Service
Form **2433** (Rev. Sept. 2001)

Notice of Seizure

Name and Address
Caitlin Estill
123 Main Street
Denver, CO 80222

Under the authority in section 6331 of the Internal Revenue Code, and by virtue of a levy from the Area Director of Internal Revenue of the area shown below, I have seized the property below for nonpayment of past due internal revenue taxes.

Due from	Amount	Internal Revenue Area and Territory
Caitlin Estill	$122,333	Denver, CO

Description of property

Real Estate located at : 123 Main Street
Denver, CO 80222

Legal Description:
Lot 14, Block 1
Griffin Heights Subdivision
Denver Township
Denver, CO

	Address	Date
Signature of Revenue Officer making seizure	600 17th St, Denver CO	11-15-02
Signature of accompanying employee	600 17th St, Denver CO	11-16-02

Part 1— Taxpayer Copy   Cat. No. 21680C   www.irs.gov   Form **2433** (Rev. 9-2001)

property is sold at the sale, the IRS is required to give you an accounting of the sale proceeds (in writing). This accounting must show where the sale proceeds were applied, along with the remaining balance on the account, if any.

The Tax Reform Act of 1998 added provisions to IRC §6331 to prohibit no-equity seizures in the future. In no-equity seizures, IRS expenses associated with the seizure (including the commission to the auctioneer) exceeded the value of the property. Thus, after the sale, the taxpayer no longer had the asset but also had no reduction in the amount owed to the IRS. The IRS has used these seizures quite often in employment tax collection cases in an attempt to put the business taxpayer out of operation so that the business could not incur more tax liabilities in the future.

If you receive a notice of a levy and seizure and cannot work with the IRS to resolve the situation, you are faced with letting the sale go through and losing the asset or filing for bankruptcy and stopping the sale. The bankruptcy option is discussed in chapter 13.

5.2.f What if you disagree with the levy notice?

The IRS will, on some occasions, attempt to seize property that it is not legally authorized to seize. Thankfully, you do have rights in this area and they should be used whenever possible. Once you receive an IRS Notice of Intent to Levy, you have 30 days from the date of the notice to request an Appeals hearing. This is known as a Collection Due Process (CDP) hearing. The following is a list of some of the more common defenses or issues that you may raise at the CDP hearing:

★ You have not had an opportunity to dispute the assessed tax liability (i.e., you are not liable for some or all of the alleged tax liability).

★ You wish to discuss other collection options and have not been given a satisfactory opportunity to do so.

★ The IRS failed to follow its own legal requirements for seeking the levy (such as providing you with proper notification).

★ The IRS failed to properly assess the tax (and without a valid tax assessment there can be no collection activities).

★ The IRS failed to collect the tax before the 10-year Statute of Limitations expired.

★ The IRS is attempting to seize assets while you are paying the IRS via an Installment Agreement.

★ The IRS is attempting to seize assets while you have an Offer in Compromise pending.

★ The IRS has not considered a valid spousal defense (such as innocent or injured spouse).

★ The IRS is attempting to collect the tax liability while you are in Bankruptcy (this is a violation of the automatic stay provisions).

★ You have already paid the tax liability in full.

There are many other possible defenses available to you and you should always consider filing a request for a CDP hearing, as nearly all appeals officers are much more reasonable than are revenue officers. After your CDP hearing ends, the appeals officer will make his or her decision. If you disagree with this decision, you have 30 days after the date of the determination to file suit in the US tax court (or a US district court in some situations).

You have the right to a CDP hearing in any of the following circumstances:

★ Whenever the IRS files a Federal Tax Lien for the first time on any given tax period

★ Whenever the IRS attempts to seize a State tax refund

★ Before the IRS sends the first levy on your property for any given tax period

★ Whenever the IRS issues a jeopardy levy

In order to request a CDP hearing, you must complete Form 12153 (see Sample 25) and send it to the address listed on the lien or levy notice. This must be done within 30 days of the date shown on the notice. You should also include a copy of the lien and/or levy notice with your Form 12153.

Once the IRS receives Form 12153, it will immediately stop the collection activities until the appeal is decided. This is the good news — the bad news is that the IRS will also suspend the 10-year Statute of Limitations for collections while the appeal is pending. Fortunately, most appeals are decided relatively quickly, so this should not be a major negative factor when deciding whether or not to file the request for a CDP hearing.

If you happen to miss the 30-day deadline, all is not lost. You are still permitted to file the request late and you will still be entitled to a hearing. The penalty, however, is that you will have to live with the decision that the appeals officer makes, as you are not permitted to challenge this decision in court.

FORM 12153 (REQUEST FOR A COLLECTION DUE PROCESS HEARING)

Request for a Collection Due Process Hearing

Use this form to request a hearing with the IRS Office of Appeals only when you receive a **Notice of Federal Tax Lien Filing & Your Right To A Hearing Under IRC 6320**, a **Final Notice - Notice Of Intent to Levy & Your Notice Of a Right To A Hearing**, or a **Notice of Jeopardy Levy and Right of Appeal**. Complete this form and send it to the address shown on your lien or levy notice for expeditious handling. Include a copy of your lien or levy notice(s) to ensure proper handling of your request.

(Print) Taxpayer Name(s): Sara Estill

(Print) Address: 111 First Avenue, Denver, CO 80123

Daytime Telephone Number: 303-555-1111   Type of Tax/Tax Form Number(s): 1040

Taxable Period(s): 2000

Social Security Number/Employer Identification Number(s): 111-22-3333

Check the IRS action(s) that you do not agree with. Provide specific reasons why you don't agree. If you believe that your spouse or former spouse should be responsible for all or a portion of the tax liability from your tax return, check here [__] and attach Form 8857, Request for Innocent Spouse Relief, to this request.

_____ **Filed Notice of Federal Tax Lien (Explain why you don't agree. Use extra sheets if necessary.)**

X **Notice of Levy/Seizure (Explain why you don't agree. Use extra sheets if necessary.)**

The IRS is attempting to seize my assets while I have an offer in compromise pending. The offer was filed on October 3, 2002, with the Memphis service center and I have received a letter (copy enclosed) that the offer is being processed. The IRS is not permitted to seize my assets while I am trying to get an offer accepted.

I/we understand that the statutory period of limitations for collection is suspended during the Collection Due Process Hearing and any subsequent judicial review.

Taxpayer's or Authorized Representative's Signature and Date: Sara Estill   11-30-02

Taxpayer's or Authorized Representative's Signature and Date: _____

IRS Use Only:

IRS Employee *(Print)*: _____   IRS Received Date: _____

Employee Telephone Number: _____

Form **12153** (01-1999)   Catalog Number 26685D   Department of the Treasury – Internal Revenue Service

(Over)

In addition, the IRS has established a Collection Appeals Program (CAP) that is available under more circumstances than is the CDP hearing. The CAP procedures are available for the following:

★ *IRS tax liens.* You are permitted to appeal after the IRS files a lien and whenever the IRS denies a request to discharge, withdraw, subordinate, or nonattach the lien.

★ *IRS levies.* you are permitted to appeal after the IRS places a levy on your wages, bank accounts, or other property. You can also appeal after the IRS has actually seized your property. You must do this within 10 days of receiving the Notice of Seizure.

★ *Installment Agreements.* You can use the CAP procedures to appeal whenever the IRS denies or terminates your monthly payment plan.

In order to use the CAP procedures, you must file a Form 9423 (see Sample 26) with the IRS. You can file this form only after an IRS employee and his or her manager have refused to accept your solution to the tax problem and thus continue to assert that the IRS is proceeding correctly. Once you file the CAP appeal, the IRS will stop all collection activities until the appeal is heard. The CAP procedures are generally quite favorable to taxpayers, with one major exception: you are not permitted to challenge the appeals officer's decision in court should you disagree with it. For this reason, I would recommend using the CDP hearing procedures if you qualify, with the CAP procedures to be utilized as a back-up plan if you don't qualify.

5.2.g Collections and businesses

Business collection issues, especially if the business is still operating, receive the most serious treatment by the IRS. At the top of the list of business collection tax issues are the trust fund taxes that I discussed in chapter 10. In addition, the IRS is also concerned with compliance checks on business taxpayers for filing purposes and making sure that all tax deposits (for Form 941) are made on time.

The IRS gets involved in trust fund tax collection cases as soon as the problem appears, often after only one or two quarters have passed. The revenue officers who handle these cases are trained to be very aggressive with the business as they pursue the taxes owed. The first thing a revenue officer will do is obtain financial information (Form 433-B) from the business. The revenue officer needs this information for two reasons:

SAMPLE 26
FORM 9423 (COLLECTION APPEAL REQUEST)

Collection Appeal Request

1. Taxpayer's Name: Sara Estill	2. Representative: (Form 2848, Power of Attorney Attached) —

3. SSN/EIN: 111-22-3333	4. Taxpayer's Business Phone: 303-555-2222	5. Taxpayer's Home Phone: 303-555-3333	6. Representative's Phone: —

7. Taxpayer's Street Address
111 South Second Street

8. City: Denver	9. State: CO	10. Zip Code: 80222

11. Type of Tax (Tax Form): 1040	12. Tax Periods Being Appealed: 2000	13. Tax Due: $7,322.66

Collection Action(s) Appealed

14. Please Check the Collection Action(s) You're Appealing:

☐ Federal Tax Lien	☒ Denial of Installment Agreement
☐ Levy or Notice of Levy	☐ Termination of Installment Agreement
☐ Seizure	

Explanation

15. Please explain why you disagree with the collection action(s) you checked above and explain how you would resolve your tax problem. Attach additional pages if needed. Attach copies of any documents that you think will support your position.

The IRS has denied my proposed $200 per month installment agreement request, even though my financial forms (433) that I submitted to the IRS show this is the maximum amount that I can pay each month. The IRS will be paid in full before the collection Statute of Limitations expires in 2011 and the IRS is legally obligated to accept this payment plan as it is the only way I can pay my tax liability.

Under penalties of perjury, I declare that I have examined this request and the attached documents, and to the best of my knowledge and belief, they are true, correct and complete. A submission by a representative, other than the taxpayer, is based on all information of which preparer has any knowledge.

16. Taxpayer's or Authorized Representative's Signature: Sara Estill	17. Date: 10/28/02
18. Collection Manager's Signature:	19. Date Received:

Form **9423** (Rev. 01-1999)   Catalog Number 14169I   **(Over)**   Department of the Treasury – Internal Revenue Service

(a) To determine if the business can immediately pay the taxes owed

(b) To make sure the business is in good enough financial shape to stay in business and not continue to add to the trust fund tax liabilities

To determine if the business can immediately pay the taxes owed, the revenue officer will demand that the business sell any assets or borrow whatever is necessary to cover the tax liability in as short a period of time as is practical or reasonable. You should always consider borrowing the money to pay for the taxes, as selling assets may directly interfere with your ability to remain in business (i.e., if you have to sell computers or delivery trucks to pay the IRS, how will you conduct business in the near future?).

If the business's cash-flow situation has improved since the tax problems first appeared, you should try to negotiate a short-term Installment Agreement (less than one year) with the revenue officer so that the taxes, interest, and penalties can be paid over a relatively short period of time. Most revenue officers will agree to this only if they are convinced that the trust fund tax liabilities are a one-time problem and will not be repeated in the future. You should be prepared to explain why the trust fund tax situation occurred — and why it will not occur again — if you expect the revenue officer to grant the business a short Installment Agreement to pay for the taxes owed. Many revenue officers will agree to the Installment Agreement if the one-time problem was an unexpected business problem such as a strike or losing an important customer.

It is important that your business remain current in the payment of all taxes that come due after the delinquent taxes are owed. The IRS will never a permit a business to "pyramid" (add more quarters of taxes owed onto what is already owed) its employment tax liabilities. It does not matter how the business is organized; all corporations, partnerships, and sole proprietorships that owe trust fund tax liabilities are treated the same. However, if the business is a partnership or sole proprietorship and the Form 433-B does not demonstrate how the business will pay the taxes, the IRS will require a Form 433-A from each of the partners or owner(s). The owners of a partnership or sole proprietorship will immediately have all their personal assets exposed to the IRS for the payment of the business's past-due employment taxes. This is another reason to consider incorporating any business entity.

A revenue officer is required to examine the business's current financial situation whenever a trust fund tax situation arises. If it appears the business is solvent, the IRS will work with it to get the taxes paid as quickly as possible (and the business will cooperate so as to get the IRS out of its financial affairs as soon as possible). If it appears to the revenue officer that the business cannot pay the taxes currently owed as well as the current operating expenses of the business, the IRS will not allow it to stay in business. All of us have seen the advertisements for business property the IRS has seized: "GOING OUT OF BUSINESS: AUCTION BY ORDER OF THE IRS — ALL BUSINESS EQUIPMENT AND ASSETS MUST BE SOLD." The IRS will do what it can to seize assets and get what money it can before the inevitable bankruptcy or dissolution of the business occurs.

The Tax Reform Act of 1998 recognized the severity of IRS seizures of business assets (i.e., if the assets are seized and the business can no longer operate, many people may lose their jobs and other businesses are likely to be affected) and added additional requirements that must be met before business assets can be seized. In addition to showing the business has tax liabilities and is not able to pay them, the IRS employee wishing to seize the assets must also obtain the approval of the district director (or the assistant district director), in writing. Before the director can give this approval, he or she must first determine that the business does not have a sufficient amount of "other assets" that could be used to pay the taxes owed.

These changes make it more difficult than before for the IRS to seize business assets, but it is certainly not impossible. If you find yourself facing a seizure of business assets, I strongly advise you to set up a meeting with the revenue officer who wants to make the seizure, along with the district director (who will ultimately have to approve the seizure). It is very likely that you will be able to work out a satisfactory resolution of the collection issues at the meeting such that a seizure will not be necessary.

Finally, it is important for you to understand that the recent changes in the tax law do not apply if the IRS determines that the collection of the business tax liabilities is in "jeopardy." For instance, if the IRS learns or believes that you are going to close down your business, load all your property onto trucks, and try to escape the liability, it will immediately move to seize your assets and can do so without the district director's approval.

5.2.h Collection problems for married persons

Many married couples experience unique tax collection issues, especially when one spouse owes tax to the IRS while the other spouse does not. This situation is often the result of one spouse accumulating tax liabilities before the marriage, or during the marriage if the couple files separate tax returns.

The revenue officer is trained to resolve the tax situation in as short a time as possible and may unintentionally use enforced collection measures against a spouse who doesn't owe any tax liabilities. I have seen many instances where a revenue officer seizes assets of a nonliable spouse (including retirement plans) to satisfy the tax liability of the liable spouse. This can obviously have very serious ramifications on the marriage itself, especially if the nonliable spouse was not aware of the other spouse's tax liabilities (which is often the case).

If a married couple jointly owns property, and one spouse alone has the tax problems, the revenue officer must be made aware of this situation before instigating any enforced collection activities. The reason for this is that the US Supreme Court, in *United States v. Rogers*, ruled that if the IRS seizes and then subsequently sells jointly held property to satisfy the tax liabilities of one of the spouses alone, 50% of the sale proceeds must go to the nonliable spouse and cannot be used to pay the tax liability of the liable spouse.

For example, if the husband owes the IRS $70,000 in back tax liabilities and the wife owes nothing, the IRS could seize the $100,000 house that the couple owns together and sell it at an auction sale to pay for the husband's tax debts. However, the IRS would receive only $50,000 of the sale proceeds, as the other $50,000 must go directly to the wife (because she didn't have any outstanding tax obligations).

When only one spouse has a tax debt, a married couple should not file joint income tax returns unless the nonliable spouse doesn't mind having any refund he or she may receive applied to the outstanding tax debt. For instance, using the figures from the previous example, if the husband did not earn any income one year and the wife did, if the couple filed a joint tax return any refund that they would have received would be applied to the husband's tax debt, even though the refund was due completely to the wife's employment.

Furthermore, the recent tax reform bills have made it much easier for one spouse to request innocent spouse relief if the tax liability at issue is the result of one spouse only (i.e., the other spouse is "innocent"). Under IRC §6015(b) and (f), the innocent spouse may escape any tax liabilities if he or she was not responsible for the error which created the tax liability or if it would be unfair or inequitable to hold him or her liable for the debt.

If you are considering marrying someone with tax liabilities, consult a competent tax advisor before filing any tax returns together or holding assets jointly.

5.2.i Collection issues for divorced persons

The Tax Reform Act of 1998 has given divorced taxpayers additional weapons in collection disputes concerning tax liabilities accrued during a marriage. The act expanded the innocent spouse rules originally found in IRC §6013 (and now moved to IRC §6015 and greatly expanded) to make them more favorable to taxpayers, especially in the collection area. It is up to taxpayers to notify the IRS that they want to challenge the joint tax liabilities and have them recomputed as if they had filed separate tax returns during the marriage. In order to qualify to make this election, you must show the following:

(a) At the time of making the election, you were divorced, legally separated, or living apart for at least 12 months from the person with whom you originally filed a joint tax return

(b) You can allocate items of income between you and the person with whom you originally filed a joint return

(c) You were not aware of an understatement of tax for any of the years in which there is a joint tax liability, or that you knew about the understatement but were forced to sign the tax return under some threat or duress

This is a potentially major opportunity for all divorced taxpayers who owe money for tax liabilities accrued during a marriage. Any elections must be made within two years after the IRS begins any collection activities.

5.2.j The Fourth and Fifth Amendments and the Collection Division

Courts have consistently rejected taxpayers' arguments concerning the IRS and its violations of the US Constitution. Although it is not spelled out anywhere in the constitution, most constitutional protections for US citizens apply to all governmental agencies except the IRS. Some courts have gone so far as to say that the IRS is basically above the law because it is responsible for funding all of the government's services. Without the IRS, this so-called logic goes, the country as we now know it would cease to exist.

While many taxpayers would disagree with this position, the fact remains that you should not hope to get much mileage out of using constitutional arguments, including those based upon the Fourth or Fifth Amendments, in any tax collection case with the IRS.

The Fourth Amendment prohibits the government from using unreasonable searches and seizures against its citizens. As I previously indicated, this amendment applies to the IRS only in very limited circumstances (generally only when a taxpayer's private property that is not open to the general public is involved).

The Fifth Amendment, relating to self-incrimination, does not usually apply in the collections area. If a taxpayer does not want to disclose the information to the IRS, he or she does not have to, but by refusing to disclose complete financial or other information, the taxpayer forfeits any opportunity for meaningful negotiations with the revenue officer. Courts have indicated that the choice belongs to the taxpayer and that any disclosure is "voluntary" and not compelled, and therefore there is no self-incrimination. Taxpayers would be wise to use arguments other than those based upon the constitution when dealing with a revenue officer.

5.3   The Federal Tax Lien

A Federal Tax Lien is a notice to all creditors that the IRS has a claim against a taxpayer's property for a specific tax debt. It is applied automatically after the IRS has made a tax assessment for which the taxpayer has previously been given notice and has not paid. After the taxpayer is notified, he or she has 30 days by which to appeal the decision to file a tax lien (the appeal process is the same as was discussed in **5.2**). The tax lien attaches to all property and rights to property belonging to the taxpayer at any time during the period of the lien, including any property or rights to property acquired by the person after the lien arises. The tax lien must be filed and recorded in the county where the property is located or where the taxpayer lives before it becomes a public record.

The tax lien will remain in place until the taxpayer pays the bill in full or until the ten-year collection period expires. Once the IRS receives full payment or determines that the time for collection has expired, the IRS must release the lien within 30 days.

The IRS likes to file Federal Tax Liens against taxpayers. It filed 426,166, 482,509, and 548,683 liens against taxpayers for the years 2001, 2002, and 2003, respectively. A Federal Tax Lien recorded against you has several negative consequences.

First, having a tax lien on your credit report causes major problems for you if you are attempting to borrow money. Most lenders simply refuse to lend funds if the credit report displays a tax lien. Other lenders will make a loan, but subject to much higher interest rates and other fees than usual.

You should always negotiate with the IRS to keep it from filing a tax lien. If a tax lien has been filed, you should make every effort to get it removed.

Second, a tax lien makes it difficult, if not impossible, for you to sell assets to satisfy the tax debt. While a lien will probably not affect the sale of smaller assets (such as furniture or clothing), it most certainly will affect the sale of any real property located in the county where the tax lien was filed.

5.3.a Discharge of Federal Tax Lien

A discharge of the tax lien simply means that the IRS has agreed to remove the Federal Tax Lien. The most common way to have a lien discharged is, of course, to pay your tax debt. The IRS is required by law to release the lien within 30 days of full payment (IRC §6325 (a)).

The IRS will also discharge the Federal Tax Lien when a taxpayer makes an application for discharge. There are four situations in which the IRS will agree to do this:

(a) *You make a partial payment to the IRS in an amount at least as much as the value of the IRS lien.* The payment need not cover all the tax liabilities as long as it covers the value of the tax lien. It is important for you to realize that a tax lien typically does not cover all liabilities, especially if you accrue additional tax liabilities after the lien is filed. If the IRS does not record multiple liens, the new tax liabilities are not considered to be part of the old tax lien.

(b) *The IRS determines that its interest in the property has no value.* This situation may occur when there are one or more mortgages or judgments recorded before the tax lien, and the value of the property does not exceed the value of everything recorded before the tax lien. For example, if a home is worth $150,000 and the total amount owed on a first and second mortgage is $175,000, the IRS will likely consider the value of its lien to be worthless, as a sale of the property would not provide any money to the IRS.

(c) *The IRS receives the proceeds from the sale or refinance of the property at the closing of the sale or refinance (or to be held in escrow by the closing company).* The IRS will release the lien to permit the buyer or new lender to obtain the property or to refinance the mortgage(s) with a title clear of the tax lien.

(d) *You submit another piece of property with a fair market value at least double the amount of tax owed.* You may wish to do this in order to remove a tax lien from your personal residence and have the lien transferred to rental or investment property.

In order to submit an Application for a Certificate of Discharge of Federal Tax Lien, you must send the following information to the district director (Attention: Chief, Special Procedures):

★ Your name and address, along with the applicant's name and address (if you are not the applicant)

★ A detailed description of the property to which the discharge will apply

★ A statement describing the transaction

★ A copy of the Federal Tax Lien(s) currently in place and recorded against the property

★ A list of all encumbrances on the property, such as mortgages and judgments, that were filed before the Federal Tax Lien

★ The amount of tax currently owed

★ An estimate of the fair market value of the property

★ The name of the escrow agent, if any, or a description of how the IRS will receive the proceeds of the transaction

★ Any other information necessary to assist the IRS in reviewing the application

The application must be signed under the penalties of perjury. A statement that reads "Under penalties of perjury, I declare that I have examined the facts presented in this statement and any accompanying information, and, to the best of my knowledge and belief, they are true, correct, and complete" will satisfy any penalty of perjury request from the IRS. The IRS may also request additional information that it believes to be necessary to make a decision. Sample 27 shows a letter to the IRS requesting a discharge of the tax lien.

5.3.b Subordination of Federal Tax Lien

In some instances, you may want to refinance a mortgage or obtain completely new financing, but cannot find a lender willing to loan money due to the presence of the Federal Tax Lien. The priority system in place under US law states that mortgages or liens are ranked according to when they were recorded. The priorities determine which creditors get paid if the property is sold, either voluntarily or by a foreclosure sale. For example, assume the following situation:

SAMPLE 27
LETTER REQUESTING DISCHARGE OF A FEDERAL TAX LIEN

July 1, 20—

Internal Revenue Service
Attention: T.X. Collector
600 17th Street
Mail Stop 5333DEN
Denver, CO 80202

Re: Herman H. Munster, SSN: 123-45-6789

Application for Certificate of Discharge of Property from Federal Tax Lien pursuant to IRC§§6325(b)(2)(A) and 6325(b)(2)(B)

Dear Mr. Collector:

This letter constitutes our formal request for the IRS to issue a certificate of discharge of the tax lien filed with respect to the property described below. In support thereof, we hereby submit the following:

1. The name and address of the taxpayer is:

Herman H. Munster
1313 Mockingbird Lane
Denver, CO 80222

2. Legal Description:

North 100 feet of Lot 13 and west 44 feet of Lot 1, Block 13, Spooky Heights, City and County of Denver

3. A copy of the federal tax lien is enclosed for your review.

4. The encumbrances on the property, along with the current amounts owed, are as follows:

First Deed of Trust 1/88	$100,000
Second Deed of Trust 1/95	$ 25,000
Total before Federal Tax Lien:	$125,000

5. The current fair market value of the property is $135,000.

6. The fair market value was established by an appraisal which is included with this application.

7. A summary of the history of the property while it has been owned by the taxpayer is set forth below:

The residence in question was purchased by Mr. Munster during January 1988. A second mortgage was taken out during January 1995. The tax lien was placed on the property as the result of Mr. Munster's wife's tax obligations (which are separate from Mr. Munster's obligations). The taxpayer is submitting this application to permit him to pay his share of the equity in the real estate (1/2) and have the IRS discharge its tax lien.

8. The taxpayer will furnish any other specific information the district director requests.

9. The total amount that will be paid to the IRS is $5,000. This amount was computed by taking the fair market value ($135,000) and subtracting the current encumbrances ($125,000) and dividing the balance ($10,000) by two, as the taxpayer does not currently owe the IRS any funds.

10. The daytime telephone number of the taxpayer is (303) 555-1212.

Under penalties of perjury, I declare that I have examined this application, including any accompanying schedules, exhibits, affidavits, and statements, and to the best of my knowledge and belief it is true, correct, and complete.

Sincerely,

_____

Herman H. Munster

Enclosures: As stated

Encumbrance	Date Recorded	Amount
First mortgage	2/1/97	$100,000
Second mortgage	2/1/98	$ 25,000
Federal Tax Lien	3/1/98	$ 25,000

If the property is now worth $150,000, the taxpayer has $25,000 in equity in the property above the tax lien ($150,000 - $125,000 = $25,000). The taxpayer may want to get a new mortgage to replace the first and second mortgages, but no lender will give this because the new mortgage will be recorded after 3/1/98 and will thus have a lower priority than the Federal Tax Lien.

The IRS will allow a subordination of its lien to occur to permit a mortgage company to have its new mortgage recorded ahead of the IRS lien. If the new lender agrees to loan $140,000, the first $125,000 will be used to pay off the first two mortgages. The remaining $15,000, assuming no closing costs, will go to the IRS. The new recording situation will look like this:

Encumbrance	Date Recorded	Amount
New mortgage	11/1/99	$140,000
Tax lien	11/2/99	$ 10,000

Like the discharge procedure, all subordination requests must be sent to the district director (Attention: Special Procedures). The same information submitted to get a discharge should be sent with the subordination application (see **5.3.b**). Give the IRS at least three weeks before the anticipated closing date to review the request, and more time if possible. In addition, the request must be signed under the penalties of perjury. While the IRS is not required to subordinate its lien, it will often do so, especially if it will get paid, in full or in part, at the closing. Sample 28 is an example of an Application for a Subordination of the Federal Tax Lien.

5.3.c Release of Federal Tax Lien

There are situations in which the IRS is legally obligated to release a tax lien, but, for some reason, refuses to do so. For example, the IRS employee may be incompetent or is using the lien as a means of continued harassment, even after the tax debt has been satisfied. If this happens, you can

SAMPLE 28
LETTER REQUESTING SUBORDINATION OF A FEDERAL TAX LIEN

January 1, 20—

District Director
Internal Revenue Service
Attn: Chief, Special Procedures
600 17th Street
Denver, CO 80202

APPLICATION FOR CERTIFICATE OF SUBORDINATION OF FEDERAL TAX LIEN

Re: Herman H. Munster
SSN: 123-45-6789
1313 Mockingbird Lane
Denver, CO 80222

To the Commissioner:

Pursuant to Internal Revenue Code §6325(d)(2), the above-referenced taxpayer hereby respectfully submits this Application for Certificate Of Subordination of Federal Tax Lien. In support thereof, the taxpayer states as follows:

1.   Location of property:

   1313 Mockingbird Lane
   Denver, CO 80222

   Legal description:

   North 100 feet of Lot 13 and west 44 feet of Lot 1, Block 13, Spooky Heights, City and County of Denver.

2.   Copies of Federal Tax Liens are attached for your reference.

3.   The taxpayer currently has a first mortgage (with ABC Bank, 888 South Peaceful Drive, Lakewood, CO 80226) and a second mortgage (with Colorado Bankrobber Bank, 100 Criminal Boulevard, Lakewood, CO 80226) on the property ahead of the Federal Tax Lien (based on priorities).

The taxpayer is submitting this Application because he has been in contact with Mr. Lou Grant, the president of ABC Bank. Mr. Grant has indicated that his bank is willing to

SAMPLE 28 — CONTINUED

refinance the property and pay all liens ahead of the IRS, with the IRS receiving all cash due the taxpayer at the closing. By permitting the taxpayer to accomplish this subordination, the IRS will realize all funds at the closing by subordinating its lien and permitting the refinance to occur.

4.   Encumbrances currently with priority over the Federal Tax Lien:

   a. Name and Address:
   ABC Bank
   888 South Peaceful Drive
   Lakewood, CO 80226

   Description of Encumbrance:
   First Mortgage

   Date of Agreement:
   July 1, 1990

   Recorded:
   Denver County, Colorado

   Original Amount:
   $100,000

   Current Amount Owed:
   $95,111 (see attached statement from ABC Bank)

   b. Name and Address:

   Colorado Bankrobber Bank
   100 Criminal Boulevard
   Lakewood, CO 80226

   Description of Encumbrance:
   Second Mortgage

   Date of Agreement:
   July 1, 1996

   Recorded:
   Denver County, Colorado

   Original Amount:
   $25,000

Current Amount Owed:

$24,100 (see attached statement from Bankrobber Bank)

5.   Estimate of Fair Market Value of the real property at issue:

$135,000 (based on appraisals performed in connection with the refinance application). A copy of the appraisal is included for your review.

6.   By subordinating the Federal Tax Lien to the new proposed refinanced mortgage with ABC Bank, the Internal Revenue Service will facilitate collection of the amount owed by allowing the taxpayer to cash out some of his equity in the property and pay the IRS. The amount that the Internal Revenue Service will net from this transaction is as follows:

Loan Amount	$135,000.00
Less:	
Settlement Charges	$ 2,000.00 (estimate)
First Mortgage Payoff	$ 95,111.50
Second Mortgage Payoff	$ 24,100.00
Total Disbursements:	$121,211.50
Amount to Internal Revenue Service at closing:	$13,788.50

Under the penalties of perjury, I declare that I have examined this application, including any accompanying schedules, exhibits, affidavits and statements, and, to the best of my knowledge and belief, it is true, correct and complete.

Respectfully submitted,

_____

Herman H. Munster

Enclosures: As stated

sue the IRS for damages associated with its refusal to release the tax lien in a timely manner. You must file such a suit within two years from the date that the lien should have been released. The mere threat of a lawsuit will often be enough to get the IRS to do the right thing, although certainly not always.

5.4 IRS accounts as currently not collectible

In many instances, taxpayers have not paid the IRS because they simply have no money to do so. Even the IRS recognizes this fact of economic reality. In these circumstances, the IRS will place a hold on the account because the account is currently not collectible.

This does not reduce the amount owed. In fact, interest and penalties add more dollars to the bill. However, placing the account in an uncollectible status does give the taxpayer some breathing room. The IRS will not attempt to collect the tax liability for a relatively short time (usually one year or less). The IRS can attempt to collect the debt until the collection statute of limitations (ten years) expires.

The IRS makes its decision to classify an account as not collectible based on financial information the taxpayer submitted on Forms 433-A and/or 433-B. If the taxpayer's allowable expenses exceed his or her monthly income, the account is considered to be currently not collectible. Before agreeing to classify any accounts as not collectible, the IRS will make sure that all tax returns that are currently due have been filed (this is called a compliance check). When the IRS agrees to classify the account as not collectible, it will usually file a Notice of Federal Tax Lien to protect the IRS's claim to the amount of taxes owed.

Tax Points

★ It is usually to your advantage to delay collection activities for as long as possible.

★ Never ignore IRS collection notices.

★ Obtaining an Installment Agreement is a good short-term solution for all taxpayers who owe the IRS for past-due taxes.

★ Always designate where all payments made to the IRS should be applied. If this is not done, the IRS will apply any payments in a way most beneficial to the IRS.

★ All tax returns must be filed before the IRS will negotiate in the collections area.

★ Always meet all deadlines imposed in the collection area.

★ Attempt to offer the IRS solutions before it offers you solutions.

★ Always fill out IRS collection forms away from IRS offices. The financial disclosures being made are important and there are high levels of stress associated with filling out the forms on hostile territory.

★ You should rarely agree to extend the statute of limitations for the IRS to collect a tax now due.

★ Don't agree to allow the IRS to receive a percentage of your future income (a collateral agreement) unless it is absolutely necessary in the negotiation process.

★ Always cooperate to avoid any summons or enforced collection matters.

★ Be aware of the sources of assets the IRS is most likely to seize and plan accordingly.

★ Obtain a not collectible status to buy time to resolve the situation if you cannot make any payments to the IRS in the near future.

★ You do have rights and have a lot of say in how and when the IRS will get its money (and usually it will get some if not all of the money owed).

CHAPTER 12

HOW TO PAY PENNIES ON THE DOLLAR: THE OFFER IN COMPROMISE PROGRAM

You can't have a government like this without an income tax, but we don't want a government like this.
    Congressman Ronald E. Paul (R-Texas), Libertarian candidate for
                                                president in 1988

Taxes and increased spending by any other names still smell.
        Representative Bill Archer (R-Texas) on March 23, 1993

Millions of US taxpayers end up owing the IRS a great deal of money as the result of audit changes and the huge penalties and interest that can accumulate over time. For instance, a taxpayer who owes the IRS $15,000 may see this amount double to $30,000 or more after interest and penalties are added to the tax due.

Often the taxpayer will attempt to dig out of the tax debt by paying the IRS through a monthly payment plan, but the payments come from money that should have been saved for the current year's taxes. Come April 15, the taxpayer now owes the IRS for another year on top of what was already owed. The taxpayer becomes buried in tax debts and cannot even pay the interest that is accruing. The end result is that the taxpayer will often owe the IRS more money than was owed at the beginning. The taxpayer cannot win.

The IRS sees situations like this all the time, and it is permitted to "compromise," or reduce, the amount that a taxpayer owes. This process is known as an Offer in Compromise or OIC. Under IRC §7122, the IRS can compromise any tax liability, including interest and penalties, as long as the taxpayer or the case has not been referred to the Justice Department for a possible criminal prosecution for a tax crime.

Unfortunately, not enough taxpayers take advantage of one of the most favorable programs the IRS offers them, as Table 10 shows.

TABLE 10
NUMBER OF OFFERS IN COMPROMISE

Year	Number of Offers Filed with IRS	Dollar Value of Offers Accepted
1996	134,000	Not Available
1997	114,000	Not Available
1998	105,000	Not Available
1999	97,000	Not Available
2000	109,000	$316,214,000
2001	125,000	$340,778,000
2002	124,000	$300,296,000
2003	128,000	$243,942,000

IRS statistics show that the IRS received only 97,000 offers in 1999, but this number increased to 128,000 in 2003. While the number of offers is increasing (based upon IRS projections), it is not increasing nearly enough. Congress, which recognizes the benefits of the Offer in Compromise program for both the taxpayer and the IRS, and has told the IRS to make changes to make the program more flexible. These changes, which are now finally in place, include the following:

(a) *Hardship Offers.* The IRS has established Hardship Offers (also known as Effective Tax Administration, or ETA Offers), thus adding a third class to Offers (with Doubt as to Collectibility or Liability being the other two [see section **1** below]). To qualify for an ETA Offer, you will have to demonstrate the hardship connected to having to pay the taxes (e.g., that you will have to decide between paying taxes and obtaining necessary medical care for a family member). The IRS usually requires great hardship before it will consider lightening the taxpayer's tax burden. This type of offer is discussed in detail later in this chapter.

(b) *Administrative Review process.* The IRS has added an Administrative Review process to review any rejected offers. Before this

An Offer in Compromise allows the IRS to compromise a tax liability, including interest and penalties.

process was added, your only recourse was an appeal with the Appeals Division if the offer was rejected. Now you can have a management review in the Offer Division before any appeals hearings. This gives you one more shot at having your case reviewed.

(c) *90-day payment.* If you are able to make a cash offer (i.e., one in which the balance will be paid within 90 days of acceptance), the IRS will calculate your future ability to pay based on 48 months (four years) and not 60 months (five years) as I describe in section **2.1.** below. This may reduce the overall amount you need to offer the IRS to reach a compromise and would end your dealings with the IRS as soon as possible.

While the IRS has not done a good job to date of promoting the Offer in Compromise program, it is essential that anyone who owes the IRS money consider whether the program will work for them. In this chapter I discuss how the Offer in Compromise process works and what you should expect both before and after filing an Offer in Compromise with the IRS.

1. When Can You Make an Offer in Compromise?

According to the IRS, the purpose of the Offer in Compromise program is to benefit both the taxpayer and the IRS, while providing a fresh financial start to the taxpayer. The basic premise of the program is that IRS will agree to take less money from the taxpayer than the IRS claims the taxpayer owes and write off the rest of the alleged tax debt.

★ If the IRS believes that it is unlikely to collect the full amount of the debt, it will agree to collect something rather than nothing. In this respect, the IRS is actually acting as a regular business would act. Most businesses understand that it is generally a good idea to resolve collection and liability issues through an agreement, or compromise, and get something from the person who owes it money. Under IRC §7122, the IRS is permitted to treat tax debts like any other business would treat its debts.

★ This being said, the IRS does not accept *all* offers from taxpayers. For example, the IRS will not accept an offer based *solely* on sympathy, hardship, or other equitable considerations. In addition, it will not accept offers if it believes it could collect more money in the near future than what the taxpayer has offered to resolve the debt.

You can use an Offer in Compromise if —

• you disagree with the amount the IRS says you owe and can prove that your dispute is valid; or

• you agree that you owe the amount the IRS claims, but you cannot pay it in full (either now or in the near future).

The IRS will reject an Offer in Compromise if it fears that public knowledge of the offer will negatively influence other taxpayers to avoid paying taxes.

★ As with most other issues involving the IRS, the decision to reject an offer may not be reasonable or reflect the likelihood of the IRS ever collecting a penny from the taxpayer. I have seen the IRS reject Offers in Compromise in which the money offered was greater than the amount that the IRS could ever hope to collect in the future. The IRS has even admitted as much, but it states that it will reject an offer if it believes that public knowledge of the accepted offer (and all accepted offers are public documents) would be seriously detrimental to voluntary compliance. In other words, the IRS reasons that it will not accept an offer if it would make the taxpaying public so upset that many taxpayers would not want to file their tax returns on time and pay their share of the taxes due.

The Offer in Compromise program deals with three distinct situations:

(a) The taxpayer owes the money but cannot pay (called "doubt as to collectibility")

(b) The taxpayer believes that he or she doesn't owe the money (called "doubt as to liability")

(c) The taxpayer owes the money and can pay the money, but doing so will create a tremendous hardship (called a Hardship Offer or "Effective Tax Administration").

In any of these situations, the IRS will eliminate the tax debt and allow the taxpayer a fresh start if the taxpayer can prove certain items to the IRS.

1.1 Doubt as to collectibility

If an Offer in Compromise is based on doubt as to collectibility, it means that your debt with the IRS is more than you can pay. There are two separate components involved in determining what you can now pay to the IRS:

(a) Your equity in your assets

(b) Your future ability to pay

For your equity in your assets, the IRS wants to know how much money you could raise if you sold everything you owned. This list of assets includes real estate, automobiles, furniture, stocks and other investments, retirement savings, and anything else you possess that has any value.

Concerning your future ability to pay, the IRS is interested in figuring out how much you could pay the IRS in the next five years on a monthly Installment Agreement.

The forced sale value of an asset is what you would get if you had to sell the asset at an auction or other distress type sale. The quick sale value of an asset is what you would get if you had to sell the asset in a hurry.

The IRS reviews all this information on the Form 433-A financial statement, which is required in an offer based upon doubt as to collectibility. (This financial statement is discussed in detail in chapter 11.) See section **2.1.** below for suggestions on how to use these two components to determine how much to offer the IRS.

One question that comes up in nearly every Offer in Compromise case is what an asset is actually worth. Obviously the IRS will claim that an asset is worth more than a taxpayer will. One reason this occurs is because each side is using a different approach to value the asset.

For example, if you were selling your car in an ordinary transaction, you might get $5,000 for it. The IRS will claim that this is what the car is worth. However, if the IRS seizes the car and sells it, it would probably get closer to $2,500 than $5,000. This value, called the forced sale value, is what you should claim the car is worth. Often you can reach a compromise with the IRS by using what is commonly referred to as the quick sale value, which is what the car would be worth if you had to sell it in a hurry (but not at an auction or other forced or distress type of sale). Thus, the car will probably be "worth" approximately $3,500 to $4,000 for purposes of the offer.

Asset values are usually negotiable. Even the IRS admits as much; it trains its investigators that the valuation of an asset, except for cash and the like, is not an exact or precise science and that a negotiated value should be used whenever possible.

1.2 Doubt as to liability

If you are applying for an Offer in Compromise based on doubt as to liability, you must demonstrate that, under the tax laws or specific facts of the case, you do not owe any additional money to the IRS. In other words, you are claiming that the alleged tax liability is erroneous and should be removed from your account. You must have records or some documentation to support your assertion that you really don't owe the tax liability.

There are several common situations in which you can successfully use an argument based upon doubt as to liability. These situations include the following:

(a) *You accepted a tax examiner's decision that was incorrect, but you failed to appeal the incorrect decision (for whatever reason).* This is perhaps the most common reason why a doubt as to liability argument would work. What you are really telling the IRS is that the incorrect audit determination was never legally challenged. In this case, you must have records to support the reasons why the IRS was incorrect during the original audit.

(b) *You qualify as an innocent spouse under the IRC.* Under IRC §6015 (IRC §6013(e) prior to the recent tax reform laws), a spouse is considered to be an "innocent spouse" and relieved of a tax liability that occurred as the result of filing a joint return with his or her spouse and that had an understatement of tax (either by not reporting all income or overstating expenses or deductions), as long as the one spouse did not know and had no reason to know of the extent of the understatement and that it would be inequitable to hold that spouse liable. This reflects a change made in the Tax Reform Act of 1998, when Congress eliminated the requirement that the understatement needed to be "substantial" (which, in the past, made it more difficult for some innocent spouses to be able to successfully claim this type of relief). The most common situation is one in which a taxpayer gets a divorce and is left with all the tax debt of the ex-spouse. The innocent spouse rule will also work if the couple is still married, although it may not have much benefit if both spouses own the couple's assets jointly.

(c) *You failed to file tax returns and the IRS prepared returns for you that are clearly incorrect.* Perhaps the IRS did not use the correct filing status or did not consider all allowable credits, expenses, and/or deductions. If you have the appropriate records to prepare an accurate tax return, the IRS will often accept the compromise due to the doubt as to liability, as long as the corrected tax return is prepared and filed with the Offer in Compromise.

Any time you file an Offer in Compromise based upon doubt as to liability, the IRS will presume that the tax liability is correct. It is up to you to produce sufficient proof to overcome the presumption (i.e., to change the IRS's view concerning the actual liability). If a court has already ruled on the liability issue, even if the taxpayer believes that the court was wrong, the IRS will not accept an Offer in Compromise on the basis of doubt as to liability.

For example, if you take the IRS to the tax court and lose, you cannot claim doubt as to liability in a future offer, even if the tax court was wrong and you do not file an appeal. According to the IRS, the tax court decision conclusively established that you owed the money and therefore there is no doubt as to liability. You could, however, file an offer based upon doubt as to collectibility or Effective Tax Administration, assuming that you qualify under these categories.

1.3 Effective Tax Administration

The third type of offer, the Effective Tax Administration (ETA) Offer, is a recent addition to the Offer in Compromise program. With the ETA Offer, you agree with the IRS that the tax liability is correct and that you can pay the liability in full, but to do so would create a severe hardship to you or your family. You must file a Form 433-A with this offer and provide a very detailed statement as to the exceptional circumstances involved in your case that would make paying the tax liability an economic hardship or would otherwise be unfair or inequitable. The IRS will consider this type of offer only after it determines that you do not qualify for an offer based upon either doubt as to liability or collectibility. The IRS is also required to review your past history of filing and paying your taxes, so that if you have a lengthy history of tax problems, the IRS will probably conclude that you do not qualify for this type of offer.

The IRS has listed three types of situations that will often (but not always) support a finding of economic hardship. These are as follows:

★ The taxpayer has a major medical condition, disability, or illness that makes it difficult for him or her to earn a living, and it is reasonable to assume that his or her financial resources will be exhausted in providing for the medical care.

★ Even though the taxpayer has sufficient assets to pay off the tax liabilities, to do so would leave him or her unable to pay for basic living expenses (such as food, shelter, clothing, medicine, etc.).

★ Even though the taxpayer has sufficient assets to pay off the tax liability, he or she cannot borrow against these assets and the IRS cannot, for whatever reason, realistically seize the asset(s) to pay off the taxes due.

Examples of taxpayers who can successfully utilize the ETA Offers include those with life-threatening illnesses (or family members with such medical conditions), those who are living on limited fixed-income assets (such as pensions and retirement accounts), and business owners who would have their businesses shut down if they had to pay the tax liabilities (and it was not their fault with respect to why there was an underlying tax liability).

2. How Do You Make an Offer in Compromise?

All Offers in Compromise begin when you complete and file a Form 656 (Offer in Compromise) (see Sample 29) with the IRS. This relatively simple form tells the IRS what tax years and types of taxes you are attempting to have compromised, along with how much money you are offering to the IRS to compromise the tax debt. In addition, you should submit as much supporting information and documentation as possible, as this will increase the odds that the IRS will accept the offer.

Effective November 1, 2003, the IRS began imposing a $150 filing fee for all Offers in Compromise. According to the IRS, this fee was necessary to limit the number of "frivolous" offers and to assist with the cost of administering the Offer program. If the filing fee presents a hardship to you, a waiver is possible by filing a Form 656-A with your Offer.

If you are submitting the offer based upon your inability to pay or for effective tax administration, you are also required to submit complete financial information (on forms 433-A and/or B). This request is reasonable: the IRS cannot be expected to evaluate your claim that you cannot pay or should not be required to pay without knowing your current financial situation.

If you have an Installment Agreement in place with the IRS at the beginning of the offer process, you should ask the IRS to waive the payments due under the agreement while the offer is being investigated. While the IRS is not required to accommodate this request, it never hurts to ask.

2.1 How do you decide how much to offer?

According to the IRS, the average amount collected on an Offer in Compromise is 14% of the total amount of the tax due. Use the formula "Equity in Assets + Future Ability to Pay = Amount to Offer" to compute the amount to offer.

After establishing that you are a candidate for an Offer in Compromise (i.e., you cannot pay, are not liable for the tax debt, or to pay the tax debt would create a serious financial hardship), you then have to figure out how much money to offer the IRS to get rid of the tax liability. According to the IRS, the average amount collected on an Offer in Compromise is 14% of the total amount of the tax due. Of course, each Offer in Compromise is unique and this figure should be used as a guideline for the amount to offer.

In general, you must offer the IRS more than the IRS could get through its own collection efforts. For example, if the IRS could seize your home and net $10,000 (after the mortgage and other liens are paid and the costs of the foreclosure sale are subtracted), you could not offer less than $10,000 and expect the IRS to accept the offer (unless an economic

FORM 656 (OFFER IN COMPROMISE)

⊕ IRS

Department of the Treasury
Internal Revenue Service

www.irs.gov

Form 656 (Rev. 5-2001)
Catalog Number 16728N

Form 656

Offer in Compromise

IRS RECEIVED DATE

Item 1 — Taxpayer's Name and Home or Business Address

Sara Estill
Name

Name

111 North Broadway
Street Address

Denver   CO   80111
City   State   ZIP Code

Mailing Address *(if different from above)*

P.O. Box 862
Street Address

Denver   CO   80112
City   State   ZIP Code

DATE RETURNED

Item 2 — Social Security Numbers

(a) Primary   111-22-3333

(b) Secondary

Item 3 — Employer Identification Number *(included in offer)*

Item 4 — Other Employer Identification Numbers *(not included in offer)*

Item 5 — To: Commissioner of Internal Revenue Service

I/We (includes all types of taxpayers) submit this offer to compromise the tax liabilities plus any interest, penalties, additions to tax, and additional amounts required by law (tax liability) for the tax type and period marked below: (Please mark an "X" in the box for the correct description and fill-in the correct tax period(s), adding additional periods if needed).

☒ **1040/1120 Income Tax** — Year(s) 1997, 1999, 2000

☐ **941 Employer's Quarterly Federal Tax Return** — Quarterly period(s)

☐ **940 Employer's Annual Federal Unemployment (FUTA) Tax Return** — Year(s)

☐ **Trust Fund Recovery Penalty as a responsible person of** (enter corporation name) _____,
for failure to pay withholding and Federal Insurance Contributions Act Taxes (Social Security taxes), for period(s) ending _____.

☐ **Other Federal Tax(es)** [specify type(s) and period(s)]

Note: If you need more space, use another sheet titled "Attachment to Form 656 Dated_____." Sign and date the attachment following the listing of the tax periods.

Item 6 — I/We submit this offer for the reason(s) checked below:

☐ **Doubt as to Liability** — "I do not believe I owe this amount." You must include a detailed explanation of the reason(s) why you believe you do not owe the tax in Item 9.

☒ **Doubt as to Collectibility** — "I have insufficient assets and income to pay the full amount." You must include a complete Collection Information Statement, Form 433-A and/or Form 433-B.

☐ **Effective Tax Administration** — "I owe this amount and have sufficient assets to pay the full amount, but due to my exceptional circumstances, requiring full payment would cause an economic hardship or would be unfair and inequitable." You must include a complete Collection Information Statement, Form 433-A and/or Form 433B and complete Item 9.

Item 7

I/We offer to pay $ 3,500 — (must be more than zero). Complete Item 10 to explain where you will obtain the funds to make this offer.

Check one of the following:

☒ **Cash Offer** (Offered amount will be paid in 90 days or less.)

Balance to be paid in: ☐ 10; ☒ 30; ☐ 60; or ☐ 90 days from written notice of acceptance of the offer.

☐ **Short-Term Deferred Payment Offer** (Offered amount will be paid in MORE than 90 days but within 24 months from written notice of acceptance of the offer.)

$_____ within_____ days (not more than 90 — See Instructions Section, Determine Your Payment Terms) from written notice of acceptance of the offer; and

beginning in the _____ month after written notice of acceptance of the offer, $_____ on the _____ day of each month for a total of _____ months. (Cannot extend more than 24 months from written notice of acceptance of the offer.)

☐ **Deferred Payment Offer** (Offered amount will be paid over the life of the collection statute.)

$_____ within_____ days (not more than 90 — See Instructions Section, Determine Your Payment Terms) from written notice of acceptance of the offer; and

beginning in the first month after written notice of acceptance of the offer, $_____ on the _____ day of each month for a total of _____ months.

NOTE: Signature(s) of taxpayer required on last page of Form 656.

Item 9 — Explanation of Circumstances

I am requesting an offer in compromise for the reason(s) listed below:

Note: If you are requesting compromise based on doubt as to liability, explain why you don't believe you owe the tax.
If you believe you have special circumstances affecting your ability to fully pay the amount due, explain your situation.
You may attach additional sheets if necessary.

I incurred these tax liabilities when I was going through a divorce and my expenses greatly exceeded my income. As the enclosed Form 433-A demonstrates, I do not have the means to pay my $25,000 tax liability for the 3 years at issue. I have filed all tax returns and did not owe anything on my 2001 tax return. This offer is submitted in good faith and would permit me to obtain a fresh financial start. Thank you for your consideration of this offer.

Item 10 — Source of Funds

I/we shall obtain the funds to make this offer from the following source(s):

Gifts/loans from friends

Item 11

If I/we submit this offer on a substitute form, I/we affirm that this form is a verbatim duplicate of the official Form 656, and I/we agree to be bound by all the terms and conditions set forth in the official Form 656.

Under penalties of perjury, I declare that I have examined this offer, including accompanying schedules and statements, and to the best of my knowledge and belief, it is true, correct and complete.

Sarra Estill

11(a) Signature of Taxpayer

4/10/02

Date

11(b) Signature of Taxpayer

Date

For Official Use Only

I accept the waiver of the statutory period of limitations for the Internal Revenue Service.

Signature of Authorized Internal Revenue Service Official

Title

Date

NOTE: Signature(s) of taxpayer required on last page of Form 656 hardship is involved). An offer is usually considered to be adequate if it "reasonably reflects collection potential."

Of course, what is seen as a reasonable reflection of collection potential varies from person to person. The Internal Revenue Manual permits Offer in Compromise investigators to consider your assets, earning power, and assets available to you that are beyond the government's reach in determining the collection potential. It is safe to assume that if the amount offered is greater than the value of your assets and earning power, then the offer would be considered reasonable.

Use the formula "Equity in Assets + Future Ability to Pay = Amount to Offer" to compute the amount to offer. For the "future ability to pay" portion of the equation, the IRS typically looks at what you could pay the IRS on a monthly Installment Agreement over the next four or five years. As well, the IRS will consider several factors, including your age, health, education, and occupation. The IRS does this to determine the likelihood that your income may increase in the future, a factor that would obviously affect the amount of your offer. A young taxpayer who is in good health will have a more difficult time getting the IRS to accept an offer than would an elderly individual in poor health, mainly due to the young person's potential ability to earn money in the near future (i.e., the next five years). Likewise, a highly educated physician will have a much more difficult time getting an Offer in Compromise accepted than would a restaurant busboy with little chance for advancement. Remember that each offer is unique and is decided on a case-by-case basis.

When you compute your future ability to pay, remember that the value of money today is not the same as the value of money in the future. This theory, often called a "present value" analysis, is simple to understand if you think in terms of someone owing you money. If that person owes you $100 today and pays you the money today, you have the ability to invest the $100 so that five years from today you would have more than the original $100. In submitting an offer, you are permitted to use present value tables with respect to the future ability to pay. It is beneficial for you to use this type of analysis because the IRS will take less money today to resolve the situation rather than waiting for up to five years to get all of the money. Table 11 lists present value factors for one to five years, which you can use when submitting an offer.

To use this table, take the number listed in the column that corresponds to the current interest rate, and multiply it by the amount that you are able to pay every month to determine a starting point for the offer. For instance, if you can afford a payment of $50 per month and will make this payment for five years (60 months), you would pay the IRS a total of

TABLE 11
PRESENT VALUE FACTORS

Interest Rate						
Year	7%	8%	9%	10%	11%	12%
1	11.57	11.51	11.46	11.40	11.35	11.29
2	22.38	22.17	21.97	21.76	21.57	21.37
3	32.49	32.04	31.61	31.19	30.78	30.37
4	41.93	41.18	40.45	39.75	39.07	38.41
5	50.76	49.64	48.57	47.54	46.54	45.59

$3,000 over these five years (60 months x $50 = $3,000). However, if you were to submit an Offer in Compromise at a time when the interest rate was 8%, you could offer the IRS $2,482 ($50 times the 49.64 figure in Year 5) to resolve the tax debt (based upon the "future ability to pay" part of the equation).

As well as ability to pay, you must also consider the value of your assets to determine if an offer is appropriate. Sample 30 shows a situation where a taxpayer owes the IRS $50,000 but wants to figure out if an Offer in Compromise would be a realistic and acceptable way to reduce the amount owed.

In this example, the taxpayer would have to pay $10,964 to compromise the tax debt. Many taxpayers cannot afford to pay the IRS this kind of lump sum and wonder if the IRS will permit a payment plan to cover the amount offered. The answer is a very qualified "yes." The IRS is permitted to give the taxpayer up to a maximum of 24 months after the offer is accepted to pay the amount offered in full.

In spite of this, I strongly advise you to pay all the money at once, as one of the primary benefits of the offer to the IRS is the immediate payment of the money. If the IRS knows that it will have to wait up to two years to get all its money, it is much more likely to reject the offer. If you need to make payments to complete the Offer in Compromise, you should offer to pay the IRS at least 50% of the total amount within 30 days of acceptance of the offer, with the balance to be paid in monthly installments.

Note that the IRS will not release any tax liens until all payments are made. In addition, interest on the amount offered accrues from the date that the offer is accepted until the date the final payment is made to the IRS. These are just two more reasons to avoid making payments or to pay the IRS in as short a time as possible. Always remember that the Offer in Compromise process is a two-way street and that the IRS must benefit in some way or it will not approve the offer.

DETERMINING THE AMOUNT OF YOUR OIC

Assets	Value
Automobile	$2,500
Household furniture	1,000
Cash	100
Checking account	200
Camera equipment	200
IRA/retirement	2,000
Total assets	$6,000
Future Ability to Pay	
Current monthly income	$2,500
Current monthly expenses	2,400
Surplus income per month	100
Owed to the IRS:	$50,000
Interest rate: 8%	

The IRS looks at the taxpayer's ability to pay over five years (or 60 months), which in this case is $6,000 (60 months x $100 per month = $6,000), not using the present value analysis. When we take the present value analysis into account, the $6,000 amount actually becomes $4,964 (49.64 x $100 = $4,964).

By adding the equity in assets ($6,000) with the future ability to pay ($4,964), this taxpayer realizes that he or she must offer the IRS at least $10,964 to compromise the tax debt.

While this is a large amount of money for most taxpayers, it is a great financial advantage if the taxpayer can come up with this amount of money, as it means the taxpayer could persuade the IRS to eliminate $50,000 of tax debts in return for a payment of $10,964. The taxpayer would save over $39,000 in taxes owed to the IRS.

While this example is rather simplistic, it does demonstrate how an Offer in Compromise should always be considered as a method of resolving a tax controversy with the IRS.

2.2 Documents you need to submit an Offer in Compromise

You should locate the following documents before submitting any Offers in Compromise to the IRS:

★ The last three years of tax returns, including all supporting documentation

★ Bank or other financial institution statements for the previous 12 months

★ Completed IRS financial forms (Forms 433-A and/or B) (While these must be submitted with any offer based upon doubt as to collectibility or effective tax administration, you should retain copies and, if necessary, update the forms during the course of the offer. Many offers take several months to work through the IRS bureaucratic system, and finances can certainly change over that time.)

★ Proof of income and expenses for the previous 12 months, including canceled checks, paycheck stubs, invoices, and credit card statements

★ Evidence to support any unusual items involved in the offer (e.g., proof of bankruptcy, lawsuits, medical bills and/or physicians' statements, deaths in family)

2.3 Disadvantages of filing an Offer in Compromise

Filing an Offer in Compromise automatically extends the statute of limitations for the IRS to collect the tax for one year plus the time that the Offer in Compromise was pending. This means that the usual ten-year collection period is made longer, sometimes by as much as two years.

There are disadvantages to filing an Offer in Compromise, although generally the advantages far outweigh the disadvantages. Perhaps the most important disadvantage is that filing an offer automatically extends the statute of limitations for the IRS to collect the tax for one year plus the time that the Offer in Compromise was pending, even if the Offer in Compromise is later rejected by the IRS. What this means is that the usual ten-year collection period that the IRS has to legally collect a tax debt is made longer, sometimes by as much as two years. The good news is that this negative provision expires December 31, 2002, so that it would not apply to any offers filed in 2003 and beyond. Instead, you will now need to waive the statutory period (usually three years) for the IRS to assess any additional tax due for any of the years. This is not a major concession on your part.

In addition, an offer provides the IRS with a detailed road map for identifying assets it could seize from you. This list of assets comes from the completed financial forms and includes real estate, bank accounts, stocks and other investments, and vehicles. The IRS will typically not seize any assets while it investigates your financial affairs during the offer process. For most taxpayers, this is not really a concern as they had to provide the IRS with this financial information as soon as the revenue officer became involved in their case (especially if they attempted to get an Installment Agreement at any point during the collection process). As long as you fill out the financial forms completely and honestly, you have little need to worry that the IRS will seize your assets during the offer process.

The IRS will also keep any refunds that you may be entitled to receive for tax returns filed while the Offer is being reviewed. This includes any refunds that may arise during the calendar year that the IRS accepts the Offer. For instance, if the IRS accepts your Offer on March 3, 2003, any refund that you may have been entitled to receive when you file your 2003 tax return on April 15, 2004, will be forfeited to the IRS. Obviously, you should monitor your payments to the IRS very carefully once your Offer has been accepted to minimize the chance of this actually happening.

Finally, the IRS generally takes well over six months to process an offer, as it must determine whether the offer is able to be processed (i.e., if it meets the minimum requirements) and then investigate the offer. Be patient during the offer process, as it rarely goes as fast as you would like or expect. Interest on the tax liability continues to accrue during this time, and there is no certainty that the offer will ultimately be accepted. However, by this stage of the game most taxpayers have resigned themselves to the fact that the IRS moves slowly and that the accumulation of interest doesn't really matter because the debt could never be paid in full anyway.

3. The IRS Investigation Process

Once the IRS receives the Form 656, along with any other documents you submit, it will assign the offer to an investigator, usually a revenue officer or offer specialist, who will determine if the offer should be accepted. The first thing that the investigator will do is decide if the offer can be processed. All offers are considered processible unless they have one of the following problems:

★ The taxpayer or tax liabilities are not properly identified

★ An out-of-date Form 656 was used (or the terms on the printed Form 656 were changed)

★ No amount of money is offered (the taxpayer must offer the IRS something)

- ★ Required financial statements (Forms 433-A and/or 433-B) are not provided or are otherwise incomplete or missing required signatures

- ★ The amount offered is less than the value of the taxpayer's assets

- ★ The IRS does not have any record of a tax liability (I have never seen this happen but the IRS claims that it does!)

- ★ A Social Security or Employer Identification Number is missing, incomplete, or incorrect

- ★ The Offer is not properly signed

- ★ The Offer is submitted to delay or impede IRS collection efforts (i.e., it is not submitted in good faith)

If one of these conditions is met, the offer will be rejected immediately and returned to you with the reason for the rejection. You are permitted to correct the problem and resubmit the offer to the IRS, which will start the process all over again.

If the offer is processable, the investigator will review the entire offer package and contact you in writing with a list of any additional information the IRS needs from you to complete its investigation. Most document requests are for the following information:

- ★ Copies of tax returns for all years at issue in the offer

- ★ Copies of titles to automobiles or other property

- ★ Copies of bank statements for a certain period of time (often four to six months)

- ★ A current inventory of furniture and other household goods (if they are quite valuable, such as antiques or artwork)

- ★ Current pay statements (usually the last three months so the offer investigator can see patterns in your wages)

- ★ Copies of any life insurance policies (to prove the value of the policy, especially with whole-life policies)

- ★ Documentation concerning all stocks, bonds, mutual funds, and other investment accounts (for valuation purposes)

- ★ Documentation concerning all pension, retirement, and profit-sharing plans (also for valuation purposes)

- ★ Copies of deeds to all real estate

- ★ Copies of appraisals used to value property

★ Copies of all judgments and liens recorded against you (those recorded before the IRS recorded its Federal Tax Lien)

You will be given a deadline by which to have the information to the IRS. A failure to get the information to the IRS on time will almost always result in the offer being rejected. This is just one more reason why all IRS deadlines should be strictly observed.

Once the investigator receives all the relevant information and has an opportunity to review it, he or she will contact you with the results of the investigation. The IRS response to your offer will be one of the following:

(a) The IRS can accept the amount offered.

(b) The IRS cannot accept the amount offered and will reject the offer.

(c) The IRS cannot accept the amount offered but could accept the offer if it were increased.

Response number three is the most common, as nearly all offers involve some form of negotiations. The fact that the IRS is willing to negotiate is usually a positive sign. Negotiations often lead to an amount that both you and the IRS can be happy with. As long as both sides want to reach some sort of agreement, you can usually achieve one.

3.1 What if the IRS accepts the offer?

If the IRS accepts an Offer in Compromise, you obviously must make good on paying the IRS the full amount of the offer. It is generally acceptable for you to deposit 5% to 10% of the amount offered when you submit the Offer in Compromise to the IRS, and you are expected to pay the balance from 10 to 90 days after the IRS accepts the offer, as long as this was stated clearly in the offer.

As soon as the IRS receives the full amount from you, the IRS will adjust your account as if payment in full was received. This means that collection efforts are stopped and all Federal Tax Liens are released within 30 days of the completed offer. I recommend that you order a transcript of account 90 to 120 days after you pay the IRS in full, just to make sure that all account balances have been eliminated and all Federal Tax Liens have been removed. (The process for ordering the transcripts is discussed in chapter 2.)

Be sure to file and pay in full all tax returns due in the five-year period after the offer is accepted. This is a major requirement and one that cannot be ignored or forgotten. If you fail to do this, the IRS can subsequently reject the offer, based upon a default of the terms of its acceptance, and you are back to square one. The IRS adds this condition to all offers to make sure that the taxpayer will not owe the IRS any tax liabilities for at least five years.

In recent years a common problem involved married taxpayers. A couple would have an Offer in Compromise accepted, the couple would get divorced, and one of the ex-spouses would fail to comply with the five-year requirement for timely filing of tax returns and/or making the required payments. Until the Tax Reform Act of 1998 was passed, the one delinquent spouse in effect defaulted the Offer in Compromise for both spouses. The new law has cleared up this problem, and the default will only affect the spouse who didn't comply with the five-year requirement. It is now safe to file an Offer in Compromise with your spouse, even if divorce is imminent or has already occurred, without having to worry about whether your spouse will hold up his or her end of the bargain.

3.2 Collateral agreements

There are some instances where the IRS will require you to sign a collateral agreement before it agrees to accept an offer. A collateral agreement is your agreement to pay a percentage of future income to the IRS, or to waive your ability to use net operating losses or other losses, in exchange for the compromise of the tax liability.

While it does not require collateral agreements in the vast majority of offers, the IRS seems to use these agreements when dealing with taxpayers whose income fluctuates greatly from year to year. For example, a real estate agent or stockbroker may have bad years when the markets are down and very good years when the markets are up. In these instances the IRS may request a collateral agreement in which 20% of all income earned over $50,000 shall be paid to the IRS for each of the three years following acceptance of the offer.

In this instance, if the taxpayer earns less than $50,000, he or she would pay nothing to the IRS in addition to what was already offered. If the taxpayer has a good year, both the taxpayer and the IRS would benefit financially.

If the IRS suggests a collateral agreement, you should try to negotiate it out of the final resolution of the offer. Many taxpayers lose the incentive to earn as much money as possible when the IRS is going to get a percentage of that income. In addition, the collateral agreement keeps the IRS in your life for the length of the agreement, and it does not let you make a financial fresh start, which is the purpose of the Offer in Compromise program in the first place.

> After an offer is accepted, you must timely file and fully pay all tax returns for the next five years. A failure to do this will result in the offer being retroactively rejected.

Taxpayers almost always benefit from agreeing to a payment period that is as short as possible, as this gets the IRS out of the taxpayer's life as soon as possible.

3.3　What if the IRS rejects the offer?

The IRS is never required to accept an offer. If the IRS decides to reject the offer, it must tell you the reason for the rejection. If the offer was rejected because the amount offered was "too low," it is certainly appropriate to ask the IRS investigator what amount would be acceptable.

If you and the IRS are unable to come to a mutually satisfactory agreement, you can request an administrative review of the rejection. If you are still not satisfied after this review, you should appeal the rejection to the IRS Appeals Division. The appeals procedure is exactly the same as that for appealing a disagreed audit case, discussed in detail in chapter 6. You have 30 days from the date of the rejection letter to file your appeal.

In the appeal, it is important that you state the reasons for your disagreement with the IRS. Many offers are rejected simply because the investigator was unreasonable or applied inflated values to the taxpayer's assets. You have a good shot at winning in appeals, especially if you can prove the offer was rejected because the revenue officer was being unreasonable. The Appeals Division tries to solve problems that other divisions of the IRS couldn't or wouldn't solve, and the offer situation is no different from any other appeals.

The Appeals Division is your last chance to get the IRS to accept the offer, as you are not permitted to file a lawsuit to compel the IRS to accept the offer, even if the IRS is completely unreasonable in its determination.

If you are unable to convince the IRS Appeals Officer to accept your position, you are permitted to submit another Offer in the future. Simply because you lost in the first round does not mean that you cannot win in round two. You should increase the amount of the Offer for the second attempt unless you can show that your overall financial situation has taken a turn for the worse. You are also required to submit new financial statements when you file a new Offer.

Tax Points

★ An Offer in Compromise is an excellent way to pay the IRS much less money than you owe and eliminate your tax debt.

★ An Offer in Compromise should be considered by all taxpayers who cannot pay the IRS in full and who do not have enough assets to sell or future earnings to pay the tax debt.

★ An Offer in Compromise can also be used by any taxpayer who disagrees with the amount of the tax that the IRS claims is owed.

★ All asset values, except cash, used in determining how much money to offer the IRS are completely negotiable.

★ The IRS will accept offers that reasonably reflect the collection potential of the tax debt.

★ All taxpayers who have an Installment Agreement in place with the IRS at the beginning of the offer process should ask the IRS to waive the payments due under the Installment Agreement while the offer is being investigated.

★ An acceptable amount of money to offer the IRS is the total of your equity in your assets plus your near-future earning potential (the excess of income over necessary living expenses).

★ When considering your future earning potential, always use a present value analysis in computing the amount that could be paid in the four-year period.

★ The filing of an offer extends the time the IRS legally has to assess a tax debt.

★ The IRS will have access to detailed financial records of all taxpayers who submit offers based on their inability to pay (i.e., doubt as to collectibility).

★ You will need to stay current with all filing and paying requirements for five years after the IRS accepts your Offer in Compromise.

★ An Offer in Compromise can be used in situations in which paying the tax liabilities will create a severe economic hardship to you or your family.

CHAPTER 13

BANKRUPTCY LAW AND TAXES: FORCE THE IRS TO SAY YES

You will see and deal with so much dirt that you will assume that everyone is guilty.
Sheldon S. Cohen, commissioner of the IRS in a speech to new IRS agents, quoted in *Government Executive* (May 1990)

A government that is big enough to give you all you want is big enough to take it all away.

Senator Barry Goldwater (R-Arizona)

Many taxpayers end up owing the IRS far more money than they could ever hope to pay. If you are in this situation, you will typically try to work out a reasonable monthly payment plan with the IRS or submit a fair Offer in Compromise (see chapter 12), but sometimes neither of these effectively resolves the situation. In some cases, the revenue officer refuses to be reasonable and demands a monthly payment amount that you could never pay. The Offer in Compromise may be rejected, again because of an unreasonable IRS employee.

At this point the IRS sees that you are out of options, and it begins to lean on you for payment of the tax liability or threatens to seize your assets. You start to feel the situation is hopeless and wake up every day wondering what the IRS will do next to create more stress and discomfort.

When all else fails, you should consider whether bankruptcy would resolve your tax liability. Bankruptcy laws in the United States are meant

Bankruptcy laws in the United States are meant to permit a debtor to get a fresh financial start without having any more harassment from creditors or too much debt.

to permit a debtor (the person filing the bankruptcy petition) to get a fresh financial start without having any more harassment from creditors or too much debt. However, the Bankruptcy Code, at least with respect to taxes, is potentially confusing and, like almost everything else concerning the IRS, actually favors the IRS over nearly every other creditor.

This chapter is meant to provide only a brief overview of the potential use of bankruptcy to deal with a tax debt and is not meant to provide specific legal advice concerning this complicated issue. Any taxpayer considering bankruptcy as a means to eliminate or reduce a tax liability should seek legal counsel, preferably with an attorney who specializes in bankruptcy and tax matters, before actually filing bankruptcy.

In determining the effect of filing bankruptcy on your tax liabilities, you will ultimately need to consider the following:

★ The type of tax involved (such as employment, income, excise, etc.)

★ The age of the tax liability (i.e., when it was incurred)

★ Whether a tax return was filed

★ The chapter of the Bankruptcy Code under which you filed

1. Types of Bankruptcy

For purposes of this chapter, I will only consider Chapter 7 and Chapter 13 bankruptcies.

1.1 Chapter 7 bankruptcy

In a Chapter 7 bankruptcy, the debtor is attempting to liquidate his or her assets and obtain a fresh financial start by discharging (eliminating) his or her debts. Each state and the federal government has its own rules about how much property a debtor may keep (called "exempt property") without having to lose the property to his or her creditors. For example, all states allow debtors to keep their homes, as long as there is not too much equity in the house. Clothing, furniture and household goods, and many other types of property are considered "exempt," again with specific dollar limitations on the value of the property, which differ greatly from state to state. Check the laws of your particular state to determine how much property you could keep if you file a bankruptcy petition.

Once the Chapter 7 case works its way through the system and you obtain a discharge, all dischargeable debts are wiped out, and the creditors cannot try to collect the debt in the future. However, please be aware that Congress is trying to legislate changes to the Chapter 7 laws to make it more difficult for debtors to file Chapter 7 (and forcing them into Chapter 13 so they must pay some money to their unsecured creditors). At this point, there have been no major reforms, but sometime in the near future this is expected to occur in some form or another (and definitely not in your favor; the changes are being aggressively pursued by banks and credit card companies).

1.2 Chapter 13 bankruptcy

In a Chapter 13 bankruptcy case, the debtor is attempting to reorganize his or her financial affairs and pay off creditors through a bankruptcy plan. The debtor proposes a plan to pay off creditors over a certain period of time, usually between three and five years (with court approval). The payments must begin within 30 days after the plan is filed with the bankruptcy court. If the debtor follows the plan and makes all payments, the bankruptcy court will grant the debtor a discharge, and the debts that remain unpaid at the end of the plan are wiped out. In certain hardship situations, the bankruptcy court may permit a discharge even though all the plan payments have not been made.

Some tax debts that would not be dischargeable in a Chapter 7 bankruptcy can be discharged in a Chapter 13 case, as long as the bankruptcy plan contains some provisions for the tax debts. This last fact makes a Chapter 13 bankruptcy case very attractive to some taxpayers because of the so-called "super discharge" provisions under Chapter 13.

There are special rules concerning Chapter 13 cases and tax debts. Most of these rules concern whether the IRS is entitled to a priority position in the bankruptcy case. A priority position means that the tax debts are considered to be more important than other types of debts, such as credit cards, and that the IRS gets paid before many other creditors are paid. The bankruptcy plan must make sure that the IRS gets paid in full for these priority tax debts or the court may not approve the plan.

Many taxpayers use a Chapter 13 case to force the IRS to accept a payment plan for the taxes owed. As I previously discussed, the IRS may refuse to allow the taxpayer a payment plan, often because the revenue officer believes the taxpayer can pay the IRS more, either in a lump sum or on a monthly basis. The revenue officer may be being unreasonable, but the taxpayer lacks any alternative within the IRS. A Chapter 13 bankruptcy is an alternative outside the IRS.

Under Chapter 7 bankruptcy, debtors may keep their homes, clothing, furniture, and household goods — but there are specific dollar limitations on the value of the property.

In a Chapter 13 bankruptcy, debtors may reorganize their financial affairs and pay off creditors over a certain period of time.

2. Discharge of Taxes in Bankruptcy

Not all taxes can be discharged in bankruptcy. This is the case no matter under which chapter of the Bankruptcy Code you file your case. In general, personal taxes owed to the IRS or the state taxing authority are dischargeable if the bankruptcy is filed more than three years after the due date of the return, including any extensions. This assumes, however, that the tax return in question was actually filed with the IRS on or before the due date for the return (including any extensions).

For example, if a tax return for 2003 was filed on April 15, 2004 (the due date), the tax due would not be dischargeable in bankruptcy until after April 15, 2007. In this situation, you would have to wait until April 16, 2007, or later, to file a bankruptcy petition.

If you filed a late tax return, the return must have been filed at least two years before you file the bankruptcy petition in order to discharge the tax liability. For example, if you filed your 2003 return (due April 15, 2004) on July 10, 2005, you could not file for bankruptcy before July 11, 2007, if you wanted to discharge the 2003 tax liability. If you had filed this tax return on time, the tax debt could have been discharged at any time after April 15, 2007.

Keep the IRS assessment date in mind when considering the effect of filing a bankruptcy petition. In most cases, the date the tax return is filed is the assessment date (based upon a self-assessment of tax on the return itself). However, the IRS can make assessments on its own, as it does when an audit or a tax court proceeding produces additional tax, interest, and/or penalties due. In these instances of additional tax assessments, the three-year rule would not discharge the tax liability until at least 240 days have passed from the date of the new tax assessment prior to filing of the bankruptcy petition (even if the return was filed at least three years before the bankruptcy petition was filed).

For example, if you file your tax return for 2003 on the due date (April 15, 2004), the tax liability would normally be dischargeable after April 15, 2007 (three years). However, if an audit resulted in an additional tax due from you on March 15, 2007, you would have to wait until November 11, 2007, to file bankruptcy if you wanted to discharge the additional tax assessment (an additional 240 days from the date of the most recent tax assessment).

If the IRS refuses to discharge any taxes that are clearly dischargeable after the bankruptcy case has ended, you should first contact the IRS Special Procedures Division in writing and give the IRS an opportunity to correct

Under Chapter 13 bankruptcy laws, the IRS assumes priority position among creditors, and thus gets paid before many other creditors.

the mistake. Usually the IRS will correct the problem and prepare a Form 3870 to abate the taxes, penalties, and interest as a result of the bankruptcy action.

If the IRS still refuses to correct the problem, it may be necessary for you to go back to the bankruptcy court to get a court order on the dischargeability of the tax liabilities. Many bankruptcy court judges have found the IRS to be in contempt of court when it fails to stop its collection efforts after the tax liabilities have been discharged in bankruptcy.

2.1 Taxes not dischargeable in bankruptcy

Not all taxes can be discharged in bankruptcy. The following types of taxes are currently not dischargeable:

(a) Employment taxes (Form 941).

(b) Taxes due on unfiled tax returns. The clock on the two- or three-year rules does not start to tick until you actually file a tax return.

(c) Taxes due on a fraudulent tax return. If the IRS can prove fraud in the bankruptcy case, no taxes associated with the fraudulent return are dischargeable.

(d) Taxes assessed less than 240 days from the filing of the bankruptcy petition.

(e) Taxes due on returns filed late and within two years of the filing of the bankruptcy petition.

(f) Trust fund recovery penalties under IRC §6672 (see chapter 10).

(g) Taxes due on timely filed returns filed within three years of the filing of the bankruptcy petition.

If a tax is not discharged, you will remain liable for the tax, along with any penalties and interest on the tax, after the bankruptcy case is over. It is thus very important to understand, before filing the bankruptcy case, which taxes will be eliminated and which will remain owed to the IRS after the bankruptcy case is over.

2.2 Effect of bankruptcy on a Federal Tax Lien

If the IRS has filed a tax lien before the bankruptcy petition is filed, the tax lien attaches to all property that you owned before filing the bankruptcy case. After the bankruptcy petition is filed and a discharge is obtained, the Federal Tax Lien still remains attached to any of your property it was attached to at the time the bankruptcy petition was filed. The tax liability can be collected from the property subject to the Federal Tax Lien, even after the bankruptcy proceedings have ended. However, the IRS will usually remove a tax lien after a bankruptcy case if the debtor/taxpayer no longer has equity in any property to which the tax lien attached.

3. Advantages of Bankruptcy

Filing bankruptcy often makes sense as the only way to eliminate old tax debts, especially if the IRS is acting unreasonably regarding the collection of those debts, an all-too-common scenario. In addition to receiving the discharge of taxes available under the Bankruptcy Code, you can also stop the IRS from continuing its collection activities and may be able to force the IRS to accept a payment plan for nondischargeable taxes. I will discuss each of these advantages in turn.

3.1 Automatic stay

An automatic stay applies in every bankruptcy case and simply prevents your creditors, including the IRS, from trying to collect a debt after you file a bankruptcy petition. The types of collection actions that are not permitted under the automatic stay provisions include lawsuits (whether beginning or continuing), enforcement of judgments or liens, seizure of property, or any other collection measures. If a creditor, including the IRS, wants to continue any collection efforts, it must first get permission from the bankruptcy court for relief from the automatic stay.

The automatic stay does not stop the IRS from continuing an audit or assessing any future tax amounts, only from attempting to collect past-due tax debts. If the IRS violates the automatic stay, you are permitted to file suit to recover any actual damages you suffered, along with court costs and attorneys' fees.

3.2 Redetermination of taxes due

Under Section 505 of the Bankruptcy Code, the bankruptcy court is permitted to redetermine the amount of tax you owe to the IRS, including any penalties. If you believe that the IRS is wrong in its tax debt calculations, this is a good opportunity for you to have that amount reviewed by a judge, even if you previously contested the matter in tax court and lost. For example, if an audit produced an additional $25,000 in tax due and you lost an appeal in tax court, you can have a bankruptcy court judge review the issue to determine the correct amount of tax due for purposes of the bankruptcy case.

3.3   Elimination of tax debts after discharge is received

This is usually the reason why people file bankruptcy in the first place, as having all tax debts, including penalties and interest, eliminated is really the only way for some taxpayers to receive a fresh financial start. Before you file the bankruptcy case you should know which taxes will be dischargeable, as the IRS often makes incorrect decisions concerning the dischargeability of taxes (not usually in your favor, of course). You may have to ask the bankruptcy court for a court order determining the dischargeability of taxes, especially if the IRS is acting unreasonably.

3.4   Forcing the IRS to accept a payment plan

In Chapter 13 bankruptcy cases, you must submit a plan to the court outlining how you will pay your creditors over time. The IRS is included in these creditors. Many Chapter 13 cases are filed solely because the IRS refuses to agree to a reasonable payment plan for the tax debts. By filing a Chapter 13 bankruptcy case, you can force the IRS to accept a payment plan. The IRS does not have to approve the plan before you file it with the bankruptcy court. Instead, it will be up to the bankruptcy court judge to decide if the plan should be approved. This feature is quite attractive, as most taxpayers would not file a Chapter 13 bankruptcy if the IRS approved a payment plan on its own.

A Chapter 13 filing may be the only way to get the IRS to agree to a reasonable solution to the problem, as many revenue officers become much more reasonable about your case when you threaten them with a possible bankruptcy. If your threat does not work and the revenue officer remains unreasonable, you must be willing to go ahead with the bankruptcy.

4.   Disadvantages of Bankruptcy

Filing bankruptcy should always be regarded as a last resort because of the expenses associated with bankruptcy, the negative consequences to your credit rating, and the fact that the IRS is given additional time to collect taxes as soon as you are finished with the bankruptcy case.

4.1   Incurs expense

It is ironic that it can be very expensive to file bankruptcy, as a person wouldn't be filing bankruptcy if he or she had money. The filing fee alone

An automatic stay applies in every bankruptcy case and simply prevents your creditors, including the IRS, from trying to collect a past-due debt after you file a bankruptcy petition.

The filing of a bankruptcy case will show up on your credit report. This may be to your detriment should you try to borrow money in the near future.

is $175, and lawyers commonly charge $500 or more (sometimes much more) for their legal services, depending on the type and complexity of the bankruptcy.

4.2   Results in a negative credit report

The filing of a bankruptcy case will show up on your credit report and will be a major negative factor should you try to borrow money in the near future. However, if you are considering bankruptcy as a possible solution to a debt problem, you likely already have a poor credit rating, especially if the IRS has filed a Federal Tax Lien. In this case, the bankruptcy may not cause any more damage to what is already a bad situation.

4.3   Increases IRS collection time

Filing a bankruptcy case increases the amount of time that the IRS has to assess or collect taxes by adding 60 days for assessments and six months for collection, plus any time that the bankruptcy case is pending. If you are close to the end of the statute of limitations for the IRS to collect a tax debt, it may be better for you to wait and see what the IRS does in the time remaining on the limitations period before actually filing bankruptcy.

4.4   Incurs trustee fees

In a Chapter 13 case, the trustee will take 10% of all payments made under the plan as an administrative fee for collecting and disbursing the plan payments. This obviously adds to the overall expenses associated with filing a bankruptcy petition. However, like the filing and legal fees, this trustee's fee should not be a reason, in and of itself, not to file the case.

While filing a bankruptcy petition is not a magic cure for all IRS tax problems, it certainly should be considered if you have tried to deal with the IRS but have had no success. In some instances, it may be the only way to deal with an unreasonable revenue officer. It may also be a perfectly reasonable way to eliminate old tax debts, especially if the IRS has refused to consider your request to pay the IRS something on a monthly basis or through an Offer in Compromise.

Tax Points

★ Bankruptcy should always be considered an option for any taxpayer who owes the IRS for taxes more than three years old.

★ Bankruptcy stops the IRS and any other creditor from continuing with any collection activities while the bankruptcy case is pending.

★ Bankruptcy can force the IRS to accept a payment plan if the IRS is being unreasonable.

★ Bankruptcy can eliminate taxes, penalties, and interest owed to the IRS.

★ Not all taxes can be eliminated in a bankruptcy case.

★ Bankruptcy may not affect the taxpayer's property that is secured by a Federal Tax Lien.

★ Bankruptcy will appear on a credit report and will have a negative effect on the taxpayer's overall credit rating.

CHAPTER 14

THE CRIMINAL INVESTIGATION DIVISION: BEWARE THE AGENTS WITH GUNS

Taxes cause crime. When the tax rate reaches 25%, there is an increase in lawlessness. America's tax system is inspired by Karl Marx.

Ronald Reagan, former president of the United States
(1980 – 1988)

The income tax created more criminals than any other single act of government.

Senator Barry Goldwater (R-Arizona) in an interview for PBS
Firing Line, November 18, 1989

We don't pay taxes. Only the little people pay taxes.

Leona Helmsley, who made this claim before being convicted of
criminal tax evasion, a conviction affirmed by the Court of Appeals
in July 1991

As complicated as the tax laws are in this country, it is in your interest to obey them. Taxpayers who do not comply with the tax laws can be hit with criminal penalties, including time in prison and very large fines. The IRS Criminal Investigation Division (CID) is responsible for investigating potential criminal violations under the IRC. The individuals responsible for criminal tax investigations within the CID are called special agents.

A special agent's main focus is to determine whether there is sufficient evidence to recommend a taxpayer be prosecuted for criminal offenses or to recommend imposing the civil fraud penalty. CID agents are considered to be law enforcement personnel and are the only IRS employees permitted to carry weapons. You should always treat the presence of a special agent very seriously, as the agent's goal is to see that any taxpayer violating tax laws does time in prison.

> A Criminal Investigation Division special agent investigates criminal violations under the Internal Revenue Code. A special agent is considered to be a law enforcement officer and may carry a weapon.

1. How Many IRS Criminal Investigations Occur Each Year?

IRS criminal investigations are highly publicized events. It is not mere coincidence that every year, in anticipation of the April 15 filing deadline, the IRS issues numerous press releases describing high-profile criminal investigations. It is also amazing how many well-known individuals have been criminally prosecuted by the IRS. For example, you no doubt have heard of Al Capone, Leona Helmsley, Darryl Strawberry, John Gotti, Pete Rose, Jim Bakker, Heidi Fleiss, Spiro Agnew, and countless others who believed that the tax laws, whether civil or criminal, did not apply to them. The IRS thrives on the free publicity it gains from these cases, knowing that the media will carry the stories and taxpayers will hear or read them.

The media coverage that the IRS generates during the first few months of every year makes it appear the number of criminal tax prosecutions is very high. The IRS uses this tactic to encourage the public to comply with the tax laws. In fact, the decision to investigate and prosecute a taxpayer for criminal tax violations is a relatively rare event, as Table 12 shows.

TABLE 12
NUMBER OF IRS CRIMINAL INVESTIGATIONS

Year	New Investigations	Discontinued	Referred for Prosecution	Number of Convictions	% to Prison
1995	5,000	1,649	3,614	2,948	79.58
1996	5,334	1,557	3,605	2,915	77.60
1997	5,335	1,437	3,817	3,110	80.19
1998	4,655	1,298	3,527	3,000	81.13
1999	3,952	1,143	3,120	2,713	81.48
2000	3,372	1,065	2,434	2,249	80.88
2001	3,284	1,005	2,335	2,251	83.95
2002	3,906	1,011	2,133	1,926	82.20
2003	4,001	1,225	2,541	1,824	84.00
(Statistics from the IRS Annual Data Books)					

The New Investigations column in Table 12 represents the number of new IRS criminal investigations during the year for the entire United States, while the Discontinued column contains all investigations discontinued during the year, whether they were started in an earlier year or in the same year. The Referred for Prosecution column represents all cases that the IRS CID referred to the Department of Justice (through the IRS area counsel) for possible prosecution. Not all of these cases actually get prosecuted. The Number of Convictions column represents the total number of federal tax convictions, with most of the convictions the result of investigations begun in previous years (most investigations take more than one year to get through the legal system). The % Sent to Prison column represents the percentage of all taxpayers convicted of tax-related crimes who received some prison time as a result of their conviction.

As you can see, the IRS is being much more selective in the types of cases it chooses to investigate, which is certainly good news. In addition, the quality of cases from the IRS' perspective is increasing, as shown by the much higher percentage of taxpayers who are convicted and serve at least some time in prison. This shows that CID is making good choices and effective use of its limited resources — something most other IRS divisions cannot claim.

> The limited number of criminal investigations by the IRS should not be viewed as a license to cheat on taxes.

While it is unlikely that the IRS will start a criminal investigation against any particular taxpayer, this does not mean you should be unconcerned about possible criminal violations. In other words, the limited number of criminal investigations should not be viewed as a license to cheat on taxes.

The IRS claims that the tax system is "voluntary" and that it is up to US citizens to self-assess the tax due by filing a tax return. The question then becomes: What happens if you don't "volunteer"? Most of us know the answer to this question. The nonvolunteers will often, but not always, end up in the middle of an IRS investigation, and at that point they had better hope that the investigation does not lead to criminal charges.

In this chapter I describe IRS criminal investigation procedures and the types of criminal tax crimes under the IRC.

2. IRS Criminal Investigation Procedures

The IRS receives information about potential tax crimes from a number of sources. The IRS special agent also has a couple of different options available to him or her for pursuing a criminal investigation.

2.1 The referral process

All criminal tax cases begin with a referral to the CID, unless the CID discovers the criminal activity on its own (usually through undercover operations or in-house informants). The CID gets referrals from several different sources.

2.1.a Other IRS personnel

In the course of performing audit or collection work, IRS employees are trained to recognize criminal violations and must make a referral to the CID if they suspect any potential criminal violations. This is perhaps the most common way that criminal tax cases get started, which is just one more reason why you should never violate one of the basic rules when dealing with the IRS: never lie to the IRS or any of its employees. Many IRS employees wouldn't recognize a technical or complex criminal violation if it jumped up and hit them in the face, but they do understand that a taxpayer will lie to cover up something the taxpayer doesn't want the IRS to discover. In short, a lie is a sure way to invite a visit from a not-so-very-friendly CID agent.

2.1.b Paid informants

Under IRC §7623, the IRS is permitted to pay individuals for information leading to the successful prosecution of persons guilty of tax-related crimes. Under current IRS policy, the information must be "specific and responsible" and must lead to a direct recovery of additional tax. There can be no reward money without the IRS recovering additional tax that it would not have otherwise known about. What this reward program means is that you should think twice about telling anyone about your tax situation, including whether returns have been filed or if the filed returns were accurate. Simple comments such as "I didn't report $20,000 of cash and the IRS will never know about it," or "I never file tax returns and the IRS has never said anything about it to me" are likely to come back to haunt you. Many people, including former employees, business partners, friends, relatives (including spouses in some instances), and other individuals, may use that information in an attempt to collect "reward" money from the IRS.

The IRS may offer a reward for specific information that leads to the successful prosecution of tax criminals.

The IRS makes it difficult to collect reward money, as the list of situations in which it won't pay is long and seems to cover more situations than not. For example, the IRS will not pay any reward money if it determines that the information was not valuable, was already known to the

IRS (and how is the informant ever to prove that the IRS didn't know about it?), that the informant also participated in the criminal activity, that the payment would be contrary to state law, or that the informant was a government employee who obtained the information as part of his or her official job duties. In any event, it is always better not to take any chances, as the IRS will have the information even if no reward money is ever paid.

2.1.c CID undercover operations

CID agents are permitted under the law to engage in undercover operations to assist in obtaining a criminal tax conviction. An undercover operation is simply a way for special agents to disguise their identity when making contact with potential tax criminals. For example, if the special agent suspects a taxpayer of engaging in money laundering (i.e., taking money from illegal sources, such as drug dealers, and making it appear to be from legal business sources) and/or not reporting taxable income, the special agent can pose as a drug dealer to see how the taxpayer responds. This is perfectly legal as long as the special agent doesn't induce the taxpayer to commit a crime that he or she would not otherwise have committed. If the special agent does induce an innocent taxpayer into committing a tax crime, the taxpayer would be able to use the defense that he or she was a victim of entrapment. It is not entrapment if the special agent helps a taxpayer to commit a crime as long as the criminal activity was the taxpayer's idea.

2.1.d Other governmental agencies

All banks, financial institutions, and any other businesses that receive more than $10,000 in cash in a transaction or series of related transactions must report the cash payment to the IRS.

Several federal agencies, including the Federal Bureau of Investigation (FBI), Securities and Exchange Commission (SEC), and Drug Enforcement Administration (DEA), investigate potential crimes that deal with money. For example, in the course of a drug investigation, the DEA may find out that a drug dealer sold cocaine and made a $100,000 profit on the sale transaction. While the DEA is not concerned with tax crimes, it may make a referral to the IRS, suggesting it investigate whether the drug dealer reported the profits from the cocaine sale on his or her tax return. Given that few persons who earn illegal income actually report the income on a tax return, the drug dealer will likely be facing tax evasion charges in addition to the drug charges.

Many state and local law enforcement agencies report possible tax violations to the CID. State or local law enforcement agencies often share this information to collect "reward" money from the IRS (the agencies see the IRS as a funding source for new squad cars and computers).

2.1.e Banks and other financial institutions

Surprisingly, the IRS receives several good investigative leads every year from banks and other financial institutions in this country. All banks, financial institutions, and any other businesses that receive more than $10,000 in cash in a transaction or series of related transactions must report the cash payment to the IRS. If they fail to report these cash transactions, they are subject to their own criminal and civil penalties.

The IRS monitors this cash transaction information closely because many illegal businesses generate large amounts of cash in their day-to-day operations. If the IRS sees a pattern develop with respect to any particular taxpayer, it will likely begin an investigation to make sure that all tax laws are being properly followed.

2.2 Rules for criminal investigations

While each criminal investigation is unique, there are certain rules that any taxpayer under criminal investigation must follow. Briefly, these rules are as follows:

(a) *Do not cooperate with the IRS CID without first obtaining advice from legal counsel.* An individual under a criminal investigation, unlike those in other tax investigations such as audits, is not required to cooperate with the IRS and should not cooperate in most instances.

(b) *Always exercise your Fifth Amendment rights and remain silent (never talk to a special agent without an attorney present).* An IRS special agent is trained to get you to make damaging statements. By always remaining silent, you will never provide the IRS with the ammunition to gun you down. It is also important for you to remember that the IRS has the burden of proof in all criminal cases (i.e., it must prove that you are guilty), and you should never make the IRS's task of satisfying its burden of proof any easier than it already may be.

(c) *Always get competent counsel, experienced in IRS criminal investigations, if any tax investigation turns criminal.* A criminal investigation is never the place to experiment with representing yourself.

2.3 Types of IRS criminal investigations

There are two ways for an IRS special agent to investigate potential tax crimes:

(a) *Administrative investigation.* In an administrative investigation, the special agent attempts to get all information and evidence on his or her own, usually by talking to witnesses and getting documents through a summons or search warrant. After all evidence is received and reviewed, the special agent makes a recommendation as to whether to prosecute or not.

(b) *Federal Grand Jury.* A grand jury investigation is similar to an administrative investigation, except that the Department of Justice and the grand jury will assist the special agent in the investigation. Grand jury investigations are commonly used when the special agent is having problems getting witnesses to cooperate or where the subject of the investigation is well known. Furthermore, a grand jury is almost always used when the person is suspected of violating nontax criminal laws, such as the drug or bribery laws.

Under either type of investigation, if the special agent believes there is enough evidence to prosecute the taxpayer, he or she must refer the case to area counsel (the IRS in-house legal staff) for review. If area counsel agrees with the special agent, the case is forwarded to the Department of Justice in Washington for review. If a prosecution is still recommended, the Department of Justice sends the case to the US Attorney Office for the actual criminal prosecution.

If you are under investigation, you have an opportunity to meet with the government at each stage in the process to try to get the prosecution dropped. It is usually a good idea to meet with the government as many times as possible (through legal representation), because each meeting provides an opportunity to learn more about the government's case, to provide defenses to the proposed charges, and to establish a pattern of cooperating with the investigation.

Tax evasion
(a criminal offense)
is not the same as tax
avoidance, which involves
legal ways of reducing the
overall taxes due.

3. Types of Criminal Tax Violations

Several different sections of the IRC relate to criminal tax violations. Following are the most common types of tax crimes that special agents tend to investigate.

3.1 Criminal tax evasion

Tax evasion is perhaps the tax crime most familiar to the general public. It is the most serious tax crime that the IRS can charge a taxpayer with committing, and it is also the most difficult for the government to prove. Under IRC §7201, a taxpayer commits tax evasion if he or she "willfully attempts in any manner to evade or defeat any tax." Note that tax evasion is not the same thing as tax avoidance. Every individual has the right to avoid paying taxes if it's done legally according to the IRC. For instance, it is perfectly legitimate to maximize all permissible deductions, claim all valid exemptions, and write off every business expense that the IRC allows. It is also absolutely reasonable to use well-thought-out tax and estate planning to shift the tax responsibilities to someone in a lower tax bracket, or to otherwise reduce the overall taxes due. Tax evasion is criminal; tax avoidance is legal.

To convict an individual of criminal tax evasion, the government must prove, beyond a reasonable doubt, that the taxpayer —

(a) owes additional tax,

(b) willfully failed to pay the tax, and

(c) attempted to evade or defeat the tax.

Most defenses to a criminal tax evasion charge relate to willfulness or the attempt to evade or defeat the tax, as the government is almost always able to show that an additional tax is due. For purposes of the criminal tax laws, willfulness is considered to be a voluntary, intentional violation of the law, as opposed to an unintentional mistake. Therefore, many taxpayers will claim that any violation of the tax laws was unintentional or simply a mistake.

Courts have held that a taxpayer's misunderstanding of the tax laws, as long as the mistake was made in good faith and was not intentional, is enough to defeat the government's criminal tax evasion case. This "good faith" misunderstanding does not have to be "reasonable" to be successful. Claiming that the tax laws are unconstitutional would not be a valid defense in this type of case. Furthermore, negligence, no matter how reckless it may have been, is not sufficient to establish a taxpayer's willfulness. The only time that the IRS can use negligence, or ignorance of the tax laws, to support its criminal case is if you purposefully decided to avoid finding out all of the facts or the correct interpretation of the law before filing your tax return.

Taxpayers have successfully defeated IRS criminal tax evasion charges by claiming that they relied on the advice of a tax preparer or attorney in filing the return. This defense works only if you tell the preparer or attorney all the facts and if it was the professional, and not you, who made the mistake. If you did not give the preparer or attorney all the facts, the defense will not be successful.

You may also use any other defense that demonstrates you were not "willful" in the evasion of your tax liability.

The government rarely has any direct evidence of your intent to evade taxes, such as a confession ("I know I should have reported that $20,000 cash payment but I didn't think the IRS would ever find out about it"). Instead, the government will usually rely on your conduct to show that you intentionally tried to evade a tax known to be due and owing. Examples of conduct that the courts have accepted to show this type of intent include the following:

★ Keeping a double set of books and records

★ Destroying books, records, or other relevant tax documents

★ Altering records used to support the tax return

★ Making false invoices, receipts, or other documents used to prove some item on the tax return

★ Filing false employee withholding forms (W-4) with an employer to eliminate any tax withholding

★ Concealing assets from the IRS

★ Hiding sources of income (i.e., not reporting income from a moonlighting job)

★ Using fictitious names on bank accounts

★ Using cash to avoid a paper trail without any legitimate business reasons (i.e., going to currency exchanges when you have a bank account available)

These are just some of the possible activities the government will use as evidence to try to get a criminal tax evasion conviction. If the government obtains a conviction, the court can sentence you to up to five years in prison and/or a fine of up to $100,000. The court will almost always order some prison time for a conviction in tax evasion cases.

3.2 Filing a false return

The IRS can criminally prosecute any taxpayer who files a false tax return, statement or other document with the IRS. Under IRC §7206(1), any person who willfully files any tax return or other document with the IRS knowing that it is false can be convicted of a felony. This criminal section applies to many different types of documents that can be filed with the IRS, including tax returns, financial statements (Forms 433-A and B), Offers in Compromise (Form 656), and any other document signed under the penalty of perjury.

For the government to convict you on a charge of filing a false return, it must prove each of the following elements beyond a reasonable doubt:

(a) You signed a return or other document that was false and signed the document under the penalties of perjury. All tax returns and many other IRS forms contain a clause (called a jurat) that states: "Under penalties of perjury, I declare that I have examined this return and accompanying schedules and statements, and to the best of my knowledge and belief, they are true, correct, and complete. Declaration of preparer (other than taxpayer) is based on all information of which preparer has any knowledge."

(b) You knew the return or other document was false as to some material matter.

(c) You signed the return or other document willfully with the intent to violate the law.

Nearly all defenses to this criminal violation center on your knowledge, willfulness, and intent when you filed the document with the IRS. The IRS realizes that most taxpayers will claim that any mistakes on the tax returns were unintentional and that they never would intentionally file a false tax return with the IRS. To combat the "mistake" defense, the IRS will usually only prosecute those taxpayers who have a pattern of filing false tax returns. To establish a pattern, the IRS will want at least three years of false tax returns, mainly because one year may be an unintentional mistake or omission, but three or more years is probably intentional.

To demonstrate that the tax return was false as to some "material" matter, the IRS will usually try to show that it was unable to determine the accuracy of the return and the correct amount of income tax due because of the false information. For example, if you or your tax preparer accidentally spelled your name wrong (and did not do it to mislead the IRS), it would not be material because the IRS could still determine whether the

> The IRS will usually only prosecute taxpayers who have a pattern of filing false taxes returns (i.e., at least three years of false returns).

tax return was accurate. However, if you failed to report all income or business receipts (even if reporting them would not result in any additional tax due), it would be enough to support a false return conviction because the mistake would be considered "material."

In addition, you should always correctly report the source and type of any income received during the year. It is not a crime to report income from illegal sources as "other" income on the return and refuse to disclose the source (because disclosing the source may then lead to prosecution for the illegal activity). It is, however, a crime to try to report illegal income as being from a legal source (such as calling income from illegal pornography sales as income from a pizzeria), even if it makes no difference as far as the total tax due for the year.

Given that a conviction is a felony under IRC §7206(1), the court is permitted to sentence any taxpayer found guilty of filing a false tax return to a maximum of three years in prison and/or a fine of up to $100,000. Many taxpayers convicted of this offense will do some time in a penitentiary, although it is certainly not required.

3.3 Criminal failure to file a tax return

Under IRC §7203, the IRS can prosecute individuals who willfully fail to file a tax return. In deciding whether to prosecute an individual under this section, the IRS will usually look at the following information:

★ *The number of years that you have not filed tax returns.* The IRS tries to develop a pattern — usually over three or more years — to counter many of the available defenses.

★ *The amount of tax owed.* The less tax owed, the less likely a criminal prosecution will be initiated.

★ *Your occupation and education.* If you are a CPA, the IRS will likely prosecute, because a CPA probably would have been, or should have been, aware of the filing responsibilities.

★ *Your previous tax return filing history.* If you filed tax returns in the past but recently stopped filing, there may be a reason for the failure to file that will not support a criminal prosecution or conviction — such as a serious illness or a death in your family.

★ *Your cooperation with the criminal investigation.*

To successfully prosecute an individual for the criminal failure to file tax returns, the government must be able to prove all of the following, again beyond a reasonable doubt:

(a) You were required to file a tax return. (See chapter 3 for a discussion of who must file tax returns. The IRS must be able to prove that you made at least the minimum income required before a tax return is legally due.)

(b) You failed to file a return on or before its due date.

(c) The failure to file was willful.

The first two elements are generally easy for the government to prove, as it is obvious whether a person was required to file and did not file. It is the third element, whether the failure to file was willful, that is often the only issue to resolve in these criminal cases. The IRS again must be able to prove that you knew you were required to file a tax return but intentionally decided not to file the return.

You have many potential defenses available for a failure-to-file criminal charge — limited only by your imagination. The most common are the following:

★ You genuinely believed that you did not legally have to file a tax return.

★ You genuinely believed that certain receipts of money were not considered to be taxable income (and thus did not understand the tax laws).

You are not permitted to claim that you did not file a tax return because you were exercising your Fifth Amendment right not to provide evidence against yourself. This situation comes up when taxpayers make money from some illegal source and are afraid if they report the money they will be caught. In these instances, you must still file a tax return, but you do not need to disclose the source of the income.

In addition, many tax protestors intentionally fail to file tax returns, often using the Fifth Amendment to support their nonfiling position. Again, this defense will not work, as tax protestors are certainly not immune to potential criminal prosecutions for willfully failing to file income tax returns.

If you are found guilty of this offense, the court can impose a sentence of up to one year in prison and/or a fine of up to $25,000. While a violation under IRC §7203 is a misdemeanor, the possible punishment is serious enough to make taxpayers think twice before intentionally deciding not to file tax returns.

3.4 Other tax-related crimes

3.4.a Conspiracy — 18 USC §371

Tax conspiracy involves two or more individuals working together to defraud the IRS. For example, a tax-related conspiracy may be an agreement between two businesspersons to hide assets and produce false business receipts.

Another common form of tax-related conspiracy involves efforts to make illegal income appear to be from a legitimate source. A drug dealer may work out a deal with a local restaurant owner whereby the dealer will give the restaurant owner $5,000 in cash and the owner will give the dealer a check for $4,500 in exchange. The restaurant owner will probably report the $5,000 as business receipts for the restaurant and call the $4,500 amount a payment for some business expense, such as wages or commissions. Both the restaurant owner and drug dealer have violated 18 USC §371 by engaging in a tax-related conspiracy (and may have also violated the money-laundering laws, discussed briefly below).

The conspiracy statute tries to discourage people from making agreements to violate the law and then making the agreement a reality. In the tax area, the government does not have to prove that the individuals involved understood the tax consequences of the conspiracy. As long as the individuals' reasons for the conspiracy are tax related, the IRS is interested in prosecuting. Taxpayers found guilty of engaging in a tax-related conspiracy can be sent to prison for up to five years.

3.4.b Submitting false statements or documents to the IRS — 18 USC §1001

The IRS frequently tries to punish taxpayers who submit false documents or statements to the IRS during the course of a tax case (usually during an audit or collections case). The basis for the criminal prosecution is 18 USC §1001. This section is more general than IRC §7206(1) (filing a false return) in that it covers *any* document provided to the IRS that turns out to be falsified (i.e., you knew it was false when it was submitted), whether or not you signed or submitted the document under the penalties of perjury. This section of the US Code states:

> *Whoever, in any matter within the jurisdiction of any department or agency of the United States, knowingly and willfully falsifies, conceals or covers up by any trick, scheme, or device, a*

material fact, or makes any false, fictitious, or fraudulent state-
ments or representations, or makes or uses any false writing or
document knowing the same to contain any false, fictitious, or
fraudulent statement or entry, shall be fined under this title or
imprisoned not more than five years, or both.

This section is the criminal sanction for lying to the IRS. I have re-peated the number one rule over and over: Never lie to the IRS. If the IRS finds out that you have falsified a receipt, altered an invoice, provided a fraudulent statement, or submitted any other false statement or document to the IRS, you will be the subject of a criminal referral.

Normally referrals are made by revenue agents, because most docu-ments that are falsified are done so during the course of an audit. How-ever, it is not uncommon for revenue officers to obtain false documents during the course of a collections case. As long as the government can prove that you knew that the document submitted was false, the IRS will prosecute and will often win the case. And your loss can again mean up to five years in prison.

3.4.c Money laundering — 18 USC §1956 and §1957

The IRS has recently begun to pursue all individuals who help other indi-viduals in financial transactions involving "dirty money." For purposes of the money-laundering laws, "dirty money" is considered to be money from a "specified unlawful activity." Specified unlawful activities include all drug and organized crime offenses, along with most other federal crimes (e.g., murder, kidnapping, arson, robbery, extortion, bribery, coun-terfeiting, racketeering, dealing in narcotics). Most of the time, dirty money involves proceeds from illegal businesses, such as drug sales, but it can involve any criminal activity that produces income for the criminal or the criminal enterprise.

The government must be able to prove that the individual knew the money came from an illegal activity before there can be a money-laundering violation. In addition, the government must also prove that the transac-tion involving the illegal activity took place in interstate commerce and that it was intended to conceal or disguise the true nature of the financial transaction. If the government is successful in a money-laundering prose-cution, the person who committed the crime can receive up to 20 years in prison and/or a fine up to $500,000 (or twice the value of the funds in-volved in the laundering, whichever is greater). Money-laundering charges are extremely serious and should always be handled by an experienced criminal tax attorney, as this is certainly not an area where any mistakes can be made.

4. Statute of Limitations

The IRS has six years to prosecute individuals for criminal violations of the tax laws. The six-year period begins on the date that the tax return is due, taking into account any extension requests. For example, if a 1997 tax return was due on August 15, 1998, because the taxpayer received an extension of time to file the return, any criminal prosecution relating to this return must be filed before August 15, 2004, or the government cannot prosecute the taxpayer for any criminal activity relating to this return. For charges that a taxpayer submitted a false document to the IRS in violation of 18 USC §1001, the government has five years from the date that the false document is submitted to begin prosecution.

5. Taxpayer Rights During Criminal Investigations

Contrary to what the IRS may tell the public or believe itself, you must understand that you, and not the government, have rights during a criminal investigation. These rights include the following:

(a) *You have a Fifth Amendment privilege against self-incrimination.* This means that a CID special agent cannot force you to speak to him or her, or force you to give any documents to the special agent that may provide evidence to convict you of a crime.

(b) *You have a right to receive* Miranda *warnings if you are in custody and to receive a statement explaining your rights if not in custody. Miranda* warnings include those informing you of your right to remain silent and to consult with an attorney, amongst other rights, before any statements can be used against you in court. CID special agents carry a card they must always read to a criminal tax suspect before they can do any questioning. This statement reads:

> *As a special agent, one of my functions is to investigate the possibility of criminal violations of the Internal Revenue laws, and related offenses. In connection with my investigation of your tax liability (or other matter), I would like to ask you some questions. However, first I advise you that under the Fifth Amendment to the Constitution of the*

United States I cannot compel you to answer any questions or to submit any information if such answers or information might tend to incriminate you in any way. I also advise you that anything which you say and any documents which you submit may be used against you in any criminal proceedings which may be undertaken. I advise you further that you may, if you wish, seek the assistance of an attorney before responding.

These rights must be read before any question-and-answer sessions with the taxpayer can begin.

(c) *You have the right to counsel during all phases of the criminal investigation under the Sixth Amendment to the US Constitution.*

You should realize, however, that the Taxpayer Bill of Rights (see chapter 16) does not apply in criminal tax investigations. These rights only apply in audits, collection cases, or any other noncriminal IRS matter.

Tax Points

★ Never lie to the IRS or any of its employees.

★ Always report all income, even if the income is from illegal sources.

★ Never discuss your confidential tax situation with anyone, including friends and relatives, as anyone can become a paid IRS informant.

★ Never speak to an IRS special agent without an experienced criminal tax attorney present.

★ Do not cooperate with an IRS special agent before first obtaining legal advice.

★ Never make up documents to support your tax return. It is better to lose the issue during the audit or collection case than to go to prison for submitting false documents to the IRS.

★ Do not file a false tax return with the IRS. It is better not to file a return at all than to file a false return.

★ Never assist other individuals who are involved in illegal businesses, no matter how much money they are offering you; it is not worth the high risk of serving time in jail for the assistance.

CHAPTER 15

FIGHT THE IRS IN COURT

The government is mainly an expensive organization to regulate evildoers, and tax those who behave; government does little for fairly respectable people except annoy them.

Edgar Watson Howe (1853 – 1937), US writer, in *Notes For My Biographer* (1926)

If mass murderer Jeffrey Dahmer is innocent until proven guilty, why in God's name isn't a taxpayer?

Representative James A. Traficant Jr. (D-Ohio), discussing House Resolution 3261 on April 21, 1994

It is never easy to fight the IRS in court, as Congress has created laws that make it difficult for taxpayers to sue the IRS in any court and win. The usual reason given by Congress for enacting these laws is that the government cannot operate without money, and it is up to the IRS to collect the money for the government. Therefore, according to Congress, the IRS must get special treatment whenever it comes to taxpayer lawsuits.

This does not mean, however, that a taxpayer cannot beat the IRS in court. In this chapter I discuss several different types of suits available to taxpayers in their battles with the IRS.

1. The US Tax Court

The US tax court is set up to hear taxpayer challenges to IRS notices of tax deficiencies. A tax deficiency normally occurs when the IRS wants to increase a taxpayer's tax due after an audit of one or more tax returns. After the IRS issues a Notice of Deficiency, you have 90 days to challenge the IRS by filing a petition with the US tax court. It currently costs $60 to file the petition. Under tax court Rule 20(b), the court may waive the filing fee for taxpayers who cannot pay. In order to waive the filing fee, you must submit a financial affidavit demonstrating your inability to pay.

While the tax court is located in Washington DC, it hears cases in cities all over the United States. The tax court's mailing address is: 400 Second Street NW, Washington DC, 20217. The clerk of the court can be reached by telephone at (202) 376-2754.

The tax court currently hears regular cases in the following cities: Albuquerque, Anchorage, Atlanta, Baltimore, Biloxi, Birmingham, Boise, Boston, Buffalo, Charleston, Chicago, Cincinnati, Cleveland, Columbia, Columbus, Dallas, Denver, Des Moines, Detroit, El Paso, Hartford, Helena, Honolulu, Houston, Indianapolis, Jackson, Jacksonville, Kansas City, Knoxville, Las Vegas, Little Rock, Los Angeles, Louisville, Lubbock, Memphis, Miami, Milwaukee, Mobile, Nashville, New Orleans, New York, Oklahoma City, Omaha, Philadelphia, Phoenix, Pittsburgh, Portland, Reno, Richmond, Salt Lake City, San Antonio, San Diego, San Francisco, St. Louis, St. Paul, Seattle, Spokane, Tampa, Washington DC, Westbury, and Winston-Salem. There are some additional cities not listed here that the tax court uses for "S" cases. The taxpayer tells the tax court where he or she would like the case to be heard by filing a Designation of Place of Trial with the Court. Sample 31 is an example of a tax court petition, while Sample 32 is a Designation of Place of Trial.

After the petition is filed with the tax court, the IRS, through its attorneys at area counsel, will file an answer in the case. The answer simply tells the court, and the taxpayer/petitioner, which sections of the taxpayer's petition the IRS agrees and disagrees with. The court will now know what issues will be contested should the parties not reach a settlement in the case.

After the answer is filed, the case is considered to be at issue and a trial date will be set, often several months in the future. In the time before the trial date, the IRS, through its Appeals Division, will contact the taxpayer and attempt to settle the case without having to go to trial. Most tax court cases are settled by the parties without having to go to trial. If a settlement cannot be worked out, the parties must present their cases to the tax court and let the court decide.

Once a petition has been filed with the tax court, the IRS Appeals Division will try to settle the case with the taxpayer without having to go to trial.

SAMPLE 31
TAX COURT PETITION

UNITED STATES TAX COURT

HERMAN H. MUNSTER	)
	)
Petitioner,	)
	)
	)
V.	) DOCKET NO.
	)
	)
COMMISSIONER OF INTERNAL REVENUE	)
	)
	)
Respondent.	)

PETITION

1.   Petitioner disagrees with the tax deficiency for the taxable year 1995 as set forth in the NOTICE OF DEFICIENCY dated November 22, 1998, a copy of which is hereby attached. The notice was issued by the Office of Internal Revenue Service at Ogden, Utah.

2.   Petitioner's taxpayer identification number is: 123-45-6789.

3.   Petitioner disputes the following:

Year	Deficiency Disputed	Additions Disputed	
1995	$15,111.00	IRC §6662(a)	$3022.20

4.   Petitioner respectfully disagrees with the following adjustments contained in the Notices of Deficiency:

a. The Commissioner of Internal Revenue improperly disallowed Petitioner's Schedule A deductions in the amount of $12,020 by claiming that petitioner failed to substantiate his medical expense and taxes paid during 1995.

b. The Commissioner of Internal Revenue improperly claimed that Petitioner received Non-Employee Compensation/Schedule C receipts in the amount of $18,433 without giving Petitioner his ordinary and necessary business expenses under IRC §162.

c.   The Commissioner of Internal Revenue improperly applied an addition to tax for the taxable year 1995 under IRC §6662(a).

WHEREFORE, Petitioner respectfully requests that this Honorable Court determine that he owes no additional tax or additions to tax for the taxable year 1995.

Respectfully submitted,

_____

Herman H. Munster
Petitioner
1313 Mockingbird Lane
Denver, CO 80222
Telephone: (303) 555-1212

SAMPLE 32
DESIGNATION OF PLACE OF TRIAL

UNITED STATES TAX COURT

HERMAN H. MUNSTER   )
)
        Petitioner,   )
)
)
        V.   )   DOCKET NO.
)
)
COMMISSIONER OF INTERNAL REVENUE   )
)
        Respondent.   )

DESIGNATION OF PLACE OF TRIAL

Petitioner hereby designates DENVER, COLORADO, as the place of trial in this case.

Respectfully submitted,

_____

Herman H. Munster
Petitioner
1313 Mockingbird Lane
Denver, CO 80222
Telephone: (303) 555-1212

1.1 Burden of proof issues

The IRS has a good historical track record when cases actually go to trial, primarily because the taxpayer has had the burden of proof in most cases. This means the taxpayer had to prove he or she did not owe the taxes.

The Tax Reform Act of 1998 changed the burden of proof requirement in the taxpayer's favor by shifting the burden to the IRS in cases in which the taxpayer has submitted all records to the IRS to support his or her position. Now, under IRC §7491, it is up to the IRS to prove you owe the taxes, but only after you have done the following:

(a) Complied with all substantial requirements of the IRC (In general, this means that you must have records relating to every expense or deduction claimed on the tax return.)

(b) Cooperated with all reasonable requests that IRS employees made for documents, information, witnesses, and meetings/interviews

Congress made these changes to eliminate the public's correct perception that taxpayers are guilty until and unless they prove their innocence. In reality, shifting the burden of proof will not affect a great number of tax court cases, as in the past the IRS would usually concede issues whenever the taxpayer had the required supporting documentation and cooperated with the audit. Notwithstanding this, it is clear that this change in the burden of proof requirements will assist some taxpayers, so the change is certainly most welcome.

The Tax Reform Act of 1998 also changed the proof requirements and placed the burden squarely on the IRS whenever it asserts additional income for a taxpayer by utilizing statistical information (as discussed in chapter 5). This is a major victory for all taxpayers, as there are no requirements for record maintenance or cooperation with this change.

Finally, Congress also changed the burden of proof requirements any time penalties are asserted against a taxpayer. Under the old laws, the IRS could assert a penalty and sit back and see if the taxpayer could disprove the penalty. Now the IRS is required to produce some evidence that the penalty is justified before the taxpayer will have to prove anything. This change should cut down on the large number of penalties that the IRS has asserted in the past.

Even with these recent changes, it is interesting to see what kind of success the IRS has in the relatively rare case that actually goes to trial. According to IRS statistics, in 1996 there were 1,227 trials from 28,757 new cases. The IRS won 650 of these trials but lost 119, and there were split decisions in 458 trials. For whatever reason, the IRS has not released any more recent statistics on its tax court "batting average."

1.2 Advantages to filing a tax court petition

There are several advantages to filing a tax court petition after you receive a 90-day letter:

(a) *The IRS cannot continue the examination process because the case is now under the control (jurisdiction) of the tax court.* Whatever conclusions the examiner reached before the 90-day letter was sent out are it as far as the examination process is concerned.

(b) *The IRS probably will not raise any new issues in the case after the tax court petition is filed, mainly because it has the burden of proof with any new issues raised.* This means that the IRS will have to prove that you are liable for additional tax based on the new issue(s) raised in the tax court case. For instance, if the 90-day letter claimed that you owed an additional $5,000 in tax for unreported gambling income, and the IRS wants to add a new allegation that you also failed to report $2,000 in dividend income, the IRS would have to prove that you did in fact fail to report the dividend income. It would still be up to you to prove that the IRS was wrong concerning the gambling income issue (assuming that the IRS doesn't have the burden of proof on this issue as well, under the changes in the Tax Reform Act of 1998). The IRS will rarely raise additional issues, because it is often very difficult to develop a new case under the time pressures associated with tax court cases.

(c) *You will be given at least two more chances to settle the case to your satisfaction.* In most cases you are given another chance to meet with the Appeals Division, and also with the area counsel attorney, before going to trial. You should never refuse any opportunity to reach a settlement with the IRS. A settlement is more likely, because of the time pressures associated with the tax court. Furthermore, many area counsel attorneys rarely, if ever, try a case in the tax court. This is surprising, especially when this is one of the primary job functions of an area counsel attorney. Many attorneys enjoy the lack of pressure associated with a government job and do not like to have their routines disrupted with the pressures of a trial. Other area counsel attorneys are sincerely afraid of losing the case and will do almost anything to stay out of court. While many area counsel attorneys are excellent trial lawyers in tax court, you should definitely not assume that this is the case.

1.3 Disadvantages of filing a tax court petition

There are several disadvantages to filing a tax court petition after you receive a 90-day letter:

(a) *You must prepare a formal tax court petition and pay the $60 filing fee to the court.* This is not necessarily difficult, as Sample 31 shows that the petition can be very straightforward and does not require a law degree to prepare.

(b) *You must be prepared to go to trial if the case cannot be settled.* If you are not mentally prepared to go to trial, you will likely have to accept a less favorable settlement from the IRS to resolve the case. On the other hand, if you are prepared to go to trial, you can stick to your settlement position, knowing that the worse that will happen is that the case will actually go to trial.

(c) *The IRS can raise new issues that would not have been raised had a petition not been filed.* While this is possible, it is not likely, and you should never base your decision not to file a petition solely on this reason. Of course, if the IRS completely messed up an audit and missed several issues that you thought would be problems, you would be wise to think twice about filing a petition, as you should not give the IRS a chance to correct its mistakes. In these circumstances, you would do well to control your desire for tax retribution and look at the potential financial downside to having the truth come out if new issues are raised in tax court.

(d) *There are no jury trials in tax court.* Congress was probably wise when it determined that the IRS would never win in tax court if juries were permitted to make the final decision. (How many juries would ever rule in favor of the IRS?)

In nearly all cases, the advantages of filing a petition and fighting the IRS in tax court outweigh the disadvantages. If you have any doubt as to what to do, you should consult a competent tax attorney well before the 90-day period for filing a petition expires. Unless the tax court petition would be considered frivolous (which would subject you to a possible penalty of up to $25,000), you should nearly always file a petition and try to reach a more favorable settlement with the IRS. Examples of frivolous tax court petitions include using tax protestor rhetoric (such as the tax laws are unconstitutional), disagreeing with well-settled tax law, or making factual assertions which are completely baseless or outrightly false.

1.4   Representing yourself in tax court

You are always permitted to represent yourself in tax court. While this may not be the wisest decision, it is sometimes the only way to challenge the IRS (for financial reasons, many people cannot afford to hire a tax attorney). If you do decide to represent yourself in court, follow these general rules:

(a) *Be organized at all times.* The tax court does not treat taxpayers (or IRS attorneys) kindly when they are disorganized during the valuable time that the court has allocated to any particular case. It is difficult enough to beat the IRS in court without having to overcome the hurdle of an angry judge.

(b) *Always respect the court (even if the judge seems to favor the IRS).* This means:

(i) Stand when speaking. The court will give you more respect if you always follow this rule.

(ii) Be professional to the IRS attorney. Remember that this is only a business or financial matter for the IRS attorney. You should assume that the IRS attorney has nothing against you personally and is in court simply because a settlement agreeable to the IRS was not reached.

(iii) Never interrupt the judge. I have seen many taxpayers interrupt a judge to correct what the taxpayer believes to be an incorrect statement. This only makes the judge angry, which is not a good thing to do when it is this judge who ultimately decides the case. Most judges will give you an opportunity to correct any statements or make any arguments at some point during the trial.

(iv) LISTEN first, then speak.

(c) *Be concise.* Don't take up more of the court's time than is necessary to prove your point. Tax court judges will often cut off taxpayers or witnesses who ramble, which may mean that the court will not hear an important part of your story.

(d) *Research the law before the trial.* It is especially important that you are aware of any relevant sections of the IRC prior to trial. You should also be familiar with any major court cases or IRS regulations that relate to the issues in the case.

(e) *Understand the facts, including those facts that go against you.* A thorough understanding of the facts will eliminate many problems that can occur during the trial.

2. Types of Tax Court Cases

There are two different types of tax court cases: those that are considered regular cases and those designated as S cases.

2.1 Regular cases

With regular cases, all tax court rules and the Federal Rules of Evidence apply. These rules cover important matters before, during, and after trials, including court deadlines, what evidence is admissible, and the procedures for both sides to follow at all times during the trial process.

2.1.a Discovery

The tax court rules entitle both you and the IRS to discover what information the other side possesses before the trial starts. For example, you could serve the IRS with a Production of Documents Request to find out what documents the IRS has in its possession. Other discovery techniques include Interrogatories (which are basically questions that the other side must answer), Depositions (which are live interviews of a potential witness with a court reporter present), and Requests for Admissions (which are statements that the other side must admit or deny).

You should read the tax court rules as soon as the case is scheduled for trial, as there are very specific deadlines that must be observed if you are going to use any of the discovery tools.

2.1.b Before the trial

After all discovery is complete, the parties must meet to decide which facts are agreed upon and which ones are still subject to a disagreement. All agreed facts are listed on what is called a Stipulation and given to the court before the trial. The purpose of the Stipulation is to reduce the number of issues at the trial to the absolute minimum so that the parties do not waste the court's time.

The court may order a pretrial conference to assist the parties in narrowing the number of issues for trial. The court may also want to see if the parties need the court's assistance in reaching a settlement so that a trial may not be necessary.

Once all the pretrial proceedings are completed, and assuming that a settlement cannot be reached, the parties are ready for trial. Shortly before the trial is set to begin, each party must submit a Trial Memorandum to the court. A Trial Memorandum gives the court an idea of what the issues are, who will likely testify for each side, how long the trial is likely to take, and an overview of the law applicable to the issues in the case. Sample 33 is an example of a Trial Memorandum.

When you prepare a Trial Memorandum, you should make sure that all potential witnesses are listed, as the failure to list a witness may mean that the witness will be denied the opportunity to testify. Both you and the IRS may subpoena witnesses to make sure that the witnesses show up for the trial.

2.1.c The trial

The trial itself is conducted by a judge, without a jury, and is recorded word-for-word by a court reporter. Besides the fact that no jury is present, the trial and courtroom look like those for any other legal proceedings in the United States. The party that bears the burden of proof (in the past the taxpayer, although the recent changes in the Tax Reform Act of 1998 will certainly shift the burden of proof to the IRS in some cases) will go first at the trial. The following is a typical order of a tax court trial:

(a) *Opening statements.* Both sides are permitted a short amount of time at the beginning of the case, usually five to ten minutes, to give the judge a brief glimpse of what they each will prove during the trial. You should always take advantage of this opportunity to make a favorable first impression on the judge by making an effective opening statement. There is generally no reason why you would want to waive your right to make an opening statement.

(b) *Witness testimony.* You have the right to call witnesses listed in the Trial Memorandum. The IRS attorney will have the opportunity to question any witnesses you call to testify. This questioning is called cross examination. Any witness who will testify for you should be well prepared before the trial, as it is important that you know exactly what the witness will say before he or she gives testimony in court.

The IRS will also call witnesses it listed in its Trial Memorandum. You should try to anticipate what these witnesses will testify about and have questions prepared for them before the trial.

Always take advantage of any opportunity to make a favorable first impression on the judge: try making an effective opening statement.

SAMPLE 33
TRIAL MEMORANDUM

Date: July 1, 1998
Place: Denver, CO

TRIAL MEMORANDUM FOR PETITIONER

Case: Herman H. Munster v. Commissioner of Internal Revenue
Docket No: 12345-97

Attorneys:

Petitioners: None Respondent: Alice Cheatum
Telephone: None Telephone: (303) 844-3258

AMOUNTS IN DISPUTE:

	Deficiency	Additions	
1995	$15,111.00	IRC §6662(a)	$3022.20

Stipulation of Facts: Completed__X__   In Process____

ISSUES:

1.   Whether the Commissioner of Internal Revenue improperly disallowed Petitioner's Schedule A deductions in the amount of $12,020 by claiming that Petitioner failed to substantiate his medical expense and taxes paid during 1995.

2.   Whether the Commissioner of Internal Revenue improperly claimed that Petitioner received Non-Employee Compensation/Schedule C receipts in the amount of $18,433 without giving Petitioner his ordinary and necessary business expenses under IRC §162.

3.   Whether the Commissioner of Internal Revenue improperly applied an addition to tax for the taxable year 1995 under IRC §6662(a).

WITNESSES:

1.   Petitioner Herman Munster

Petitioner will testify concerning his business, Munster's Funeral Home, including, but not limited to, his profit motive, start-up expenses, business purpose, and overall business picture for the taxable year at issue.

2. Sam Numbers, Return Preparer and Accountant

Mr. Numbers may testify, if necessary, regarding Petitioner's consultations with him, including his overall profit motive and questions about the maintenance of proper books and records for accounting and/or tax purposes.

3. Wilma Worker, Part-time Employee

Ms. Worker will testify as to her part-time position with Petitioner's business and his business expenses incurred to operate his business.

CURRENT ESTIMATE OF TIME OF TRIAL: 2-3 hours

SUMMARY OF FACTS:

During the taxable year 1995, Petitioner owned and operated a funeral home called Munster's Funeral Home. Petitioner received some proceeds from this business, but also incurred numerous business expenses, including rent, advertising, labor, taxes, licences, cleaning supplies, office supplies, and miscellaneous expenses.

During 1995, Petitioner also incurred large medical expenses as the result of having screws placed into his neck (for a chronic spine problem). Petitioner provided copies of all medical invoices, along with proof of payment, to the IRS during the audit and subsequent phases of this trial process. To date, no IRS employee has provided a reason as to why the medical expenses should not be permitted. In addition, petitioner incurred deductible expense for taxes paid during this year. Again, no IRS employee has told Petitioner why these tax bills are not permitted as a deduction.

BRIEF SYNOPSIS OF LEGAL AUTHORITIES:

According to the Notice of Deficiency, the IRS has determined that Petitioner has not substantiated the deductions claimed on his tax return and did not incur any business expenses in the ordinary course of his business. It is of course well known that a taxpayer is entitled to these deductions under IRC §162 and §212.

Case law generally indicates that _____.

With respect to the addition to tax under IRC §6662 (a), Petitioner is not liable for this because he was not negligent or did not disregard the tax rules or regulations. Petitioner properly reported all income and expenses and obtained the advice of an independent accountant at the beginning of his business endeavor and was informed that everything he was doing satisfied the tax code. Petitioner does not possess a tax background and by consulting a tax professional on these very issues, he was not negligent or careless with respect to the tax laws.

EVIDENTIARY PROBLEMS: None anticipated

DATE: _____   _____

Herman H. Munster
Petitioner
1313 Mockingbird Lane
Denver, CO 80222
(303) 555-1212

(c) *Closing statements.* At the end of the trial, after all witnesses have testified and all evidence is presented, the parties are permitted to make a brief closing statement to the court. In the closing statement you summarize your position and make a final plea to the court concerning your case. Again, you should not waive your right to a closing statement and should always use the opportunity to make a final impression on the judge as to why you should win the case (i.e., why the IRS is wrong).

At the end of the trial the judge usually does not make a decision one way or the other. Instead, he or she will ask the parties to submit briefs. A brief is a legal document that lists the applicable facts and law and the reasons why the judge should rule for the taxpayer (or the IRS, as the case may be). These briefs usually must be filed within 75 days after the trial has ended, unless the judge sets a different due date.

After all briefs have been filed, the judge will review all evidence and the briefs and make a decision, in writing, concerning who wins the case. The written decision will be published in the Tax Court Reports (TC) or Tax Court Memorandum Decisions (TCM), so that other taxpayers can see how the tax court ruled on a particular issue. The tax court decides which court reporting book the decision will be reported in. Except for the most important decisions, most decisions are published as TCM decisions.

2.1.d Appealing a tax court decision

If the tax court decision is in favor of the IRS, you can file an appeal with the US Court of Appeals. Of course, if you win, the IRS is also permitted to file an appeal if it believes that the tax court was wrong in ruling in your favor. To file an appeal you must file a notice of appeal, along with the filing fee for the appeal, with the tax court (see Sample 34). This must be done within 90 days after the tax court's decision becomes final. If no appeal is filed, the tax court decision becomes final and the parties are bound by the court's decision.

Once the Notice of Appeal is filed, the case rests within the jurisdiction of the Court of Appeals and the tax court no longer has anything to do with the outcome of the case.

2.2 "S" cases

The tax court also has a procedure for cases that it calls "small" cases, or those cases in which the amount at issue with the IRS is $50,000 or less for any one tax year. (The amount was recently increased from $10,000 as a part of the Tax Reform Act of 1998.) By electing this procedure, the taxpayer is able to treat the tax court case like a small claims case (or something similar to *The People's Court*). Making this election is not permanent; you may ask the tax court to remove the small case designation at any time before the trial begins. There are certain advantages and disadvantages to making the "S" election when filing a petition with the tax court.

2.2.a Advantages of "S" cases

Some advantages of "S" cases include the following:

(a) *Informal court procedures.* The rules of evidence are relaxed and the court will admit any evidence that has "probative value" (as stated in tax court Rule 177 (b)). In general, any evidence that relates somehow to the tax controversy will be allowed at the trial.

(b) *There is limited or no discovery available to the parties.* Most "S" cases thus do not have Interrogatories, Requests for Production of Documents, or the like, as the court is trying to keep these cases as simple and straightforward as possible. This benefits you because the IRS will not be able to serve a lot of discovery requests on you in the hopes of burying you with legal paperwork.

(c) *The IRS is more likely to settle the case in your favor than it would in a regular case.* This is because the IRS, especially the attorneys at area

The judge usually only makes a decision after having reviewed the evidence and the written briefs.

UNITED STATES TAX COURT

HERMAN H. MUNSTER) Petitioner,) V.) DOCKET NO. COMMISSIONER OF INTERNAL REVENUE) Respondent.)	

NOTICE OF APPEAL

Notice is hereby given that Herman H. Munster hereby appeals to the United States Court of Appeals for the 10th Circuit from the decision of this Court entered in the above-captioned proceeding on the 10th day of February, 200-.

Respectfully submitted,

_____

Herman H. Munster
Petitioner
1313 Mockingbird Lane
Denver, CO 80222
Telephone: (303) 555-1212

counsel, often considers these cases to be nuisances and wants to get rid of them without devoting much time to the case. However, this view may change now that the amount in question has been increased from a maximum of $10,000 to $50,000. With more money at stake, the IRS likely will devote more resources to these cases.

2.2.b Disadvantages of "S" cases

Some disadvantages of "S" cases include the following:

(a) *The tax court decision is final, so you (or the IRS) cannot appeal it*. If the tax court makes a decision that is completely unreasonable and goes against all the facts in the case, there is nothing that either party can do about the decision.

(b) *The case may not receive as much attention from the judge because it is not considered as "important" as a regular case*. While this is not always the case, and may not even be the case a majority of the time, I have seen numerous situations where the court tried to get rid of as many "S" cases as possible by strongly encouraging the parties to reach a settlement. The court is sometimes forced into taking this position because there are far too many cases scheduled for trial, with not nearly enough time to try most of the cases.

(c) *The case is heard by a special trial judge and not a regular tax court judge (although this may not actually be a disadvantage)*. Many IRS attorneys, along with tax attorneys in private practice, think this is a disadvantage because the special trial judge is often relatively new to the court and thus does not have a track record. This means the attorneys cannot predict how he or she will rule in the case. For taxpayers representing themselves this does not really matter, and it may work to their advantage, as the IRS may offer a more favorable settlement due to the uncertainties associated with a relatively new judge.

2.2.c Choosing "S" case procedures

In general, I recommend you use the "S" case proceedings whenever possible, as I believe you have a greater advantage over the IRS in "S" cases than in regular cases. The major advantage, in my opinion, is that the IRS is very likely to settle these cases at all costs. The reason for this is simple: the IRS has limited resources and cannot take all cases to trial. Given that a trial is still a trial no matter how much money is involved, it only makes sense that the IRS would devote more resources to those cases with the most amount of money involved.

For example, if the IRS claims that you did not report gambling winnings from a casino, it will certainly pursue you much harder if you owe $500,000 in tax than if you owe $5,000, even though the issues are exactly the same. Thus, the gambler who "only" owes $5,000 may be able to settle with the IRS for half of that amount, while the same settlement would not likely be offered to the "luckier" gambler.

2.3 Legal costs

Under either the "S" or regular case proceedings, you can force the IRS to pay your legal fees if you have "substantially prevailed" in the case. In general, the tax court will award this extra bonus when the IRS takes an unreasonable position in the court proceedings. While it is possible to get the IRS to pay your legal bills in cases where you settle without a trial, the IRS will often make the settlement conditional upon you paying your own legal fees. Although the occurrence is relatively rare, you would certainly have reason to celebrate if you beat the IRS in tax court and then forced the IRS to pay for your legal representation.

3. US District Court

Nearly all other suits in which taxpayers are suing the IRS are filed in the district court. While taxpayers also have the right in some instances to sue the IRS in the US court of claims, they typically do not do so. Perhaps the primary reason is that jury trials are not permitted in the claims court.

For the discussion in this section, I will consider in turn each of the suits that may be filed in the district court. Remember that you will have the burden of proof in these suits (i.e., the IRS doesn't have to prove anything) in order to win the case.

3.1 Suits for refund

The IRS often attempts to collect, or does collect, taxes from individuals who do not really owe the taxes. For instance, perhaps you moved and did not notify the IRS of your new address. The IRS would have sent a Notice of Deficiency to your last known address, but if the notice was not forwarded to your new address, you would not have found out about it until after the 90-day period expired and could not have filed a tax court petition. In such a situation you can bring a suit against the US government for a refund of any taxes improperly assessed or collected.

Before filing a lawsuit, you must give the IRS an opportunity to correct the problem. In most cases, this means that you must file a claim for refund (Form 843) with the IRS. After filing the claim for refund, you must then wait six months before filing a suit, unless the IRS rejects the claim sooner than six months. Under any circumstances, you have two years to file a suit after the IRS rejects the claim.

After you file a refund suit, the government attorney (in the Justice Department) will consider whether or not to settle the case. Most of the time the government attorney will consider the likelihood that you will win (and maybe set a precedent for all other taxpayers) when he or she decides how much to offer you to end the case.

3.1.a Advantages of filing suit for refund

There are several advantages to filing a suit for a refund:

(a) *A jury trial is possible.* This is the number one reason why you would want to file a suit for refund against the IRS.

(b) *Government attorneys are not IRS attorneys and may not understand the tax laws as well as IRS attorneys would.* The government attorneys are from the Tax Division of the Department of Justice. However, some Department of Justice attorneys have very strong tax backgrounds, either through their education or prior work experience with the IRS area counsel.

(c) *You can get the IRS to pay your attorney fees and court costs if you win at trial (see IRC §7430).* Reasonable litigation costs include attorney fees, court costs, expert witness expenses, and the costs of reports or studies necessary for the preparation of your case.

(d) *There is a good possibility that the case will be settled after you file suit.* The IRS may have been unreasonable when it denied your claim for refund. The odds are very low that the Department of Justice attorney will also be unreasonable. Furthermore, if the case is a close one and could go either way at trial, the Department of Justice attorney can consider what the hazards of litigation might be for the government when he or she decides what the case is worth for settlement purposes.

Always give the IRS a chance to correct its mistakes before filing a suit to force the IRS to correct its mistakes.

3.1.b Disadvantages of filing suit for refund

Some disadvantages of filing a suit for a refund include the following:

(a) *You must pay the tax (or a portion of the tax) before filing suit.* Without paying at least some of the tax, there would be nothing for the government to "refund" should you be successful with the lawsuit.

(b) You must exhaust your administrative remedies (Form 843 claim) within the IRS before filing a suit. This is not necessarily a disadvantage, as the IRS does grant a taxpayer's claim for refund in some instances. In any event, you should always make it a point to give the IRS a chance to correct its mistakes before filing a suit to force the IRS to correct its mistakes.

(c) *You will often need to hire a competent tax attorney to handle the case.* This is by far the greatest disadvantage, as the legal fees can be quite high in these cases. However, without legal representation it is difficult, but certainly not impossible, for you to comply with all of the court's rules and still win the case. In addition, most Department of Justice attorneys are excellent trial lawyers and make very formidable opponents should the case not settle and go to trial.

> You should take advantage of the laws when the IRS makes a mistake.

3.2 Suits for improper disclosure under IRC §6103

By law, all information contained in a tax return is considered to be confidential and the IRS is not permitted to disclose this information to anyone without the taxpayer's written consent (see IRC §6103). The confidential information includes everything on a tax return, including the identity of the taxpayer. You can consent to release the confidential tax information by executing a Power of Attorney (Form 2848) with the IRS (see Sample 35). There are, of course, numerous exceptions to this disclosure rule, with most exceptions having to do with the need of the IRS to disclose information to enforce federal, state, and local tax, criminal, and other laws.

If an IRS employee makes an improper disclosure of confidential tax information, you are allowed to file a suit against the government in the district court. Under IRC §7431, you are entitled to a minimum amount of $1,000 for each unauthorized disclosure, or more money if actual damages can be proved. Actual damages may be suffered if the IRS improperly disclosed confidential tax information to one of your business customers and you lost business as a result of the unauthorized disclosure.

SAMPLE 35

FORM 2848 (POWER OF ATTORNEY)

Form **2848** (Rev. January 2002) Department of the Treasury Internal Revenue Service	**Power of Attorney and Declaration of Representative** ▶ See the separate instructions.	OMB No. 1545-0150

For IRS Use Only
Received by:
Name _____
Telephone _____
Function _____
Date ___/___/___

Part I Power of Attorney (Type or print.)

1 Taxpayer information. Taxpayer(s) must sign and date this form on page 2, line 9.

Taxpayer name(s) and address

Sara Estill
123 Main Street
Denver, CO 80222

Social security number(s)
123 45 6789

Employer identification number

Daytime telephone number
(303) 555-5555

Plan number (if applicable)

hereby appoint(s) the following representative(s) as attorney(s)-in-fact:

2   Representative(s) must sign and date this form on page 2, Part II.

Name and address

Joe Accountant
10 North 1st Street #101
Denver, CO 80111

CAF No. 1111-22222R
Telephone No. (303) 222-3333
Fax No. (303) 222-3344
Check if new: Address ☐   Telephone No. ☐

Name and address

CAF No. ....
Telephone No. ....
Fax No. ....
Check if new: Address ☐   Telephone No. ☐

Name and address

CAF No. ....
Telephone No. ....
Fax No. ....
Check if new: Address ☐   Telephone No. ☐

to represent the taxpayer(s) before the Internal Revenue Service for the following tax matters:

3   Tax matters

Type of Tax (Income, Employment, Excise, etc.) or Civil Penalty (See the instructions for line 3.)	Tax Form Number (1040, 941, 720, etc.)	Year(s) or Period(s)
INCOME	1040	1999, 2000, 2001

4   Specific use not recorded on Centralized Authorization File (CAF). If the power of attorney is for a specific use not recorded on CAF, check this box. See the instructions for **Line 4. Specific uses not recorded on CAF.** . . . . ▶ ☐

5   Acts authorized. The representatives are authorized to receive and inspect confidential tax information and to perform any and all acts that I (we) can perform with respect to the tax matters described in line 3, for example, the authority to sign any agreements, consents, or other documents. The authority does not include the power to receive refund checks (see line 6 below), the power to substitute another representative, the authority to execute a request for a tax return, or a consent to disclose tax information unless specifically added below, or the power to sign certain returns. See the instructions for **Line 5. Acts authorized.**

List any specific additions or deletions to the acts otherwise authorized in this power of attorney: ....
....

Note: In general, an unenrolled preparer of tax returns cannot sign any document for a taxpayer. See Revenue Procedure 81-38, printed as Pub. 470, for more information.

Note: The tax matters partner of a partnership is not permitted to authorize representatives to perform certain acts. See the separate instructions for more information.

6   Receipt of refund checks. If you want to authorize a representative named on line 2 to receive, **BUT NOT TO ENDORSE OR CASH,** refund checks, initial here _____ and list the name of that representative below.

Name of representative to receive refund check(s) ▶

For Paperwork Reduction and Privacy Act Notice, see the separate instructions.   Cat. No. 11980J   Form **2848** (Rev. 1-2002)

Form 2848 (Rev. 1-2002)   Page **2**

7   Notices and communications. Original notices and other written communications will be sent to you and a copy to the first representative listed on line 2 unless you check one or more of the boxes below.

a If you want the first representative listed on line 2 to receive the original, and yourself a copy, of such notices or communications, check this box . . . . ▶ ☐

b If you also want the second representative listed to receive a copy of such notices and communications, check this box ▶ ☐

c If you do not want any notices or communications sent to your representative(s), check this box . . . . ▶ ☐

8   Retention/revocation of prior power(s) of attorney. The filing of this power of attorney automatically revokes all earlier power(s) of attorney on file with the Internal Revenue Service for the same tax matters and years or periods covered by this document. If you **do not** want to revoke a prior power of attorney, check here . . . . ▶ ☐
YOU MUST ATTACH A COPY OF ANY POWER OF ATTORNEY YOU WANT TO REMAIN IN EFFECT.

9   Signature of taxpayer(s). If a tax matter concerns a joint return, **both** husband and wife must sign if joint representation is requested, otherwise, see the instructions. If signed by a corporate officer, partner, guardian, tax matters partner, executor, receiver, administrator, or trustee on behalf of the taxpayer, I certify that I have the authority to execute this form on behalf of the taxpayer.

▶ **IF NOT SIGNED AND DATED, THIS POWER OF ATTORNEY WILL BE RETURNED.**

Sara Estill	11-11-02	—
Signature	Date	Title (if applicable)

Sara Estill
Print Name

—	—	—
Signature	Date	Title (if applicable)

—
Print Name

Part II	**Declaration of Representative**

Caution: *Students with a special order to represent taxpayers in Qualified Low Income Taxpayer Clinics or the Student Tax Clinic Program, see the separate instructions for Part II.*

Under penalties of perjury, I declare that:
- I am not currently under suspension or disbarment from practice before the Internal Revenue Service;
- I am aware of regulations contained in Treasury Department Circular No. 230 (31 CFR, Part 10), as amended, concerning the practice of attorneys, certified public accountants, enrolled agents, enrolled actuaries, and others;
- I am authorized to represent the taxpayer(s) identified in Part I for the tax matter(s) specified there; and
- I am one of the following:

a Attorney—a member in good standing of the bar of the highest court of the jurisdiction shown below.
b Certified Public Accountant—duly qualified to practice as a certified public accountant in the jurisdiction shown below.
c Enrolled Agent—enrolled as an agent under the requirements of Treasury Department Circular No. 230.
d Officer—a bona fide officer of the taxpayer's organization.
e Full-Time Employee—a full-time employee of the taxpayer.
f Family Member—a member of the taxpayer's immediate family (i.e., spouse, parent, child, brother, or sister).
g Enrolled Actuary—enrolled as an actuary by the Joint Board for the Enrollment of Actuaries under 29 U.S.C. 1242 (the authority to practice before the Service is limited by section 10.3(d)(1) of Treasury Department Circular No. 230).
h Unenrolled Return Preparer—an unenrolled return preparer under section 10.7(c)(1)(viii) of Treasury Department Circular No. 230.

▶ **IF THIS DECLARATION OF REPRESENTATIVE IS NOT SIGNED AND DATED, THE POWER OF ATTORNEY WILL BE RETURNED.**

Designation—Insert above letter (a–h)	Jurisdiction (state) or Enrollment Card No.	Signature	Date
B	CO	_Joe Accountant_	11-11-02

*U.S. Government Printing Office. 2002 — 474-353   Form **2848** (Rev. 1-2002)

The IRS is very sensitive about the disclosure of confidential tax information and will usually not violate the disclosure laws, but this does not mean it never happens. This is one area of the tax law where the IRS can actually be held accountable for its improper actions, and you should take advantage of the laws when the IRS makes a mistake.

3.3 Suits to stop seizure or sale of assets

The IRS has, from time to time, attempted to seize (levy) and sell property belonging to an individual who in reality owes no additional tax. This usually occurs when the IRS claims that the property is owned by someone who owes tax, but the property is really owned by an innocent person. The IRS makes this mistake because its employees have been sloppy in checking ownership records or because they make incorrect assumptions.

When an improper seizure occurs, the innocent person may bring suit against the IRS for its conduct in seizing the assets. Often the mere threat of such a suit will cause the IRS to take a second look at the situation and release the levy on its own. This can be a powerful weapon for innocent taxpayers to use against the IRS bureaucracy.

3.4 Suits to stop IRS collection activities

Taxpayers are generally prohibited from suing the IRS to stop the IRS from collecting taxes. This prohibition is known as the anti-injunction statute and can be found at IRC §7421. The IRS must be permitted to collect taxes with a minimum of interference from the courts, especially when the entire government's ability to function is directly related to the IRS's ability to collect tax revenues. The IRS is well aware of this rule, which may lead some of its employees to break the law in their collection efforts, since they know they generally can't be sued.

Courts may agree to stop IRS collection activities if the IRS is prohibited from collecting taxes but tries to collect them anyway, regardless of whether or not they are owed. For example, the IRS may not collect any taxes due during the 90-day period after a Notice of Deficiency is issued or during the time that the case is under the control of the US tax court, assuming that the taxpayer filed a petition with the tax court. If the IRS does try to collect any tax relating to the years under controversy in the tax court, the taxpayer can file a suit to stop the improper IRS collection activities.

Other courts have held that the anti-injunction statute may not apply if the IRS has no legal possibility of collecting the tax because the tax is not legally due. In general, to win this kind of suit you must prove that the government cannot win under any circumstances and that you would suffer an "irreparable harm" for which there is no other remedy available. This is a very difficult burden for a taxpayer to overcome.

3.5 Suit when IRS fails to release a Federal Tax Lien

Under IRC §6325, the IRS is legally required to release all tax liens against a taxpayer within 30 days after the tax debt has been paid or becomes legally unenforceable. The tax debt is "legally unenforceable" after the collection statute of limitations expires (generally ten years from the date that the tax was assessed). When the IRS fails to release the lien in a timely fashion, whether intentionally or not, you can file suit in the district court to collect damages. As with nearly all other types of suits against the IRS, you must first give the IRS an opportunity to correct the problem before filing suit. Usually the IRS will perform a quick investigation and agree to release the lien on its own, without any judicial interference. The mere threat of a suit is often enough, as long as you know that this type of suit is available.

3.6 Suit for improper browsing

A recent addition to the Tax Code (IRC §7213A) provides a criminal and civil penalty for any IRS employee caught browsing or looking at any taxpayer's tax return without proper authorization. This new provision is an attempt to protect the confidentiality of tax returns, and the information in the returns, from snooping IRS employees. The IRS employee who is guilty of violating this section will be fired from his or her position with the IRS and can be sent to prison for up to one year. In addition, the IRS is required to inform taxpayers when an IRS employee is charged with violating this section of the IRC, presumably because the taxpayer is then permitted to file a suit seeking damages from the now ex-IRS employee who violated the confidentiality laws. This law is still new and there are few court cases to indicate how the courts will interpret this section of the IRC.

3.7 Suit for improper collection actions

Perhaps the one power that the IRS most frequently abuses is its ability to collect taxes. Too often improper collection tactics are used, usually by overly aggressive revenue officers. This improper conduct can include harassment of taxpayers, improper use of enforced collection activities (e.g., liens, garnishments and other levies), and just about anything else that you can imagine.

When improper collection activities occur and the IRS won't correct the problem, you are permitted to sue the IRS for damages. Congress recently raised the maximum amount of damages that taxpayers can collect from the IRS from $100,000 to $1,000,000, perhaps recognizing the amount of damage that the IRS can do to taxpayers if it really wants to. In order to win a suit for improper collection actions, you must show that the IRS employee recklessly or intentionally disregarded the tax laws.

Congress also changed the law to permit taxpayers to file suit against IRS employees who negligently disregard the Internal Revenue Code or tax regulations. While the amount of potential damages you can win is capped at $100,000, this is a major change in the tax law in the taxpayers' favor. It is much easier to show that an IRS employee was negligent (i.e., careless or made a mistake) than it is to show that he or she intentionally or recklessly disregarded the tax laws or regulations. Taxpayers can use this knowledge as leverage against the IRS whenever the revenue officer or other collection personnel gets overly aggressive or makes a mistake in their handling of a collection case.

4. Waiver of Rights

In recent years, more taxpayers have become aggressive in pursuing legal actions against the IRS and its employees. Several IRS employees fought back by refusing to resolve any of a taxpayer's tax matters until the taxpayer agreed not to file a suit against the employee for the improper conduct.

Congress realized that this appeared as if the IRS was holding a gun to the taxpayer's head by forcing him or her not to file suit (even though the taxpayer had the legal right to do so). In the Tax Reform Act of 1998, Congress specifically prohibited any IRS employee from requesting any taxpayer to waive a right to sue the IRS employee as a condition to getting the tax matters resolved, unless —

(a) either the taxpayer knowingly and voluntarily agrees to give up the right; or

(b) the waiver request is made to the taxpayer's representative, either orally or in writing.

In general, I would not advise you to give up this possibly valuable right unless you are getting something valuable in return. For instance, if an auditor is willing to close an audit as a "no change" and you were expecting an increase in your tax, then it may make sense for you to agree to waive your rights. However, why should you give up this valuable right if only the IRS or its employees will benefit? You are in control here and should not give up this control without some compelling reason for doing so.

5. Termination of Employment

Although this is not another way for a taxpayer to file suit against the IRS for misconduct, you should know that IRS employees can be terminated from their employment with the IRS for various forms of misconduct.

Congress recently added provisions for termination of employment due to the widespread (and often accurate) perception that IRS employees are not held accountable for their own misconduct. Now IRS employees can be fired if there has been a judicial (court) or administrative (often within the IRS) determination that the employee did any of the following:

★ Violated any of your constitutional rights

★ Violated any of your civil rights (usually discrimination based upon age, race, gender, or disabilities)

★ Willfully failed to get the required signatures before seizing your home, business assets, or personal property

★ Provided any false statements while under oath (usually in a court proceeding) concerning a material tax matter

★ Violated the Internal Revenue Code for the purpose of harassing or retaliating against you

★ Falsified or destroyed any document to cover up a mistake made by any IRS employee

★ Committed assault or battery against you (and was convicted of the offense in court)

★ Threatened to audit you for a personal (and not professional) reason

These new changes may provide you with additional information to use against an IRS employee, as long as you realize that these are protections for you and should not be used to threaten any IRS employees. Remember, the employees cannot be fired for incompetence, only illegal conduct.

Tax Points

★ Filing a petition with the US tax court gives you at least two more opportunities to reach a settlement with the IRS.

★ If the amount in controversy with the IRS does not exceed $50,000 in any given tax year, you should consider filing a petition with the tax court as an "S" case.

★ The IRS can and should be sued for any unauthorized disclosures of confidential tax information.

★ The IRS can and should be sued for collecting any tax amounts that you do not legally owe.

★ It is extremely difficult to file a suit to stop the IRS from using legal means to collect a tax owed, even if you will suffer some financial harm as a result of the IRS's actions.

★ You should force the IRS to release all Federal Tax Liens when the law requires the liens to be released. If the IRS will not release a lien, you should make the IRS explain to a judge why it is not following the law.

★ You should consider filing suit whenever any IRS collection employees negligently, intentionally, or recklessly fail to follow current tax laws or regulations.

★ You should not waive your right to file suit against the IRS or one of its employees unless the IRS is willing to give you something in return.

CHAPTER 16

THE TAXPAYER ADVOCATE:
WHEN ALL ELSE FAILS

I am extraordinarily sorry.
> Michael Dolan, acting IRS commissioner, in testimony to the US
> Senate concerning IRS mistakes and the impact on US citizens
> (1997)

For taxpayers who must deal with the IRS, it's often a David vs.
Goliath fight that leaves David the taxpayer without a slingshot.
> Representative Nancy L. Johnson (R-Connecticut), September 12,
> 1995

Even though there are numerous appeal and review mechanisms in place within the IRS, many cases fall through the cracks. This is often simply a bureaucratic problem: no one at the IRS wants to make a decision. Many IRS employees seem to think, "If I, as an IRS employee, do nothing, nothing bad can happen to me. But if I do the right thing and give the taxpayer what he or she is entitled to, I can end up having to report the changes to my supervisor, and with this comes the filling out of mountains of additional paperwork. And if I do the right thing, someone else at the IRS will look bad for letting this problem get as far as it did without being resolved."

The IRS recognizes that there are many problems within its bureaucracy, with the taxpayer ultimately paying for these problems. To try alleviate these problems, the IRS established the Taxpayer Advocate's Office (formerly known as the Problem Resolution Program), while Congress drafted the Taxpayer Bill of Rights and implemented the Taxpayer Assistance Order to help taxpayers struggling with the IRS.

1. The Taxpayer Advocate Program

The Taxpayer Advocate program deals with instances where the IRS has made mistakes and where the taxpayer is unable to deal with the IRS through normal channels. This program is also known as the Problem Resolution Program (PRP).

The Taxpayer Advocate was set up, in theory, to insure that taxpayers are given an advocate to help them resolve problems through regular IRS organizational channels. If this doesn't work, the advocate can go outside regular channels and enlist whatever source(s) he or she deems necessary to get the problem resolved correctly (whether it is in the taxpayer's favor or not). The Taxpayer Advocate program is also supposed to recommend changes to the way that the IRS conducts its business in the future. Each Taxpayer Advocate office has a at least one taxpayer advocate officer who generally has the authority to do whatever is necessary to correct the problem.

During 1996, over 355,000 cases were referred to the Taxpayer Advocate offices throughout the United States. According to the IRS, the taxpayer was contacted within one week of the referral in 89.5% of the cases. Presumably, the number of cases in the Taxpayer Advocate's office would have been much higher had all taxpayers who needed this service actually known about this program. If you think that the Taxpayer Advocate may benefit you, request IRS Publication 1546 (The Taxpayer Advocate Service of the IRS), then contact the Taxpayer Advocate. A list of all district offices for the Taxpayer Advocate is included in Appendix 2 at the end of this book.

> If your Taxpayer Advocate officer is unhelpful, you can always ask for IRS management assistance.

The Taxpayer Advocate is generally available for the following situations:

★ You are currently suffering, or about to suffer, a significant hardship as a result of IRS actions

★ You will suffer an irreparable injury or long-term adverse impact as the result of IRS actions

★ You have experienced a delay of at least 30 days to resolve the issue

★ The IRS employee is not responding to you or working your case despite promises to the contrary

★ You will incur a significant cost as a result of the IRS action (including legal or professional fees)

★ You are facing an immediate IRS threat of adverse action (such as a property seizure)

Once the Taxpayer Advocate receives your case, the IRS promises that the following will occur:

★ The Taxpayer Advocate employee will provide a "fresh look" at your problem

★ You will receive an acknowledgment that your case has been received, along with the name and phone number of the employee assigned to your case

★ You will receive periodic progress reports from the employee

★ You will be given time frames for action, including deadlines for you to follow

★ You will receive a quick resolution and courteous service from the taxpayer advocate employee

I have found this list to be true much more often than not, as the Taxpayer Advocate usually does an excellent job overall.

The following table shows the success that taxpayers have had with getting assistance.

TABLE 13
TAXPAYER ASSISTANCE STATISTICS

	2000	2001	2002	2003
No. of Applications for Taxpayer Assistance	237,885	248,011	234,327	196,619
Assistance Provided to Taxpayers (%)	68.8	68.1	69.0	65.9
Assistance Not Provided (%)	31.2	31.9	31.0	34.1
Reasons for No Assistance (%)				
Relief Requested Not Appropriate	25.5	21.5	17.4	20.2
No Response from Taxpayer	1.5	4.8	7.2	6.8
Relief Already Provided Before TAO	2.5	2.5	3.1	3.6
No Hardship Proven	0.7	2.2	1.9	0.8
Tax Law Doesn't Permit Relief	1.0	0.8	0.7	0.8
Taxpayer Withdrew Request	0.0	0.2	.6	1.1

While the Taxpayer Advocate is a good service, I have found that some Taxpayer Advocate officers are not interested in helping taxpayers, but instead seem to be more concerned with covering up for their fellow IRS employees' mistakes and errors of judgment. If you find that this is the case with your tax problem, do not give up, as there are other avenues available to you (which I discuss in this chapter). At the very least, you can request that another Taxpayer Advocate officer help with the problem or ask for IRS management assistance. Always follow all IRS administrative procedures before requesting assistance from the Taxpayer Advocate.

A Taxpayer Advocate employee is permitted to do the following on any case:

★ Release Federal Tax Liens and levies if a substantial hardship is created

★ Temporarily stop collection activity until a solution to the problem is reached

★ Find out what happened to tax refund checks

★ Clear up miscommunications within the IRS, especially if the miscommunication was causing or contributing to your problem

★ Resolve problems associated with incorrect IRS notices

★ Remove penalties and interest as permitted by law

★ Credit tax payments to your account if the payments have been misapplied

Taxpayer Advocate officers cannot help you prepare a tax return, and they cannot provide any legal advice concerning the interpretation of the tax laws.

If you decide it is necessary for you to contact the IRS through the Taxpayer Advocate program, you should include the following information in the initial letter:

★ Your name, address, and social security number

★ Your current daytime telephone number

★ Copies of all notices and other correspondence received from the IRS

★ Copies of all documents and correspondence sent to the IRS

★ A copy of the tax return(s) for the year(s) at issue

★ A letter outlining the problem and the solution to the problem (i.e., what the IRS should do about the problem)

You can make the initial contact with the Taxpayer Advocate office by telephone in an emergency situation, such as when the IRS is attempting to seize your property. After the Taxpayer Advocate program receives your request, an officer will contact you and explain what will happen next. The Taxpayer Advocate office tries to resolve all cases within 30 days, although this is not always possible. But under most circumstances, this program does seem to resolve cases much faster than any other division of the IRS. This does not mean, however, that you should expect the Taxpayer Advocate officer to do everything and anything to help you out. The Taxpayer Advocate's job is to correct problems created within the IRS and not to fix every situation in which you were dissatisfied with the IRS. (If this were the officer's job, there would need to be more officers in the IRS than any other type of employee.)

2. Taxpayer Bill of Rights

Remember that you, and not the IRS, have rights during all phases of the tax game. The IRS has the authority to do what it does, but it never has the right to do anything. For instance, taxpayers have constitutional, statutory, and common law rights (developed over the course of the more than 200 years of US existence), while the IRS is limited to the directives set forth in the IRC.

Congress has recently begun to recognize what taxpayers have known for a long time: the IRS is often out of control and inflicts numerous hardships on taxpayers. On July 30, 1997, Congress and the president enacted the Taxpayer Bill of Rights 2. This new law provides taxpayers with increased rights in all dealings with the IRS. The following are some of the more important rights:

(a) *The Office of Taxpayer Advocate was established.* This office was set up to do the following:

★ Assist taxpayers who are now suffering a significant hardship due to the way the IRS is administering the tax laws

★ Resolve problems when the IRS is being more unreasonable than usual

★ Many times, the Taxpayer Advocate officer will come to the taxpayer's aid by issuing a Taxpayer's Assistance Order (TAO). These orders are discussed in detail in section **3.**

(b) *The IRS's ability to abate (reduce or eliminate) interest has been expanded to include interest caused by IRS delays or errors in dealing with a taxpayer's case.* For instance, the IRS may now eliminate interest that has accrued if the IRS loses or misplaces a file, if the IRS employee is not available to resolve a case for an extended period of time (such as being on an extended leave due to illness or training), or for any other reason for which the IRS is at fault. This provision, however, applies only to tax years beginning after July 30, 1996.

(c) *The IRS has been given additional reasons to release a Federal Tax Lien (before it is paid in full) or to return seized property to the taxpayer even though he or she still owes the IRS money.* There are basically four situations in which the IRS will release or return property, each of which obviously benefits the taxpayer:

(i)   If the Federal Tax Lien or seizure was premature or did not comply with IRS administrative procedures

(ii) If the taxpayer has agreed to make monthly installment payments to resolve the tax liability

(iii) If the withdrawal of the tax lien or seizure will make it easier for the IRS to collect the tax liability in the future

(iv) If the withdrawal of the tax lien or seizure would be in the government's best interests

(d) *The IRS is now permitted to disclose its collection activities with respect to divorced spouses if the joint tax liability was accrued during the marriage.* For example, a married couple filed a joint Form 1040 for the 1997 tax year in which a balance was owed. The couple then divorced in 1999. Either the husband or wife can now write to the IRS and request information relating to the IRS's attempts to collect any tax due from the other spouse, the general nature of the collection activities, and the total amount of tax collected to date. The IRS is required to provide this information in writing after the request is received.

> You do not have to tolerate hardship at the hands of the IRS. Instead, you are eligible for relief within the IRS.

This is a welcome change for taxpayers who were married and then went through a divorce not knowing how the tax liabilities would be paid. The IRS traditionally would go after the spouse from whom collecting the money would be the easiest. Often, this meant that a spouse who was employed would be at a major disadvantage over a spouse who did not work, as his or her wages could be easily levied to satisfy the joint tax liability. I strongly encourage all divorced taxpayers who owe the IRS money to take advantage of this new policy and get all the information concerning the joint tax debt directly from the IRS.

3. Taxpayer Assistance Order

Congress recognizes that sometimes the IRS will inflict terrible financial punishment upon taxpayers and has provided, in IRC §7811, for the taxpayer to obtain relief (called a Taxpayer Assistance Order, or TAO) if he or she is suffering or about to suffer a "significant hardship" as a result of the IRS actions.

In the Tax Reform Act of 1998, law makers added language to IRC §7811 in an attempt to provide some guidance as to what actually constitutes a "significant hardship." For example, Congress specifically recognized that an IRS threat of "adverse action," a delay of more than 30 days in resolving your account problems, irreparable injury to you, "significant" costs incurred by you while you wait for the IRS to do something, or anything else that may have a negative long-term impact on you are examples of significant hardships.

You do not have to tolerate hardship at the hands of the IRS. Instead, you are eligible for relief within the IRS. This relief, which will usually come from the office of the National Taxpayer Advocate or a Taxpayer Advocate officer, can take many different forms, including the release of levies or seizures, an enforced collection hold, or any other act that is necessary to put an end to the significant hardship. It is up to you to file an Application for Taxpayer Assistance Order (cleverly called a Form 911) to request this relief from the IRS (see Sample 36). The collection statute of limitations is suspended while the IRS is considering your Form 911 request.

The problem with this relief program is that it is sometimes difficult to convince the IRS that you are about to suffer a significant hardship. You will likely consider every hardship you face a significant one. For instance, it is not enough to show that you will suffer economic or personal inconvenience as a result of the IRS's actions. If an IRS wage levy will force you to cut back on your restaurant bills, it will not be considered to be a significant hardship. On the other hand, if you are unable to pay for necessary medical supplies, it likely will be considered a significant hardship. Every situation is considered on a case-by-case basis.

There are several factors and loopholes available to the IRS that make the granting of a TAO a somewhat rare event. For example, the IRS will consider whether you will be able to retain housing; pay for food, medical treatment, clothing, education and utilities; retain your job; and be able to get to and from work as a result of the IRS action. If you will not be able to do each of these things due to the IRS, then a significant hardship is probably occurring or about to occur and a TAO will probably be issued.

SAMPLE 36

FORM 911 (APPLICATION FOR TAXPAYER ASSISTANCE ORDER)

OMB No. 1545-1504

Department of the Treasury – Internal Revenue Service

TAXPAYER ADVOCATE SERVICE

Application for Taxpayer Assistance Order (ATAO)

Form **911**
(Rev. 3-2000)

Section I.   Taxpayer Information

1. Name(s) as shown on tax return Caitlin Estill	4. Your Social Security Number 123-45-6789 6. Tax Form(s) 1040
	5. Social Security No. of Spouse — 7. Tax Period(s) 2000 and 2001
2. Current mailing address (Number, Street & Apartment Number) 123 Main Street	8. Employer Identification Number (if applicable) N/A
	9. E-Mail address Caitlin @ xyz. net
3. City, Town or Post Office, State and ZIP Code Denver, CO 80111	10. Fax number 303-555-1111
11. Person to contact Caitlin Estill	12. Daytime telephone number 303-555-5555 13. Best time to call 9 AM - 5 PM

14. Please describe the problem and the significant hardship it is creating. *(If more space is needed, attach additional sheets.)*

The IRS is holding my tax refunds in the amounts of $6,250 and $2,100 for 2000 and 2001, respectively, due to a tax debt of my ex-husband. I did not file joint tax returns with him and do not personally owe any money to the IRS. I have tried to resolve this with the Service Center but have had no success. The lack of refunds is creating a major financial hardship for me now.

15. Please describe the relief you are requesting. *(If more space is needed, attach additional sheets.)*

Release the refunds of $6,250 and $2,100, along with an interest I am entitled to receive, as soon as possible so I can eliminate this financial hardship.

I understand that Taxpayer Advocate employees may contact third parties in order to respond to this request and I authorize such contacts to be made. Further, by authorizing the Taxpayer Advocate Service to contact third parties, I understand that I will not receive notice, pursuant to section 7602(c) of the Internal Revenue Code, of third parties contacted in connection with this request.

16. Signature of taxpayer or corporate officer Caitlin Estill	17. Date 11/25/02	18. Signature of spouse —	19. Date —

Section II.   Representative Information (if applicable)

1. Name of Authorized Representative	3. Centralized Authorization File Number (CAF)
2. Mailing Address	4. Daytime telephone number
	5. Fax number
6. Signature of Representative	7. Date

Cat. No. 16965S

Form **911** (Rev. 3-2000)

If there are any doubts regarding whether a TAO should be granted, the decision should be made in the taxpayer's favor. In fact, the changes made in 1998 to the tax laws require that the Taxpayer Advocate consider all facts in the light most favorable to you whenever an IRS employee fails to follow applicable IRS guidelines. While this change may appear to be common sense, the reality is that it will now make it much easier to obtain relief from some of the harsh IRS treatment that would have been tolerated in the past.

When making a request for a TAO, spell out precisely what hardship(s) you are facing and how the IRS action has affected you and your family. You should let the IRS know if its actions will cause bankruptcy, lead to a potential suicide, force your family out of its home, or endanger a life because of a lack of funds to pay for prescription medicine.

The IRS's response to what appears to you to be an obvious need for a TAO may not be kind and understanding. The IRS instructs its employees that your inability to pay both rent and the tax liability is not a significant hardship if you will not be evicted for nonpayment of the rent. In other words, you should pay your taxes before the landlord, because lowering a tax liability is more important than shelter. Of course, if you will be evicted for not paying rent, a significant hardship will occur. It may be necessary to include a letter from the landlord when you submit the Form 911 to show that the situation is serious and that an eviction is imminent.

You should also let the IRS know about your past history with the IRS, especially if you have been in compliance with the filing requirements and were faithfully paying taxes until some event occurred that caused the tax problem. Let the IRS know why the significant hardship has occurred and offer the IRS potential solutions to the problem (if you know how to resolve the situation). It never hurts to offer a solution or solutions to the problem; you haven't lost anything if the IRS says no. In other words, give the IRS as much information and documentation (including copies of the IRS notices and your responses, if any) as possible. You are much more likely to get a positive result when you make the Taxpayer Advocate employee's job as easy as possible.

Before submitting a request for a TAO, you should make sure that you have reached a roadblock within the IRS and have no other place to turn for assistance. You generally must show that you have tried to resolve the situation with the IRS but that the IRS employee, often a revenue officer trying to collect a tax liability, is being unreasonable or simply cannot resolve the problem. Typical types of problems that the Taxpayer Advocate's office is designed to straighten out include refunds from the IRS (when the

IRS won't refund money to the taxpayer after several attempts by the tax-payer), responses to IRS notices that go unanswered by the IRS, or any other situation in which the taxpayer simply cannot get the IRS to respond. However, a TAO can only delay IRS collection enforcement action and cannot be used to forgive or reduce a tax liability (you must use the Offer in Compromise program to do this. For a discussion of this program, see chapter 12).

The Taxpayer Advocate will not respond to inquiries if you are currently under criminal investigation, have already received a response from the IRS, have been labeled a tax protestor (or whatever the new term will be) by the IRS, or if the issue was already resolved. If the Taxpayer Advocate will not review the case, you will be informed of the reason and what the next step in the process is. Many problem resolution officers will offer taxpayers some suggestions as to potential ways to resolve the situation through the normal IRS channels. It is usually wise to consider these suggestions, as many problem resolution officers are very experienced and know what it takes to get cases resolved.

4. Use Your Representative in Congress

If you receive no assistance from the Taxpayer Advocate officer or any other offices within the IRS, it is sometimes worthwhile to go outside the IRS and use a member of Congress to work for your benefit. Representatives in Congress need as many votes as possible at election time and should work for their constituents during the years of their elected terms. When the IRS won't resolve an issue that should be resolved in your favor, contact your Congressperson. Sometimes, simply getting a telephone call from a Senator's or Representative's staff member will be all that is necessary to light a fire under the IRS and get some action. At least the IRS will know that it is being watched by someone who will ultimately determine its budget for the next fiscal year.

While contacting a politician may have some benefit, it should be noted that most, if not all, of the 435 members of the House and the 100 Senators do not understand the tax laws that they have created. Many politicians themselves are also privately afraid of the IRS and will not want to stir up too much trouble when helping out a taxpayer. It is therefore unreasonable to expect a great deal of help, unless you happen to be very wealthy and generous with your campaign contributions. Like anything else, money talks and can sometimes get results that most of us can only dream about.

Most, if not all, of the 435 members of the House and the 100 Senators do not understand the tax laws that they have created.

Tax Points

★ The Taxpayer Advocate Program was established to assist tax-payers who cannot resolve their cases through regular IRS channels.

★ Taxpayers should ask the Taxpayer Advocate to resolve collection cases in which the revenue officer is being unreasonable in his or her collection tactics and is unwilling to reach a reasonable resolution of the case.

★ The Taxpayer Advocate officer can stop collection activities, release liens and levies, and basically do whatever is necessary to clear up the case.

★ You should use Form 911 whenever the IRS has or is about to inflict a significant hardship on you or your family.

★ Taxpayers, and not the IRS, have rights, and taxpayers should use all rights listed in the Taxpayer Bill of Rights to their advantage whenever possible.

★ When the Taxpayer Advocate program won't help, and if it is also being unreasonable, consider contacting a member of Congress for assistance. The IRS often listens to Senators and Representatives, as these individuals approve the IRS's budget for every fiscal year.

CHAPTER 17

CONCLUSION

If you don't drink, smoke, or drive a car, you're a tax evader.
Thomas S. Foley, US Congressman and Speaker of the House
(D-WA), *Time Magazine*, June 18, 1990

On April 15, just try telling the Internal Revenue Service you just don't feel like "contributing" this year.
Robert H. Michel (R-Illinois), US House Minority Leader,
February 1993

Former House Speaker Foley's comments should not seem that unusual at this point, whether he was being sarcastic or was serious. Most members of Congress have given the IRS the benefit of the doubt throughout the relatively brief, but controversial, history of the income tax and the IRS. Over time, Congress has decided to virtually exempt the IRS from the US Constitution, has made taxpayers prove their innocence rather than having the IRS prove their guilt, raised income tax rates, and made the Tax Code impossible to understand, often in the name of "tax reform." Congress has managed to give the IRS a vast amount of power and financial resources, which the IRS has used and abused throughout its history in such a way that it frustrates, harasses, and generally annoys taxpayers of all races, nationalities, religions, and political affiliations. The IRS does not discriminate: the IRS is a problem for everyone.

I hope this book has provided you with a starting point for fighting back against the IRS. Specifically, you should now realize that no tax situation is hopeless. Many tax situations deteriorate because you do not know what options are available to you, and the IRS rarely discusses any options that may actually benefit you. Once you understand your options, the game changes and the tax situation will improve until it is eventually resolved, hopefully in your favor. The following are some key points to keep in mind whenever the IRS is attempting to interfere with your life.

(a) *Taxpayers, and not the IRS, have rights.* You should explore and use these rights whenever possible. Included in these rights are the following:

★ The right to obtain all information from the IRS, with very limited exceptions, concerning you and your case against the IRS. You are always permitted to obtain current account information for any year(s) by requesting a transcript of account, and you can get almost any other information from the IRS through a Freedom of Information Act request.

★ The right to tape-record any meeting with the IRS to limit the opportunity for any misunderstandings to occur in the future. In order to do this, you must give the IRS at least ten days' written notice.

★ The right to obtain management assistance whenever an IRS employee is unreasonable or incompetent. You are also permitted to speak to the manager's supervisor if the manager turns out to be either unreasonable or incompetent.

★ The right to be represented by counsel at any IRS meeting. The counsel is of your choice and can be an attorney, CPA/accountant, or enrolled agent.

★ The right to appeal any incorrect IRS decision. Many taxpayers who exercise their appeal rights, either within the IRS Appeals Division or with the US court system, wind up with a much better overall result than do those taxpayers who give up and fail to appeal any incorrect IRS decision.

★ The right to use the Taxpayer Advocate Program to resolve any cases that cannot be resolved through the normal IRS channels. Many times, a Taxpayer Advocate officer will come to the aid of a taxpayer who is being treated poorly by an unreasonable or incompetent IRS employee.

(b) *The IRS will negotiate with taxpayers, and all taxpayers should be prepared to negotiate with the IRS.* To be prepared to negotiate with the IRS, you should do the following:

No tax situation is hopeless. Once you understand your options in dealing with the IRS, you can beat the IRS at its game.

★ Thoroughly understand the law and facts before any meeting or negotiation session with the IRS.

★ Be organized and have solutions for the tax problems. Having a solution for the tax situation usually makes the IRS employee's job much easier. Whenever you help out the IRS employee, you will usually benefit in the end. In addition, you will receive a better result by proposing a solution than by waiting for the IRS employee to propose a solution for you.

★ Understand exactly what you want before meeting with the IRS. The pressures associated with an IRS meeting mean that it is no place for you to make complicated settlement or negotiation decisions.

(c) *Taxpayers should use all available weapons to fight the IRS.* You often get only one shot at the IRS, and you should make sure that the shot is a good one. In order to win any battle, you must understand what weapons you have before beginning the battle. For instance, in a collection battle, you should explore the possibilities of an Installment Agreement, having the account placed into an uncollectible status, filing an Offer in Compromise, or declaring bankruptcy if you cannot pay the account in full at any time in the near future. Analyze all battles with the IRS in this way, and bring out all applicable weapons whenever necessary.

(d) *Taxpayers should always stand up to the IRS and not be intimidated by its power, threats, or use of force.* The IRS is not used to dealing with taxpayers who are not intimidated or afraid of it. Taxpayers who understand their tax rights tend to be much more confident and less likely to be intimidated. These taxpayers also tend to be much more successful at beating the IRS. Never let the IRS dictate what is happening during the tax game and always challenge the IRS whenever something does not seem quite right. You can be successful in challenging the IRS during any audits, collection cases, proposed penalty assessments, or any other phase of the tax game.

I leave you with the final list in this book: 15 Rules for Success in Dealing with the IRS. I hope you will use these rules, along with all other information contained in this book, to defeat the IRS at the tax game. The IRS is certainly a monster, but like all monsters, it can be slain. Good luck!

15 Rules for Success in Dealing with the IRS

1. *Always use the IRS bureaucracy to your advantage.* A patient taxpayer is often a taxpayer who will win in the end. If you are in a hurry to get a case resolved, you should be prepared to pay for your impatience.

2. *Never miss a deadline with the IRS.* Missing a deadline only gives the IRS a further reason to cause problems, and problems with the IRS will never benefit you.

3. *Never lie or attempt to intentionally deceive the IRS.* It is never worth losing your freedom over an IRS tax problem.

4. *Always report all income that the IRS knows about or can find out about.* Unreported income is the primary reason why taxpayers have any contacts with the IRS in the first place. Reducing the chance of an IRS contact should be your goal.

5. *Always file tax returns on time and be able to prove that they were filed on time.* It is up to you to prove that a tax return was filed on time to avoid any late filing penalties. In addition, it is better to file on time even if you cannot pay any or all of the balance due on the tax return.

6. *Always be organized for all meetings with the IRS and act professionally when with the IRS employee.* Remember, the IRS employees takes few tax situations personally. You will usually benefit by keeping the case professional and businesslike.

7. *Never ignore an IRS notice or letter.* A tax problem will not simply go away if you ignore the IRS. The problem may remain dormant for a short time, but when it reappears it will be much worse than it was before.

8. *Never volunteer information to the IRS.* The IRS will usually use any information against you if it can. The only time that it is acceptable to volunteer any information is if you are certain that the information can only help, and not hurt, your case. This is a very rare event.

9. *Always ask the IRS questions.* IRS employees are not used to having taxpayers ask them questions,and they may be uncomfortable answering the questions. However, you have a right to ask questions and the IRS has an obligation to answer the questions truthfully. You will always benefit by having the greatest amount of information at your disposal, and it never hurts for you to know what the IRS knows or is planning to do as soon in the game as is possible.

10. *Always get the IRS to agree.* The IRS is often willing to agree, especially to minor points in your favor. Even if the agreement helps you in a relatively minor way, you have benefited. Once the IRS starts to agree, it will often continue to agree.

11. *Never discuss confidential tax information with anyone.* This includes friends, family members, and business associates. Everyone is a potential IRS informant and should be treated as such.

12. *Never trust the IRS or its employees.* While most IRS employees are honest and fair, there are enough IRS employees who aren't to make a bad name for the other employees by lying to taxpayers, harassing taxpayers, and doing whatever is necessary to collect the greatest amount of tax from an unsuspecting taxpayer. Be safe, not sorry: don't trust any IRS employee.

13. *Always appear willing to cooperate with the IRS.* Taxpayers who publicly cooperate with the IRS fare much better than those taxpayers who demonstrate their unwillingness to cooperate. Failure to cooperate will generally make your ride with the IRS both rough and long.

14. *Never assume that the IRS understands the tax laws.* The members of Congress who wrote the tax laws, along with all the people who make their living as tax professionals, do not completely understand the complex mess of tax laws in effect today. Unfortunately, this means that the IRS, the federal agency in charge of administering the tax laws, also does not understand the laws.

15. *Never assume that the IRS knows anything about you other than what you reported on your tax return.* All information the IRS initially has comes either from you or from information reported to the IRS by other individuals (such as employers who report their wages to the IRS or banks that report the interest paid to its account holders). The IRS will learn more about you only by working the case from start to finish.

IRS DISTRIBUTION AND SERVICE CENTERS

a. Distribution Centers

Western United States

Western Area Distribution Center
Rancho Cordova, CA 95743-0001

Central United States

Central Area Distribution Center
P.O. Box 8903
Bloomington, IL 61702-8903

Eastern United States

Eastern Area Distribution Center
P.O. Box 85074
Richmond, VA 23261-5074

b. Service Centers

Location	For use by residents of:
Andover Service Center Andover, MA 05501	Connecticut, Maine, Massachusetts, New Hampshire, New York (parts), Rhode Island, Vermont
Atlanta Service Center Atlanta, GA 39901	Florida, Georgia, South Carolina

Austin Service Center
Austin, TX 73301

Kansas, New Mexico, Oklahoma, Texas

Brookhaven Service Center
Holtsville, NY 11742

New York

Cincinnati Service Center
Cincinnati, OH 45999

Indiana, Kentucky, Michigan, Ohio,
West Virginia

Fresno Service Center
Fresno, CA 93888

California (parts), Hawaii

Holtsville Service Center
Holtsville, NY 00501

New Jersey, New York (parts)

Kansas City Service Center
Kansas City, MO 64999

Illinois, Iowa, Minnesota, Missouri,
Wisconsin

Memphis Service Center
Memphis, TN 37501

Alabama, Arkansas, Louisiana,
Mississippi, North Carolina, Tennessee

Ogden Service Center
Ogden, UT 84201

Alaska, Arizona, California (parts),
Colorado, Idaho, Montana,
Nebraska, Nevada, North Dakota,
Oregon, South Dakota, Utah,
Washington, Wyoming

Philadelphia Service Center
Philadelphia, PA 19255

Delaware, District of Columbia,
Maryland, Pennsylvania, Virginia,
Guam, Puerto Rico, Virgin Islands,
American Samoa

IRS DISTRICT OFFICES (TAXPAYER ADVOCATE)

ALABAMA
801 Tom Martin Drive
Room 150-PR
Birmingham, AL 35211
Fax: (205) 912-5091

ALASKA
949 East 36th Avenue
Anchorage, AK 99508
Fax: (907) 271-6824

ARIZONA
210 East Earll Dr.
Mail Stop 1005 PX
Phoenix, AZ 85012
Fax: (602) 207-8250

ARKANSAS
700 West Capital Avenue
Mail Stop D:P
Little Rock, AR 72201
Fax: (501) 324-5183

CALIFORNIA
Laguna Niguel District
24000 Avila Road, Room 3362
Laguna Niguel, CA 92677
Fax: (949) 389-5033

Los Angeles District
300 North Los Angeles Street,
Room 5206
Los Angeles, CA 90012
Fax: (213) 576-3141

Sacramento District
4330 Watt Avenue
North Highlands, CA 95660
Fax: (916) 978-5902

San Francisco District
1301 Clay Street, Suite 1540 S
Oakland, CA 94612
Fax: (510) 637-2715

San Jose District
55 South Market Street,
Room 710
San Jose, CA 95113
Fax: (408) 817-6851

COLORADO
600 17th Street
Mail Stop 1005 DEN
Denver, CO 80202
Fax: (303) 446-1011

CONNECTICUT
135 High Street
Mail Stop 219
Hartford, CT 06103
Fax: (860) 756-4559

DELAWARE
409 Silverside Road,
Room 152
Wilmington, DE 19809
Fax: (302) 791-5945

DISTRICT OF COLUMBIA
31 Hopkins Plaza, Room 620A
Baltimore, MD 21201
Fax: (410) 962-9340

FLORIDA
Ft. Lauderdale District
7850 SW 6th Court
Room 285
Plantation, FL 33324
Fax: (305) 424-2483

Jacksonville District
400 West Bay Street, Room 116
Jacksonville, FL 32202
Fax: (904) 665-1818

GEORGIA
401 West Peachtree Street, NW
Summit Building
Mail Stop 202-D, Room 1520
Atlanta, GA 30370
Fax: (404) 338-8096

HAWAII
300 Ala Moana Blvd., Room 2104
Box 50089
Honolulu, HI 96850
Fax: (808) 539-2859

IDAHO
550 West Fort Street
Box 041
Boise, ID 83724
Fax: (208) 334-1977

ILLINOIS
Chicago District
230 South Dearborn Street,
Room 3214
Chicago, IL 60604
Fax: (312) 886-1564

Springfield District
320 West Washington Street
Springfield, IL 62701
Fax: (217) 527-6373

INDIANA
575 North Pennsylvania Street
Indianapolis, IN 46204
Fax: (317) 226-6222

IOWA
Mail Stop 2
210 Walnut Street
Des Moines, IA 50309
Fax: (515) 284-6645

KANSAS
271 West 3rd Street, North
Mail Stop 1005 WIC
Wichita, KS 67202
Fax: (316) 352-7212

KENTUCKY
600 Dr. Martin Luther King Jr. Place
Federal Building
Room 622
Louisville, KY 40202
Fax: (502) 582-6463

LOUISIANA
600 South Maestri Place
Mail Stop 12
New Orleans, LA 70130
Fax: (504) 558-3492

MAINE
68 Sewall Street
Room 313
Augusta, ME 04330
Fax: (207) 622-8458

MARYLAND
31 Hopkins Plaza,
Room 620A
Baltimore, MD 21201
Fax: (410) 962-9572

MASSACHUSETTS
JFK Federal Bldg.,
Room 775
Government Center Plaza
Boston, MA 02203
Fax: (617) 316-2700

MICHIGAN
477 Michigan Avenue
Mail Stop 7
Detroit, MI 48226
Fax: (313) 628-3669

MINNESOTA
316 North Robert Street, Stop 1005
St. Paul, MN 55101
Fax: (651) 312-7872

MISSISSIPPI
100 West Capitol Street
Mail Stop 31
Jackson, MS 39269
Fax: (601) 292-4821

MISSOURI
Robert A. Young Bldg.
1222 Spruce Street
Mail Stop 1005-STL
St. Louis, MO 63103
Fax: (314) 612-4628

MONTANA
Federal Building
301 S. Park
Helena, MT 59626
Fax: (405) 441-1045

NEBRASKA
1313 Farnam Street
Mail Stop 1005 OMA
Omaha, NE 68102
Fax: (402) 221-3051

NEVADA
4750 West Oakey Blvd.,
Room 303
Las Vegas, NV 89102
Fax: (702) 455-1216

NEW HAMPSHIRE
Federal Office Bldg.
80 Daniel Street
Portsmouth, NH 03801
Fax: (603) 430-7809

NEW JERSEY
955 South Springfield Avenue
Springfield, NJ 07081
Fax: (973) 921-4355

NEW MEXICO
5338 Montgomery Blvd. N.E.
Mail Stop 1005 ALB
Albuquerque, NM 87109
Fax: (505) 837-5519

NEW YORK
Albany District
Leo O'Brien Federal Bldg.,
Room 354
Clinton Avenue & North Pearl Street
Albany, NY 12207
Fax: (518) 427-5494

Brooklyn District
10 MetroTech Center
625 Fulton Street
Brooklyn, NY 11201
Fax: (718) 488-3100

Buffalo District
201 Como Park Blvd.
Buffalo, NY 14227
Fax: (716) 686-4851

Manhattan District
290 Broadway, 7th Floor
New York, NY 10007
Fax: (212) 436-1900

NORTH CAROLINA
320 Federal Place, Room 125
Greensboro, NC 27401
Fax: (910) 378-2495

NORTH DAKOTA
657 Second Avenue, N.
Stop 1005-FAR
Fargo, ND 58107
Fax: (701) 239-5323

OHIO
Cincinnati District
550 Main Street, Room 3530
Cincinnati, OH 45202
Fax: (513) 263-3257

Cleveland District
1240 East Ninth Avenue
Cleveland, OH 44199
Fax: (216) 522-2947

OKLAHOMA
55 North Robinson
Mail Stop 1005 OKC
Oklahoma City, OK 73102
Fax: (405) 297-4056

OREGON
1220 S.W. 3rd Avenue,
Room 681
Portland, OR 97204
Fax: (503) 326-5453

PENNSYLVANIA
600 Arch Street, Room 7426
Philadelphia, PA 19105
Fax: (215) 861-1613

Pittsburgh District
1000 Liberty Avenue,
Room 1102
Pittsburgh, PA 15222
Fax: (412) 395-4769

RHODE ISLAND
380 Westminster Street
Providence, RI 02903
Fax: (401) 525-4247

SOUTH CAROLINA
1835 Assembly Street,
Room 571, MDP 03
Columbia, SC 29201
Fax: (803) 253-3910

SOUTH DAKOTA
115 4th Avenue Southeast
Aberdeen, SD 57401
Fax: (605) 226-7246

TENNESSEE
801 Broadway
Room 481
Nashville, TN 37202
Fax: (615) 250-5001

TEXAS
Austin District
300 East 8th Street
Mail Stop 1005 AUS
Austin, TX 78701
Fax: (512) 499-5687

Dallas District
1100 Commerce Street
Mail Stop 1005 DAL
Dallas, TX 75242
Fax: (214) 767-0040

Houston District
1919 Smith Street
Mail Stop 1005 HOU
Houston, TX 77002
Fax: (713) 209-4779

UTAH
50 South 200 East
Mail Stop 1005 SLC
Salt Lake City, UT 84111
Fax: (801) 779-6957

VERMONT
Courthouse Plaza
199 Main Street
Burlington, VT 05401
Fax: (802) 860-2006

VIRGINIA
400 North 8th Street
Room 916
Richmond, VA 23240
Fax: (804) 916-3535

WASHINGTON
915 Second Street
Mail Stop 405
Seattle, WA 98174
Fax: (206) 220-6047

WEST VIRGINIA
425 Juliana Street
Parkersburg, WV 26101
Fax: (304) 420-6682

WISCONSIN
310 West Wisconsin Avenue,
Room M-28
Milwaukee, WI 53203
Fax: (414) 297-3362

WYOMING
5353 Yellowstone Road
Room 206A
Cheyenne, WY 82009
Fax: (307) 633-0918